Magistrates Manual
of Papua New Guinea

Magistrates Manual of Papua New Guinea

by

EDWARD R HILL BA, LLB

Lecturer in Law and Law Clinic Supervisor,
School of Law, University of the South Pacific

Barrister and Solicitor of the Supreme Court of British Columbia and the High Court of Fiji

Formerly Lecturer, Faculty of Law, University of Papua New Guinea

and

GUY POWLES BA, LLM (Hons), PhD

Fellow of the Faculty of Law, Monash University

Barrister and Solicitor of the Supreme Court of Victoria and
of the High Court of New Zealand

Formerly Judge of the Appellate Division of the Supreme Court
of the Federated States of Micronesia
and Magistrate in Samoa

with Forewords by

THE HONOURABLE SIR ARNOLD AMET KB, CBE, LLD

Chief Justice of Papua New Guinea

and

MR GEORGE MANUHU LLB

Chief Magistrate of Papua New Guinea

UPNG PRESS AND BOOKSHOP, 2010

Magistrates Manual of Papua New Guinea

Originally published in Sydney by Lawbook Co.
100 Harris St, Pyrmont NSW 2009

2010 - This reprint by the University of Papua New Guinea Press and Bookshop is by kind permission of the original publisher and of the Copyright Holder (**Copyright Advice Request Number—13201)**

It is produced from final proofs provided by Professor Kwa and these have been checked against a copy of the Lawbook text.

ISBN 9980-939-52-4

Copies available from:

UPNG Press and Bookshop
Box 413
University Post Office
NCD 134
Papua New Guinea

Foreword to the Series

This is one of a series prepared under the auspices of the Access to Laws in Papua New Guinea Project funded by the Australian Government through the Australian Agency for International Development (AusAID). The Access to Laws Project comprised three components aimed at improving access to the laws of this country. The Project involved updating and authenticating all the current legislation of Papua New Guinea and the extensive case law developed by the courts. The legislation and judicial decisions have been produced in the modern electronic CD-ROM format. Equally importantly, the Project included the production of a number of legal textbooks to record the distinctive developments in the laws of Papua New Guinea.

The book publishing component of the Access to Laws Project was under the direction of the Publications Committee that I had the pleasure of chairing. The other members of the Publications Committee were: the Commissioning Editor, Professor Don Chalmers, the Chief Magistrate, Mr George Manuhu, the Deputy Chief Magistrate, John Numapo, the Hon the Attorney-General, Mr Francis Damen (previously Mr Sao Gabi, Mr Michael Gene), the Access to Laws Project Manager, Mr Bruce Fulton, the Project Team Leader, Mr Eric Kwa (previously Dr Val Haynes), representatives of AusAID (Mr Stuart Schaefer, Ms Pauline Doonar, Ms Debbie Bowman, Mr John Prescott, Ms Katherine Ruiz-Avila), a representative of the PNG Law Society, Ms Catherine Davani and the Dean of the Law School, Mr Eric Kwa (previously Mr Gerry Linge). The Publications Committee was responsible for choosing authors, settling the contents, assessing the quality and appointing referees for each of the texts. At an early meeting of the Publications Committee it was decided that it was appropriate that Papua New Guinean authors or authors with considerable experience in Papua New Guinea should be chosen.

I am delighted that Ted Hill and Guy Powles have agreed to accept the invitation of the Commissioning Editor on behalf of the Publications Committee to write this text. I commend the learned authors for their work and scholarship and I am confident that this text, with the others in this series, will be of great value to judges, magistrates, legal practitioners, academics, students and the citizens of Papua New Guinea. If the underlying law is to be developed according to the precepts and principles embodied in our *Constitution* and *The Underlying Law Act* 2000, it is essential that the Papua New Guinea community has access to texts which can state the law of this country concisely, authoritatively and accurately. On behalf of the Publications Committee, I commend the authors for their contribution to this important endeavour.

The Hon Sir Arnold Amet, Kt, CBE, LLD

Chief Justice of Papua New Guinea,

Chair of the Publications Committee,

Access to Laws in Papua New Guinea

Port Moresby 2001

Foreword to the Manual

I am delighted that Magistrates in Papua New Guinea now have a Magistrates Manual. The earlier publication (*The Criminal Jurisdiction of Magistrates in Papua New Guinea* by N K F O'Neill and R N Desailly, 1982) covered the criminal jurisdiction only and is out-of-date and unavailable. The new Manual is, therefore, a significant development for Magistrates in Papua New Guinea.

The Manual is intended not only to provide Magistrates with guidance as to how court proceedings should be conducted according to the relevant law and procedure, but also as to a Magistrate's personal approach to his judicial responsibility.

An important feature of the preparation of this Manual has been the consultative process by which groups of Magistrates have met with the authors in order to consider draft chapters and to make suggestions as to how topics might best be treated in the Manual, and generally to provide valuable input. For their part, the authors have produced a text that takes into account local advice. I am grateful to AusAID for making the funds available for the two consultative workshops held in Port Moresby. The result is what Papua New Guinean Magistrates can be proud to call a "home-grown" Manual.

I am further delighted for reasons of institutional responsibility and the desire to respond appropriately to the public demand for quality and the timely resolution of disputes coming before Magistrates. As we enter the new Millennium, after 25 years of independence of a nation as diverse as ours, major socio-economic developments have brought with them all types of disputes with varying complexities that must be dealt with by the courts.

On 18 August 2000, legislative amendments merging the grades of Magistrates and abolishing the Local Courts came into effect. This has permitted Magistrates, previously limited by jurisdictional barriers, to deal immediately with disputes that they would not otherwise have attended to. Magistrates have been encouraged and are being trained to improve their judicial writing and general skills. It is worth mentioning that alternative dispute resolution, pursuant to these legislative amendments, is now a formal aspect of the hearing of most, if not all, civil matters before the District Court. All these matters emphasise the importance of the drive to improve judicial skills.

The Magistrates Manual is no exception. It was appropriately given priority at the beginning of the Access to Laws Project. Its completion is an achievement. I am confident that the Manual will be warmly received by Magistrates and I sincerely believe that it will have a profound impact on how Magistrates apply their judicial skills in the resolution of disputes and, for that matter, make an important contribution to the administration of justice. In addition to its value to Magistrates, it will be indispensable for training purposes. Altogether, the Manual will greatly advance the quality improvement of the Bench in Papua New Guinea.

May I also stress the developmental aspect of this publication. I hope that, as Magistrates become familiar with the Manual and can test it in its operation over time, they will provide me with information and comments that will assist in the drafting of future editions.

I sincerely thank the authors for their commitment to the Manual and their friendship in the process. I also commend the Magistrates who assisted the authors during the consultative process.

George Manuhu

Chief Magistrate

Papua New Guinea

May 2001

Table of Contents

[References are to page numbers]

PART 5: ENFORCEMENT AND COSTS

PART 6: MAGISTRATES' CIVIL LIABILITY AND CASE MANAGEMENT

PART 7: SETTLEMENT, DECISIONS AND APPEALS

Table of Cases

[References are to page numbers]

Table of Statutes

[References are to page numbers]

References to the *District Court Act* have not been included in the Table of Statutes. The major concepts covered will be dealt with in the Index.

Introduction

The Magistrates of Papua New Guinea perform a vital role in society. A vast amount of criminal, civil and family litigation passes through the courts in which they serve. Without an ethical, knowledgeable and motivated magistracy, the country would be placed at an enormous disadvantage.

Many Magistrates have, over the years, been required to perform their duties without ready access to legal materials. This manual is intended to redress this deficiency. It is hoped that it will become a helpful day-to-day reference and a source of information that will refresh and supplement the working knowledge of Magistrates. It is intended to be a practical book. Footnotes have not been used and extensive case citations have for the most part been avoided. Important Papua New Guinea decisions are referred to, but foreign authorities are not cited.

This book has been written to form part of a series of texts on the laws of Papua New Guinea. Others in the series have been written simultaneously. It is hoped that the contents of this manual in relation to criminal law, land law and the law of evidence will be complemented by other texts devoted exclusively to these subjects. Relevant statutes and provisions of the *Constitution* are referred to throughout the manual, and will provide a guide to lead Magistrates to the applicable legislation. The *Bench Statute Book*, a companion to this manual, is intended to be the primary source on which Magistrates should rely.

It is impossible in a book of this nature to cover exhaustively all of the matters that come before Magistrates. Such a book would require several volumes. It has been necessary to be selective in the coverage of topics. The coverage has been determined with a view to maximising the practical benefit that it will provide in the most common types of cases that Magistrates preside over. Serving Magistrates have been of great assistance in determining the coverage of the manual.

Part 1 of the manual includes chapters that are relevant to Magistrates in all types of cases and extending beyond their professional lives. Judicial ethics and conduct pervade the entire range of judicial duties. Matters of jurisdiction, basic principles underlying court hearings presided over by Magistrates, matters of natural justice, representation of parties and the step-by-step procedure of criminal and civil hearings are considered in Chapters 1-4. Part 2 (Chapter 5) deals with evidence. This chapter is intended to provide a readily accessible reference to the most common issues that arise in the law of evidence in Papua New Guinea. Part 3 consists of chapters dealing with criminal jurisdiction and responsibility, criminal procedure and principles of sentencing. Part 4 begins with two chapters relating to civil litigation and civil procedure generally. Then a chapter is devoted to each of family and children's matters, Land Courts and Village Courts. Chapter 19 is divided into four sections, covering (a) Coroners inquests, (b) disputes arising out of elections and electoral rolls, (c) the surety of the peace and good behaviour jurisdiction and (d) motor vehicle deaths compensation. Part 5 is concerned with enforcement and costs, and Part 6 with Magistrates' civil liability and case management. Finally, Part 7 deals with settlements and dispute resolution, writing and delivering decisions, and appeals.

The laws of Papua New Guinea are dynamic. As this manual was being written, the Local Courts were abolished and the *District Courts Act* and the *Village Courts Act* were amended. Parliament can be expected to pass new laws that affect the operation of the Magistrates' Courts and practice directions and rules may be made. The role of alternative dispute resolution can be expected to increase. Case law can be expected to clarify the meaning of existing legislation. Subsequent editions of this manual may be required to take into account changes in the law. The use of this edition over a period of time can be expected to reveal matters which will require further attention. Revision will then compensate for any lack of accuracy or completeness which appears in the present edition.

Much of the legislation that is currently applied by Magistrates is in need of amendment or outright repeal and replacement with new legislation. One need look no further than Pts VI, IX and X of the *District Courts Act* to find provisions which are archaic, unclear and arguably inappropriate to the realities of the justice system or wider Papua New Guinean society. Much of the law that is applied in District Courts calls out for reform. However, these are matters for Government and Parliament. Magistrates have an obligation to uphold and apply the law as it presently exists. Accordingly, the authors have refrained from extensive commentary on the law or its underlying policy except in so far as it assists Magistrates in discharging their duties.

The authors are indebted to a large number of people whose expertise and willing assistance was provided – particularly the Chief Magistrate Mr George Manuhu, the Deputy Chief Magistrate Mr John Numapo and Magistrates Mr Steven Oli, Ms Regina Sagu, Ms Dessy Magaru, Mr Paul Beu'u, Mrs Ibonigu Kapigeno, Mrs Christine Anawe, Mr John Gesling, Mr Brian Pebo and Mr Mark Selefkariu. These Magistrates contributed the benefit of their experience and ideas during two intensive workshops held at Port Moresby in the first half of 2000. The manual is the better for their input, they have put their stamp upon it, and indeed their involvement in the creation of the manual demonstrates that this publication belongs truly to them.

The authors also wish to recognise the roles played by Professor Don Chalmers and Dr Val Haynes, and the support of members of the Publications Committee of the "Access to Laws" project of which this manual is part. In many practical ways, representatives of Thomson Legal and Regulatory Group and members of the Port Moresby office of the "Access to Laws" project gave valuable assistance to the authors.

To the best of their abilities the authors have attempted to state the law as it existed on 31 August 2000.

PART 1

Judicial Independence, the Legal System, Conduct of Court Matters and Court Hearings

CHAPTER 1 – JUDICIAL INDEPENDENCE, ETHICS AND CONDUCT

1.1 INTRODUCTION

A judicial system plays a vital role in any society founded upon the rule of law. Without an effective judicial system, a society would quickly deteriorate into a state of chaos or repression.

In a society such as Papua New Guinea, which is founded on principles of individual rights, democracy and the rule of law, a judicial system must be independent. The independence of the courts in Papua New Guinea finds its source in s 157 of the *Constitution*:

> "Except to the extent that this *Constitution* specifically provides otherwise, neither the Minister responsible for the National Justice Administration nor any other person or authority (other than the Parliament through legislation) outside the National Judicial System has any power to give directions to any court, or to a member of any court, within that System in respect of the exercise if judicial powers or functions."

The effect of s 157 is that the duties of Magistrates may only be directed by legislation or by the lawful directions of their superiors within the judicial system. The needs, preferences or directions of anyone else (apart from proper considerations relating to the parties in a matter before the court), regardless of their position in society, cannot influence a Magistrate in the discharge of his or her duties.

1.1.1 Judicial declaration

This limit of external influence and control of the judicial system requires a greater amount of internal control and self-regulation. Members of the judiciary are entrusted with a responsibility that goes beyond that of an ordinary citizen or employee. This responsibility is reflected in the solemn declaration taken by each Magistrate and Judge upon appointment. The words of this declaration are set out in Sch 4 of the *Constitution*. They are significant:

> "I ___________, do promise and declare that I will well and truly serve the Independent State of Papua New Guinea and its people in the office of ___________, that I will in all things uphold the *Constitution* and the laws of the Independent State of Papua New Guinea, and I will do right to all manner of people in accordance therewith, without fear or favour, affection or ill-will."

The words of the declaration serve more than just a symbolic purpose. In a condensed way they reflect the independence of the judiciary, the role of each Magistrate in preserving and maintaining this independence and a fundamental requirement of natural justice. It is useful to consider some of the words of the declaration separately:

"All manner of people" means everyone who comes before the court. Everyone is entitled to be treated with equal care and concern. Nobody is above or below the law regardless of his or her status in society, gender, race, place of origin or tribe.

"Without fear" means that no threat, either express or implied, can influence the way a Magistrate hears or decides a case.

"Without favour" means that a Magistrate is not amenable to any express or implied benefit from a member of the public in return for taking certain interests into account in hearing or deciding a case.

"Without affection" means that a Magistrate will not allow any personal preference that favours a person or group to influence the way a case is heard or decided.

"Without ill will" means that a Magistrate will not allow any personal bias against a person or group to influence the way a case is heard or decided.

The words of the declaration require not only that a Magistrate be independent of outside influences, but also that his or her professional duties be discharged in a way that is independent of pre-existing personal feelings or beliefs, for or against a cause, that would affect the outcome of any judgment.

1.2 RULES OF CONDUCT

It is not sufficient for a judicial system to be independent. People must have the *perception* that the judicial system is independent and have confidence in the integrity of those who work within the system. This requires a standard of conduct of Magistrates that ensures that a member of the public (whether a party before the court or not) will not have a reasonable suspicion that a Magistrate's independence is compromised in any way. Ensuring that this public perception is maintained requires constant vigilance on the part of a Magistrate in both personal and professional life.

There is a Code of Conduct for Magistrates in Papua New Guinea. This Code of Conduct is a guide to Magistrates in the conduct of both their professional and personal lives. The code has been reduced to five basic rules. Most of these rules can be traced back to the words of the judicial declaration of office.

- **Rule 1: A Magistrate shall uphold the integrity and independence of the judiciary.**
- **Rule 2: A Magistrate shall avoid impropriety and the appearance of impropriety in all of the Magistrate's activities.**
- **Rule 3: A Magistrate shall perform the duties of judicial office impartially and diligently.**
- **Rule 4: A Magistrate shall so conduct the Magistrate's extra-judicial activities to minimise the risk of conflict with judicial obligations.**
- **Rule 5: A Magistrate shall refrain from inappropriate political activity.**

1.3 RULE 1: A MAGISTRATE SHALL UPHOLD THE INTEGRITY AND INDEPENDENCE OF THE JUDICIARY

This is a general rule. It relates to the ongoing personal commitment that a Magistrate must have to a high standard of ethical and professional conduct. This commitment is just as important to the discharge of duties as is a technical knowledge of the law.

Magistrates must recognise that public confidence rests on the conduct of each Magistrate, and must have the personal commitment to upholding public confidence through the ethical and independent discharge of judicial duties. Rules 2-5 elaborate on the requirements of this commitment.

1.4 RULE 2: A MAGISTRATE SHALL AVOID IMPROPRIETY AND THE APPEARANCE OF IMPROPRIETY IN ALL OF THE MAGISTRATE'S ACTIVITIES

Magistrates must accept the fact that they are exposed to close public scrutiny both in their professional and personal lives. Because of this, a Magistrate must accept restrictions on his or her conduct which might not apply to ordinary citizens.

For example, an ordinary citizen (for instance a nurse, PMV driver, pilot or village farmer) would not be likely to attract criticism for associating with persons who have a questionable reputation or who have served a criminal sentence. Similarly, an ordinary citizen would be unlikely to attract criticism for associating with a politician. The ability of people to perform their jobs is not usually judged by the people they associate with away from their jobs. Even if such an association did attract criticism, an ordinary citizen would be entitled to take the view that it is the *criticism* that is unwarranted, not the association. A Magistrate does not have the luxury of acting on this basis. No-one would dispute that a Magistrate has a *legal* right to make such an association. However, a Magistrate should forgo such a legal right if it would generate negative public perception about the Magistrate's integrity as a member of the judiciary.

Similarly, an ordinary citizen might not be judged adversely for minor infringements of laws or regulations. For example, if an ordinary citizen forgets to have his or her motor vehicle registration renewed and inadvertently drives for a few days after the expired date, no-one is likely to make an adverse judgment about the person or the person's ability to perform his or her duties. Any busy person might forget to renew a vehicle registration on time. A Magistrate on the other hand must be aware that adverse judgments could readily be made against the Magistrate's professional abilities in exactly these circumstances.

A Magistrate must be careful to separate his or her personal affairs from the professional office he or she holds. Judicial office must never be used to gain advantage, either directly or indirectly for a Magistrate or anyone else. For instance, judicial letterhead must never be used in personal correspondence. A Magistrate must maintain a completely "hands off" relationship with any court proceedings or pending proceedings that affect his or her own interests or the interests of a family member or friend.

Section 55 of the *Constitution* provides that all persons have the same rights regardless of "race, tribe, place of origin, political opinion, colour, creed, religion or sex." A Magistrate must be careful to avoid any associations with people or groups that discriminate on any of these grounds. Support for, or even indirect association with, such an organisation by a Magistrate could create negative perceptions in the minds or members of the public about a Magistrate's ability to uphold s 55 of the *Constitution* in court.

This restriction is not absolute and the Magistrate's own judgment is required to determine how far it extends in particular circumstances. For instance, it does not prevent a Magistrate from belonging to a particular church. Nor would it be improper for a Magistrate to belong to an organisation that is dedicated to the preservation of religious, ethnic or cultural values of legitimate common interest to its members.

1.5 RULE 3: A MAGISTRATE SHALL PERFORM THE DUTIES OF JUDICIAL OFFICE IMPARTIALLY AND DILIGENTLY

This rule is directed at the manner in which a Magistrate behaves in the discharge of his or her professional duties. It affects a Magistrate's dealings with superiors, persons appearing in court (parties, counsel and witnesses) and with members of the courthouse staff.

Diligence requires a continuing effort. Despite a sometimes onerous caseload, a Magistrate must not refuse to hear a case that is assigned unless there is a legitimate reason to disqualify oneself.

A Magistrate must remain competent and up to date in the law. Although not all Magistrates have access to a complete law library, every Magistrate should make full use of the library materials that are available.

1.5.1 Maintaining a professional bearing

In court, a Magistrate must display patience and courtesy. Court proceedings are stressful to parties and others, especially those without any previous experience. A Magistrate will take this into account and project a sense of calm authority in the courtroom. It must be remembered that non-verbal communications, including facial expressions, can create a perception of bias, impatience, or anger that could bring the judicial system into disrepute.

A Magistrate must maintain civility and decorum in the courtroom and ensure that those appearing in court display these qualities, both towards the court and towards others appearing before the court.

A Magistrate must be alert to the challenges faced by those who are illiterate, without legal representation or dealing with a language barrier.

In an adversarial system of justice, it is not up to the Judge or Magistrate to adduce evidence or examine witnesses: see 2.9.4. Occasionally counsel, for some reason, conducts an examination in an obviously unsatisfactory way. This may leave the Magistrate with unanswered questions about relevant facts. It is proper for a Magistrate to ask questions in such circumstances in order to clarify the state of the evidence.

Also, when the evidence is complex, such as when an expert is giving opinion evidence, it is frequently necessary for a Magistrate to ask questions.

Ideally, questions from a Magistrate should wait until counsel has finished the examination or cross-examination as the case may be. Sometimes, however, questioning from the Magistrate is required during the course of an examination of a witness.

Too many questions from the bench can distort the proceedings and create an impression that the Magistrate is in fact biased: see 2.9.4. This issue arose in the case of *Birch v The State* [1979] PNGLR 75. During the prosecution of that case the Magistrate asked 186 questions compared to 123 which were asked by the prosecutor. The accused appealed his conviction for sexual offences on the basis that "there was undue participation by the Magistrate in the trial of such a nature and extent that justice did not appear to be done."

The Supreme Court in *Birch v The State* acknowledged that a court must be careful that it does not interfere in proceedings to an excessive extent. However, it also acknowledged that it can be difficult, especially in cases of alleged sexual offences, to get young female complainants to "come out with their version of the complaint" in court. The court went on to say (at 80):

> "In the circumstances of the country it may become necessary ... for a Magistrate to hold the balance between the interest of the State in enforcing the law and that of the accused in defending himself against a charge by intervention of a rather more detailed and prolonged nature than would be called for or proper in other more sophisticated settings."

A Magistrate has the power to recall witnesses who have already given evidence. This would be done where the interests of justice require. However, just as there is a limit on the degree to which a Magistrate should interfere with the proceedings by asking questions, so too the recalling of witnesses by a Magistrate would not occur on a regular basis. The following remarks were made in *Birch v The State* (at 85):

> "The other matter was the recall of three witnesses by the Magistrate. His Honour had every right to do this ... It is permissible. Of course, one has to take care and it is not something done lightly."

1.5.2 Ex parte proceedings

A Magistrate must be mindful of the basic rule of fairness (natural justice) that each party shall be given a right to appear in a case in which they have a legal interest: see 2.6.2. Parties normally should not appear before a Magistrate in the absence of the other party. Each party to a dispute has a right to be present, to be heard and to have a chance to answer the allegations and submissions made against him or her.

Some circumstances may justify the hearing of an application ex parte. For instance, a party in a civil matter may be taken to have *chosen* not to appear. Some applications by their nature are best made on an ex parte basis. An application for a Mareva injunction is one example. An application for a restraining order under Pt X of the *District Courts Act* where the applicant is under real physical threat by the respondent is another.

In cases where ex parte proceedings are justified, the party or parties who are not present must be given the first available opportunity to apply to set aside the order made against them. This requires that any order made ex parte includes a provision that it be served on absent parties and that they be entitled to apply to vary or vacate the order. A discussion of ex parte hearings is found in Chapter 14.

1.5.3 Restricting all communications to open court

It is improper for a Magistrate to speak out of court, either publicly or privately, about a pending case. It is improper for a Magistrate to meet with or communicate with parties or witnesses outside of court, unless such communications are part of the court proceedings or have been consented to by the parties. A Magistrate may confer with other Magistrates about a case, unless the other Magistrate is someone who would be disqualified from hearing the case.

An exception to the rule is found in situations where a Magistrate attempts to assist the parties by acting as a mediator: see Chapter 24. However, if mediation is unsuccessful, a Magistrate may be disqualified from presiding at a contested hearing: see *District Courts Act*, s 22C.

Once a case has been decided and a judgment given, a Magistrate must not elaborate or qualify the decision in any out of court communications. The judgment speaks for itself. Further involvement creates confusion rather than clarity. Pronouncements by a Magistrate, even if made out of court, can be interpreted by parties as an invitation to make further response. This only complicates matters further.

Proper communication of decisions and reasons for decisions is important, but takes place in court, in accordance to specific criteria and constraints: see Chapter 25.

Courthouse staff should be reminded of their duty of confidentiality in relation to all communications with a Magistrate regarding all matters that come before the court. Of course matters heard in open court, unless subject to an order to the contrary, are by their nature public. Nevertheless, staff should be instructed that it is unprofessional to needlessly gossip about what goes on even in open court: see 4.6. Other employees under the direction of a Magistrate must be instructed to display standards of professional conduct in the discharge of their duties.

1.5.4 Efficient use of time and resources

In conducting court proceedings, a Magistrate must be mindful of the need to use time efficiently. This is not only in the interests of the justice system. It is also in the interests of parties who are often put to great expense and inconvenience to appear and take part in court proceedings. See Chapter 23 for a discussion of efficient case management.

The efficient use of time means that hearings should always begin at the appointed time. Apart from being discourteous, delays in commencing hearings, especially if they are habitual, send messages to members of the public that it is not necessary for *them* to be punctual. This leads to further waste of court time as well as damaging the image of the justice system.

Efficient use of the court's time means that cases which require adjournment should, whenever possible, be adjourned to a specific time and place. If witnesses who are present in court will be required, an order should be made that they appear at the next court date. This eliminates the need for parties and registry staff to determine an appropriate court date and go through the trouble of serving parties and witnesses with summonses or notices.

A Magistrate who has supervisory responsibilities over other Magistrates must ensure that court resources are used efficiently by those Magistrates.

1.5.5 Dealing with misconduct of others

A Magistrate sometimes becomes aware of improper conduct on the part of another Magistrate or on the part of a lawyer appearing before the Magistrate. Where the conduct is repeated or serious, it is improper for a Magistrate to ignore such conduct.

The seriousness of a lawyer's misconduct might vary from relatively trivial (such as being five minutes late or not providing a copy of a document to other sides) to more serious (such as making a misrepresentation to the court or acting in clear conflict of interest). The response of a Magistrate will depend on the seriousness of the misconduct. A warning in court, a reprimand in chambers (with both sides represented) or a written complaint to the Papua New Guinea Law Society would be appropriate responses in different circumstances: see 3.4 regarding conduct of lawyers. A Magistrate should report to a senior Magistrate when such a step has been taken or when in doubt about what step is appropriate.

Where a Magistrate becomes aware of serious or repeated misconduct on the part of another Magistrate, it creates a difficult and challenging situation. The Magistrate in question may be a close associate or friend. This can create a conflict of interest. However, the conflict must be resolved in favour of the integrity of the justice system. Depending on the seriousness of the conduct, appropriate responses range from a conversation with the Magistrate in question pointing out the inappropriateness of the conduct to immediately reporting the conduct in writing to the Chief Magistrate.

1.5.6 Disqualification for conflict of interest

Occasionally a matter that comes before a Magistrate creates a conflict of interest. It is important that a Magistrate be quick to recognise a conflict of interest and to take appropriate action. Conflicts of interest can arise in a variety of circumstances. One example is where a Magistrate has a financial interest in the outcome of a case. This includes cases where a close friend or family member of the Magistrate has a financial interest.

Another type of conflict of interest is where a Magistrate's personal beliefs prevent him or her from being impartial. For instance, a Magistrate might have a strong religious conviction that it is wrong to procure a miscarriage. Perhaps the Magistrate is active in an anti-abortion campaign. In such a circumstance, a Magistrate has a duty to declare the conflict. If this belief would affect the Magistrate's ability to preside impartially in a case then the Magistrate has a duty to disqualify himself or herself from presiding over the proceedings.

Another example of a conflict occurs where a Magistrate presides at a trial and learns in the course of evidence that a person other than the accused is guilty of an offence. That other person may later be charged, come before the court and plead not guilty. The Magistrate would not be able to preside at the trial of this charge and should disqualify himself or herself.

Conflict of interest is a matter of degree. For instance, if a Magistrate owns a significant share in a company that is a party to a case, it would clearly be a conflict. However, suppose the Magistrate has a routine bank account at the Papua New Guinea Banking Corporation. Presiding over a case in which the Papua New Guinea Banking Corporation is a party would not in ordinary circumstances be a conflict, even though in a remote or theoretical way a Magistrate's financial interest could possibly be affected.

1.5.7 Disqualification for appearance of conflict

In addition to being alert to actual conflicts and taking steps to deal with them, a Magistrate must also be aware of circumstances that could be *perceived* by others as constituting a conflict of interest. When this is recognised, a Magistrate must take appropriate steps to deal with it.

Case law has established guidelines for Magistrates in Papua New Guinea in situations where there may be a perception of conflict of interest.

In the case of *Boateng v The State* [1990] PNGLR 242, the wife of a Magistrate sat in court next to the prosecutrix in a rape trial and spoke to the prosecutrix during adjournments of the case. The Magistrate's wife did not speak to anyone about these conversations. There was no suggestion that the Magistrate was biased or acted improperly in any way. The Magistrate's wife had a perfect right to attend court and to speak to whomever she pleased.

The conviction was overturned on appeal on the ground that the Magistrate should have disqualified himself from continuing to hear the case. The Supreme Court said:

> "Whether or not a Magistrate's wife actually influences the outcome of the case is important but is not the case here. The point here is the reaction of a reasonable man or woman knowing the relevant facts that justice might have miscarried because of such association in or in the precincts of the court."

The Court adopted the test in *R v Liverpool Justices; Ex parte Topping* [1983] 1 WLR 119:

> "Would a reasonable and fair minded person sitting in a court and knowing all the relevant facts have a 'reasonable suspicion that a fair trial for the appellant was not possible'?"

Whether a Magistrate should apply such a test in any given case depends on the circumstances. In Papua New Guinea, *wantokism* is often regarded as a basis of divided loyalties between people. This may become a factor in court that could cause a reasonable suspicion that a fair trial is not possible. However, the fact that a Magistrate might come from the same part of the country as a party is not of itself a sufficient basis for a Magistrate to become disqualified.

The case of *Fidelis Agai v Buckly Yarume* [1987] PNGLR 124 provides a guide for Magistrates in dealing with the question of disqualification over possible *wantokism*.

In that case, the prosecutor and the presiding Magistrate were from the same province. It was alleged on this ground that the Magistrate should have disqualified himself. The National Court disagreed. The court recognised the principle that it is not necessary to prove that a Magistrate is biased and that "it is enough to show a real likelihood of bias, or at all events that a reasonable person advised of the circumstances might reasonably suspect that a judicial officer was incapable of being impartial and detached".

However, the court went on to say (at 126):

> "It will often happen that a Magistrate will have someone from his own province before him as prosecutor or defence counsel and he may have someone from his own province as defendant or as the victim of a crime. The administration of justice would come to a standstill if every time a prosecutor and victim (or for that matter defence counsel and defendant) came from the same province as the Magistrate a party could have the Magistrate barred for bias."

If the association between the Magistrate and a party is more than simply that they are from the same province, for instance, if they live in the same small town, know each other well and see each other often, a Magistrate would likely disqualify himself or herself on the basis of the tests set out in *Fidelis Agai v Buckly Yarume* and *Boateng v The State*.

Where circumstances satisfy the test for disqualification on the basis of what a reasonable person might think, but the Magistrate feels that no conflict in fact exists, parties may consent to the Magistrate presiding. A Magistrate should ensure that he or she does not influence the parties in deciding whether to consent and that their consent is expressed clearly and recorded.

In cases of emergency, where an application cannot wait and there is no other Magistrate available, necessity may take priority over the question of disqualification. However, such circumstances would be extremely rare.

1.5.8 Prompt rendering of judgments

The expression "justice delayed is justice denied" is the basis of the obligation of Magistrates to render judgments as soon as possible after a matter has come before the court. Parties are entitled to a decision on the merits as soon as possible. Not only is this an ethical duty, but it reduces stress and backlogs of work for Magistrates. See Chapter 25 for a full discussion of writing judgments.

1.6 RULE 4: A MAGISTRATE SHALL SO CONDUCT THE MAGISTRATE'S EXTRA-JUDICIAL ACTIVITIES TO MINIMISE THE RISK OF CONFLICT WITH JUDICIAL OBLIGATIONS

A Magistrate should be mindful at all times of the fact that extra-judicial activities could create a doubt about the Magistrate's ability to act impartially. It is neither possible nor desirable for a Magistrate to live a life of isolation. What is required is the exercise of judgment in deciding when and what activities to engage in and what affiliations to maintain.

Where involvement with an activity could create a reasonable doubt about a Magistrate's ability to act impartially, or where it might otherwise cast the justice system into disrepute, a Magistrate should not engage in the activity.

1.6.1 Public communications relating to the justice system

It is permissible for a Magistrate to take part in speaking, writing and teaching activities that have to do with the law or the legal system. Magistrates are in a unique position to promote public understanding and acceptance of the legal system. When engaging in such activities, a Magistrate should avoid making statements that criticise members of the judiciary. Any comments regarding the justice system generally should be made in as constructive and objective a fashion as possible.

1.6.2 Involvement with government, community service or charitable activities

A Magistrate must not become involved in a governmental position (paid or unpaid) except in very limited circumstances. One such circumstance would be a position that is concerned with the legal system or the administration of justice. Another occasion would be where a Magistrate is asked to represent Papua New Guinea in a ceremonial capacity or in relation to educational or cultural activities.

However, before accepting any such appointment a Magistrate should obtain the permission of a superior and ensure that the appointment will not strain the available judicial resources or delay the movement of cases through the court.

As long as no negative perceptions would arise about a Magistrate's ability to act impartially, a Magistrate may serve as an officer, director, trustee or non-legal adviser in a governmental or non governmental agency that is devoted to the improvement of the law. He or she may also serve in a similar capacity in a charitable, religious or educational organisation that operates on a non-profit basis.

However, a Magistrate must not become involved in any organisation if it is likely that the organisation will be engaged in contested proceedings that come before the Magistrate in court.

1.6.3 Non profit fund raising and recruiting membership

Even where it is permissible for a Magistrate to be associated with an organisation, the Magistrate must not become involved in fund raising activities for the organisation. To do so would risk creating the impression that the Magistrate is using his or her judicial position to pressure others to contribute money. The only exception is that a Magistrate is permitted to solicit funds from fellow Magistrates provided that the soliciting Magistrate is not the supervisor of those being solicited.

A Magistrate who is associated with an organisation may take part in the management and investment of the organisation's funds.

Sometimes recruitment of members of an organisation can appear to outsiders to be like fund raising. If there is a likelihood of this, a Magistrate must refrain from engaging in the recruitment of members for any organisation he or she is associated with.

Under no circumstances should a Magistrate use the prestige of judicial office for fundraising or membership recruitment.

1.6.4 Financial activities

In the course of performing judicial duties, a Magistrate might become aware of financial opportunities. For instance, if a Magistrate knows that a businessman is likely to be sentenced to a term of imprisonment, there could be an obvious financial advantage in buying or investing in the businessman's competitor. There are many other circumstances where this type of potential advantage could arise.

A Magistrate must never take advantage of financial opportunities that he or she becomes aware of through the position of Magistrate. This extends to members of a Magistrate's family or any other person.

Subject to the limitations set out above, it is permissible for a Magistrate to hold and manage investments belonging to himself or herself or members of his or her family. On the same basis, it is permissible for a Magistrate to be engaged in a business that is closely held by the Magistrate or members of the Magistrate's family. However, such engagement should not require time away from judicial duties or otherwise place the Magistrate in a position of potential conflict.

1.6.5 Gifts and loans

A Magistrate must be very careful when accepting gifts. It is easy for even a minor gift to appear as a bribe or an attempt to influence a Magistrate in the discharge of judicial duties. It can raise questions about the Magistrate's impartiality and the integrity of the judicial office. This applies to gifts to the Magistrate or to family members residing with a Magistrate.

The only gifts that a Magistrate should accept are:

- Complimentary materials relating to the law (such as books, tapes CD Roms or other resource materials) supplied by publishers.
- An invitation to a Magistrate and spouse or guest to attend a bar related function or other activity relating to the legal system or administration of justice.
- A gift or loan from a relative or close personal friend where such a gift would not require a Magistrate to disqualify himself or herself from a case.
- A loan from a lending institution which is made in the usual course of business and on the same terms that are offered to other members of the public.
- A scholarship or fellowship awarded on the same terms that it is offered to other members of the public.
- A gift from a person who is not a party to court proceedings and is not likely to come before the Magistrate in future proceedings. This precludes any gift from a lawyer or law firm, and from any clients of law firms if they are likely to appear before the Magistrate.
- The Code recommends that even if a gift is permissible, if it is of a value greater than K100 and is not from a close family member, it should be reported to a senior Magistrate.

1.6.6 Professional services

A Magistrate must not engage in professional activities related to the law that fall outside the professional duties as a Magistrate. This means that a Magistrate must not act as a private mediator or arbitrator or engage in the practice of law.

It is permissible for a Magistrate to act on his or her own behalf in a legal capacity to give legal advice to and draft legal documents for members of the Magistrate's family, so long as no compensation is received.

If a Magistrate engages in any professional services that are not related to the law and are not otherwise prohibited, the Magistrate may receive compensation and reimbursement for *expenses* provided that it does not exceed what a non-Magistrate would receive and provided expense money does not exceed that actual cost of food, lodging or travel reasonably incurred by the Magistrate.

1.7 RULE 5: A MAGISTRATE SHALL REFRAIN FROM POLITICAL ACTIVITY

A Magistrate may participate as a voter in the political process. However, further involvement in politics is improper.

This means that a Magistrate shall not:

- act as a leader or hold an office in a political organisation;
- publicly endorse or oppose a candidate for public office;
- make political speeches;
- attend political gatherings; or
- engage in fundraising for a political cause, contribute to a political cause, or purchase tickets for political dinners or other political fundraising events.

If a Magistrate wishes to become involved in political affairs or run for political office, it is necessary to resign from the position of Magistrate before doing so. A further reason for Magistrates to remain aside from politics is that they may be called upon to rule on election disputes: see Chapter 19B.

1.8 PROTECTION FROM LIABILITY

Although the duties and obligations of a Magistrate pursuant to the Code of Conduct are extensive, they are not the end of the matter. Questions concerning the legal liability of a Magistrate may arise. It is important to note that a Magistrate who observes the Code of Conduct and acts in good faith may enjoy some protection from liability for his or her actions: see Chapter 22 for discussion of the issues.

CHAPTER 2 – THE MAGISTRATES' COURTS IN CONTEXT

2.1 THE NATIONAL JUDICIAL SYSTEM

Magistrates sit mainly in the provincial District Courts which are part of Papua New Guinea's National Judicial System as provided for by the *Constitution* of the independent state: s 155. The District Court is established by its own statute under the authority given to Parliament by s 172(1) of the *Constitution*. Other courts and inquiries usually presided over by Magistrates include the Local Land Court, the Provincial Land Court, the Children's Court and Coroner's hearings.

The *Constitution* vests "the judicial authority of the people" in the National Judicial System and requires that "in interpreting the law, the court shall give paramount consideration to the dispensation of justice": s 158.

2.2 THE MAGISTRATES' COURT AS A CREATURE OF STATUTE

Unlike Judges of the Supreme and National Courts, Magistrates have no inherent authority and can act only in accordance with those powers which are expressly conferred on them by statute. For example, because the only power which Magistrates have to punish a person for contempt of court is provided in the statutes (see 3.1.3), a Magistrate must follow the wording of the section carefully and does not have the wider powers of a Judge.

2.2.1 The principal Act

The District Courts were established by the *District Courts Act* 1964, with both criminal and civil jurisdiction. Until repealed in April 2000, the *Local Courts Act* provided for a Local Court jurisdiction and junior Magistrates sat in Local Courts throughout Papua New Guinea. The reforms of 2000 rationalised the magistracy and the lower court system. The grading of Magistrates was abolished: see below. The jurisdictional powers of a District Court depend on whether the Magistrate who hears the case is a Principal Magistrate or a District Court Magistrate. For example, while District Court Magistrates may deal with summary offences, only Principal Magistrates may also try certain indictable offences which have been declared to be punishable on summary conviction: *District Courts Act*, s 20 and *Criminal Code Act* 1974, Sch 2.

2.2.2 Other legislation

Magistrates of the District Court also have powers and responsibilities under the *Village Courts Act* 1989. Magistrates may be called upon to decide whether to endorse certain Village Court orders (*Village Courts Act*, ss 68 and 75) and to hear appeals and conduct reviews (*Village Courts Act*, Div 11). In addition, Magistrates have powers and responsibilities under such statutes as the *Land Disputes Settlement Act*, the *Coroners Act*, the *Deserted Wives and Children Act*, the *Inter-Group Fighting Act*, the *Organic Law on National and Local-level Government Elections* and the *Motor Vehicles (Basic Protection Compensation) Act*.

2.2.3 Concurrent jurisdiction and transfer between courts

The proclamations establishing District Courts and Village Courts define the area within which each court may operate. Because of geographic overlap between the courts, parties may have some choice of court and the relevant statutes facilitate transfer of cases from one court to another of the same name or to a different court: *District Courts Act*, s 24 and *Village Courts Act*, s 97. See also further discussion of transfers and venues in Chapter 4.

2.2.4 Appointment, removal and conditions of service

Full-time Magistrates are appointed by a constitutional body, the Judicial and Legal Services Commission (*Constitution*, ss 172(3) and 175), and in accordance with the *Magisterial Service Act*. The Commission determines the qualifications for appointment as Magistrate and appoints the offices of Chief Magistrate, two Deputy Chief Magistrates, Principal Magistrates, a Senior Magistrate for each province and the District Court Magistrates: *Magisterial Service Act*, ss 5-7 and 8. The salaries and conditions of service are determined by the Commission after consultation with the head of the Department of Personnel Management: *Magisterial Service Act*, s 10. The judicial declaration made by Magistrates prior to taking office is set out in Chapter 1 of this manual.

Magistrates are members of the Magisterial Service (*Constitution*, s 173) headed by the Chief Magistrate who, subject to the direction of the Commission, is responsible for its "efficient functioning and operation" and has wide powers in relation to Magistrates' postings and duties: *Magisterial Service Act*, s 2.

Full-time Magistrates may be removed from office only for "incapacity or misbehaviour (including, if applicable, misconduct in office)": *Constitution*, s 172(3).

2.3 SOURCES OF LAW

2.3.1 The Constitution

Since independence in 1975, the laws of Papua New Guinea are subject to the provisions of the *Constitution*, which, together with the organic laws, are the supreme laws of the nation. All acts (whether legislative, executive or judicial) that are inconsistent with these supreme laws are, to the extent of the inconsistency, invalid and ineffective: *Constitution*, s 11. The hierarchy of laws set out in s 9 of the *Constitution* reads:

(a) *Constitution*;

(b) Organic Laws;

(c) Acts of National Parliament;

(c) Emergency Regulations;

(d) Laws made or adopted under the *Constitution*, including subordinate legislation; and

(e) Underlying Law.

2.3.2 Organic laws

These laws of National Parliament are made for limited purposes and amended by special procedures: *Constitution*, ss 12, 14 and 17. Organic laws have been passed on provincial governments, the electoral process, electoral boundaries and the Ombudsman Commission.

2.3.3 Acts of National Parliament

The legislative power of the people is vested in the National Parliament, which, subject to the *Constitution*, has unlimited powers of law-making and is responsible for making laws "for the peace, order and good government of Papua New Guinea and the welfare of the People": *Constitution*, ss 99, 100 and 109.

2.3.4 Emergency regulations

The Head of State, on the advice of the National Executive Council, can declare a national emergency and make regulations which can override most laws of the country, including some, but not all, provisions of the *Constitution*: *Constitution*, ss 246-266.

2.3.5 Laws made by provincial legislatures

Certain areas of activity in the provinces are governed by laws of provincial governments, but, generally speaking, laws relating to the courts and justice and criminal offences are national statutes that apply throughout the country.

2.3.6 Adopted and subordinate legislation

On independence, all prior statutes in force, including a few from Australia and England, were adopted in Papua New Guinea and made subject to the *Constitution*. Subordinate legislation such as regulations and rules made under the authority of statutes is construed subject to those statutes as well as the *Constitution*.

2.3.7 Interpretation of written laws

The *Underlying Law Act* 2000 has placed two obligations on the courts when they are interpreting "any word, expression or proposition in the written law", namely:

Custom: "the Court shall give effect to any relevant customary practice, usage or perception recognised by the people to be affected as a result of the interpretation": s 23(1).

Foreign jurisdictions: "subject to subsection (1), the Courts may consider how the Courts in foreign jurisdictions have interpreted similar or identical provisions, words, expressions or propositions": s 23(2).

2.3.8 Underlying law

2.3.8.1 Constitutional requirements

The "underlying law" is the body of unwritten law, such as "custom" and "common law and equity", which applies to any question on which there is no legislation. Under ss 20 and 21 of the *Constitution*, Parliament was required to declare the underlying law and provide for its development. In the meantime, the provisions of Sch 2 of the *Constitution* were to fulfil this function.

2.3.8.2 The Underlying Law Act 2000

Progress with development of the underlying law should now occur in accordance with the *Underlying Law Act* 2000, which was passed in order to:

(a) state the source of the underlying law;

(b) provide for the formulation of rules of the underlying law; and

(c) provide for the development of the underlying law: *Underlying Law Act* 2000, preamble.

The *Underlying Law Act* appears to replace most, if not all, of Sch 2 of the *Constitution*. When considering what is said about the Act, here and elsewhere in this manual, it should be borne in mind that any difficulties which there may be in interpreting and implementing the Act had not been considered by the courts at the time of writing the manual.

2.3.8.3 Sources of underlying law and their application

The detailed provisions of the *Underlying Law Act* should be referred to, but they may be summarised briefly in the following manner:

1. In every case, the court must apply the laws of Papua New Guinea in the following order:

   (a) written law;

   (b) the underlying law (if it has been formulated);

   (c) the customary law; and

   (d) the common law: see ss 6 and 7.

2. The sources of underlying law are the customary law and the common law as defined in s 1 of the Act. They must to be adopted and applied to form part of the underlying law in accordance with the qualifications set out in s 4 of the Act.

3. A court that refuses to apply a principle or rule of customary law, or decides to apply a principle or rule of common law, under s 4, must give reasons for its decision: s 4(4), and see 25.6.4.

4. Rules for the ascertainment and application of customary law are set out in ss 16 and 17, and should be read with the *Customs Recognition Act*: see 2.4 below.

2.3.8.4 Further responsibility for development of the underlying law

1. It is the responsibility of the courts, especially the Supreme and National Courts, to ensure that the underlying law develops as a coherent system: *Underlying Law Act*, s 5.

2. Where a court, other than the Supreme or National Court, has made a decision applying the underlying law, the customary law or the common law in the manner set out in s 7, it must forthwith send a copy of the decision to the Chief Justice and the Chairman of the Law Reform Commission, to be dealt with by either of these under ss 12, 13 and 14.

3. The National Court and the Law Reform Commission have wide powers in relation to the review of decisions, as set out in ss 12, 13 and 14.

4. Counsel appearing in a proceeding which raises a question of whether or not the customary law applies, is under a duty to assist the court by calling evidence and obtaining relevant information and opinion that would assist the court in determining:

   (a) the nature of the relevant rules of customary law; and

   (b) whether or not to apply those rules in the proceedings: ss 15 and 16.

2.4 CUSTOM

2.4.1 Custom: its nature

Custom is a system of rules, usually unwritten, intertwined with the way of life of the community, which people living in that community obey without the formal laws and courts of the state. In Papua New Guinea, under the constitutional definition, "custom" means:

> "the customs and usages of indigenous inhabitants of the country existing in relation to the matter in question at the time when and the place in relation to which the matter arises, regardless of whether or not the custom or usage has existed from time immemorial": *Constitution*, Sch 1.2(1); *Underlying Law Act* 2000, s 1.

2.4.2 Custom: its application

2.4.2.1 Custom as a source of law

Custom has wide effect outside the formal legal system but it is also one of the main sources of law which is recognised as having force in circumstances specified by statute: see 2.3.8 above. Custom may not be applied in the courts except as provided by the relevant statutes.

The main statutes are the *Underlying Law Act*, discussed above at 2.3.8, and the *Customs Recognition Act*, which deals with proof of custom (a topic discussed in Chapter 5 on Evidence) and its application generally. Where these two Acts are inconsistent, the usual rule of interpretation applies so that the later Act overrides the former.

Subject to the above two Acts, customary law must be applied by all courts. However, it may be rejected in a particular case if:

[QUALIFICATIONS ON THE USE OF CUSTOM]

- it is inconsistent with a written law (the *Constitution* or statute - see 2.3.1 above);
- its application and enforcement would be contrary to the National Goals and Directive Principles and the Basic Social Obligations established by the *Constitution*; or
- its application and enforcement would be contrary to the basic rights guaranteed by Div III.3 (Basic Rights) of the *Constitution* (*Underlying Law Act*, s 4).

2.4.2.2 Custom in criminal matters

The main limitations on the application of custom are to be found in ss 4 and 5 of the *Customs Recognition Act*. In criminal matters, the state alone can punish people, and it can do so only for crimes defined by state law: *Constitution*, s 37(2). A person cannot be convicted for doing something which is an offence against custom unless it is also an offence under statute or regulation. Conversely, people may be guilty of breaking the state law while doing something which custom allows them to do.

The Act requires that courts are not to take custom into account in criminal cases except to determine:

[DESPITE LIMITED SCOPE, CUSTOM MAY BE VERY RELEVANT]

- whether a person had the state of mind required by law (see 7.4-7.6, 7.15 and 7.16);
- where the law allows reasonableness to be relevant, whether an act or omission, or an excuse given by a person, was reasonable or unreasonable (see Chapters 7.13, 7.15 and 7.16);
- in accordance with any other law, whether to proceed to the conviction of a guilty party; or
- the penalty (if any) to be imposed on a guilty party,

or except where the court thinks that by not taking the custom into account injustice may be done to a person (see s 4).

2.4.2.3 Custom in civil and other cases

Subject to the *Underlying Law Act*, the application of custom is also restricted in cases other than criminal cases.

Custom may be taken into account only in relation to the matters listed in s 5 of the *Customs Recognition Act*. To summarise the more important matters briefly, custom may be applied to determine:

[CUSTOM MAY BE DECISIVE IN CIVIL AND OTHER MATTERS]

- the ownership of customary land, including any thing in or on it, or its produce, and rights of hunting or gathering;
- the ownership of rights in the sea or reef, including the bed of the sea, a river or lake, and rights of fishing;
- the ownership by custom of rights to water;
- the devolution of interests in customary land;
- trespass by animals;
- marriage, divorce or the right to custody or guardianship of infants under a customary marriage;
- a transaction that the parties intended, or justice requires, should be regulated wholly or partly by custom and not by law;
- the reasonableness of an act, default or omission by a person;
- the existence of a state of mind of a person,

or it may be applied where the court thinks that by not taking the custom into account injustice may be done to a person. In the case of guardianship and custody of infants and adoption, custom must always be taken fully into account in deciding questions before the court.

2.4.2.4 Conflict between customs

Where a question arises as to which particular customary law should apply, the court must determine the matter in accordance with the rules set out in s 17 of the *Underlying Law Act*.

2.4.3 Custom in other recognised applications

2.4.3.1 Customary law rules and procedures

In two jurisdictions, under the *Village Courts Act* and the *Land Disputes Settlement Act*, the courts are free to follow customary procedures in order to arrive at settlements or decisions in accordance with custom, even if that is inconsistent with other statutes or laws.

2.4.3.2 Custom specifically recognised

Customary institutions are allowed to operate under statute in certain situations.

For example:

- the *Marriage Act* recognises customary marriages;
- the *Wills, Probate and Administration Act* preserves customary succession rules; and
- the *Business and Land Groups Incorporation Acts* recognise customary groups as bodies which can do business or hold land for the purposes of state law.

2.4.4 The recording of custom

As a further means of developing the underlying law of Papua New Guinea, Magistrates in the District Courts and Land Courts are encouraged to record their findings as to what the custom is in particular cases (see Chapter 25), and are required to give reasons and send copies of their decisions to the Chief Justice and the Law Reform Commission in accordance with the *Underlying Law Act* (see 2.3.8 above).

2.5 COMMON LAW AND EQUITY

The principles and rules of common law in force in England immediately before 16 September 1975 are declared to be a source of, and must be adopted and applied as part of, the underlying law of Papua New Guinea, provided the common law in question is:

consistent with written law;

applicable and appropriate to the circumstances of the country;

consistent with customary law applied under the *Underlying Law Act*;

and

its application and enforcement would not be contrary to the National Goals and Directive Principles and the Basic Social Obligations established by the *Constitution*; and

its application and enforcement would not be contrary to the basic rights guaranteed by Div III.3 (Basic Rights) of the *Constitution*: *Underlying Law Act*, s 4.

Because statutes and custom do not cover all aspects of commercial, administrative and private law, the courts are constantly applying common law and equity: see 2.8.1 below.

An exception is the Village Court jurisdiction where case law is seldom referred to. If custom does not apply, the court is required to decide all matters before it in accordance with "substantial justice": *Village Courts Act*, s 58. It is helpful to think of "substantial justice" as the justice of the decision itself – the outcome of the case – while "natural justice", discussed below, relates to the process or procedures leading to the decision.

2.6 CONSTITUTIONAL GUIDANCE

2.6.1 National Goals and Directive Principles

The statements of National Goals and Directive Principles and of Basic Rights and Social Obligations which appear in the preamble to the *Constitution* are not law to be applied directly, but they are able to provide guidance in the administration of justice. The *Constitution* says that where any law or power can reasonably be understood, applied or enforced in such a way as to give effect to the National Goals and

Directive Principles, it should be understood, applied or enforced in that way. Of course, the intentions of the *Constitution* and Parliament are always paramount: *Constitution*, s 25.

The preamble contains several statements which may be useful to the courts in explaining the reasons behind existing laws and the ways in which they should be applied. For example, the statements emphasise the equality of all citizens; their rights of equal access to government and the courts; rights to participation in the consideration of matters affecting their interests; the value of the family unit, equality of partnership and responsible parenthood; preservation of natural resources; and the protection of culture, language and traditional villages.

2.6.2 Natural justice

The principles of natural justice have been developed by the English common law and recognised in the drafting of the *Constitution.*

Good examples of what natural justice requires are:

- the rights of a person charged with an offence, as listed in s 37(4); and
- the rights of parties in civil disputes specified in s 37(11)-(13).

It is intended that the principles of natural justice should be part of the rules of the "underlying law". Section 59(2) adds:

> "The minimum requirement of natural justice is the duty to act fairly and, in principle, to be seen to act fairly."

Although the *Underlying Law Act* has replaced Sch 2 of the *Constitution* dealing with development of the underlying law (referred to in s 60 of the *Constitution*), s 59 read with s 24(1) of the *Underlying Law Act* seems to keep alive the high status of the principles of natural justice in Papua New Guinea.

Natural justice is not merely an abstract concept. Every time a magistrate has a discretion as to a matter that affects the process of a case (for example, decisions whether to adjourn a case and for how long) natural justice considerations are relevant. In the Village Courts, the Magistrate's powers and procedures must be exercised "in accordance with the principles of natural justice": *Village Courts Act*, s 59(2). Just how natural justice should be applied depends on the nature of the case, and a useful summary is set out in 4.1.3.

2.7 CONSTITUTIONAL RIGHTS

The *Constitution* guarantees certain rights which must be respected and applied in the courts. This summary is only a set of signposts to assist the reader to find the law relevant to the case in hand.

2.7.1 Types of rights

2.7.1.1 Fundamental rights

- **Right to Freedom** – This makes it clear that:
  - every person has the legal right to do anything that does not injure or interfere with the rights and freedoms of others, and is not prohibited by law; and
  - no person is obliged to do anything that is not required by law: *Constitution*, s 32.
- **Right to Life** (s 35) and **Freedom from Inhuman Treatment** (s 36)
- **Right to Protection of the Law** – Every Magistrate should be familiar with these detailed provisions for the protection of the accused, including, for example, the right to a fair hearing within a reasonable time by an independent and impartial court: s 37. A full summary of these rights as applicable to criminal cases is set out below in Chapter 6. As to civil cases, see Chapter 14.

2.7.1.2 Qualified rights

The following rights may be restricted by statute on certain grounds, and to the extent that is reasonably justifiable in a democratic society (ss 38-40):

- **Liberty of the Person** – These rights, concerning arrest and detention, as well as the next two, are also particularly relevant for the criminal jurisdiction (see Chapter 6): s 42;
- **Freedom from Forced Labour**: s 43;
- **Freedom from Arbitrary Search and Entry**: s 44;
- **Freedom of Conscience, Thought and Religion**: s 45;
- **Freedom of Expression**: s 46;
- **Freedom of Assembly and Association**: s 47;
- **Freedom of Employment**: s 48;
- **Right to Privacy**: s 49.

2.7.1.3 Citizen-only rights

While all persons in Papua New Guinea possess the above rights, those that follow are granted only to citizens:

- **Right to Vote and Stand for Public Office**: s 50;
- **Right to Freedom of Information**: s 51;
- **Right to Freedom of Movement**: s 52;
- **Protection from Unjust Deprivation of Property**: s 53;
- **Right to Equality of all Citizens** – regardless of race, tribe, place of origin, political opinion, colour, creed, religion or sex: s 55;
- **Rights to Vote and Acquire Freehold Land**: s 56.

2.7.2 Enforcement of rights

The above rights or freedoms may be enforced in the Supreme or National Court. If Magistrates, on their own initiative or at the request of a party or person interested, think there has been an infringement of a right or freedom, or there is reasonable probability of infringement, they may adjourn the proceedings before them in order to allow the question to be decided by the superior court. Damages may be awarded for infringement: ss 57 and 58.

2.7.3 Group rights and responsibilities

Some of the statements of the National Goals and Directive Principles and of the Basic Rights and Social Obligations include recognition of the importance of families and wider groups in Papua New Guinea. They stress reciprocal rights and obligations. In keeping with these values, a Village Court may recognise a group as if it were a natural person and make orders for or against it: *Village Courts Act*, ss 98-100. Under other legislation also, such as the *Land Disputes Settlement Act* and the *Inter-Group Fighting Act*, the Magistrate may be required to consider the rights and responsibilities of traditional tribes, clans, customary kinship groups and communities. In these situations, the group becomes a party, and its interests may take priority over the interests of an individual member.

2.8 CASE LAW IN THE MAGISTRATES' COURTS

2.8.1 Case law

Whenever a court interprets a statute or applies a rule of common law and equity, or a rule of customary law, it is making "case law" in the sense that its decision will help another court decide a similar case in the future. When the reasons for a judgment are written down they are an example or "precedent" which others may follow. Over the years, and from precedent to precedent, a body of law is built up in this way and continues to grow (for example, the *Papua New Guinea Law Reports*). Now it is useful to look at what a precedent is, and when it is binding.

2.8.2 The ratio of the case

A decision alone, such as a finding of "guilty", is not a precedent, because you need to know the facts of the case and the legal reasons for the decision before it is of any help in the future. So the findings of fact and the court's opinion of the law and legal consequences together make up the "ratio decedendi" or precedent. Sometimes a judge will express opinions which are not necessary for the actual decision in the case, and these are not part of the precedent and are called "obiter dicta". Also, if judges in a case do not agree, it is only the ratio of the judgments of the majority view which are the precedent.

2.8.3 Binding precedent

The rule is that a court must follow the precedents set by the decisions of those courts that have power over it. A court will normally follow its own previous decisions in later cases, but it is not bound to do so. Decisions of the Supreme and National Courts are binding on all other courts: *Underlying Law Act*, s 19. Sections 20-22 of the *Underlying Law Act* set out rules for dealing with conflict between precedents, considering decisions of foreign and pre-independence courts, and the overruling of decisions, so that in special cases new decisions may be prospective in operation only.

It is helpful for Magistrates to collect decisions of the District Court as guidance, and to try to produce, as far as possible, a consistent set of decisions and a body of law in the areas with which the Magistrates are frequently dealing. The importance of good reasoning in decisions is discussed below in Chapter 25.

2.9 THE ROLE OF THE MAGISTRATE IN ADVERSARIAL PROCEEDINGS

2.9.1 Procedural rules

The *District Courts Act* does not say much about how Magistrates should run their courts and conduct cases. The importance of impartiality and professional bearing has been stressed in Chapter 1. Some rules of procedure and evidence are laid down in the Act, and others appear in the *Evidence Act* and the *Criminal Code*, but the rules do not deal fully with such issues as:

- **what Magistrates should actually say to parties, lawyers and witnesses throughout a case;**
- **precisely who may speak in court, and when;**
- **how much control Magistrates should exercise over these people – for example, as to how long a witness may have to speak, and how long the witness may be cross-examined, what sorts of things people may say and, more importantly, what they should not say in the hearing;**
- **when and for what reasons Magistrates should interrupt or intervene in what is happening.**

The answers to these questions, and many others that arise during a hearing, come from written and unwritten rules that govern courts generally in the "common law" world. Some guidance in relation to these issues will be found in this manual. Of course, a lot depends on whether a party has a legal representative: see 3.2-3.5. Here is a brief explanation of the Magistrate's role.

Magistrates are responsible for administering justice, under the *District Courts Act* and other statutes, in the matters that are brought to the courts by the police, other government authorities or members of the community. The courts must decide matters if the parties are unable to resolve them or settle the disputes between themselves: see Chapter 24 on settlement. Court proceedings will be commenced by the prosecution (where an offence is alleged) or by the aggrieved person in civil and other matters. The courts in Papua New Guinea have inherited the English and United States "common law" system in which the Judge or Magistrate has no power to begin proceedings. The court cannot conduct its own inquiry, and, even after a case has been started, it cannot call for people to be brought to the court as witnesses unless a party requests it. Powers of inquiry under the *Coroner's Act*, the *Deserted Wives and Children Act*, the *Inter-Group Fighting Act* and the *Motor Vehicles (Basic Protection Compensation) Act* are exceptions.

The role of a Magistrate who is acting as mediator in civil matters is very different: *District Courts Act*, ss 22B-22D. Also, different rules apply to a Magistrate who is exercising the jurisdiction of a Village Court. The technical rules of evidence do not apply (*Village Courts Act*, s 38) and the Village Court has primary responsibilities with regard to keeping the peace, mediation and resolution of disputes and the application of custom: *Village Courts Act*, ss 43, 51, 53 and 57.

2.9.2 Reasons for the adversarial system

Under the "common law" system, the court is the place where the parties present and defend their arguments as to fact and law, and it is up to the parties to decide how to run their side of the case. This applies to criminal as well as all other types of cases. The theory is that the best way to test the truthfulness of a witness's evidence and "how good is the party's case?" is to allow the other side to attack it. The proceedings are called "adversarial" because the opposing parties are pitted against each other. They may refuse to disclose documents or call evidence unless the rules of evidence require it. The parties may use strategies to try to outwit the opponent. Only the prosecution side in criminal cases has a duty actively to assist the opponent (the accused) by giving him or her details of evidence to be called. The result of the contest may not give the court the whole truth, but, if the procedural rules have been followed and the principles of natural justice have been observed, we usually say "justice has been done".

2.9.3 Disadvantages of the system

A result of the existence of these procedural rules is that the adversarial contest is often uneven – one side is usually stronger than the other. The duty of disclosure on the prosecutor recognises that the prosecution has the power of the state behind it. The strength of a party might come from high status (chief or official), wealth (businessman), large physique (a husband) or from being able to have a lawyer in court. The field of battle is seldom level. Also, unfortunately, witnesses may lie, parties may try to avoid the rules of evidence by concealing documents or evidence, and parties and lawyers may try to mislead the other side and the court in many ways.

2.9.4 The role of the Magistrate

The responsibility of the Magistrate is to ensure that:

- the Magistrate does not hear a case where the Magistrate might be seen to be biased (for example, as the relative of a party) (see the discussion of impartiality in 1.5);
- if there are prospects of settlement (civil) or agreement as to plea (criminal) the parties are given reasonable opportunities to avoid a contest in court;
- the parties will follow the rules governing the order of giving evidence and making submissions so that the rules of evidence as to burden of proof can be observed (except that the technical rules of evidence do not apply in the Village Court);
- the trial or hearing is fair to all parties, for example, by giving them time to be heard, stopping unfair questioning and remarks, dealing firmly with attempts to mislead the court (see the discussion of natural justice above and in 4.1.3);
- where a party is obviously weaker than the opponent (perhaps because the party needs, but cannot afford, a lawyer), that party is allowed more time to present the case and is given necessary assistance (see 3.2);
- the Magistrate limits his or her questioning from the bench unless the circumstances of the case clearly require it, or questioning by parties or counsel is unsatisfactory (see 1.5.1);
- whenever it seems appropriate, people in court are reminded that the purpose of the hearing is to do justice;
- the friendly atmosphere of the court (including the Magistrate and staff) encourages all parties and witnesses to come forward and participate willingly; and
- apart from ensuring fairness in the above manner, the Magistrate does not interfere in the conduct of the case (see the discussion of "professional bearing" in 1.5.1).

Finally, the Magistrate must give a decision based only upon:

- the legal issue or matter which the prosecution or aggrieved party has brought to the court; and
- the evidence presented in the trial or hearing.

This is the way in which the *Constitution* intends that the court should dispense justice: see s 158 (referred to in 2.1 above) and also s 59 on natural justice (in 2.6.2).

CHAPTER 3 – MAGISTRATES' POWERS, REPRESENTATION OF PARTIES AND THE CONDUCT OF MATTERS IN COURT

3.1 THE MAGISTRATE IN COURT

3.1.1 The atmosphere of the court

The court's function is to do justice. The Magistrate sets the tone of the proceedings by ensuring that not only is the law administered justly with fairness and compassion, but that this is seen to be done: see also the discussion in Chapters 1 and 2.

It is important to remember that the court is a government service to the public acting on behalf of the people of Papua New Guinea in order to enforce the law and resolve disputes. All parties, witnesses and other members of the public should be helped to feel at ease and as comfortable as possible in a place which is often very stressful for many people and where emotions often run high.

The dignity of the court is maintained better by encouraging people to understand its procedures and respect its fairness, rather than by causing people to fear its authority.

The court is an open environment to which the public is entitled to have access, unless special circumstances arise: see 4.6.

Magistrates' approach to their work not only sets the tone of the court hearings, but it also reflects the commitment of Magistrates to their duties. It is often said that that commitment may be demonstrated by patience, courtesy, punctuality, and generally the appearance of doing right.

3.1.2 The authority of Magistrates

Magistrates are in charge of the courtroom and are expected to control proceedings so that they are just and fair. The procedure of hearings is discussed in Chapter 4. As a general rule, the Magistrate should allow parties to conduct their cases as they think fit: see 2.9 for the Magistrate's role in adversarial proceedings. However, the Magistrate is like a referee who should politely but firmly control the individual behaviour of parties, lawyers and witnesses if that behaviour interferes with the opportunities of others to present their cases. Just as a referee can send a player off the field, the Magistrate can order a person to sit down, be quiet or, in extreme circumstances, leave the courtroom.

Magistrates have certain statutory powers to assist them to keep order in court. Because the court is a creature of statute, the sanctions Magistrates can use to assist them maintain order in court are found in the *District Courts Act* and *Village Courts Act*.

3.1.3 Contempt of court

3.1.3.1 The Magistrate's approach to contempt

This is the most powerful tool available to the Magistrate and should be used only when it is absolutely necessary. The reason for this is that if the Magistrate is obliged to punish somebody for contempt, that may be an indication that the Magistrate has not been careful to anticipate problems in the court and to take less drastic steps to maintain order in the court. For example, if a party, lawyer or witness has lost his or her temper, or is inclined to persist in arguing with the Magistrate, the Magistrate should quietly adjourn the case for an hour or two or until the afternoon, or even the next day, to enable people to quieten down. The Magistrate could go on to deal with other cases in the meantime. An adjournment is better than a shouting match, and, on resuming the case, the Magistrate can state that such unruly conduct is unbecoming and cannot be permitted.

Above all, the Magistrate must be decisive and act with dignity. The case can be carried on, but if the disturbance continues then the Magistrate should deal with it as a matter of contempt.

Contempt is an offence, and so must be proved beyond reasonable doubt to have been committed in the manner alleged.

Contempt can be divided into four categories, two "in court" and two "out of court":

In court – within Magistrate's power

1. Disturbing the conduct of the court while the court is sitting.
2. Disobeying an order of the court after the case is finished.

Outside court – Magistrate has no power

3. Publishing in newspapers or by other means, before the case is heard, such things as statements which might prejudice parties in the case.
4. Making a serious personal criticism of the Magistrate, or conduct of a case, out of court.

Magistrates must follow the statutes in relation to the first two categories of "in court" contempt but, unlike the National and Supreme Courts, Magistrates have no power to deal with contempt committed "out of court" (the third and fourth categories).

3.1.3.2 In the District Court

Section 277 of the *District Courts Act* creates the following offences, committed by a person who:

- wilfully interrupts the proceedings of a court; or
- conducts himself or herself disrespectfully to the court during the sittings of the court; or
- obstructs or assaults a person in attendance, or an officer of the court, in view of the court; or

- wilfully disobeys an order made by the court that witnesses other than the complainant and defendant should go and remain outside and beyond the hearing of the court until required to give evidence: s 63.
- On being found guilty, the person:
- may be ordered to leave; and
- be excluded from the court; and
- fined up to K200: s 277(1).

In addition, a person who, in the opinion of the court, wilfully prevaricates in giving evidence may be found guilty and fined up to K100: s 277(2).

It is important to note that where any such offence appears to have been committed in the presence of the court, the Magistrate may rely on his or her own knowledge or may call any person to the stand to give evidence as a witness. If the court convicts the offender a fine may be ordered, but, if before the court arises the offender makes an apology which the court considers satisfactory, the fine may be remitted wholly or in part: s 277(4). The enforcement of court orders is dealt with in Chapter 20.

3.1.3.3 In the Village Court

The Village Court has somewhat different powers.

A person commits an offence who:

- wilfully interrupts, interferes with or disturbs the proceedings of a Village Court; or
- wilfully obstructs a Village Court official or other person acting under the *Village Courts Act*: *Village Courts Act*, s 62(1).

Instead of a penalty of up to six months imprisonment, the court may order community work (s 62(2)) or impose a fine. If imprisonment is ordered, it cannot take effect unless endorsed by a Magistrate: s 68. A similar set of provisions applies if a person fails to obey certain orders of a Village Peace Officer or a Village Court: s 73. Throughout, the court is obliged to carry out its procedures in accordance with the principles of natural justice: s 59.

3.1.4 Order to leave and be excluded from the court

The power to order a person to leave the court (*District Courts Act*, s 277(1)) can be exercised without imposing a fine for contempt. Of course, if it is the defendant in a criminal matter who wilfully disrupts the proceedings, care must be taken to ensure that the defendant's conduct has been so disruptive "as to render the continuance of the proceedings in his absence impracticable": *Constitution*, s 37(5). Otherwise, the defendant has the constitutional right to be present at the trial throughout (*Thomas*

Kavali v Thomas Hoihoi [1986] PNGLR 329), unless it is a simple offence not involving imprisonment: see *District Courts Act*, s 125.

A Village Court has no statutory powers to exclude a person from court unless s 62, above, has been breached.

The public's general right to be present in "open court" is discussed in Chapter 4.

3.1.5 Costs order against a party

A costs order is a sanction available to a Magistrate where one of the parties behaves in such a way as to cause harm or serious inconvenience to other parties. For example, a party, personally or through an agent or lawyer, might wilfully mislead the court and another party, might delay proceedings without reasonable excuse, or might be responsible for causing the case to be adjourned.

The District Court has a general power to award costs when entering a conviction or dismissing an information, when making an order in favour of the complainant or defendant, when adjourning a case, and when dealing with witnesses expenses: *District Courts Act*, s 260.

The Magistrate has discretion whether to award costs against a party. The amount must be "just and reasonable", it must not exceed prescribed amounts in criminal matters, and it must be in accordance with s 260A in the case of a successful defendant in criminal proceedings.

A Village Court has no statutory powers in this regard. For further discussion of costs, see Chapter 21.

3.1.6 Conduct of legal representatives

The Magistrate's contempt powers (above) apply to lawyers and others authorised to represent parties (as defined in *District Courts Act*, s 59).

Before taking action to deal with legal representatives, it is important to remember that:

- **a person charged with an offence is entitled to appear in person or by a legal representative (*Constitution*, s 37(4)(e));**
- **the District Courts Act entitles complainants and defendants to be represented (*District Courts Act*, s 59);**
- **the District Courts generally allow parties in all types of cases to be legally represented; and**
- **lawyers are not permitted to appear in the Village Court (*Village Courts Act*, ss 38 and 80).**

Sometimes legal representatives make the Magistrate's task difficult. While most lawyers take their duty to assist the court seriously, a Magistrate's patience may be tested by a lawyer who argues with the court, or refuses to accept the Magistrate's advice to stop asking a witness irrelevant questions, or who persists in using discourteous language when referring to parties and witnesses. In these circumstances, the Magistrate should try to remain calm and preserve the dignity of judicial office. Because of the party's right to be represented, the Magistrate should allow the lawyer considerable latitude. However, if the interests of justice are clearly interfered with, the Magistrate may warn the lawyer and, if the conduct continues, may adjourn the case and retire from the courtroom or order the lawyer to leave the court. Conviction of a lawyer for contempt would be an extreme course of action.

Breaches of professional conduct and ethics should be reported by the Magistrate to the Lawyers Statutory Committee of the Law Society in Port Moresby: see 3.4.3 below.

3.1.7 Delay

Magistrates are responsible for the efficient flow of cases from issue to final determination: see Chapter 23. The old saying "justice delayed is justice denied" holds true today. The *Constitution* requires that the hearing of a charge shall be "within a reasonable time": s 37(3). It is part of the four-sided right of the accused – to a **fair** hearing within a **reasonable time** by an **independent** and **impartial** court. Apart from anything else, an accused who denies the charge is entitled to have his or her name cleared: *The State v John R Kaputin* [1979] PNGLR 532 at 535.

The discretion of Magistrates to adjourn cases is discussed in Chapter 4, and in deciding whether to grant an adjournment the constitutional right is always a factor to be considered. As Batari AJ observed in *The State v Jeffrey Balakau* (1996) N1528:

> "it is incumbent on those responsible for the fair administration of justice; the courts, judges, magistrates, lawyers, police and correctional officers to bring the [accused's] case to speedy fruition. In the event of breach, he is entitled to the protection of his right under *Constitution* s 37(3)."

What is a reasonable time? Every case must be decided on its merits and there is no "rule of thumb". The Magistrate's responsibility is always to hear both parties on the question of adjournments and, if it appears the constitutional right has been contravened, the Magistrate may either dismiss the charge or order the matter to be brought to trial by a specified date.

In both criminal and civil cases, once a hearing is under way and evidence begins, the Magistrate is "seized of the case" and has the responsibility personally to hear the case and decide it. The Magistrate is responsible for keeping a close eye on the time taken by the prosecution or the civil complainant to bring their case to a conclusion. Delay on their part may be inconsistent with the constitutional right to a fair hearing. Effective case flow management is discussed in Chapter 23. Where parties are legally represented, Magistrates should be on their guard against attempts by lawyers to manipulate the court process in order to delay matters.

A Magistrate has no control over delay in charging or issuing proceedings against the accused from the time an offence is alleged to have occurred, but there are statutory time limits for these steps: see Chapters 6 and 8. Of course, this type of delay may contribute to a larger picture of failures on the part of the prosecution in a particular case.

Delay on the part of the police and prosecution which is prejudicial to the rights of the accused to a fair trial may be grounds for dismissal of the charge. Indeed, the Magistrate is obliged by statute to dismiss an information if the defendant appears on the appointed day and, having had notice, the prosecution does not: *District Courts Act*, s 124. Further, substantial delay on the part of the prosecution is a matter which the Magistrate may take into account in passing sentence, especially if the accused has been kept in custody.

3.1.8 Disobedience of court orders

In addition to the procedures that are available to a party to enforce court orders (see Chapter 20), the proper running of a case may mean that a Magistrate is asked to enforce procedures such as the attendance at court of the defendant (*District Courts Act*, ss 93 and 125 and *Village Courts Act*, ss 81(1) and 91) or witnesses (*District Courts Act*, ss 113 and *Village Courts Act*, ss 81(2) and 91).

The many provisions outlined above give the Magistrate ample authority to control the conduct of matters in court, but at all times control must be exercised within the powers conferred by the statutes and in accordance with the principles of natural justice.

3.2 THE MAGISTRATE AND UNREPRESENTED PARTIES

3.2.1 Generally

In exercising authority in court, the Magistrate should remember that most parties have little or no knowledge of the law and court procedures. If they have no legal representation, the Magistrate should be alert to the possibility that justice may not be done unless the Magistrate provides some assistance to the parties concerned. To begin with, the Magistrate should consider the ability of the defendant to act for himself or herself and, where appropriate, the defendant should be supplied with paper and pencil and invited to sit at the bar table. If a defendant wishes to have a person other than a lawyer to provide some assistance on the day, the Magistrate should consider the issues raised under 3.5.3 below.

Next, the Magistrate may decide to explain to an unrepresented party the implications of proceeding or not proceeding in a particular way. For example, after the court has heard a key witness against the defendant, he or she may sit silent not understanding the importance of cross-examination, unless the Magistrate points out how damaging to the defendant the evidence appears to be.

For the same reason, where the defendant is unrepresented, the Magistrate may have to take a more active role in questioning witnesses in order to bring out facts which will assist the Magistrate to make a just decision. As is pointed out in Chapters 1 and 2.9.4, the court should not conduct an extensive inquiry, but, where parties are unrepresented, the Magistrate may have to intervene more than would otherwise be the case in order to ensure justice is done.

A difficult situation arises if it appears that an accused who is called upon to plead to an indictment may be unable to understand the proceedings. This is not a question of language. It is more likely to arise due to mental illness or some unusual circumstances, and s 569 of the *Criminal Code* provides a procedure to be followed.

The Magistrate would also be mindful of the importance of assisting the parties to reach agreement on factual issues and to settle the case: see Chapter 24.

Of course, the Magistrate should always be careful not to appear to prefer one party over the other. As discussed in Chapters 1 and 2.9.4, impartiality must be preserved.

3.2.2 The unrepresented accused

Here, the Magistrate has a clear duty to inquire and determine whether the accused has the ability to act for himself or herself.

As far as possible, the Magistrate should ensure that the unrepresented accused understands:

- the significance of pleading guilty or not guilty (see 4.3.2.1 and 4.8 checklist 6-12);
- his or her right to cross-examine witnesses for the prosecution;
- at the end of the prosecution case – the right to have the charge dismissed if there is no case to answer, and to choose whether to give evidence or to make an unsworn statement, and whether to call witnesses; and
- the right to address the court at the close of all the evidence.

- An unrepresented accused will almost always need advice on the question of whether the defendant has a case to answer: see 4.8 checklist 17-19 and Chapter 5.

If, at the end of the prosecution case, the Magistrate has decided that there is a case to answer, the next step is to give to the unrepresented defendant information which may be usefully summarised in the following words:

> "You have heard the evidence against you. Now is the time for you to make your defence. You have a choice:
>
> 1. You may go into the witness box and give evidence on oath and be cross-examined like any other witness, and you may call witnesses in your defence – but you are not obliged to do this: you do not have to give or call any evidence.
> 2. Instead, you may remain silent, or you may make an unsworn statement to the court.
>
> Whichever you decide, you may address the court before the court makes a decision on the evidence."

The Magistrate must then ask the defendant –

> "Do you wish to give evidence yourself?" and "Do you wish to call witnesses?"

The procedure laid down for dealing with committals in the District Court for trial of indictable offences requires a form of words to be used by the court whether or not the defendant is represented: *District Courts Act*, s 96.

3.3 THE REPRESENTATION OF PARTIES

3.3.1 The right to legal representation in criminal matters

In criminal cases, the accused has a constitutional right:

- to be represented at his or her own expense by a legal representative of his or her own choice; or
- if entitled to legal aid, to be represented by the Public Solicitor or another legal representative assigned to him or her: *Constitution*, s 37(4)(e).

The right does not extend to the Village Court: see 3.3.3 below.

Legal representation for the accused provides essential protection for the rights of the citizen in a legal system where prosecution and defence are adversaries, and the resources of the state are available to one side only. As discussed in 2.7.2, under this system the court is supposed to arrive at the truth of the matter through the testing of evidence given by witnesses in the course of examination and cross-examination. An accused unskilled in the art of questioning is at a serious disadvantage. So also is an accused who is unaware of the intricacies of the law and procedure.

3.3.2 Representation in the District Court

The *District Courts Act* goes further than the *Constitution*. It provides that a party, whether in a criminal or a civil case, is entitled to be represented by a lawyer if they wish, or, as discussed below under 3.5, they may be represented by a trainee lawyer, law student or other person authorised by law or with the leave of the court: *District Courts Act*, s 59.

3.3.3 In the other courts

In the Village Courts, a party to proceedings in criminal, civil or enforcement matters is not entitled to legal representation, but may be represented by any other person: see 3.5 below. Section 80 of the *Village Courts Act* refers to Pt V, Divs 3, 4 and 9. Curiously, s 80 is silent as to Divs 5, 6 and 7 relating to the Village Court's preventive jurisdiction, mediatory jurisdiction and joint jurisdiction, respectively. The usual rules of statutory interpretation would have the effect of permitting a party to be represented by a lawyer or any other person in relation to these three jurisdictions.

Legal representation is not permitted at all in a Local Land Court, and is only permitted in a Provincial Land Court where the court considers that the case before it involves "a matter of unusual difficulty or complexity" and all parties agree with the court that it is necessary that all parties should have the right to legal representation: *Land Disputes Settlement Act*, s 72. In other cases, a Local or Provincial Land Court may permit a group to be represented by a member of the group. It may also permit an infant, a severely disadvantaged person or a person for whom representation is required by custom, to be represented by a person other than a lawyer: *Land Disputes Settlement Act*, s 72.

3.4 LEGAL REPRESENTATION

3.4.1 The significance of legal representation

Representation by a lawyer is of great assistance to a party and may also facilitate the work of the court. Legal representation gives a party a distinct advantage. If only one party to a dispute has a lawyer, the Magistrate may be obliged to ensure that the unrepresented party is not unfairly disadvantaged.

It is important for Magistrates to have some understanding of the lawyer's professional role, and also his or her obligations to the client and to the court. The Magistrate should know what are the limits of acceptable conduct on the part of members of the legal profession. A useful guide is the set of *Lawyers' Professional Conduct Rules* 1989 made under the *Lawyers Act* 1986.

3.4.2 Role of the lawyer

While a lawyer is engaged to represent his or her client as a party with determination and without fear, the legal training and practical skills that the lawyer brings to the court can be of great assistance to the Magistrate in the conduct of the case in hand. Lawyers are often facilitators whose knowledge of the parties and the background facts can fill gaps in the Magistrate's understanding of the case. In appropriate cases, the lawyer will clarify the issues of fact and law, and may present argument that assists the court to reach a just decision.

Further, in cases where a question arises as to whether custom applies, counsel is under a statutory duty to call evidence and obtain information and opinion that would assist the court in determining the nature of the relevant rules of customary law, and whether or not to apply those rules in the case: *Customary Law Act*, s 15. "Existence and content" of custom is a question of law, and the range of material that the court may consider is set out in s 16.

For these reasons, a Magistrate who develops good professional relationships with the lawyers appearing in a case can benefit significantly and improve the throughput of cases. The Magistrate's virtues of patience, courtesy and appropriate firmness have been mentioned in 3.1.1 above. Tactics used by lawyers, which run against the interests of justice, must be dealt with firmly as soon as they become apparent. The Magistrate has certain powers to deal with lawyers' conduct in court, and suggestions for how to deal with a lawyer whose behaviour is making the Magistrate's task difficult are discussed in 3.1.6 above.

3.4.3 Rules of professional conduct

The lawyer's duty to the client requires that the client's instructions must be carried out with competence and with loyalty to the interests of the client. The lawyer owes an over-riding duty of *confidentiality* to the client which may prevent disclosure of matters to the court unless the client agrees. Loyalty also means that the lawyer may not act for a client if there is a conflict between the interests of that client and another present or former client: *Lawyers' Professional Conduct Rules*, rule 10.

Rules 15 and 16 set out a number of the lawyer's duties to the court and the administration of justice, while pointing to the right balance between those duties and the lawyer's obligations to the client. These rules may be summarised as follows:

1. Subject to the rules, a lawyer must conduct each case in such manner as he or she considers will be most advantageous to the client.
2. A lawyer must not knowingly deceive or mislead the court.
3. A lawyer must appear formally and tidily dressed, act with due courtesy to the court and conduct himself or herself in a professional manner.

4. A lawyer must use his or her best endeavours to avoid unnecessary expense and waste of the court's time, and, in particular, must:
   (a) when requested, inform the court of the probable length of a case;
   (b) inform the court of the possibility of a settlement (without mentioning the content), but must obtain the client's clear instructions before settling the case;
   (c) not delay proceedings that have been set down for trial only for the reason that money has not been received on account of his or her costs;
   (d) inform the court of any relevant decision on a point of law or any relevant legislative provision of which he or she is aware, whether the decision or legislation is for or against the interests of his or her case; and
   (e) if a procedural irregularity comes to the knowledge of a defending lawyer before verdict, he or she must inform the court as soon as practicable, and must not wait with a view to raising the matter later on appeal.
5. In cross-examining a witness, a lawyer must not question the credibility of the witness by attacking his or her character, unless there are reasonable grounds to support the line of questioning. Similarly, a defending lawyer in a criminal case must not, in a plea in mitigation, make any allegation that is merely scandalous or calculated to vilify or insult any person.
6. A lawyer must always exercise his or her own independent judgment as to the substance and form of statements made and questions asked in court, and, in particular, must not allow himself or herself to be the channel for statements or questions intended to insult or annoy the witness or any other person.
7. While a witness is under cross-examination, no lawyer should communicate with the witness without the leave of the court.
8. While a case is pending or likely to be pending before a court, a lawyer representing an interested party must not communicate with the Magistrate about the facts or issues unless he or she has first informed the other interested party or lawyer and given them the opportunity to be present.
9. In a civil case, if a client informs the lawyer before judgment that the client has committed perjury, the lawyer must not inform the court without the client's consent, but must not take any further part in the case unless the client authorises him or her to inform the court of the perjury.
10. Subject to these rules, a lawyer must defend his or her client and endeavour to protect the client from being convicted, irrespective of any opinion which the lawyer may have formed as to the guilt or innocence of that person.

11. If a client has made a clear confession of guilt in respect of a charge before the proceedings have commenced, the lawyer may decide whether or not to act for the client. If, however, the confession is made during the proceedings, the lawyer must continue to act for the client, on condition that a lawyer who has heard a confession of guilt must not:

    (a) set up an affirmative case inconsistent with the confession;

    (b) assert or suggest that some other person committed the offence; or

    (c) call evidence in support of an alibi.

12. A lawyer may advise the client as to the plea in a criminal charge, if necessary in strong terms, but the client must be allowed complete freedom of choice as to the plea he or she wishes to make. Similarly, while a defending lawyer may advise the client about giving evidence in his or her own defence, the client alone must decide whether to give evidence or not.

13. A defending lawyer must be present throughout the trial unless there are exceptional unforeseeable circumstances and, with the client's consent, a competent deputy who is well informed about the case takes the lawyer's place.

The Magistrate should be aware of the special difficulty (the subject of paragraphs 10 and 11 above) which can arise when a lawyer is acting for someone the lawyer knows, or suspects, to be guilty of the charge. The lawyer to whom the client-defendant has privately admitted his or her guilt is bound by rules of confidentiality not to inform the court unless the defendant agrees. Further, it is the obligation of the lawyer to put the prosecution/complainant case to the test and to argue the sufficiency of evidence called against the defendant: *Nai'U Limagwe v The State* [1976] PNGLR 382. It is for the court to determine the question of guilt beyond reasonable doubt, according to law. The lawyer is not a judge. However, the lawyer must be careful not to put forward an alibi or positive defence which is inconsistent with the defendant's private admission of guilt. That would amount to misleading the court, and is a serious breach of professional ethics.

If a lawyer has deliberately misled the court or a party, or wilfully delayed or disrupted proceedings, or otherwise interfered with the court's ability to do justice in a case, the Magistrate may make a written report on the matter and send it to the secretary of the Lawyers Statutory Committee of the Papua New Guinea Law Society, which has authority under ss 52-54 of the *Lawyers Act* to inquire into and deal with complaints of improper conduct on the part of a lawyer.

In short, the vigilance of the Magistrate is important. While the parties' interests, as well as those of the court, are usually protected by the involvement of lawyers, it should not be forgotten that lawyers are subject to professional discipline for breaches of rules of ethical conduct.

3.5 REPRESENTATION BY PERSON OTHER THAN A LAWYER

3.5.1 Law trainees/students

Trainees at the Legal Training Institute and law students at the University of Papua New Guinea, all of whom must be properly certified under the *District Courts Act* (s 59(1)), are entitled to represent parties who request their services for Magistrates' Court proceedings.

Their participation helps to meet the need for representation in the courts, and it also provides valuable training experience for people who have been studying law and need practical experience.

The Magistrate should always check the certification of trainees and students before they appear, and should be aware that they lack experience and may make mistakes. On the other hand, they might appreciate feedback on their performance in court, if given to them informally after the court has risen. The Magistrate should be aware that misconduct may be reported to the University Dean or to the Head of the Institute. The Magistrate may also order that a student (but not a trainee) be prohibited from representing a party if, in the opinion of the Magistrate, the student's conduct is detrimental to the interests of that party. The Magistrate must give the reason for such an order: s 59(3).

3.5.2 Authorised by law

A person authorised by statute to represent a party in the courts may do so (s 59(1)), for example, health, customs, companies and fisheries officers under their respective statutes.

On the hearing of an information, the informant may be represented by a police officer: s 59(2).

3.5.3 Other persons

The Magistrate also has the discretion to permit any suitable person to represent a party: s 59(1)(d). The leave which may be granted to such a person applies only to the one sitting of the court and is limited to the one proceeding. Subject to the cautions indicated, a grant of leave may be justified in two main types of situations:

[ASSISTING A DISADVANTAGED PARTY]

If the party has a disability, such as one which affects hearing or speaking, or is too young, old, ill-educated or otherwise weak or disadvantaged to represent himself or herself, the Magistrate should consider the situation carefully. In the first place, the Magistrate should weigh up the considerations referred to in 3.2.1 above. Also, is it absolutely clear that the party wishes to be assisted by the particular person who has come forward? What is the relationship between the two? The non-lawyer representative may be able to help with advice and oral argument, but the Magistrate should always take care that the representative is acting under the instructions of the party and is not "driving the case". If there is any doubt, the Magistrate should test what the party's true position is by asking a question direct to the party.

[REPRESENTING AN ABSENT PARTY OR LAWYER]

If a party is unable to be present at a hearing or other due date, the party may seek to arrange for a person to represent the party on a particular day for limited purposes, such as asking for an adjournment. That person must seek the leave of the court to do so, and the Magistrate has an obligation to exercise his or her discretion judicially. Provided the Magistrate has made inquiries and is satisfied that it is proper to do so, it may be convenient for all concerned for the Magistrate to grant leave to appear on that day and for that limited purpose.

With regard to the representation of companies, co-operatives and other incorporated bodies, it is wise for a Magistrate to require the representative to produce an official letter, or other authentic documentation, in order to show that the person has the authority of the senior management of the company to appear in the particular matter before the court.

A more difficult question arises where the lawyer representing a party is unable to appear on a particular day and is unable to arrange for another lawyer to appear temporarily in the matter as agent. Again, it is for the Magistrate to exercise discretion under s 59 whether or not to permit a clerk or other employee of the lawyer to appear on that day for a limited purpose. One consideration may be whether the person attending court has the authority of the lawyer or client to make decisions about, or agree to, procedural steps which need to be taken in the case. For example, a Magistrate may refuse to allow a lawyer's clerk to enter an appearance for a party unless the clerk has authority to give undertakings as to the filing of documents and the length of an adjournment subject to costs or other order, so that the case can be moved along and brought to trial without delay. In other words, unless the clerk's appearance is able to assist the court, the Magistrate may decide to treat it as a "non-appearance" for the party and award costs or even judgment to the other party.

Finally, the Magistrate should be on guard to ensure that any representation or assistance provided to a party by a non-lawyer does not misrepresent the party's wishes, mislead the court, or otherwise interfere with a fair hearing. Remember that a Magistrate who has granted leave to a person under the *District Courts Act* may revoke that leave at any time, if it is in the interests of justice to do so. Further, persons other than lawyers who represent parties are not subject to professional rules. It is a breach of the *Lawyers Act* for persons other than lawyers to make it their practice or business to represent parties in court.

3.6 PROSECUTORS

3.6.1 The role of the prosecutor

Underlying the function of the prosecution is its responsibility to decide whether or not to prosecute and to retain control of that decision. A Magistrate cannot direct that charges be laid or discontinued. It is important, however, that Magistrates should understand the nature of the prosecution's responsibilities.

Although by definition an executive act, the decision whether or not to prosecute should be exercised in a quasi-judicial way. There is no rule that requires that suspected criminal offences must automatically be the subject of prosecution. The dominant consideration for the prosecution in every case is whether, by virtue of the offence itself, or the circumstances surrounding the commission of the offence, the question may be asked: "Is there enough evidence to justify putting the case before the court?" That does not end the matter, because, if the answer is "yes", there remains the question whether, in the particular circumstances of the case, public interest considerations might be persuasive against prosecution (such as, perhaps, public expense, the age of the offender, and/or that it was a victimless crime).

The prosecutor has a significant part to play in the day-to-day administration of justice. At the outset, it is the duty of the prosecution to check all informations and ensure that the correct wording of the charges is used. Then the prosecutor continues to make decisions affecting the prosecution process, such as whether or not to proceed on charges laid, whether to seek amendment and whether to agree to the reduction of charges to which the defendant will plead guilty.

The Public Prosecutor and State Prosecutors provided for under the *Public Prosecutor (Office and Functions) Act* are authorised to provide prosecutorial services, but at the level of the District Court prosecution is usually handled by members of the police force. In this manual, reference to the prosecutor and the prosecution includes prosecutorial services at all levels.

In the case of indictable offences triable summarily by virtue of s 420 and Sch 2 of the *Criminal Code*, the Public Prosecutor must decide whether the offence will be tried before a Principal Magistrate in the District Court, whether it will go through committal proceedings to the National Court (see 11.3.2 on committals and *The State v The Principal Magistrate, District Court, Port Moresby; Ex parte The Public Prosecutor* [1983] PNGLR 43) or whether the information will be withdrawn

(*District Courts Act*, s 61A and *Public Prosecutor (Office and Functions) Act*, s 4(1)(ga)).

The duties of the prosecutor are different from those of the defendant and defence lawyer. The obligations are wider, both to the court and to the public at large. As the prosecutor is obliged to present the case fairly to the court, he or she has greater independence from those who are instructing the prosecutor than is enjoyed by other legal representatives.

3.6.2 Conduct of the case

The prosecutor has a discretion as to which witnesses to call, and whether to call a particular witness in a particular case. The Magistrate should not normally interfere with the prosecutor's discretion, but the prosecutor has a duty to be fair to the accused: *The State v Theo Yandalin* (1995) N1329. For example, if the prosecutor knows of a witness whose evidence would materially assist the accused's defence, the prosecutor should advise the accused and assist the accused if there is difficulty in securing attendance of the witness at the hearing. On the other hand, there is no similar duty on the defence to disclose any details of the defence case (apart from an alibi) to the prosecution: *Awoda v The State* [1984] PNGLR 165.

It is well known that the prosecutor must conduct the case moderately, albeit firmly. The prosecutor must not:

- strive unfairly to obtain a conviction;
- press the case beyond the limits which the evidence permits; nor
- invite the court to convict the defendant on evidence which the prosecutor, in his or her own judgment, no longer sustains the charge.

For example, if the evidence of a witness is known to be unreliable, the prosecutor should not present the witness to the court as worthy of credibility. This is because the relevant information as to the reliability and background of the witnesses whom the prosecution proposes to call will be available to the prosecutor and not to the Magistrate.

3.6.3 The prosecutor in sentencing

When it comes to the sentencing process it is the prosecutor's responsibility to provide the court with such information in relation to the defendant as will enable the Magistrate to make the appropriate determination.

It is not the function of the prosecutor to ask the court to impose a particular sentence, although it is appropriate to inform the court of such matters as the prevalence of offences of the type of which the defendant has been convicted.

When the circumstances of an offence are not particularly serious, the prosecutor should assist the court with information as to alternative penalties or courses of action which might be appropriate. See Chapter 13 on sentencing.

3.7 WITNESSES IN COURT

3.7.1 Witnesses generally

It is usual for the parties to decide whether or not to call a witness or to request the issue of a witness summons, but it is the responsibility of the Magistrate, once the witnesses are in court, to ensure that the proper procedures for giving evidence are followed so that justice is done. Interpreters may be needed.

The procedures for witnesses giving evidence in court hearings, both civil and criminal, are discussed in Chapters in 4 and 5, and it has been pointed out in Chapter 1, Rule 3.1 that there may be circumstances where a Magistrate may re-call witnesses who are in the precincts of the court. The non-attendance at court of witnesses is dealt with in Chapter 9.

3.7.2 Protection of witnesses

While it is the duty of members of the public to come forward in the interests of justice and give evidence in court proceedings, they are entitled not to be treated unfairly in court. It is the responsibility of the Magistrate to protect witnesses, including the parties, from questioning on matters which are not relevant to the case in hand, and to ensure that witnesses understand their rights.

For example, the court should not allow questions:

- which are "indecent or scandalous" unless strictly relevant to the facts in issue; or
- which are "intended to insult or annoy"; or
- which are "needlessly offensive in form, even if otherwise proper in themselves": *Evidence Act*, s 27.

Further *Evidence Act* provisions govern the circumstances in which the court must decide whether:

- the party calling a witness can discredit him or her (s 21);
- a witness can be cross-examined as to credit (s 26); and
- members of the clergy and medical practitioners should refuse to divulge communications made to them in the circumstances of the case (s 19).

3.7.3 Silence or reluctance of witnesses

The accused is, of course, entitled not to give evidence if he or she wishes, and this is not to be taken as an admission of guilt. The Magistrate should be careful to ensure that an unrepresented defendant understands the implications of giving evidence in the witness box, especially in circumstances where the prosecution appears to have had difficulty in proving its case. Any pressure on the defendant to give evidence would be contrary to the principles laid down by the Supreme Court in *Paulus Pawa v The State* [1981] PNGLR 498.

Under the *District Courts Act*, s 70 deals with the situation of a witness in court who refuses to be examined. The court has certain statutory powers to deal with the situation where a person appears to give evidence on a summons or, being present, is orally required by the court to give evidence and that person:

- without lawful excuse, refuses to be examined on oath in connection with the matter; or
- refuses to take the oath; or
- having taken the oath, refuses, without lawful excuse, to answer a specific question put to him or her concerning the matter.

The court may adjourn the proceedings for up to eight days and may, in the meantime, order that the person be held in custody. The same procedure may be repeated again and again until the person consents to give evidence. The section also applies to the non-production of documents.

3.7.4 False evidence

The "contempt of court" section of the *District Courts Act* (s 277, see above) makes it an offence if a person "wilfully prevaricates" in giving evidence. This means that it is an offence for a witness to give false or evasive replies with the intention of deceiving the court. The offence carries a fine of up to K100. There is no such provision in the *Village Courts Act*.

What are Magistrate's responsibilities if it appears that a witness is deliberately lying or attempting to deceive the court? The provision in s 277 of the *District Courts Act* is useful because it does not require the laying of charges for perjury.

Perjury in judicial proceedings means knowingly giving false testimony concerning any matter that is material to a question raised in the proceedings: *Criminal Code*, s 121. That offence, and the related offence of fabricating evidence (*Criminal Code*, s 122), are indictable offences which cannot be tried in the District Court.

The Magistrate should proceed with caution. It may be advisable to warn a witness who appears to be lying that prevarication and perjury are serious offences. However, until all the evidence in the case has been given and considered carefully, the

Magistrate cannot be certain that lies have been told. Trial and conviction for prevarication or perjury will require proof of what the witness said, as well as proof of the true facts and proof that the witness knew the truth while lying to the court. The official record of what witnesses said in court might need to be supported by notes made by others in the courtroom, such as the Magistrate, the prosecutor and counsel.

If false evidence is given by a prosecution witness or witnesses, this may so discredit the prosecution case that the charge should be dismissed.

3.7.5 Interference with witnesses

If the Magistrate suspects that someone has attempted to interfere with a witness or evidence in court, it may be necessary to act quickly to deal with this form of abuse of justice.

Interference may include:

- corruption, that is to say, influencing a witness to tell lies or withhold the truth (*Criminal Code*, s 123);
- deceiving a witness with intent to affect the testimony (s 124);
- destroying evidence (s 125);
- preventing a witness from attending the court to give evidence (s 126);
- conspiring to have an innocent person charged with an offence (s 127); and
- conspiring to obstruct, pervert or defeat the course of justice (s 128).

Interference is a serious matter for the Magistrate to consider, particularly if it appears in a case that the witnesses of one party have been interfered with by the other party. For example, supporters of an accused defendant might have attempted to influence the evidence of prosecution witnesses. As soon as this is discovered, the Magistrate may decide to re-call the witnesses in order to question them further as to the true evidence which should have been given. If the interference appears to be substantiated, or if the Magistrate has serious concerns, the matter should be referred to the police for prosecution.

3.8 WORKING WITH INTERPRETERS

Parties are entitled to understand the proceedings. In civil cases it is the parties' own responsibility to provide interpreters. In criminal cases, if the accused cannot understand or speak the language used at the trial, the *Constitution* gives the right to have the assistance of an interpreter at no cost: s 37(4)(d).

Ideally, the interpreter is an independent person who serves the interests of the court. Where doubt is raised, it is the Magistrate's responsibility to ensure that, as far as possible, the interpreter is properly qualified and independent. In criminal trials interpreters should be sworn in and should state on oath, or should affirm, that they are competent in the languages involved and that they will "well and truly interpret" between the parties, witnesses and the court. In all cases, it is also important that the interpreter should not interpose his or her own opinions or give any personal explanations, unless the Magistrate asks for them.

CHAPTER 4 – COURT HEARINGS

4.1 PROCEDURE IN COURT

4.1.1 Sources of procedure

The procedure to be followed in a particular case depends upon the jurisdiction being exercised. Here is a rough guide to the sources to which District Court Magistrates may refer:

GUIDE TO SOURCES OF PROCEDURE

Criminal cases	
simple and summary offences	*District Courts Act* (*DCA*), Pts IV, V & VII *Summary Offences Act* (*SOA*) *Criminal Code* (*CC*) *Arrest Act* (*AA*) *Search Act* (*SA*) *Bail Act* (*BA*)
indictable offences triable summarily by a Principal Magistrate	*DCA*, Pt VII; *CC*
indictable committals	*DCA*, Pt VI
Civil cases	• *DCA*, Pts IV, V & VIII
Matters involving children	• *Child Welfare Act* (*CWA*)
Matters involving deserted wives and children	• *Deserted Wives and Children Act* (*DWCA*)
Land mediation	• *Land Disputes Settlement Act* (*LDSA*)
Village Court matters	• *Village Courts Act* (*VCA*)
Inter-group fighting matters	• *Inter Group Fighting Act* (*I-GFA*)
Coroner's inquests	• *Coroners' Act*
Elections: enrolment appeals and disputed returns	*Organic Law on National and Local-level Government Elections*
Motor vehicle compensation assessment	*Motor Vehicles (Basic Protection Compensation) Act*

4.1.2 Statutes and court rules

In every case where a statute provides for the procedure, that procedure must be followed. For example, criminal cases in the District Court are usually governed by the *District Courts Act* and the *Criminal Code*. However, some aspects of criminal procedure, such as the examination and cross-examination of witnesses, are not dealt with by statute, and the procedure of the National Court should be followed: *DCA*, s 131.

4.1.3 Natural justice in criminal and civil matters

The framework of statutory procedures for criminal and civil cases is constructed so as to give effect to the principles of natural justice, some of which are mentioned in the *Constitution*: see 2.6.2. There are gaps, as where the statute book fails to provide for a particular situation. More importantly, Magistrates frequently exercise discretions with regard to such matters as hearings, documentation, witnesses and issues to be tried. Where the statute does not provide a clear answer, the Magistrate is still bound by the same basic principles, as the following guide indicates.

NATURAL JUSTICE IN A MAGISTRATE'S COURT

- Adequate notice of charge, complaint or allegation, with full details, should be given to the accused or defendant.
- A civil complainant is entitled to details of the grounds of the defence.
- Adequate notice of hearing and any adjourned hearing should be given to all parties.
- The parties are entitled to a public hearing before an impartial Magistrate within a reasonable time.
- Each party has the right to call witnesses, give evidence, cross-examine opposing witnesses and address the court – and also to be present in court throughout, either in person or through a lawyer.
- A party has the right to appeal against the decision of the primary decision-maker.

4.2 CHOICE OF JURISDICTION, VENUE OF THE COURT AND TRANSFER OF PROCEEDINGS

The relevant statutes set out which jurisdiction is appropriate in criminal and civil cases, depending on the gravity of the offence alleged and the nature and amount of the remedy sought. These will determine the jurisdiction to be used (National, District or Village Court) and, in the District Courts, the status of the Magistrate who may preside over the case: see Chapter 6 for criminal jurisdiction and Chapter 14 for civil jurisdiction.

4.2.1 Concurrent jurisdiction

The National Court has concurrent jurisdiction with the District Court to hear and determine indictable offences punishable on summary conviction, being offences specified in Sch 2 of the *Criminal Code*: *DCA*, s 20. The District Court may transfer proceedings to the National Court, and the National Court has power to order District Court proceedings to be transferred to the National Court. The power to transfer proceedings between National and District Courts is dealt with under 4.2.3 below, as is the referral of a matter into or out of a Village Court. The situation is complicated by overlapping or concurrent jurisdictions and rules regarding venue. The District Courts have jurisdiction over all offences triable summarily and over civil actions at law or in equity.

4.2.2 Venue

The District Court must sit at one of the appointed places gazetted (*DCA*, s 17) within the province for which it is established. Rules for determining which courthouse should be used for a particular criminal matter within the province, and for other venues and circumstances, are set out in s 122 of the *DCA*, with power of adjournment to a different place in the province in s 123.As to the actual place where the court may sit, s 17 makes it clear that the court must use a courthouse unless:

- there is no courthouse within a convenient distance; and
- as much notice of the time and place of sitting as is practicable is given to members of the public likely to desire to attend.

Compliance with the above statutory provisions is mandatory.

As to the appropriate venue for the commencement and hearing of proceedings, see Chapter 6 for criminal proceedings and Chapter 14 for civil proceedings.

4.2.3 Transfer from one jurisdiction/court to another

The National Court may "reach down" and order the transfer of certain matters from the District Court to the National Court on certain terms: see *DCA*, s 24(2).

A Magistrate in a District Court may transfer proceedings out of his or her jurisdiction by means of:

- transfer "upwards" from the District Court to the National Court (*DCA*, s 24(1)); or
- transfer "outwards" from the District Court out to some other District Court (*DCA*, s 24(1)).

Transfer up to a more senior court is justified if the matter is particularly serious or raises major questions of legal principle or public policy. In other circumstances it is the duty of the Magistrate to endeavour to deal with the proceedings where they are instituted – to the best of his or her ability.

An unusual example of power to change the jurisdiction under which a case will be dealt with arises under s 425 of the *Criminal Code*, where a Magistrate can abstain from dealing with certain summary property offences (under ss 422-424) if he or she considers that they should be replaced with indictable offences. The Magistrate would then commit the defendant for trial in the National Court on the indictable offences.

Transfer outwards from one District Court to another may require an adjournment of the case. In civil proceedings the defendant can obtain an adjournment if he or she can satisfy the Magistrate that the complaint could "more conveniently and more properly" be heard before the other court: *DCA*, s 150. If the bringing of the action in the wrong court was "vexatious and oppressive", the Magistrate may award compensation to the defendant: *DCA*, s 151.

The case of the Village Court is somewhat different: see 18.8.9. The test is whether the proceedings could "more appropriately" be dealt with by the Village Court or some other court having jurisdiction in the matter. Under s 97 of the *Village Courts Act*, a National or District Court may refer a matter to a Village Court, and, conversely, a Village Court may refer a matter to another court.

In all of these situations, the test of what is "appropriate" requires the Magistrate to consider whether or not the matter in hand would be better heard in a Village Court having regard to:

- the special nature of the Village Court jurisdiction;
- its personnel;
- its focus on custom and land-related matters;
- its powers and procedures, particularly with regard to peace-keeping, mediation and compensation, and
- its appeal and review process.

4.3 ISSUES TO BE DETERMINED AND ROLES OF PARTIES

4.3.1 Law and facts

The Magistrate is presiding over a court of law which, in the course of doing justice, is responsible for deciding issues of law and fact. It is always the duty of the Magistrate to find the law and apply it to the relevant facts. This is how the public generally see the function of the Magistrate, and the distinction between criminal proceedings and civil (and other non-criminal) proceedings is not widely understood.

The picture is complicated by the power of the Magistrate in criminal proceedings to order monetary compensation to the party harmed by the accused's actions.

This manual is structured to demonstrate the importance of the common functions and the basic duties of Magistrates (particularly Chapters 1-5 and 20-26) while also highlighting the difference between criminal and non-criminal proceedings (in Chapters 6-19).

4.3.2 Criminal jurisdiction

The issues arise between the parties in two stages:

4.3.2.1 Determination of guilt

The guilt issue is not a choice between "guilt" or "innocence" – but whether the prosecution has established that the accused is guilty beyond reasonable doubt. The role of the prosecutor is to represent the interests of the informant, those harmed or aggrieved by the alleged offence and the wider public interest in dealing with crime. The members of the judiciary have no function in relation to decisions by the prosecution. A Magistrate cannot direct that a prosecution should be launched: see 3.6 above.

Private prosecutions may be brought for an indictable offence. In that situation, the interests of the private person alone are being pursued. Sections 616-618 of the *Criminal Code* require a private person to obtain the permission of the National Court and give security for costs before presenting an information.

If guilt is not proved, the accused is acquitted and discharged. The role of the accused is to test the evidence called against him or her and to present evidence if he or she wishes, but the accused is not obliged to give or call evidence. The accused may, at the outset, or at any time, enter a plea of guilty to the charge. A finding on the guilt issue ends the proceedings if it is an acquittal. A determination or plea of guilty leads to the second stage.

4.3.2.2 Determination of sentence

At this stage the procedures and practices of the court are designed to assist the Magistrate to carry out an inquiry as to the appropriate sentence to be passed. The Magistrate has discretion to receive evidence needed to perform this task (*Criminal Code*, s 596(4)), and should ensure that both prosecution and defence co-operate with the court as discussed in Chapter 13. Unlike a contested criminal trial (see 2.9.2), this stage of the proceedings should be non-adversarial.

4.3.3 Civil jurisdiction

At the hearing of civil proceedings, the main issues are again two-fold.

4.3.3.1 Determination of liability

A person seeking redress for harm or loss caused by the actions of another comes to the court as a complainant alleging a recognised cause of action and ready to prove facts on the balance of the probabilities. The first issue is whether the complainant can show that the facts of the case support a finding of civil liability against the defendant based on a cause of action known to law. If liability is not established, the defendant is entitled to judgment in the defendant's favour. A finding in favour of the complainant leads to the second stage.

4.3.3.2 Determination of nature and amount of remedy

Depending on the type of cause of action issued, the complainant may seek to prove entitlement to damages or the benefit of orders such as specific performance, restitution or injunction. Unlike the second (sentencing) stage of criminal proceedings, this second stage of civil proceedings requires evidentiary proof on the balance of the probabilities – to be brought to the court by the complainant in the same manner as the first stage. The proceedings are still adversarial. See Chapter 14 for further discussion.

4.4 EX PARTE HEARINGS

"Ex parte" means that the court is asked to proceed in the absence of one party, usually the defendant, in criminal or civil cases. Sometimes preliminary orders as to the service of documents or interim injunctions are made ex parte, in order to speed up the process until the full hearing takes place. The absence of the defendant is an exception to the basic principle that the defendant is entitled to be present throughout his or her trial. This is a constitutional right: *Constitution*, s 37(5).

There are three constitutional exceptions applicable to the full hearing:

1. The defendant can waive his or her right to be present, provided the Magistrate is satisfied that the defendant has been properly advised of this right, and clearly consents to the hearing proceeding in his or her absence.
2. The court can order the defendant to be removed if his or her conduct is such as to make it impracticable to proceed.
3. If the statute provides for an offence not punishable by imprisonment to be heard summarily and the defendant has been duly served with a summons, the hearing may proceed in his or her absence.

In the case of a defendant's failure to attend court on a summons for a simple offence for which the maximum penalty does not include imprisonment, the Magistrate may proceed to hear the case ex parte: *DCA*, s 125. This means that the Magistrate must hear the evidence against the defendant and decide whether or not he or she is guilty. The prosecution evidence must be given in court on oath, otherwise the constitutional requirement that there be a "hearing" is breached. In 1982, the Supreme Court struck down s 132A(b) of the *District Courts Act* (then s 138A(1)(b)) and the corresponding provision of the *Motor Traffic Act* because those provisions purported to require the Magistrate to record a plea of guilty merely on proof of service of the summons and non-attendance at court on the day: *Supreme Court Reference No 1A of 1981* [1982] PNGLR 124. See also 9.4.

If the defendant fails to attend on summons in the case of a simple offence involving imprisonment or an indictable offence triable summarily, the Magistrate may issue a warrant for arrest to have the defendant brought to court to answer the information: *DCA*, s 125.

If a case is adjourned and either or both of the parties or their representatives fails to attend at the adjourned date, the court may proceed in their absence, or, if the complainant does not attend, may dismiss the charges: *DCA*, s 130.

In relation to charges punishable by imprisonment, these sections in the *District Courts Act* should be read in light of the first and third constitutional exceptions above. They seem to require that, before a court can proceed to hear such a charge in the absence of the defendant, the defendant must have communicated his or her consent in a positive way, perhaps in writing or through a representative. The defendant's failure to appear after having been served with a summons would not be enough. Mere proof of service of the summons on the defendant would not meet the constitutional requirements. In short, in such cases the defendant should be present voluntarily, by a representative, or brought to court by a bench warrant, at least for the opening stage of the hearing.

Court decisions made ex parte may be challenged later by the party who was absent. The court has discretion to set aside a conviction or other decision and to order a rehearing of the decision on terms the court considers to be just. The court should consider all the circumstances of the case and, in particular:

- **whether the defendant had a reasonable explanation for failing to attend;**
- **whether the defendant appeared to have a good defence to the charge(s) and**
- **the seriousness of the charge(s).**

For the procedure to be followed in this situation, see s 25 of the *District Courts Act.*

In the civil jurisdiction, there is an important distinction between an ordinary complaint/summons and a default summons for a liquidated sum: see Chapters 14 and 15.

4.5 JOINT PARTIES AND SEVERANCE OF PARTIES

Courts are generally concerned to adjust rights and obligations and enforce the law between single parties. Sometimes the interests of justice may require that two or more parties, whose positions at law and on the facts are very similar, should be joined together so that their cases will be heard at the same time. For example, several complainants may join together in bringing a civil claim, and a complainant may sue several defendants who are alleged to have caused harm to the complainant in the same set of circumstances.

In criminal proceedings, the prosecution may charge two or more accused with offences arising out of the same set of facts, or closely related facts, and they may be tried together: see, for example, *Criminal Code*, ss 7, 8 and 532(6)-(9). The question of several charges alleged in a single information is a difficult issue: see Chapter 8.

On a joint indictment, if one accused pleads guilty and the other not guilty, the sentencing of the first accused should not occur until after the trial of the other has finished. If a joint hearing would prejudice the defence of one of the accused, application may be made for separate trials: *Criminal Code*, s 568. The Magistrate should consider whether the joint nature of the trial raises the real possibility that one or more of the accused will not receive a fair trial. Generally, if an accused requests a separate trial, this should be granted.

4.6 OPEN COURT

The court is a public place subject to the authority of the Magistrate, whose responsibility it is to maintain the dignity of the court while at the same time ensuring that, as far as possible, the public can see that justice is being done. Parties are entitled to a public hearing, and the guarantee in the *Constitution* (s 37(12) and (13)) adds weight to s 57 of the *District Courts Act* which requires that the room or place in which the court sits shall be "an open and public court to which all persons may have access so far as the room or place can conveniently contain them". "Open" means that the door must be open throughout the trial so that the public feel free to enter and leave as they please. Police should not stand near the door so as to block it.

Of course, the section also empowers the Magistrate to close the court or require that particular persons be excluded from it, if the Magistrate is of the opinion that the interests of public morality require it. The interests of justice may require that, during committal proceedings for an indictable offence, the taking of statements of the accused should not be in open court: *DCA*, s 58. Further, child welfare proceedings and charges against children should not be held in open court: see Chapter 16. The power to exclude does not extend to parties or their legal representatives.

As far as witnesses are concerned, it is usual for the parties to request the Magistrate (or for the Magistrate on his or her own initiative) to order witnesses to remain outside the court until they have been called. They can remain in court after giving evidence. If anyone's behaviour in court interferes with the court's ability to do justice, the Magistrate can exercise such powers as exclusion from the court and contempt of court, which are discussed in 3.1.3 and 3.1.4.

4.7 AT THE BEGINNING OF A DAY'S HEARINGS

Before the Magistrate enters the courtroom, it is wise to check arrangements with the court clerk.

PRE-COURT CHECKS

The Magistrate should ensure that:

- all the relevant court files have been made available to the Magistrate to study;
- any particular information about cases on the list, such as urgency or special difficulty or sensitivity, is made known to the Magistrate before the hearing begins (and see Chapter 22 in relation to administrative responsibilities);
- in civil cases, the clerk has called out the names of parties to check who is present;
- parties are in attendance for the first case – or at least one party is present at the front of the court;
- the courtroom is open to the public;
- the public inside are seated quietly;
- the ventilation and lighting are in order;
- the court staff are ready.

As the Magistrate enters the courtroom certain formalities are observed.

COURT ANNOUNCEMENTS

The Magistrate should take, or arrange for, the following steps:

- ask everyone to stand, people should bow and the Magistrate should return the courtesy; then everyone should remain standing until the Magistrate has sat down;
- declare the court open;
- call the names of the parties of the first case (the defendant in criminal cases).

4.8 ORDER OF PROCEEDINGS DURING THE HEARING

Once the Magistrate has entered the courtroom and the first case has been called, the parties should be asked to identify themselves, and problems arising out of the absence of any parties (see 4.4 above) should be dealt with. From that point, the order of proceedings will depend on the type of case. Here are some checklists.

MAGISTRATE'S PROCEDURE CHECKLISTS

A. Criminal cases before the District Courts

Summary offences and indictable offences triable summarily (DCA, ss 57-92 and 124-132)

(Sections 525-578 of the *Criminal Code* also provide some guidance)

PRELIMINARY

1. Check the court is open (see 4.6).
2. Examine the information form to check the offence is within jurisdiction.
3. Consider whether jurisdiction is also vested in some other court and whether the case should be transferred.
4. Call the defendant forward and check the language spoken, name, address and occupation.
5. If necessary, swear or affirm an interpreter.
6. Read the charge(s) to the defendant and ensure he/she understands it/them.
7. Ask the defendant to plead "guilty" or "not guilty" and record the reply. If it is "not guilty", proceed to trial.

GUILTY PLEA

8. If the defendant pleads guilty, note the plea provisionally.
9. The prosecutor to give a brief statement of facts.
10. Ask the defendant if he/she wishes to say anything in answer to the charge.
11. If not, enter a plea of guilty.
12. If the defendant makes a statement which raises a possible defence, change the plea to not guilty and proceed to trial. If an adjournment is necessary to a fixed trial date, consider questions of bail and surety (see 4.9 below and Chapter 10).

TRIAL

13. Order witnesses to leave the court (s 63).

14. The prosecutor to open the case and call witnesses.

In the case of each witness:

- swear/affirm an interpreter, if necessary;
- swear/affirm the witness;
- record the evidence at each stage of examination;
- allow cross-examination by the defendant;
- allow re-examination by the prosecutor only as to new matters raised in cross-examination;
- put the court's questions to the witness;
- ask the witnesses to remain in court after giving evidence. (If the Magistrate thinks there will be no reason to recall a witness later, the Magistrate may excuse the witness from further attendance.)

15. The close of the prosecutor's case.

16. Hear a "no-case" submission, if any. The defendant is always entitled to argue that the defence has no case to answer.

17. Decide whether the defendant has a prima facie case to answer. If necessary, adjourn briefly to consider the matter.

18. If no prima facie case, acquit the defendant and give reasons.

19. If there is a prima facie case, give reasons and explain rights and choices to the defendant, namely:

- to remain silent if the defendant wishes;

  (Explain that:

  silence at this stage is the defendant's right, because the burden of proof is on the prosecutor/complainant;

  the issue at this stage is only whether the defendant is guilty, and, if he/she is found guilty, there will be a later opportunity to address the court on the question of penalty;

  the defendant cannot be criticised for remaining silent);

  or

- to make an unsworn statement (explain the significance of this);

  or

- to give evidence on oath and/or, if the defendant wishes, to call witnesses.

(Explain that all such evidence can be questioned by the prosecutor/complainant and by the court, and that the defendant must decide who the witnesses will be).

20. If the defendant makes an unsworn statement, record it and do not allow any questions.

21. If the defendant wishes to present evidence, follow the steps for the prosecutor's witnesses under item 14 above.

22. Consider whether the court should recall a prosecution witness to answer any new matter raised by the defence which has taken the prosecution by surprise. Recall should follow immediately after the defence evidence.

23. The close of the defendant's case. The defendant may sum up, followed by a reply by the prosecutor. If the defendant did not give evidence, the prosecutor may sum up first, and the defendant may reply.

FINDING OF GUILTY OR NOT GUILTY

24. Consider all the evidence and decide from the facts before the court whether the defendant's guilt has been established beyond reasonable doubt. Announce a finding that the defendant is guilty as charged, or is acquitted, and record the decision. On acquittal, the defendant is entitled to leave the courtroom immediately and unhindered, unless there are other charges on which he/she can be held lawfully in custody.

CONSIDERATION OF DISPOSITION

25. Ask the prosecutor for details of any previous convictions or written report on the defendant's behaviour which the court should be aware of. Ensure that these details are shown to the defendant, and ask the defendant whether the details are admitted. Record the details.

26. Ask the defendant whether he/she wishes to address the court or call character witnesses on the question of sentence. Record the main points.

27. Consider the appropriate disposal of the case (and adjourn, if necessary, to give the matter proper attention: see 4.9 below). Review sentencing requirements and options (see Chapter 6), including whether the matter should be disposed of without conviction (s 132).

ANNOUNCEMENT OF DISPOSITION

28. The appropriate sentence will be announced in open court to the defendant (who should be standing while the Magistrate speaks to him/her). Reasons should be given for the Magistrate's decision.

29. If the defendant is sentenced to imprisonment, the police should take control of the defendant before the court rises.

THE COURT RISES

30. When the court's business is finished:

- the Magistrate should make any appropriate final remarks (perhaps to acknowledge any special assistance from lawyers or particular members of the public);
- the Magistrate or clerk should announce that the sitting of the court is adjourned to a fixed date, or until it is required (sine die);
- the Magistrate or clerk should call everyone to stand; and
- the Magistrate should rise, bow and leave the courtroom and go to a separate room or place.

WRITING UP THE DECISION

31. The Magistrate is advised to take the time immediately to make notes of the decision and the reasons for sentence imposed, and to write them up without delay (see Chapter 25).

B. Civil Cases before District Courts

(DCA, ss 57-92 and 133-159)

PRELIMINARY

- Follow steps 1-3 under A above.
- Call the parties forward and check language spoken and names.
- If necessary, swear or affirm an interpreter.
- Have the complaint read out and explained to the defendant.
- Ask the defendant whether the complaint is admitted. If so, proceed to consider the amount to be ordered or other disposition of the case.

HEARING

- Deal with application(s), if any, for particulars of claim or defence (see Chapter 14).
- If the defendant does not admit the complaint, hear the complainant followed by any witnesses called by the complainant. Follow the steps for calling and questioning witnesses set out in 14 under A above.
- Ask the defendant if he/she wishes to give evidence. If the defendant does not give or call evidence, he/she may address the court and the complainant may reply.
- If the defendant does not adduce evidence, consider whether the complainant has established the necessary facts and has the necessary legal basis for an

order, and, if so, enter a finding in favour of the complainant and consider the amount to be ordered or other disposition of the case.

- Enter judgment in favour of the complainant or the defendant, as the case may be, and announce the decision in open court, with reasons.
- If the defendant wishes to give or call evidence, follow the same steps for calling and questioning witnesses.
- At the conclusion of all the evidence, ask the complainant to address the court, followed by the defendant.
- Consider whether the complainant has established his/her case, enter judgment and deal with the matter in the manner described above.

WRITING UP THE DECISION

- The Magistrate is advised to take the time immediately to make notes of the decision and reasons, and to write them up without delay (see Chapter 25).

4.9 ADJOURNMENTS

A frequent judicial act performed by Magistrates concerns adjournments. Proceedings may be adjourned when a defendant is brought into court on a warrant.

Cases may be adjourned at these stages:

- when they are first called
- on application to set aside an ex parte order (*DCA*, s 75)
- after or part-way through the taking of evidence
- between the evidentiary stage and the decision
- between conviction and penalty or between a decision on civil liability and the fixing of compensation
- when a case is transferred to another court, and
- in diverse circumstances, such as when the Magistrate, the prosecutor, one of the parties or a lawyer falls ill or is otherwise unable to proceed on a hearing day.

The Magistrate has a general discretion as to whether to order an adjournment and, if so, for how long. See, for example, ss 88-92 and 123 of the *District Courts Act.* In every situation, the Magistrate should exercise the discretion judicially.

The Magistrate should consider:

- whether an adjournment is necessary in order to allow time to prepare the case and/or secure the attendance of witnesses – this is a fundamental principle of natural justice (see 2.6.2)

- whether the adjournment would have the opposite effect, namely to prolong the process of the case, in breach of the constitutional guarantee of "reasonable time" (see 3.1.7)
- whether the defendant is being held in custody and whether bail should be granted (see Chapter 10)
- if the adjournment is due to pressure of work in the District Court, whether the court staff are giving the case adequate priority for a hearing
- whether the court's policy on case-flow management requires the Magistrate to take a firm stand on adjournments (see Chapter 23), which may include limiting the period and refusing to grant adjournments sine die (without fixed date)
- the cost and inconvenience of an adjournment to one or both of the parties
- whether an order for costs should be made against the party who has caused the adjournment (see s 260(1)(e) and Chapter 21)
- whether the need to adjourn the case to another jurisdiction or venue was the fault of one party, who should therefore pay costs (see 4.2.3)
- the reason for an adjournment requested by a party, and whether it is a genuine reason or whether the request arises from the applicant's own fault or carelessness
- whether the adjournment application is being used to cause delay or to wear down the opponent (see 3.1.7 and 3.4.3)

4.10 CHANGE OF MAGISTRATES AND TERMINATION OF MAGISTRATE'S POWER

4.10.1 Change

When a Magistrate is unable to finish the hearing and final disposal of a case, it may be transferred to another court (see 4.2 above) or it may be heard in the same court by a different Magistrate. In both situations the case must be re-started; it must be called again and the hearing procedure must begin afresh. Preliminary matters, such as the issue of a summons or warrant, need not be repeated but, in a criminal case for example, a defendant who has pleaded not guilty must be taken through that process again by the new Magistrate.

4.10.2 Termination of power

The Magistrate exercises powers under statutory procedures. When a particular power has been exercised and finalised, the Magistrate cannot go back and exercise the same power or part of it again. This means that the Magistrate's power is exhausted (functus officio).

To give some examples, once the Magistrate has found a defendant guilty on the evidence, he or she cannot re-open the case and hear more evidence. (The defendant may have a right of appeal on the ground of fresh evidence.) The same applies to the entry of a conviction. Similarly, once the Magistrate has passed sentence, the sentencing power is exhausted and no subsequent change can be made. The only exception to the above rule occurs when there has been an obvious mistake or defect in form but not substance – which merely requires the correction of the record. There is further provision for amendment by the National Court under s 163 of the *District Courts Act*.

The importance of this "termination rule" means that if the Magistrate has any doubt as to the appropriate finding or sentence, the Magistrate should take more time for consideration or, if necessary, stand the case down or adjourn it for a short period.

PART 2

Evidence

Chapter 5 – Key Concepts in Evidence

5.1 INTRODUCTION

The law of evidence is a collection of rules that apply to the proof of facts in court. Many of the rules of evidence originate in the common law, at a time when the institution of the jury was prevalent in both civil and criminal trials. Many of the rules of evidence continue to be explainable in light of the separation in the function of a judge as the trier of law and the one who controlled the proceedings of a trial and the jury, which was a collection of people who together listened to the evidence and made findings of fact based on the evidence.

This chapter is intended as a summary of the most important rules of evidence in Papua New Guinea. It is not intended to be a substitute for case law or statutory authority. Neither is it a substitute for a text that deals exclusively and comprehensively with the law and rules of evidence.

In Papua New Guinea, the *Evidence Act* contains both common law and statutory provisions, most of which originated in England years ago. However, there are rules of evidence which exist apart from the *Evidence Act*, either pursuant to other statutes or as part of the underlying law originating in the common law. The rules of evidence are difficult to classify in a systematic way. Any two texts on the subject are likely to be organised very differently, even where the same topics are covered.

Many of the rules of evidence were originally designed to protect and guide the jury in their duty to determine the facts of a case. For instance, the rules relating to hearsay and opinion might be thought of as means of protecting unsophisticated members of a jury from relying on evidence which might result in mistaken or unreliable findings of fact.

Other rules of evidence can be explained in terms of different considerations. For instance, public policy lies behind the rules of evidence relating to privilege. Evidence may be privileged, not because it is unreliable, but because society places a higher importance on protecting the evidence from disclosure than it does on the probative value that the evidence would otherwise have. Similarly, rules concerning compellability and the presumption of innocence can be explained in terms of public policy. Convenience is a concern that lies behind other rules of evidence. For instance, rules pertaining to judicial notice provide that some facts can be established without calling any evidence at all. Such facts would often require a great deal of inconvenience and expense to prove in a conventional way. Rules relating to relevance and previous consistent statements have much to do with preventing trials from becoming even more drawn out affairs than they already are.

Although it is impossible to accurately simplify the law of evidence, it might be useful for Magistrates to keep in mind that some rules and concepts are more central than others.

The three central concepts are relevance, admissibility and weight.

- Relevance is one of the most central of the rules pertaining to the admissibility of evidence.
- If evidence is relevant then, unless some other exclusionary rule applies, the evidence is admissible.
- The major consideration that applies to admissible evidence is what weight (or credit) it should be given. The weight that evidence is given will usually determine the outcome of a case.

5.2 ADMISSIONS

A party against whom a fact would otherwise need to be proved may agree to admit that fact. When this happens, the fact may be taken by the court as having been proved without evidence being called.

Admissions may be made in both criminal proceedings (see *Criminal Code*, s 589) and civil proceedings. A Magistrate must ensure that both parties are clear and that the Magistrate is also clear on what exactly is being admitted. The purpose for which the admission is being made is also important. A fact might be admitted for one purpose but not for another.

An admission can only bind the party that is making it. For example, if there are two plaintiffs making a claim for damages arising out of a defendant's negligence, one plaintiff might admit that the defendant was sober at the time of the accident. The other plaintiff might not be prepared to make this admission. If the state of the defendant's sobriety is in issue, the admission of one plaintiff only applies with respect to that plaintiff's claim. It cannot be used to prejudice another party who does not admit the fact.

The best way to establish that an admission is being made is to have it reduced to writing and signed by the party or lawyer making the admission. This practice avoids any doubt about exactly what is being admitted. If this is not practicable then the Magistrate should write the admission word for word in his or her bench notes and then read the admission back to the party making it to ensure that what has been written is correct.

A Magistrate cannot *force* a party to make an admission even though the admission might be reasonable in the circumstances and even though not making the admission forces the other side to call evidence to prove the fact, thereby requiring delays and inconvenience.

5.3 AFFIDAVITS

An affidavit is a written statement of fact that is signed and its contents sworn to be true by the deponent. Although it is sworn, an affidavit is not automatically admissible to prove a fact in issue in a trial. Because an affidavit is sworn to be true it may be more reliable than an out-of-court statement that is not sworn. However, it is still hearsay, and the party against whom it is admitted (unless the maker of the affidavit is called as a witness) is denied the opportunity of cross-examining the maker of the statement.

Affidavits can be a convenient shortcut for adducing evidence. However, they can create difficulty for a Magistrate where credibility of the deponent is in issue. Therefore, in a situation where parties adduce inconsistent evidence by means of affidavits, and a Magistrate is forced to make a finding of fact, it may be necessary to call the deponents for cross-examination.

Affidavits are admissible as proof of the facts stated in some circumstances:

- where the party against whom the affidavit is adduced consents to its admission;
- to prove a matter that is not a substantive issue, for instance service of a document on a party;
- where a specific statutory provision allows for the admission of affidavit evidence;

where the proceedings are interlocutory in nature, and proceedings where the rules of evidence are relaxed generally, either by statutory authority or by the rules of practice. Examples are bail hearings and sentencing submissions.

There are a number of *statutory provisions* that permit the admission of affidavits as evidence. They are found in the *Evidence Act* and in various other statutes. The following are some of the most commonly relied upon provisions.

Sections 32-37 of the *Evidence Act* provide specific instances and rules governing the use of affidavits to prove facts in District Court proceedings. These sections give a Magistrate the discretion to allow evidence to be adduced by affidavit.

However, where:

- a person interested in the proceedings applies for the production of the maker of the affidavit for cross-examination;
- that person has a reasonable basis for requiring the person to be produced; and

- the maker can be produced,

a Magistrate must not allow evidence by affidavit without calling the maker for cross-examination.

Section 46 of the *Evidence Act* provides for the admission of affidavit evidence to prove a previous conviction outside of Papua New Guinea.

Sections 75-78 of the *Evidence Act* are examples of other statutory provisions that authorise the use of affidavits to prove particular facts subject to certain conditions. These pertain to documents and copies of documents.

Other statutes provide for admission of affidavits in particular circumstances. A party wishing to have an affidavit admitted as evidence should be called upon to provide authority for its admission.

An example of a statutory provision that allows for admission of affidavits is s 19 of the *Deserted Wives and Children's Act*, which provides that:

> "a woman who complains that she has been deserted by her husband or left by him without means of support shall produce direct evidence of her marriage to the defendant or, if she is unable to produce direct evidence to the satisfaction of the Court, shall make and produce an affidavit setting out the time, place and circumstances of the marriage".

5.4 BURDEN OF PROOF

The general rule is that the party who makes an allegation of fact has the burden of proving it (for exceptions see 5.21 and 5.26). This means that the plaintiff in a civil action has the burden of proving the allegations that together constitute the claim. The prosecution in a criminal case has the burden of proving the allegations that form the basis of the charge.

The burden of proof can refer to the evidential burden or the legal burden. The evidential burden is the burden that must be met by a prosecutor or a plaintiff in order to present a prima facie case. If the evidential burden is not met, a criminal case may be dismissed as a result of a no case submission. In a civil case, a similar motion, sometimes called a non suit motion, may be made: see 5.23.

In a criminal case, if a defendant wishes to rely upon some defence such as consent or self-defence, he or she must adduce some evidence that points to the existence of that defence. This imposes a burden on the defendant. However, this burden is not an onerous one. It takes only a minimal amount of evidence to discharge this burden. If a defendant raises *some* evidence (either during cross-examination of the prosecution witnesses or by calling evidence during the defence case) then a Magistrate is obliged to consider the existence of such a defence when deciding whether the prosecution has proved its case beyond a reasonable doubt.

In a *criminal* case, where a defendant wishes to rely on a statutory *excuse*, a *proviso*, *justification* or *licence* for the actions which constitute the actus rea of the offence, then a higher evidential burden is cast upon the defendant.

An example of an offence where such a defence might be advanced is s 43 of the *Summary Offences Act*, which provides that:

> "a person who, without lawful authority, in a public place ... defaces ... a building is guilty of an offence".

Other examples of offences where such a defence must be proved on the balance of probabilities are found in s 4(c) of the *Dangerous Drugs Act* and s 26(4) of the *Firearms Act*.

In a civil case, a defendant who wishes to rely on a defence (such as contributory negligence or failure to mitigate) must discharge an evidentiary burden in relation to the allegations that provide the basis of such a defence. In civil cases this burden of proof on the defendant is the same as the burden borne by the plaintiff. The evidentiary burden must be discharged on the balance of probabilities.

The *evidential* burden of proof relates to the question of whether a party has adduced a prima facie case. Generally, the evidential burden is met when there is some evidence going to each element of an offence (in a criminal case) or each ingredient of a cause of action (in a civil case): see also 5.23.

The *legal* burden is the burden of proof that a plaintiff or a prosecutor must meet in order to succeed at the end of the case after all the evidence has been called by both sides. In a criminal case it is proof beyond a reasonable doubt. In a civil case it is proof on the balance of probabilities.

5.5 CHARACTER EVIDENCE

Character evidence is evidence that shows what qualities a person has. Character evidence is usually adduced in relation to the credibility of a witness to show that a person's evidence should or should not be believed.

The common law rules relating to the admission of evidence of character have resulted in a fairly complex set of rules and exceptions. Much of this may be explained in terms of relevance. If evidence of a person's character is relevant to an issue, including credibility, then it is likely to be admissible.

Section 21 of the *Evidence Act* permits a party to test the credit of his or her own witness, but not by means of character evidence. A party may test the credit of an opposing party's witness by character evidence, provided it is probative and relevant. This applies to both criminal and civil cases.

In criminal law there are important statutory limitations to the admissibility of evidence concerning the *character of the defendant*, including evidence of a prior criminal conviction.

Section 15 of the *Evidence Act* prevents the character of the accused from being raised by the prosecution, except in certain circumstances.

One circumstance where character evidence is admissible is pursuant to s 15(c), where proof of a previous conviction is necessary to prove the commission of the offence with which the defendant is charged. An example is when a defendant is charged with escaping from lawful custody pursuant to s 139 of the *Criminal Code*. In order to prove the offence, the prosecution must prove that the custody from which the defendant is accused of escaping was lawful. If the custody that the defendant escaped from results from a sentence for the commission of a criminal offence, then it is necessary to prove that criminal offence and therefore the criminal record for that offence.

Other instances where evidence of the defendant's character is admissible are triggered by the manner in which the defendant conducts his or her defence.

If the defendant:

- gives evidence against a co-defendant;
- cross-examines any prosecution witness to demonstrate his or her bad character;
- makes suggestions about the prosecutor's bad character; or
- adduces evidence about his or her good character,

then the character of the defendant becomes an issue and evidence may be led about it by the prosecutor.

5.6 CIRCUMSTANTIAL EVIDENCE

Circumstantial evidence is sometimes called indirect evidence. It is evidence that is relevant, not because it proves a fact in issue, but because it proves another fact which makes a fact in issue more or less probable. Circumstantial evidence requires an inference to be drawn on the part of the Magistrate in order to relate it to a fact in issue.

Example: If a person is charged with breaking and entering a dwelling-house, there may be no direct evidence to prove that the person committed the offence. No-one may have seen the offence take place. However, there may be evidence that the defendant was seen close to the house a few minutes after the offence was committed. This does not prove that the accused broke into the house. The defendant may have had other reasons for being in the vicinity of the house. This is circumstantial evidence, because the fact that the defendant was close to the house shortly after the offence shows that he *could* have committed the offence. It is more probable that the offence was committed by a person who was in the vicinity of the house shortly after the offence than by a person who was a greater distance away. If it is proved that the defendant was in possession of a camera taken from the house, this too is circumstantial evidence. It does not prove that the defendant broke into the house. The defendant may have found the camera on the street or innocently bought the camera. However, the evidence does make it more likely that the defendant was the one who took the camera, especially if an explanation is not offered as to how the defendant came into possession of the camera. There may be additional circumstantial evidence in the form of fingerprints belonging to the defendant that were found in the house. Similarly, this does not prove that the defendant broke into the house, but it is circumstantial evidence which, in the absence of an explanation, allows a trier of fact to conclude that it is more likely that the defendant did break into the house. The evidence might include further circumstantial evidence. It might be in the form of evidence that the defendant was seen near the house before the break-in. It might be that the accused knew that the owners of the house would be away at the time of the break-in.

Sometimes circumstantial evidence is relevant because it makes a fact in issue *less* probable. If the defendant in the above example gave evidence that he had a friend in the neighbourhood whom he had been visiting, and that he was walking home when the break-in occurred, it would not prove that he did not commit the break in. However, it would be relevant circumstantial evidence because if accepted, it would tend to reduce the probability that the defendant committed the offence.

If there is enough circumstantial evidence of sufficient weight, a Magistrate may find that the offence is proved beyond a reasonable doubt, even without direct evidence. Sometimes, a combination of direct and circumstantial evidence proves an offence.

5.7 COMPELLABILITY

A person is compellable if that person can be forced, against his or her will, to be a witness. The general rule is that everyone who is competent is compellable. The usual means of obliging a person to give evidence is to serve the person with a summons or issue a warrant to bring them to court: *District Courts Act*, ss 66-73. Even a person who has not been summoned (the *Evidence Act* uses the word "subpoena") is compellable as a witness if he or she is "present at any legal proceeding": *Evidence Act*, s 10. If a compellable witness who is present in court refuses to give evidence, he or she may be dealt with pursuant to s 70 of the *District Courts Act*. This section gives a Magistrate the power to commit a person to custody for a period of up to eight days.

Exceptions: There are exceptions to the general rule that competent witnesses are compellable. Certain people are competent witnesses but cannot be compelled to give evidence.

The most important exception to the general rule is a defendant in a criminal case. The right to silence continues throughout a trial. Section 14 of the *Evidence Act* makes this clear in the following words:

> "A person charged with an offence shall not be called as a witness by the prosecution in any legal proceedings in connexion with the offence."

Of course a defendant in a criminal case may *choose* to give evidence: see 5.8. If the defendant chooses to do this, he or she may be cross-examined by the prosecution.

A co-accused cannot be compelled to give evidence, but may choose to do so. If a co-accused gives evidence, it may be evidence that the other co-accused was the one who committed the offence. This opens the testifying co-accused to cross-examination about his or her own character: see 5.5.

A spouse of a defendant in a criminal case is not compellable as a witness against the defendant in relation to most types of offences, unless the defendant consents: *Evidence Act*, s 13.

Some witnesses who are compellable may be permitted to refuse to answer particular types of questions. This is a matter of privilege, not compellability: see 5.29.

5.8 COMPETENCE

A person is competent to testify as a witness if the person is *permitted* by the court to testify. The general rule is that everyone is competent to testify. The importance of the rule about competence lies in the exceptions to the general rule.

The mental capacity of a person to make an oath or affirmation is the main limiting factor in deciding whether or not a person is competent to give evidence. If a person understands the meaning of an oath or an affirmation then the person is competent to give evidence. In Papua New Guinea, the *Oaths Affirmations and Statutory Declarations Act* governs the giving of an oath.

In certain circumstances a witness may give evidence without taking an oath or making an affirmation. Section 6 of the *Oaths, Affirmations and Statutory Declarations Act* provides that:

> "a person called in a civil or criminal proceeding who does not appear capable of understanding the nature of an oath or of understanding the meaning of a statutory declaration or affirmation may be permitted to give evidence".

However, this is only permitted if a Magistrate is satisfied that the person understands that he or she is liable to punishment for giving false evidence. Children often fit within the meaning of this section. This is a special category of competence, and a Magistrate must treat such evidence with extra care: see 5.10.

5.9 CONFESSION

A confession is a full admission by an accused person of the commission of a criminal offence. Although most confessions are reduced to writing, they can also be made orally.

A confession is a form of hearsay evidence. It is an out-of-court statement that a prosecutor wishes to adduce as evidence to prove the truth of what was said. Confessions may therefore be thought of as an exception to the rule against hearsay. The exception falls generally within the scope of the larger exception referred to as *statements against interest*.

Special rules govern the admission of confessions in a criminal prosecution. The party seeking to have it admitted must prove that the confession was voluntarily made, that is, that it was not induced by threats or promises: *Evidence Act*, s 28. The procedure for determining whether the prosecution can demonstrate that the confession has not been induced by threats or promises is called a voir dire: see 5.36.

The requirement that a prosecutor prove that a statement is voluntary before it can be admitted as evidence is based on the perceived risk that a person might confess to something not because it is true, but because he or she is frightened as a result of an express or implied threat, or expects to receive some benefit as a result of making a confession. The perceived benefit that induces a confession might be release from custody or a lenient sentence, or it might be directed towards some other person (protection of a friend or family member who could be charged with an offence). A prosecutor must satisfy the Magistrate that a confession does not result from these or other similar motives.

During a voir dire the issue is not whether the confession is true, nor is it whether the confession is sufficient to form the basis of a conviction. The only issue is the admissibility of the confession. Stated another way, the issue is whether the confession was made as a result of threats or promises, express or implied. The important factor is not whether threats or promises were intended to be made, but rather whether a defendant would have *perceived* a threat or a promise.

If a prosecutor demonstrates during a voir dire that the confession was *not* made as a result of perceived threats or promises, that is, that it was voluntarily made, then it *may* be admitted as evidence: see 5.20. When this happens, it is subjected to the same considerations as any other evidence in relation to the weight that should be given to it. For instance, a confession might be admissible but be of little weight. It might not be clear what the defendant is confessing to or what exactly the defendant meant by the words he or she used. These are matters of weight which can be considered *after* a decision to admit evidence has been made.

Apart from the possibility that a confession may be inadmissible because the prosecutor is unable to prove that it was not made as a result of perceived promise or threat, it may be alleged that the confession was obtained by other wrongful, illegal or unconstitutional means. This may lead to its rejection: see 5.20.

5.10 CORROBORATION

Corroborating evidence is independent evidence that *confirms* or *supports* some other evidence. It can take the form of oral testimony, documentary evidence or real evidence. It might be direct evidence or it might be circumstantial. A finding that an accused has told lies in court may amount to corroboration. However, evidence of a recent complaint by a victim of a sexual offence is not corroboration because it is *not* independent.

Section 1 of the *Criminal Code* defines "uncorroborated testimony" in relation to an accused person as "testimony that is not corroborated in some material particular by other evidence implicating him".

There are particular types of cases (both criminal and civil) where corroboration is important. These cases break down into two categories:

1. Cases where corroboration is *required* before a particular finding can be made.
2. Cases where a Magistrate may make a finding without corroboration but must first *warn* himself or herself of the danger of doing so. Rules about corroboration can be traced to what has been regarded as the inherent weakness in the types of evidence that require corroboration.

5.10.1 Where corroboration is required

The following are some instances where corroboration is required before there can be a finding made against a defendant.

Paternity cases: Sections 50, 53(2), 55(3), 58(6) and 59(8) of the *Child Welfare Act* all require that certain orders regarding affiliation and maintenance not be made solely on the uncorroborated evidence of the mother of the child in question: see 16.2.12.

Treason and perjury: A conviction for treason pursuant to s 40 of the *Criminal Code* and a conviction for perjury pursuant to s 121 of the *Criminal Code* must not be made on the uncorroborated evidence of one witness. As these charges are not heard in the District Court, it is not necessary to elaborate.

Indecent exposure: Section 23 of the *Summary Offences Act* creates the offence of indecent exposure. It also makes corroboration a requirement in convicting a defendant for this offence.

5.10.2 Where a warning is required

Where a warning is required before convicting on uncorroborated evidence, **a failure of a Magistrate to direct his or her mind properly and clearly to this rule of evidence may, on appeal, be regarded as an error of law sufficient to overturn a conviction**.

The types of cases where this warning is required are as follows:

Unsworn evidence: Section 6 of the *Oaths Affirmations and Statutory Declarations Act* gives a Magistrate discretion to allow a witness to give evidence even though he or she is unable to take an oath or make a statutory declaration or affidavit. Such unsworn evidence usually comes from a young child: see 5.8. Section 6(3) provides that nothing in the section affects the operation of any rule of law or practice relating to corroboration of evidence. The rule of law in this case is that a Magistrate has an obligation to warn himself or herself of the danger of convicting without corroboration on the evidence of a person who has not taken an oath or affirmed pursuant to the *Oaths Affirmations and Statutory Declarations Act*.

Sexual cases: The common law has historically recognised that it is often easier to make an allegation of sexual assault than it is to refute it, especially where the issue is consent. Out of this recognition has grown the need to take great care before convicting a person of a sexual offence on the uncorroborated evidence of a complainant. If a Magistrate does convict without corroboration, then the Magistrate must be careful to state in the reasons for judgment and in the bench notes that he or she is aware of the need for warning on the danger of convicting without corroboration and has in fact done so.

Evidence of an accomplice: Similar care is needed in convicting a defendant on the uncorroborated evidence of an accomplice. An accomplice may or may not be a co-accused in the case before the court. For instance, an accomplice might be a person not yet charged, or one who has already been convicted. A Magistrate who convicts on the uncorroborated evidence of an accomplice must make it clear in the reasons for judgment that he or she has warned himself or herself of the dangers of doing so, but is satisfied that such a conviction is safe in view of the strength of other evidence.

5.10.3 Illustration of corroborating evidence

Suppose a victim of an assault gave evidence that the defendant hit him with a stick on the head and the defendant gave evidence that he did not hit the victim with a stick. A Magistrate might have some difficulty in making a finding of fact. The finding would have to be made by weighing the evidence of each witness and applying the burden and standard of proof. If the evidence of one of the witnesses was corroborated (confirmed or supported by independent evidence), for instance by medical evidence that the injuries of the victim are consistent with blows by a stick, it could make the Magistrate's task easier. Where the sides appear equally credible, corroborating evidence in support of one side can assist in determining whether the burden of proof has been discharged.

5.11 CREDIT

The credit of evidence refers to the extent to which a court may give it weight or accept it as true. Similarly, the credibility of a witness refers to the extent to which a witness should be believed. A witness whose evidence is accepted as true is one who is found to be credible.

A question put to a witness in relation to his or her credit is relevant if it assists the court in deciding how much weight, if any, to attach to the witness's testimony.

Credit may be affected by a variety of factors. Among them are:

- Motive for not speaking the truth
- Memory
- Perception
- Understanding
- Inconsistencies in testimony

Sometimes evidence of credit relates to the character of a witness: see 5.5. For instance, suppose a witness was caught cheating on a school exam 10 years ago. The witness might be cross-examined by the opposing party about this. Even though the exam might have nothing to do with the case before the court, if the fact that the witness cheated on an exam 10 years ago may help to determine whether the witness is telling the truth about an issue before the court, then it is relevant. However, Magistrates are given *discretion* by s 26 of the *Evidence Act* to decide whether a witness has to answer these types of questions.

The exercise of this discretion turns on whether the answer to a question about character (used to attack the credit of a witness) would have a far greater negative effect on the character of a witness compared to the extent to which it really helps a court to decide whether the witness is telling the truth. If so, then a Magistrate is entitled to tell a witness that he or she is not obliged to answer the question.

Even if the answer to the question that the cross-examiner is seeking would only have a very small effect on the credibility of a witness, then a Magistrate has the discretion to inform a witness that he or she is not obliged to answer it. The example given above about whether a witness was caught cheating on an exam many years ago is an example of this type of question.

It is difficult to determine credibility in relation to hearsay evidence, whether oral or written: see 5.3 and 5.17.

Where documentary hearsay evidence in the form of computer-generated documents is considered for credibility, s 67 of the *Evidence Act* provides guidelines.

5.12 CROSS-EXAMINATION

5.12.1 What is cross-examination?

Cross-examination is an important tool in the search for truth in the adversary system of justice. It allows a party to test and probe the evidence that has been given by an adverse witness. There are two main purposes of cross-examination. One is to expose the weaknesses of the witness' evidence. The weight of an opposing witness' evidence may be diminished and the opponent's case therefore rendered less damaging. The other purpose of cross-examination is to elicit evidence from an adverse witness that is favourable to one's own case.

Cross-examination is distinguished from examination-in-chief mainly by the fact that leading questions are allowed. See 5.16 for description and examples of leading questions.

While a wide range of questions may be asked of a witness during cross-examination, it is not unlimited. For instance, the questions have to have some relevance.

Also, s 27 of the *Evidence Act* requires a Magistrate to disallow any question that is:

- scandalous or indecent (unless relating to a fact in issue or necessary to determine a fact in issue); or
- intended to insult, annoy or is needlessly offensive.

Other rules of admissibility also apply to evidence elicited in cross-examination.

During cross-examination, a witness may be challenged on a previous inconsistent statement: see 5.28.

5.12.2 Browne v Dunn

If a defence that is intended to be advanced involves a denial or contradiction of evidence given by a prosecution or plaintiff witness, the defence version of facts should be put to the witness in cross-examination. This is known as the rule in *Browne v Dunn* [1894] 6 R 67.

For instance, suppose a prosecution witness says that he saw the defendant in Waigani on the night of the crime. Suppose also that the defendant will be giving evidence that he was *not* in Waigani. In such a case, the proposition that the accused was *not* in Waigani on the night of the crime (that the person that the witness *thought* was the accused was really someone else, or that the witness is not telling the truth) must be put to the prosecution witness during cross-examination.

The rule in *Browne v Dunn* allows a party to know before closing their case what parts of his or her case are going to be challenged by evidence from a defence witness. A party may then decide to re-examine their own witness on this point or choose to call further evidence in support of the fact that will be disputed: see 5.34.

If a party ignores the rule in *Browne v Dunn* and later attempts to lead evidence that is inconsistent with evidence adduced by an opposing witness, a Magistrate may exercise discretion to disallow this evidence or take into account the failure to cross-examine on the point when weighing the defendant's evidence.

5.13 CUSTOM

Custom is an important source of law in Papua New Guinea. The *Constitution* and the *Underlying Law Act* give it priority to the common law: see 2.3.8 and 2.4. Where a party's case involves custom, the court must determine what is and is not custom and whether custom is applicable to the facts and issues before the court. Until recently, custom was a matter that had to be proved as a fact: see *Customs Recognition Act*, s 2. Now, however, s 16 of the *Underlying Law Act* provides that a question as to the existence or content of custom is a question of law and not a question of fact. This gives a Magistrate much wider scope for the determination of custom than previously existed.

A Magistrate, pursuant to s 16(2) of the *Underlying Law Act*, must consider the submissions on behalf of the parties, and may:

- refer to cases, books, treatises, reports and other works of reference on the customary law relevant to the proceedings;

- refer to statements and declarations of customary law made by local, provincial and other authorities in accordance with a law empowering them to make such statements;
- consider evidence and information concerning the customary law relevant to the proceeding presented to it by a person the court is satisfied has knowledge of the customary law relevant to the proceedings; or
- obtain evidence, information and opinion of his or her own motion.

In determining which particular customary law should apply to the matter in hand, the court must follow the rules set out in s 17 of the *Underlying Law Act.* For example, it may be necessary to consider which community or communities the parties belong to. The rules for ascertaining membership of a community are contained in s 1(2) of the Act.

In criminal cases, custom may *only* be taken into account for specific purposes. These purposes are set out in s 4 of the *Customs Recognition Act*. They are:

- ascertaining a person's state of mind;
- deciding the reasonableness of a person's act or omission;
- determining the reasonableness of an excuse;
- deciding whether to proceed with a conviction (or to grant a discharge); and
- determining an appropriate sentence.

See also 2.4.2.2, which deals with custom in criminal matters.

Custom in civil matters is dealt with in 2.4.2.3, and see 25.6.4 for decisions in customary matters.

5.14 DIRECT EVIDENCE

Direct evidence is evidence of one of the actual facts that must be proved in order to convict in a criminal case, or to make a finding in favour of a plaintiff in a civil case. Direct evidence does not require a Magistrate to draw an inference.

For instance, if a defendant is charged with breaking and entering a dwelling-house, and a witness gives evidence in court that he saw the defendant kick in the door and go into the house, that is direct evidence. Similarly, if a person is alleged to have left the scene of an accident and a witness at the scene of the accident gives evidence that the defendant drove away, it is also direct evidence. It is not necessary for a Magistrate to draw any inference from this evidence in order to link it to an element of the offence.

Direct evidence can be contrasted with indirect or circumstantial evidence which requires a trier of fact to draw an inference to link the evidence with a fact that must be proved: see 5.6. Because there is no risk of drawing an incorrect inference in relation to direct evidence, it is therefore considered to be inherently more reliable than circumstantial evidence (subject to the credibility of the source of the evidence).

5.15 DOCUMENTARY EVIDENCE

A document usually takes the form of a piece of paper with writing on it. However, this is not always the case. Section 1 of the *Evidence Act* defines a document to include "a book, plan, paper, parchment or other material on which there is any writing that is marked with letters or marks denoting words or any other signs capable of carrying a definite meaning to persons conversant with them, and includes any part of a document".

When deciding upon the admissibility of a document and the use to which it can be put if admitted, it is useful to think of the several categories of documents.

One way of distinguishing documents is to decide whether the document has some legal significance (for instance a lease or a contract) *or* whether the document is intended to prove the truth of assertions made in the document. The first type of document does not present a hearsay issue. The latter type does.

If the document does not present a hearsay problem (that is, it is not being adduced to prove the truth of an assertion contained in it), then its admission usually depends only on its relevance and upon it being properly identified as what it purports to be. In most cases this will require a witness to identify the document and to establish its relevance.

The *Evidence Act* provides some shortcuts in respect of some documents whereby it is not necessary to call a witness to identify the document for the following:

- Copies of laws, proclamations, orders etc: ss 38-43;
- Evidence of judicial proceedings: s 44;
- Government votes and proceedings in PNG and Australia: s 48;
- Other public documents: s 51;
- Gazettes and other government publications: ss 52-54;
- Letters of probate and administration: s 56;
- Incorporation of a company: s 58.

If a document is being offered to prove the truth of assertions contained in it then it is hearsay, and its admission may depend on it fitting within some exception to the hearsay rule.

There are a number of statutory exceptions to the hearsay rule that apply to the admission of documents. These include previous criminal records, banking documents, business records and affidavits. The following list is drawn from the *Evidence Act*:

Affidavits: s 34;

Medical reports: s 37;

Birth, death and marriage certificates: s 57;

Computerised information: ss 65 and 66;

Bankers records: s 93;

Certificate of previous convictions: *Evidence Act*, s 48 and *Penal Code*, s 581;

Business records: s 61;

Votes and Acts in Parliament: s 48;

Official statistics: s 59;

Bylaws: s 60.

See also 5.18.

Copies of documents: Often, it is not the original but the copy of a document that a party attempts to adduce in court. The best evidence rule is a common law rule which requires that if an original of a document can be produced in court that a copy should not be allowed. However, the best evidence rule is not as rigorously enforced as it once was. With computers storing original information, it is arguable that all printed documents are really copies. The main concern with producing a copy of a document as evidence is whether it accurately reflects the contents of the original. This is the major concern in relation to the admissibility of a copy.

Sections 68-90 of the *Evidence Act* set out detailed provisions providing for the admission of photocopied documents. These sections appear to be outdated and difficult to apply.

5.16 EXAMINATION-IN-CHIEF

Examination-in-chief is the process by which the party who calls a witness elicits the witness's testimony about matters in question. Examination-in-chief consists of questions and answers.

5.16.1 Rule against leading questions

The most important rule about examination-in-chief is that the person examining a witness is generally not permitted to ask leading questions.

A leading question is a question that suggests a particular answer.

There are several types of leading questions. An example of one type is: "You were present at the restaurant when the defendant walked up to the counter with a gun, weren't you?" It is obvious that the questioner is expecting the witness to answer "yes" to such a question.

A variation on this type of leading question is where the question contains detailed information that suggests what answer is expected. For instance, "When you awoke during the middle of the night after hearing a loud noise, did you react by getting out of bed immediately?" This is clearly a leading question. It suggests that the witness was awakened in the middle of the night, that the cause of the awakening was a loud noise and further, it tends to suggest that the witness got out of bed immediately upon hearing the noise.

Another type of leading question is one that implies an affirmative answer to an embedded question. For instance, if a witness is asked "Have you been driving without a licence for a long time?", an answer of either "yes" or "no" implies that the witness has been driving without a licence. It is therefore a leading question.

Leading questions are sometimes easy to detect, in that they often require the answer to be "yes" or "no". However, not all "yes" or "no" questions are leading questions. For instance, the question "Are you a citizen of Papua New Guinea?" is not a leading question. Although it demands a "yes" or "no" answer, neither answer is suggested by the question.

In court, a lawyer representing an opposing party might object to leading questions. If the lawyer does not do so, it may be assumed that the lawyer consents to the leading questions being asked. However, if the opposing party is not represented by a lawyer, no such assumption should be made. The party is unlikely to know the rules of evidence. In such a case, it is up to the Magistrate to ensure fairness in the trial by controlling the degree to which a party is allowed to ask leading questions.

5.16.2 Exceptions to rule against leading questions

1. Where a witness is being asked introductory and background questions about matters which are not in issue. For instance, the witness's name, address, profession and any other relevant background information.
2. Where the answer to the question has been established by some earlier evidence, either by the witness's own answers or by some other witness. For instance, in the example above, if the witness (who was asked about being awakened in the night by a loud noise) has already answered non-leading questions that establish that the witness was awakened by a loud noise in the middle of the night and that as a result the witness got out of bed, the questioner might want simply to establish whether the witness got out of bed *immediately*.
3. Where the opposing side does not object to the leading question. However, as mentioned above, if the other side is not represented by a lawyer it is appropriate for a Magistrate to limit the asking of leading questions.
4. Where the subject matter of the question is not in dispute.

See also 5.27, 5.19 and 5.32.

5.17 HEARSAY RULE

5.17.1 What is hearsay?

Hearsay is a statement of fact that is offered in court to prove the truth of what is asserted without the person who is making the assertion being present in court and able to be cross-examined.

The rule against hearsay, together with its exceptions, is one of the most important rules of evidence. The *purpose* for which the statement is intended to be used is important in deciding whether it is hearsay. A witness's statement or document that repeats something that was said out of court is only hearsay if the statement is repeated in court to *prove that the facts asserted in the statement are true*. If the statement is offered in court simply to prove that the statement was made, and not to prove that what is asserted is true, then it is not hearsay.

Example: Suppose a witness (let's call him Tim) is called to give evidence and says "My brother John told me that the university was closed last Saturday." If the evidence is offered as proof that the university was closed on Saturday, then it is hearsay. However, suppose Tim is a delivery person and there is an issue about the reasonableness of Tim not making a delivery to the university on Saturday. The evidence of what Tim's brother John said is not hearsay. It is not being introduced to prove that the university was closed (the truth of the assertion by John), but only to explain the reasonableness of what Tim did on being *told* that it is closed.

Other types of court statements may be repeated in court because they are not intended to prove the truth of the out-of-court statement. Such statements are not hearsay.

Statements having legal effect: An example of such a statement would be a statement that has legal effect. For instance, if a representation is made as part of a contractual relation, that statement might be adduced in court to clarify the legal obligations of the parties, not to prove that the statement is true. For instance, if Joe sells Mary his car and, in the discussions leading up to the sale, tells her that the car's air conditioner works (when in fact it does not), then if Mary sued Joe for breach of contract she may adduce the out-of-court statement, not to prove that it is true, but to prove that it was made (and that she relied upon it).

Statements disclosing state of mind: Another example is where a statement made by a person out of court is adduced as evidence in court to show the state of mind of the person. For instance, a person might say to a neighbour "If you don't stop your dog from barking, I will shoot it." This statement might be admissible in court, not to show that it is true, but to indicate the state of mind of the person who made it at the time it was made.

5.17.2 Rationale for hearsay rule

An important reason for the hearsay rule is a Magistrate's need to make findings of credibility. If a witness who actually saw an event is in court when the evidence about that event is given, that witness can be cross-examined about what he or she perceived, how well he or she remembered, or whether he or she has a motive for not telling the truth. If the witness deliberately attempts to distort the truth or is somehow mistaken, this has a good chance of being revealed. The Magistrate can also evaluate the witness' demeanour (non-verbal communication).

On the other hand, if the person who witnessed an event is not in court to give evidence about what was seen, heard or felt, but the information is passed on to court through some other person, it is difficult for a trier of fact to weigh the evidence. It is difficult or even impossible to know whether the person who witnessed the events was lying, whether he or she saw or heard the events clearly, whether he or she has a motive for not telling the truth or whether he or she has a bad memory.

Hearsay is often contained in documents. When a person presents a document in court as evidence of the truth of what the documents says, then it is hearsay, just as it is when a person reports orally what another person said outside court: see 5.15.

5.18 HEARSAY RULE - EXCEPTIONS

There are many exceptions to the hearsay rule. Some are based on statute and some are part of the common law which forms part of the underlying law in Papua New Guinea. Together they provide for instances where an out-of-court assertion may be adduced in court (either orally or in writing) to prove the truth of the assertion.

5.18.1 Common law exceptions

Res gestae: If a statement is made in a state of great emotional excitement at the time of the events to which the statement relates, then it may be admitted as an exception to the hearsay rule. The statement must be spontaneous in the sense that it is not premeditated.

> **Example:** Suppose a witness to a robbery is heard to exclaim at the time of the robbery: "Oh no, it's Willie Sam!" If the witness is not available to give evidence in court (because of death, absence or mental disability), his or her statement might be given in evidence to prove the identity of the robber as a res gestae exception.

The res gestae exception *also* covers statements made by a person about how he or she feels at the time the statement is made. For example, "I am tired" or "I have a pain in my head." Evidence that a person (who is not a witness) said such a thing may be admitted to prove that that is how they really felt, even though the evidence is hearsay.

Statements against interest: This common law exception to the hearsay rule is based on the assumption that a person who makes a statement that is against his or her own interest would not do so unless that statement is true.

The most important example of this exception is a full confession that is made in a criminal case by a defendant to a person in authority. A person who confesses to a criminal offence makes the ultimate statement against interest. There are special rules governing this exception which are designed to ensure that the confession in made voluntarily and that other prerequisites are met: see 5.9 and 5.20.

A statement against interest, other than a confession in a criminal case, does not require a voir dire: see 5.36. For instance, an accused person may make an out-of-court statement that they are 18 years of age. This is a statement against interest if their age is in question and they are being tried in an adult court. Another example in a civil case would be where a person being sued for negligence admits that they were driving too fast for road conditions at the relevant time. A further example is where a person admits out of court that they owe someone else money. This statement is against the interest of the person making the statement and would therefore be admissible as an exception to the hearsay rule.

Other common law exceptions

Statements by persons since deceased made in the course of duty are admissible as a common law exception to the hearsay rule;

Statements made in public documents are prima facie evidence of their contents;

Statements made by persons since deceased, either against their interest or made in the course of official duty;

Readings from mechanical or technical devices that may be presumed to be operating properly: see 5.26.1.

5.18.2 Statutory exceptions to the hearsay rule

Statements about cause of death: *Evidence Act*, s 20. A statement about the cause of a person's death is admissible in court if that person is competent when the statement is made and believes that their death is imminent.

Affidavits: *Evidence Act*, s 34. A Magistrate or Judge has the discretion to allow affidavit evidence or deposition evidence. Sections 35 and 36 provide for notice by a party of an intention to use an affidavit, and the right of the opposing party to object or seek the attendance of the witness (deponent) for cross-examination. These provisions help to preserve the fundamental entitlement of natural justice that a party ought to be allowed to question evidence given against him or her.

Medical evidence: *Evidence Act*, s 37. Evidence of a medical doctor may be given by affidavit. There is a provision for the opposing party to apply for the doctor to be present for cross-examination. In deciding on the application a Magistrate must balance the interests of justice against the interference that a doctor's attendance at court would have on the ability to provide an essential service to the community.

Where a defendant is being tried with an indictable offence, affidavit evidence of a medical practitioner may only be adduced against the defendant with his or her consent.

Births, deaths and marriages: *Evidence Act*, s 57. Certificate evidence of a person's birth, death or marriage is admissible in documentary form, as long as the document purports to be issued by a person authorised by law to do so. This includes certificates from Papua New Guinea or from any other Commonwealth country.

Business records: *Evidence Act*, ss 61 and 72. These sections allow the admission of business records, or copies of them, to prove the truth of facts contained in them. It is an important exception to the hearsay rule. Such a record must have been made in the "ordinary course of business". There is a discretion to disallow a business record in the interests of justice.

Computerised information: *Evidence Act*, ss 64-67. These sections provide for the admission of information stored on computers. The admission of computer records, or copies of these records, is conditional on a number of criteria being satisfied. These are set out in s 65(1). The prerequisites may be proved by a certificate pursuant to s 66. A Magistrate is guided by criteria in s 66(3) in deciding what weight to attach to evidence stored on computer that is adduced as evidence: see also 5.11.

Banking records: *Evidence Act*, ss 91-94. These sections of the *Evidence Act* provide for the admission of bankers' documents in certain circumstances. In many cases this exception to the hearsay rule eliminates the need to call employees of banks to give evidence about deposits, withdrawals and other information relating to banking transactions and bank accounts.

5.19 HOSTILE WITNESS

A hostile witness is one who may be *cross*-examined by the party who called the witness. The determination that a witness is hostile is made by the Magistrate upon application by the party who called the witness.

The prerequisite for a declaration that a witness is hostile is a finding by a Magistrate that the witness is motivated by dishonesty or malice in the giving of evidence. A witness who tries *not* to tell the truth as a result of bribery or intimidation may be declared hostile.

Lawyers will sometimes seek a declaration that a witness is hostile simply because the evidence given by the witness in examination-in-chief does not come up to proof (does not say what is expected). However, this alone does not mean that a witness is hostile. A witness is not hostile simply because the witness is forgetful, confused or in error.

5.20 ILLEGALLY OR WRONGFULLY OBTAINED EVIDENCE

A defence counsel may object to the admission of evidence that is alleged to have been obtained illegally or unconstitutionally.

A Magistrate must make a ruling on such an objection. This involves two distinct issues:

1. The first issue is to decide whether the evidence has been illegally or unconstitutionally obtained.
2. The second issue is to decide what, if any, steps should be taken as a result of the evidence having been wrongfully obtained.

A decision on the first question often involves the Magistrate having to hear (or see) the evidence and to hear evidence about how the evidence was obtained. This is typically done in the context of a voir dire: see 5.36.

A decision about what to do if a finding has been made that the evidence is wrongfully obtained raises a number of questions. One is what powers does a Magistrate have when dealing with this sort of evidentiary issue?

If it is alleged that the evidence was obtained in an unconstitutional manner and should be excluded for that reason pursuant to s 57 of the *Constitution*, the case must be adjourned so that the National Court can rule on that question. The District Courts have no jurisdiction to rule on applications for relief (in the form of an order for the exclusion of evidence or otherwise) for breaches of the *Constitution*.

However, Magistrates have discretion, based on common law, to exclude evidence which has been obtained in an unfair manner. The Judges Rules, which originated in England in 1912, provide a basis for the exercise of this discretion. They were intended to guide the conduct of police in dealing with criminal suspects. The rules provided that suspects are to be warned that they are not obliged to give evidence.

This common law discretion relates primarily to the exclusion of evidence in a criminal case. It most commonly relates to a confession or evidence that has been obtained as a result of information given to the police by a defendant. For instance, if a person was threatened or assaulted by the police and, as a result, told the police where stolen property was located (which would link that person to the offence), a discretion to exclude might be exercised. This would not be as a result of the evidence being unreliable (which is the concern underlying confessions obtained by threats or promises), but because the evidence was wrongfully obtained as a result of an assault upon the accused. In many cases the discretion to exclude evidence on this basis overlaps with the need to determine whether a confession was obtained as a result of a promise or threat: see 5.9.

5.21 JUDICIAL NOTICE

Judicial notice is a way of establishing facts in court without calling evidence. When a Judge or Magistrate takes judicial notice of a particular fact, it is established for the purposes of the hearing or trial. It is not necessary for a party to call evidence to prove a fact that has been judicially noticed.

5.21.1 Judicial notice pursuant to statute

Sections 3-8 of the *Evidence Act* set out matters of which a Magistrate or Judge is *required* to take judicial notice. These include the laws of Papua New Guinea and Australia, including regulations, by-laws, commissions, determinations, proclamations or orders made by a government official pursuant to a statute or ordinance. Judicial notice must be taken of the existence of certain public offices and office holders in Papua New Guinea or Australia pursuant to s 7 of the *Evidence Act.*

Custom is a matter that is a question of law. Section 16 of the *Underlying Law Act* provides that custom is a question of law. This allows a Magistrate to take judicial notice of custom without receiving evidence on the matter (although evidence may also be received instead of, or in addition to, judicial notice of custom: see 5.13).

5.21.2 Judicial notice of other matters

Judicial notice may also be taken of matters other than those specified in the *Evidence Act*. The common law has established criteria which can be used as a guide in deciding whether to take judicial notice of a particular fact.

A fact that is so well known to the general public that is cannot be seriously disputed may be judicially noticed. Sometimes such facts are said to be *notorious*. For instance, in Papua New Guinea it is commonly known that snow does not fall in Port Moresby. No-one would seriously dispute this fact. If this fact becomes relevant to an issue before the court, a Magistrate could take judicial notice of it. Other examples of facts that are commonly known are that there is no highway between Port Moresby and Lae, that chewing buai is a popular habit in Papua New Guinea, and that the *Post Courier* is the name of a newspaper that is published in Papua New Guinea. These are only examples of facts that are so commonly known that they cannot seriously be disputed. No-one would expect a Magistrate to require sworn testimony to establish these facts. It would be impossible to list all of the facts that a Magistrate might take judicial notice of on this basis.

In the case of *Tomalana v Drug House of Papua New Guinea* [1991] PNGLR 65, the court explained judicial notice in the following words:

> "It is as if the proposition put to any reasonable person in that locality at that time, would bring an answer 'of course' or 'obviously that is correct'."

Judicial notice may also be taken of a fact if a Magistrate is able to satisfy himself or herself of the truth of the fact by reference to a well-known authority of indisputable accuracy. For instance, a Magistrate could consult a published atlas to determine the distance between two towns. If there is a question of what day of the week Christmas fell on in 1998, a Magistrate might consult a calendar to make the determination and then take judicial notice that it fell on a Friday.

However, the scope of this type of judicial notice is restricted. In *Mesalam Tomalana v Drug House of Papua New Guinea*, referred to above, the court held that judicial notice could *not* be taken of a published article in a medical journal.

A Magistrate should be careful not to take judicial notice of a fact that is within his or her personal knowledge but is *not* commonly known. For instance, a Magistrate might know that the traffic lights at a particular intersection were not working on a particular date. The Magistrate might know this because he or she drives through the intersection on the way to work every day. However, if it is not well known to the general public, then a Magistrate should not take judicial notice of the fact. To do so would be to take the role of a witness. It is up to the party seeking to establish that fact to call evidence.

5.21.3 When judicial notice may be taken

Judicial notice can be taken at any stage of a trial or hearing. A party may request that a Magistrate take judicial notice of a fact. Alternatively, a Magistrate may take judicial notice of a fact without specifically being asked to do so. A Magistrate should make clear to all parties a matter of which judicial notice is being taken.

5.22 LEADING QUESTIONS

See 5.16 and 5.12.

5.23 NO CASE SUBMISSION

At the end of a prosecution's case in a criminal trial, defence counsel may make a no case submission (sometimes called a no case motion or a no evidence motion). A similar motion in civil proceedings is sometimes called a non suit motion. The defendant submits that no prima facie case has been made out. In other words, it is a submission that evidence of some essential element of the offence is missing in the case. This is an invitation to the court to dismiss the charge against an accused.

The question that a Magistrate must consider when a no case submission is made is this: Is there some evidence going to each element of the charge? In order to answer this, it is necessary to break an offence down into its constituent elements or parts.

A Magistrate does not need to weigh evidence or make findings of credibility in deciding a no case submission. That can wait until the end of the case when both sides have had an opportunity to present all their evidence. Rather, a Magistrate should ask himself or herself whether someone who found the evidence of the prosecution credible could *possibly* convict on the evidence adduced.

Example: Suppose a Magistrate is presiding in a case where the defendant is charged with assault. The constituent elements are the application of force against a person, the intention to apply force and the lack of consent on the part of the victim. Also, evidence linking the defendant who is present in court to the offence (identification) is an essential element of this (and every other) offence. If there is evidence that goes to each of these elements in the prosecution's case, a no case submission should fail.

If, on the other hand, there is some element of the offence that is not supported by *any* evidence, then, even if all of the evidence that has been adduced is believed at the end of the case, it would not be possible to convict. There is no point in letting the case go any further. A no case submission must succeed.

A counsel for a defendant who makes a no case submission does not forfeit an opportunity to make submissions if the no case submission fails. If a no case submission is rejected and defence counsel elects to call no evidence, then both sides must be invited to give closing submissions. These submissions would properly invite the Magistrate to draw inferences from the evidence, make findings of credibility, deal with any issues of law and ultimately whether the case has been proved beyond a reasonable doubt: see 5.4 and 5.35.

5.24 OATHS AND AFFIRMATIONS

See 5.8.

5.25 OPINION

Opinion evidence is evidence of what someone thinks rather than what someone knows as a result of direct experience. Opinion evidence can often be detected because it often begins with expressions such as "I think that ...", "In my opinion ...", "I believe that ..." or "I would say that ...". Sometimes it is difficult to determine where factual evidence leaves off and opinion evidence begins. For example, when a witness says of a person, "she looked tired" or "he appeared to be at least 60 years old" it can be characterised either as opinion evidence or as factual evidence.

As a general rule, opinion evidence is not admissible. It is considered the role of a Magistrate as trier of fact to listen to factual evidence and form opinions, where necessary, on the basis of the factual evidence. The general rule against opinion evidence is based on the idea that when witnesses give opinions, they are usurping the role of the Magistrate. However, there are important exceptions to the general rule against the admission of opinions.

5.25.1 Opinion about matters of common experience

One exception is that witnesses are allowed to give opinions on matters of common experience. This includes a description of a person's state as tired, sad, exhausted, upset, old, young, disabled, aggressive or drunk. The speed of a motor vehicle based on a witness's observation and experience is also commonly accepted as an exception to the general rule against opinion evidence.

5.25.2 Expert opinion

Another exception to the general rule against opinion evidence is that of expert opinion. Where an issue in a case concerns specialised knowledge, a person who is qualified as an expert in that area of knowledge may be permitted to give opinion evidence within the scope of his or her expertise. A very common example of this exception is when a medical doctor is permitted to give evidence about a person's medical condition, treatment, cause of the condition or effects of the condition. Other examples include fingerprint evidence, handwriting analysis, property valuation and evidence about loss of future profits or income. It would be impossible to make an exhaustive list of the areas where expert opinion evidence could be admissible.

Before expert opinion evidence is admitted, it is necessary for the Magistrate to be satisfied that the person really is an expert in the area in which he or she has been asked to give an opinion. Determining this issue requires the Magistrate to consider the qualifications of the proposed expert. Many experts gain their qualifications by formal education and professional experience. However, this is not always the case. For example, a Chief may have no formal training but be qualified to give opinion evidence concerning matters of custom in a particular area. If there is an objection to the expert's qualifications, the question of whether the witness is an expert should be resolved by way of a voir dire: see 5.36.

Once an expert is qualified to give opinion evidence he or she is permitted to give factual evidence and opinion evidence based on facts or assumptions. The evidence of the expert is led by the party calling the expert. Then the expert may be cross-examined by adverse parties.

There may be an objection to expert evidence on the basis that the other side is taken by surprise by such evidence. In such a case, a Magistrate should take care to ensure that fairness prevails. If the party calling an expert did not give notice to the opposing party that expert opinion evidence would be called, or did not give the other side an idea of what the anticipated opinion would be, then fairness may require that the opposing party be given time to prepare for cross-examination of the expert or to call its own opinion evidence. The complexity of the subject matter in which an opinion is to be offered may be a factor in determining this.

5.25.3 Opinion about custom

Section 16(2) of the *Underlying Law Act* provides that a Magistrate may accept opinion, along with several other sources of information, when determining what custom applies to a matter. The source of this opinion is not limited to an "expert" in the usual sense, and may be obtained from anyone that the Magistrate thinks fit.

5.26 PRESUMPTIONS

A presumption is a rule of law that provides that where a party proves a particular fact or facts, another particular fact is taken to be proved in the absence of evidence to the contrary. A presumption allows a party to establish one fact by calling evidence to establish another specific fact or facts.

Establishing a presumption in court can be considered a two-stage process. The first is proof of necessary pre-existing fact or facts. The second is the drawing of an inference when the pre-requisite fact or facts are proved.

5.26.1 Some common presumptions

Presumption of legitimacy: When evidence is led to prove that:

- a child was born to a married woman;
- the child was born during the marriage or within the normal period of gestation after marriage; and
- the husband was alive at the time of gestation,

then a presumption arises that the child is legitimate. Unless an opposing party calls evidence to displace the presumption, the presumption of legitimacy operates.

Presumption of marriage: When evidence is led to prove that:

- a man and a woman cohabited; or
- a man and a woman went through a form of marriage celebration,

then a presumption arises that the parties were legally married. An opposing party may adduce evidence to rebut this presumption.

Presumption of death: Where evidence has been led to prove that:

- there has been no evidence that a person is alive for a continuous period of seven years;
- anyone who is likely to have heard from the person during that period has not heard from him or her; and
- all appropriate inquiries concerning the whereabouts of the person in question have been made without success,

then the court is entitled to make a presumption that the person is dead.

The presumption of regularity: There is a presumption in law that "all things are presumed to be done rightly." The operation of this presumption has a number of applications. For instance, if a minister or priest conducts a marriage ceremony, it will be presumed that he or she had the capacity to do so. This presumption also operates in relation to mechanical devices. A person who is charged for speeding on the basis of a radar reading must rebut the presumption that the radar device was working properly if he or she wishes to avoid a conviction for speeding. Similarly, if a device for measuring the alcohol content of a person's blood gives a particular reading, it will be presumed that the blood alcohol reading is what the machine says, because of the presumption of regularity. Any of these presumptions may be rebutted. However, the onus is on the party against whom the presumption operates to adduce evidence to rebut the presumption.

Presumption of knowledge (stolen property): There is also a presumption that a person in possession of stolen property knows that the property is stolen. The facts that give rise to this presumption are that:

- the property in question is stolen; and
- the person in question is in possession.

This presumption may be rebutted by evidence that the possessor of the stolen property did not know that the property was stolen.

5.26.2 Automatic presumptions

Some presumptions exist independently of any prerequisite facts. In other words, it is not necessary to prove any specific facts in order for the presumption to arise. Here are some of the more common automatic presumptions. These presumptions may be rebutted by evidence.

Presumption of sanity: A person is presumed to be sane. In order to establish that this is not so, and to displace the presumption, it is necessary to call evidence to prove that a person is not sane: *Criminal Code*, s 27. See 5.35 and Chapter 7.10.

The presumption of innocence: This presumption is fundamental in the criminal justice system. This presumption places the onus on a prosecutor to prove that a person is guilty. The burden of proof required to overcome or discharge this presumption is proof beyond a reasonable doubt.

In certain instances this presumption is affected by the age of a person who is alleged to have committed an offence. The presumption is absolute and cannot be rebutted in relation to a person under the age of seven. The presumption in relation to a defendant between the ages of seven and 14 is only rebuttable on proof that at the time of committing the offence he or she had the capacity to know that he or she ought not to do the act (or make the omission as the case may be). A male person under the age of 14 is presumed to be incapable of carnal knowledge. This presumption is rebuttable.

The presumption of intention: This presumption holds that a person intends the natural consequence of his or her acts.

Presumption of undue influence: The presumption of undue influence holds that a person who receives a large gift from someone has exerted undue influence on the donor of the gift. This presumption may be rebutted by evidence that undue influence was not used.

Presumption regarding "ancient documents": A document that is over 20 years old is said to be an ancient document. There is a common law presumption that a document that purports to be over 20 years old (by a date or reference on its face) is the age it purports to be and that it was signed by the person purporting to sign it. Section 82 of the *Evidence Act* extends this presumption to copies of ancient documents.

Other statutory presumptions also exist. For instance, s 30(3) of the *Criminal Code* creates a presumption that a male under the age of 14 is presumed to be incapable of having carnal knowledge. This presumption is rebuttable.

5.27 PREVIOUS CONSISTENT STATEMENT

A previous consistent statement is a statement made by a witness out of court that is offered in court along with a statement to the same effect made in court under oath. The general rule is that previous consistent statements are not admissible. This means that a party is generally not able to give evidence in court which refers to the giving of substantially the same evidence out of court.

Example: Suppose a person is arrested for break and entry. When arrested at the scene, the person might protest their innocence to the arresting police officer. Later, at their trial, they might want to lead evidence that they told the arresting police officer at the time they were arrested that they were innocent. In other words, they want to give evidence that:

(a) "I am innocent."

(b) "At the time I was arrested I told the arresting officer I was innocent."

5.27.1 Exceptions to the rule against previous consistent statements

There are several important exceptions to the rule against previous consistent statements. Exceptions to the general rule, briefly stated, are set out below.

Res gestae: A remark made spontaneously in a state of excitement at the time of an event, such as an assault or an accident, is said to be a res gestae statement. Such statements are also admissible as an exception to the rule against previous consistent statements: see 5.18.

Part of an inculpatory statement: If the prosecution wishes to adduce a statement made by the accused which is against his or her interest (for example, a confession), the entire statement must be adduced, not just the part the prosecution wishes to rely on. Part of the statement might qualify the statement in an important way. Even if that part of the statement is consistent with what the defendant says in court, it is admissible.

Example: Suppose a person suspected of assault, on being arrested, makes the following statement: "Yes, I did hit the victim. I meant to hit the victim. But I did it only because I was defending myself." The prosecution might want to use the first two sentences in the statement as part of their case: see 5.9. However, the last part of the sentence must be included as well, even though it is a previous consistent statement – that is, consistent with what the defendant will say in court.

Previous identification: A witness may be asked to identify an accused in court. Further evidence might be adduced to show that the witness identified the victim earlier at a police station when asked to take part in an identification parade or on some other occasion. The earlier identification described later in court would, in effect, be a previous consistent statement. However, it falls under the previous identification exception and is admissible.

Recent complaints in sexual cases: Where a victim of an alleged sexual offence reports the offence very soon after the event, it is called a recent complaint. It is sometimes referred to as a proximate complaint. Even though later, in court, the victim will likely give evidence of what happened, evidence may also be given of what she said in her recent complaint. Evidence of a recent complaint is often adduced to rebut evidence that a victim later concocted her allegations. However, evidence of a recent complaint *is not a required element* in the proof of a sexual offence. It only goes to the *credibility* of the victim. The lack of a recent complaint is not evidence that a victim consented to the sexual assault.

To be admissible under this exception to the rule against previous consistent statements, a recent complaint must be made soon (or recently) after the event. What constitutes "recent" is a matter of reasonableness. It should be at or near the first appropriate time. A victim might not complain to total strangers but wait until later when she is with people she knows, or with some person in an official capacity such as a police officer or a nurse. The complaint may still be recent, despite this kind of delay. To fall under the definition of recent complaint, the complaint must also be made *spontaneously*. If someone has to persuade a reluctant victim to complain, it is not spontaneous and will not fall within this exception to the rule against previous consistent statements.

Rebuttal to suggestion of recent fabrication: If it is suggested to an accused under cross-examination that the accused recently made up his or her evidence and that it is a lie, the accused is able to adduce evidence to show that the same evidence was contained in an earlier recounting of the events in question. For instance, a prosecutor may ask an accused the following question: "You said in your examination-in-chief that you were invited into the house by the owner. But that's a lie. You just made that up didn't you?" An accused may then adduce evidence that he or she told someone else the same thing some time ago. This previous consistent statement is admissible to show that the accused did not just make up his or her evidence in court. It is an exception to the general rule against previous consistent statements.

5.28 PREVIOUS INCONSISTENT STATEMENT

If a person gives evidence in court that is inconsistent with or contradicts a previous statement made by the person (either in court or out of court), the previous statement is said to be a previous inconsistent statement. The party or lawyer who is cross-examining such a witness may wish to establish that the witness's sworn evidence is inconsistent with the previous statement. Cross-examination of a witness for this purpose is permitted, provided it is done properly.

Sections 22 and 23 of the *Evidence Act* govern the procedure for the cross-examination of a person about a previous inconsistent statement. The first step is to establish that a person made a previous statement. This is done by asking the witness whether he or she made a statement concerning the matter in question. The time and place of the previous statement should be put to the witness in order to give the witness an accurate reference to what statement is being referred to. Counsel might ask the witness if the previous statement was true or if it was made under oath as the case may be.

The contents of the previous statement should be put to the witness and the witness given an opportunity to either admit or deny that they made the previous statement. If the previous statement is in writing or reduced to writing, it should be shown to the witness to allow the witness an opportunity to examine the statement. If the witness admits to making the previous consistent statement, then it is not usually necessary to carry the line of questioning any further. The fact that the witness has made a previous statement that is inconsistent with the present testimony has been established. If a witness denies making the previous inconsistent statement, then evidence may be adduced to prove that in fact the witness did make the previous inconsistent statement.

Evidence of a previous inconsistent statement may have an impact on the credibility of the witness. This is because the witness has been shown to have said one thing on one occasion and then, under oath, said something inconsistent or contradictory with that statement. On the other hand, the inconsistency may be insignificant or there may be an explanation, in which case the inconsistency would have little or no impact on a witness's credibility.

Proof of a previous inconsistent statement only goes to the credibility of the witness who made it. It is not a way to prove that the previous statement is the true version of events. Even if a witness admits to having made the previous statement and it is clearly inconsistent with the testimony being given in court, the Magistrate should not automatically reject the "in-court" testimony and accept the truth of the previous statement unless there are other reasons to make such a finding of fact.

5.29 PRIVILEGE

A witness may be competent and compellable and may be asked a relevant question, but if the answer to that question is privileged, the witness may refuse to answer that question. There are several types of privilege in Papua New Guinea.

5.29.1 Lawyer-client privilege

This privilege attaches to communications that are made between a client and a lawyer who is acting in his or her professional capacity. A lawyer may properly refuse to answer questions which would force the lawyer to disclose these communications, unless the client waives the privilege (ie consents to the disclosure). It does not apply if the communications between the client and the lawyer were for a criminal purpose.

Solicitor-client privilege also applies to communications between a party or a party's lawyer and a third party if the dominant purpose of the communication is in relation to court proceedings, either underway or anticipated. This privilege often applies to doctors, accident investigators, accountants, and other witnesses who are retained to give expert opinion evidence or otherwise lend their expertise to a client's interests.

5.29.2 Spousal privilege

Communications made by a husband to a wife or a wife to a husband are privileged, and the spouse to whom the communication is made cannot be compelled to disclose such communications. Section 18 of the *Evidence Act* creates this privilege. Because this section refers to "husband" and "wife", it only applies if the parties are married at the time that the privilege is claimed. Also, it does not cover any communications made before or after a marriage.

5.29.3 Privilege against self-incrimination

This is not an absolute privilege and, when it relates to a defendant in a criminal proceeding, has to do with the issue of compellability. An accused person cannot be compelled to give evidence. If an accused decides to give evidence, then that person can be asked questions that would incriminate him or her in relation to the offence charged. However, an accused who gives evidence cannot be asked questions about any previous offence or his or her character except in limited circumstances. These circumstances are set out in s 15 of the *Evidence Act*.

Where an accused has given evidence against a co-accused, or where proof of a previous offence is necessary to show that the accused committed the offence with which he or she has been charged, then, by virtue of s 15(c) and (f) of the *Evidence Act*, the accused can be asked questions about a previous conviction. An example of a situation where proof of a previous offence would be necessary to prove the present offence is where an accused is charged with escaping from lawful custody. In order to convict, it would be necessary to prove that the accused was in lawful custody. This would involve proof of the commission of a previous offence if the person's being in custody resulted from the commission of a criminal offence: see 5.5.

The privilege against self-incrimination extends to witnesses in either civil or criminal proceedings. A witness may claim privilege in relation to questions or the production of documents which would tend to incriminate him or her. See *The Application of Graham Ellis, Constituting the Poreporena Freeway Commission of Inquiry, For Leave to Apply for Judicial Review of a Decision Made on 8 September 1992 by the Ombudsman Commission v Ombudsman Commission of Papua New Guinea* [1993] PNGLR 458.

5.29.4 Communications with clergy or medical doctor

Section 19 of the *Evidence Act* creates these two categories of privilege that do not exist at common law. A member of the clergy "must not divulge in any legal proceedings a confession made to him in his professional capacity, except with the consent of the person who made the confession." This privilege applies to both civil and criminal proceedings.

The privilege involving communications with a medical doctor is narrower. It applies only to civil proceedings and where the sanity of the patient is *not* the issue to be decided.

The privilege created by s 19 does not apply to any communication made for a criminal purpose or in relation to any communication made to or by a medical practitioner in relation to placing life insurance on a person's life.

5.30 REAL EVIDENCE

Real evidence is a thing that can be made an exhibit in court. It can be a physical object, an audio or video recording, a photograph, a map or a diagram.

In order to be admissible, real evidence must be relevant. Sometimes, the relevance of some evidence is not immediately apparent. In such a case, a Magistrate could ask counsel for an explanation of how the evidence might become relevant. If satisfied that the relevance of the evidence will be established by evidence from a subsequent witness, a Magistrate may admit the evidence, subject to its relevance later being established: see 5.33.

5.31 RECENT COMPLAINT

See 5. 27.

5.32 REFRESHING MEMORY

A witness who is being examined in chief may be unable to answer a question that is put to him or her because he or she cannot remember. However, the witness may have made a note of the information at an earlier time – when he or she did remember the events in question. The examining party may wish to have the witness refer to written notes to assist the witness in recalling the answer to the question. Several rules govern whether this is permissible and how it is to be conducted.

Before being allowed to refresh the memory of a witness by reference to notes, a party calling the witness must establish the following:

- The witness has exhausted his or her memory in relation to the question being asked.
- The witness thinks that his or her memory would be refreshed in relation to the question being asked by reference to notes.
- The notes to which the witness seeks to refer were made at or close to the time of the events to which they refer. The word contemporaneous is often used to describe this requirement. How long after an event notes may be made and still be contemporaneous depends on the circumstances. The requirement that the notes be contemporaneous is to ensure that they are made while the events being noted are still fresh in the mind of the witness.
- The notes must have been made by the witness or, if not made by the witness, they must have been seen by the witness at the time they were made and accepted by the witness as true.

Once the prerequisites are established through questions of the witness, the notes may be produced in court. The witness may read the notes before the question is repeated. When a witness refers to notes during examination-in-chief, the opposing party must be given an opportunity to look at the notes and to cross-examine the witness on the notes.

The notes that are used to refresh memory normally do not become exhibits in the proceeding. By themselves, they do not prove anything. It is the evidence of the witness after using the notes to refresh memory that may or may not prove something.

Only in rare circumstances do the notes themselves become relevant to an issue and therefore become admissible as evidence in relation to that issue. For example, it might be suggested that the notes were not really made by the witness, in which case the authenticity of the notes becomes an issue.

5.33 RELEVANCE

The fundamental prerequisite for the admissibility of evidence is that it is relevant to some issue before the court. The issues before the court are defined by the complaint or charge that gives rise to the proceedings and any defence that is raised. Section 137 of the *District Courts Act* makes this clear in relation to civil matters. In criminal matters, it is the information or complaint that defines the main issues. If evidence is not relevant, it is not necessary to go on to consider the admissibility of the evidence in relation to any other rule. However, relevant evidence may be excluded because of some other rule of evidence.

Relevance is essentially a common sense notion. If evidence is helpful in determining a fact or issue in question then it is relevant. A more technical but easily understood definition is contained in the *United States Federal Rules of Evidence*, rule 401(1):

> "'Relevant evidence' means evidence having the tendency to make the existence of any fact that is of consequence to the determination of the action more probable or less probable than it would be without the evidence."

If the relevance of evidence is not apparent, an opposing party or counsel may object to its admissibility. Even if it is not objected to, a Magistrate may ask the lawyer or party leading the evidence to explain its relevance to the court, especially if the relevance of an entire line of questioning is in doubt.

Sometimes the relevance of evidence or a line of questioning is not immediately apparent. A party or lawyer, when asked by a Magistrate how the evidence is relevant, may explain that the relevance of the evidence will become apparent when further evidence is called. In such a case, a Magistrate may allow the evidence pending the further evidence which establishes its relevance: see 5.30.

Example: Suppose that in a trial there is an issue about whether a defendant was involved in a motor vehicle accident. The first prosecution witness might describe finding a motor vehicle licence plate on the ground near the scene of the accident. The witness might identify the licence plate in court and counsel might ask that it be introduced as an exhibit. The witness might not know the significance of the plate and therefore would not be able to establish its relevance through answers to questions. However, a later witness might be able to identify it as the plate from a vehicle that the defendant was seen driving shortly before the accident. This later witness would thereby be able to establish the relevance of the real evidence introduced earlier.

5.34 RE-EXAMINATION

After a witness has been cross-examined, the party who called the witness may wish to ask further questions of the witness. The scope of questions asked in re examination is restricted to matters that were dealt with in cross-examination. It is not proper for a party to use re-examination to launch into any matter which has already been dealt with during examination-in-chief but which has not been dealt with in cross-examination. Nor is it an opportunity for a party to ask questions which could have been included in examination-in-chief but which were left out.

The *only* purpose of re-examination is the clarification of matters which have been raised in cross-examination. Often a witness during cross-examination is forced to answer "yes" or "no" without an opportunity to expand or explain the answer. Re-examination is an opportunity for clarification of those answers.

A party conducting a re-examination must adhere to the rules of questioning that apply to examination-in-chief. That means that the rule against leading questions applies: see 5.16.

5.35 STANDARD OF PROOF

The standard of proof is the degree to which a party must convince the court that a fact is true. There are two standards of proof that are used in the courts. One standard applies in civil proceedings. The other applies to criminal proceedings.

The civil standard of proof is proof on a balance of probabilities. This has sometimes been expressed as proof which establishes that a fact is more likely to be true than not true. Where an allegation in a civil trial involves criminal or morally reprehensible conduct of a person, meeting the civil standard of proof may require stronger evidence. This results from the perception that people do not ordinarily conduct themselves in illegal or immoral ways.

The criminal standard of proof is referred to as "proof beyond a reasonable doubt." This is a higher standard than the civil standard of proof. However, it is not so high as to require that a case must be proved to a standard of absolute certainty. A useful explanation of the meaning of "proof beyond reasonable doubt" is found in the judgment of Lord Denning in *Miller v Minister of Pensions* [1947] 2 All ER 372:

> "Proof beyond reasonable doubt does not mean proof beyond the shadow of a doubt ... If the evidence is so strong against a man as to leave only a remote possibility in his favour, which can be dismissed with the sentence 'of course it is possible but not in the least probable', the case is proved beyond reasonable doubt, but nothing short of that will suffice."

Proof beyond a reasonable doubt is also the standard required in a voir dire when the issue of voluntariness relating to the admissibility of a confession is being determined.

Where a defendant must prove something in a criminal case, the standard of proof is only on the balance of probabilities. The exception is insanity. If an accused wishes to advance the defence of insanity, he or she must prove insanity to a higher standard.

5.36 VOIR DIRE

A voir dire is a procedure that is followed in order to determine whether some evidence that is tendered is admissible. The expression is French and, roughly translated, it means "to look to say". It is a process of looking at or examining evidence in order to say whether it is admissible.

The issue in a voir dire is different from the main issue in a trial. It may be whether a confession has been induced by threat or promise (ie whether it is voluntary). It may be whether some evidence has been illegally or improperly obtained to the extent that it should be excluded pursuant to a Magistrate's discretion It is important that the issue be identified clearly so that it is not confused with the ultimate issue in the trial.

Sometimes a voir dire is appropriate where the competence of a witness is called into question. For example, if an expert witness is tendered to give expert opinion evidence, and the opposing party questions the expertise of the expert, a voir dire may be held to determine whether the witness has the required expertise to be able to offer an opinion on the topic in question.

During a voir dire the rules of natural justice prevail. Both parties are given an opportunity to lead evidence, cross-examine and make submissions. They must restrict their input to the issue of admissibility of the evidence (or competence of the witness as the case may be) and not the ultimate issue in the trial. The issue to be decided in a voir dire determines the relevance of questions and evidence led during the voir dire.

At the conclusion of a voir dire, a Magistrate must decide whether the evidence in question is admissible. If the evidence is not admissible, the Magistrate must completely disregard the evidence that was adduced during the voir dire. If the evidence is ruled to be admissible, it becomes part of the evidence of the trial proper (either by consent or by having it re-introduced).

5.37 WEIGHT

Weight is a concept that is closely related to credit and credibility. It deals with the degree to which evidence should be accepted as proof of what it is adduced to prove. Evidence which is highly credible will be given more weight than evidence that is less credible or not credible at all. Magistrates weigh evidence in order to determine whether a case has been made out to the required standard of proof.

A Magistrate should not make a final determination of the weight of evidence until all the evidence for both sides is given. It is not necessary to weigh evidence beforehand. It is not necessary to weigh evidence to rule on a no case submission (where the existence of a prima facie case is the issue), and it is generally not necessary to weigh evidence at a committal hearing.

PART 3

Criminal Cases in the Magistrates' Courts

Chapter 6 – Criminal Jurisdiction: A Guide

6.1 INTRODUCTION

Part 3 of the manual, which includes this chapter and Chapters 7–13, is concerned with the criminal jurisdiction of the Magistrates' Courts. Part 1 of the manual has already described the Magistrates' Court jurisdiction as a whole, and a great deal of what has been said in Part 1 applies to the criminal jurisdiction.

In Part 3, where a particular topic under consideration has already been covered in Part 1, there will be cross-references to that part.

This chapter can be used as a guide or checklist of matters which a Magistrate should consider before trying a criminal case.

6.2 PURPOSE OF THE CRIMINAL JUSTICE SYSTEM, JUDICIAL POWER AND CONSTITUTIONAL PRINCIPLES

6.2.1 Purpose

The criminal justice system is a framework of laws and procedures designed to control social behaviour through the prevention and punishment of criminal activity. The courts are expected to ensure criminal justice within their jurisdictions. Parliament is responsible for passing the laws which declare what is illegal conduct and determine maximum penalties.

In circumstances where individuals and local communities understand the law and are willing to respect it, the work of the courts will be relatively smooth. Real difficulties for the courts arise in cases of ignorance of the law, and where local community attitudes do not accept that the particular offences or penalties as set out in the statute are appropriate for local conditions (such as situations in remote areas of the country, or where custom already provides for the situation).

In difficult cases the Magistrate should be aware of four primary obligations -

- **To uphold the law**
- **To follow just procedures (natural justice)**
- **To take into account the particular circumstances of the defendant and local community attitudes – as far as possible within the law**
- **To ensure that the outcome is just (criminal justice)**

6.2.2 Judicial power

Judges and Magistrates exercise the judicial power of government in matters concerning crime and penalties. In the case of Magistrates, that power is to be found in the *Constitution* and the statutes, as described in 2.1 and 2.2.

6.2.3 Constitutional principles

The *Constitution* and statutes also provide guidance as to the application of custom (see 2.4.2.2), the principles of natural justice (2.6.2 and 4.1.3) and the important fundamental rights referred to in 2.3-2.5. For the purpose of criminal law and procedure, the key provisions of the *Constitution* are ss 37 and 42-44. As a reminder, the provisions of s 37(3) and (4) are set out here.

[CONSTITUTIONAL RIGHTS GOVERNING CRIMINAL MATTERS]

Protection of the law: Section 37 ...

"(3) A person charged with an offence shall, unless the charge is withdrawn, be afforded a fair hearing within a reasonable time, by an independent and impartial court.

(4) A person charged with an offence –

(a) shall be presumed innocent until proved guilty according to law, but a law may place upon a person charged with an offence the burden of proving particular facts which are, or would be, peculiarly within his knowledge; and

(b) shall be informed promptly in a language which he understands, and in detail, of the nature of the offence with which he is charged; and

(c) shall be given adequate time and facilities for the preparation of his defence; and

(d) shall be permitted to have without payment the assistance of an interpreter if he cannot understand or speak the language used at the trial of the charge; and

(e) shall be permitted to defend himself before the court in person or, at his own expense, by a legal representative of his own choice, or if he is a person entitled to legal aid, by the Public Solicitor or another legal representative assigned to him in accordance with law; and

(f) shall be afforded facilities to examine in person or by his legal representative the witnesses called before the court by the prosecution, and to obtain the attendance and carry out the examination of witnesses and to testify before the court on his own behalf, on the same conditions as those applying to witnesses called by the prosecution."

6.3 NATURE AND TYPES OF OFFENCES AND THE STATUTORY JURISDICTION OF MAGISTRATES IN CRIMINAL CASES

6.3.1 What is an offence?

6.3.1.1 Written law

An offence is an act or omission that makes a person liable to imprisonment: *Criminal Code*, s 2. The *Constitution* requires that offences must be defined and penalties must be prescribed by a written law: s 37(2). This means two things:

1. No common law or unwritten offence is recognised in Papua New Guinea.
2. The query "what is an offence?" is answered in the statutes, and it is not a question of morals or beliefs – nor even a question of whether an act is good or bad, or fair or unfair. The only question is whether the act is legal/lawful or illegal/unlawful.

6.3.1.2 Time: when was the act/omission declared to be an offence?

If the act or omission complained of was not an offence under the law at the time it was committed, no person can be convicted of it. If an offence was committed but the maximum penalty for it has been changed since then, the offender must not be punished to a greater extent than was permitted under the law at the time of the offence, or is now permitted at the time of the conviction. He or she is entitled to the benefit of the lesser of the two maximum penalties: *Constitution*, s 37(7); *Criminal Code*, s 11.

6.3.2 National context

Although the National Court has unlimited criminal jurisdiction, it normally deals with indictable offences only. Committal proceedings leading to the National Court trial are held in the District Court, where committal on the documents (the "hand-up brief") is a common alternative to committal following a preliminary hearing.

The National Court also hears criminal appeals from the District Courts: see Chapter 26.

6.3.3 Categories of offences

There are four categories of criminal offences in Papua New Guinea:

1. **Indictable offences** (also called "crimes or misdemeanours" in the *Criminal Code*) which may be tried in the National Court. An indictable offence is one that is declared to be such, or any offence punishable by imprisonment for more than 12 months: *Interpretation Act*, s 21.

2. **Approximately 80 indictable offences** which may be tried summarily by a Principal Magistrate (see s 420 and Sch 2 of the *Criminal Code*) under Pt VII of the *District Courts Act* (*DCA*).

3. **Summary offences** (also called "simple offences" in the *Criminal Code*) under the *Summary Offences Act* and other legislation, which may be tried in the District Court. All offences that are not indictable offences are punishable on summary conviction: *Interpretation Act*, s 22. It should also be noted that the Magistrate has power under s 425 of the *Criminal Code* to abstain from dealing with certain summary offences relating to property (ss 422-424) if he or she considers that they should be replaced with indictable offences, in which case the Magistrate may commit the defendant for trial in the National Court on the indictable offences: see 4.2.3.

4. **Offences affecting village life**, as prescribed in reg 3 of the *Village Courts Regulations* under s 41 of the *Village Courts Act* (*VCA*), which may be tried in the Village Court.

6.3.4 District Court

The Chief Magistrate, Deputy Chief Magistrate, Principal Magistrates and District Court Magistrates may sit in the District Court: see *DCA*, Pt II; *Magisterial Services Act*, s 5; and 2.2 of this manual. The District Court may be constituted by one or more Magistrates: *DCA*, s 16.

There are three types of matters over which District Courts have criminal jurisdiction:

1. All Magistrates have criminal jurisdiction over all non-indictable offences (summary or simple offences) which are punishable on summary conviction (category 1 in 6.3.3).

2. The Chief Magistrate, Deputy Chief Magistrate and Principal Magistrates may try the indictable offences referred to in category 2 in 6.3.3, provided that they are dealt with summarily.

3. Any District Court Magistrate may preside over the committal procedure (see Chapter 11).

The main limit on the sentencing power of the District Court is that which is imposed by statute in relation to each offence. However, in the case of the indictable offences triable summarily referred to in category 2, if the maximum penalty for the offence exceeds 10 years imprisonment, the maximum period which may be imposed by a Principal Magistrate is 10 years, subject to the power of the Magistrate to commit the offender to the National Court for sentence: *Criminal Code*, ss 420 and 421.

6.3.5 Village Court

Normally, the Village Court is constituted by no fewer than three Village Magistrates. In criminal cases, the Village Court may impose fines and may order the offender to perform community work. The court has no jurisdiction over motor traffic offences. Because of the particular powers of the Village Court in relation to preventive orders, mediation, compromise and compensation, the Village Court jurisdiction generally is discussed in more detail in Chapter 18.

District Court Magistrates should be fully conversant with the jurisdiction and procedures of the Village Courts, not least because of the endorsement, review and appeal responsibilities which they may be called upon to exercise from time to time.

6.4 GEOGRAPHICAL LIMITATIONS OF CRIMINAL JURISDICTION

6.4.1 District Court

The criminal jurisdiction of each Magistrates' Court is limited to a geographical area which should be observed in every case – otherwise lawful jurisdiction will not exist to deal with the case: see 2.2. The place where a court should sit within that area may also be relevant: see 4.2.2.

Generally speaking, a District Court has been established for an area proclaimed in the National Gazette to be that of each Province of Papua New Guinea. Its criminal jurisdiction is defined in relation to summary (simple) offences. Informations for such offences must be heard within the Province (*DCA*, s 122):

in which the alleged offence was committed, or, if outside the Province, within 33 kilometres of the provincial boundary;

where the defendant usually resides; or

where the defendant is at the time the information is laid.

6.4.2 Village Court

Notice in the National Gazette determines the area for which a Village Court is established. A Village Court has jurisdiction over offences committed within that area: see Chapter 18.

6.5 CONCURRENT JURISDICTION AND TRANSFER OF PROCEEDINGS

The statutory requirements governing concurrent jurisdiction and transfer from one jurisdiction/court to another have been dealt with under 4.2, because most of them apply to both criminal and civil cases.

6.6 TIME OF OFFENCES

One of the duties of a Magistrate is to check informations to determine whether they have been laid within the time prescribed by statute. In the District Court, unless a statute provides otherwise, an information for a summary (simple) offence must be laid within **six** months after the time when the matter of the information arose. No such limitation applies to indictable offences, including those triable summarily: *DCA*, s 36.

The *Summary Offences Act* also imposes an absolute limitation of six months on the laying of charges for offences prescribed under that Act: *Summary Offences Act*, s 69.

6.7 DISTRICT COURT JURISDICTION IN RELATION TO CHILDREN

The age of a young offender should be checked. When a Children's Court has been established for an area, it has exclusive jurisdiction to hear charges against children under the age of **16** for all summary offences (and also all indictable offences except those punishable by death or life imprisonment) committed within that area: *Child Welfare Act* (*CWA*), ss 32(1) and 33(1). See also Chapter 16.

There is an important exception to this. If a District Court Magistrate is satisfied that circumstances prevent the Children's Court Magistrate from dealing with the matter, and that it is in the interests of justice for the District Court Magistrate to deal with it, he or she may do so. In that case, he or she will exercise the powers of a Children's Court Magistrate: *CWA*, s 29(5). The same exercise of powers by a District Court Magistrate may occur if there is no Children's Court established for that area: *CWA*, s 33(3).

It should also be noted that the *Criminal Code* provides for the lack of criminal responsibility on the part of younger children: see 7.12.

6.8 TYPES OF SENTENCES AND ORDERS

The statutory jurisdiction and sentencing limits of Magistrates have been dealt with in 6.3 above. Sentencing principles are considered in Chapter 13. In this section it is useful to review the different types of sentences and orders available to the Magistrate.

6.8.1 Penalties generally

The only penalties which a Magistrate can impose are those prescribed by statute, and then only after the defendant has been found guilty of the offence. For the Magistrates Courts, the statutes prescribe the penalties of:

- imprisonment;
- fine;
- compensation; and
- finding security to keep the peace and/or be of good behaviour.

A fine may be imposed in addition to or instead of imprisonment. Imprisonment may be imposed for non-payment of a fine: see, for example, *DCA*, ss 167, 168 and 201.

Under the *Motor Traffic Act* the court may suspend or otherwise deal with a person's driving licence: see, for example, s 18. The Village Court may impose a fine in terms of goods or money: *VCA*, s 42.

Unless otherwise specified, the statutes are concerned to prescribe maximum penalties only, and a Magistrate may impose a lesser penalty (see *Criminal Code*, s 19) in accordance with the "sentencing principles" and "matters which must be considered" which are discussed in 13.4 and 13.5.

6.8.2 Compensation must be considered

The *Criminal Law (Compensation) Act* 1991 makes it compulsory for the court to consider compensation every time sentence is to be passed. The prosecutor must provide sufficient evidence on which compensation can be considered and calculated, in order to assist the Magistrate. The Magistrate should insist that the prosecutor is ready with the information, or should allow a short adjournment for the information to be obtained and presented to the court. The Magistrate is required to consider the several factors set out in s 3 of the Act, and is not bound by the technical rules of evidence in examining these factors. In this way, the Magistrate is making a significant contribution to the resolution of the problem that has arisen out of the offence, and to bringing about some finality between the "offender" and the "victim". An order of compensation may be regarded as a punishment, in addition to other forms of punishment which may be imposed: s 2. Because consideration of compensation is compulsory, the Magistrate should always make a note of considering it in his or her record of the sentence.

In addition to the provisions of the above Act, the criminal justice system seeks, wherever appropriate, to provide civil compensation to a person injured or aggrieved by the commission of an offence. The District Court appears to have power to order compensation: see *DCA*, ss 132 and 165. The *Summary Offences Act* empowers Magistrates to order compensation, in addition to penalties, for several offences, such as "damaging property": s 47. When a Village Court is dealing with an offence, it can, at the same time, make orders for compensation or damages in favour of the victim, for an amount up to K1,000: *VCA*, s 45.

Section 421 of the *Criminal Code* empowers the District Court, when dealing with indictable offences summarily, to order the defendant to make restitution of any property in respect of which the offence has been committed – with a scale of periods of imprisonment in default of payment of amounts awarded.

6.8.3 Restriction of movement must be considered

The Magistrate may consider that restriction of movement of an offender would be in the best interests of the community generally, or of the victim of the offence or of the offender's rehabilitation in particular. The offender may be required to stay away from a part of the country, or to return to his or her home. Parliament has approached this by inserting s 205B in the *District Courts Act*. In addition to any other punishment, the Magistrate may impose restriction of movement. It is compulsory for the Magistrate to consider whether such restriction is an appropriate punishment in the circumstances of every case before passing sentence. A note of his or her consideration of the matter must be recorded in the court file.

The relevant sections set out the requirements of an order and define the offender's "home" in a number of different ways, so as to give the Magistrate considerable discretion. However, it should be remembered that the *Constitution* guarantees the "right to freedom of movement" subject only to statutes which deal with persons convicted of offences: s 52. Any order of the court which is not strictly authorised by the relevant sections will be unconstitutional.

6.8.4 Probation order

In circumstances where supervision by a probation officer is available, the options open to the sentencing Magistrate are greatly extended.

In a probation order under s 16 of the *Probation Act*, a Magistrate who is dealing with an offence punishable by imprisonment may:

- impose sentence but suspend committing the offender to prison; or
- defer sentencing the offender to imprisonment and release him or her on probation for a specified period, between six months and five years.

A probation order must contain certain statutory requirements (s 17) together with further conditions which the Magistrate may select (s 16). The purpose of the probation service is the social rehabilitation of offenders: s 12.

6.8.5 Recognisances

6.8.5.1 "to be of good behaviour"

The District Court has, as part of its general sentencing jurisdiction, the power to discharge an offender without conviction but on condition that he or she enters into a recognisance (agreement or bond) "to be of good behaviour" and to appear for conviction and sentence when called upon within three years. The required factors and possible conditions of such an order in terms of s 132 of the *District Courts Act* should be looked at carefully.

6.8.5.2 "to keep the peace and/or be of good behaviour"

In appropriate circumstances, the District Court has jurisdiction to make a specific type of "restraining order". The court may exercise statutory power to have a person brought before it on the grounds that he or she has threatened harm and caused fear: *DCA*, ss 209-213. The Magistrate may require the defendant to enter into a bond "to keep the peace and/or be of good behaviour" or, in default, to serve up to six months imprisonment. The court may also require the defendant to find sureties: *DCA*, s 214. This power is discussed further in Chapter 19C.

6.8.6 Community work

The District Court has the power to order a convicted defendant to perform specific work for community purposes approved by the Minister by notice in the National Gazette. This order may be in addition to or instead of a fine or imprisonment. The time limits prescribed by s 199A of the *District Courts Act* must be strictly adhered to, otherwise the order will be unconstitutional as a violation of the "freedom from forced labour" provision: *Constitution*, s 43. Community work may be ordered by a Village Court instead of a fine, for defined periods and subject to such conditions as may be specified: *VCA*, s 42(2). As in the case of probation, this important sentencing option is of no value to the court unless a Probation Officer and appropriate resources are available to arrange and supervise the court's order.

6.8.7 Dismissal or conditional discharge

The ultimate discretion of the Magistrate is, in appropriate circumstances, to decide whether or not to dismiss a proven charge or to release an offender without punishment on conditions. This is an essential judicial power which enables the Magistrate to do justice in every case.

In the District Court, the Magistrate has wide powers of disposal of simple offences and indictable offences triable summarily where the charge is proved but the Magistrate is of the opinion that, having regard to certain factors, it is "inexpedient" to impose punishment. A conviction need not be entered, and the Magistrate may dismiss the charge or discharge the offender conditionally on a bond after considering carefully the provisions of s 132 of the *District Courts Act*: see also 6.8.5.1 above.

6.8.8 Costs

Orders as to costs in the disposition of criminal cases are discussed in Chapter 21.

Chapter 7 – Criminal Responsibility and General Defences

This chapter will describe the main topics briefly, and provide cross-references to the *Constitution.* There are references to the relevant sections of the *Criminal Code* (*CC*). By referring to the section in the *Criminal Law Practice and Procedure* further annotations on relevant cases can be found.

7.1 OFFENCES AND THE CRIMINAL CODE

The question "what is an offence?" has been discussed in 6.3. Criminal responsibility for, and defences to, offences under the statute law of Papua New Guinea is dealt with primarily in the *Criminal Code* (*CC*), and the *Summary Offences Act* (*SOA*) is relevant in some cases.

If there must be a guilty mind as well as forbidden behaviour, then it follows that only people free to choose between right and wrong, and who have chosen to do wrong, should be punished. It also follows that there must be special rules to exclude people unable to choose freely. For example, a person who is insane or too young to understand, or forced to act against his or her will may be excused for what would otherwise be an offence.

***Criminal Code*, Div 5:** Unlike much of the *Criminal Code*, Div 5 applies to summary offences and the criminal jurisdiction of the District Courts. Division 5 (ss 22-36) applies to all persons charged with offences against any law: s 22. Division 5 and certain other sections of the *Criminal Code* constitute a comprehensive statement of the law covering responsibility for crime in Papua New Guinea, so that the English common law approach to proving criminal intention (mens rea) does not apply. The Papua New Guinea equivalent to criminal intention is discussed in 7.4 below.

Outside Div 5, the main provisions relating to defences are:

defences to assault (ss 266-271);

the defence of property (ss 265 and 272-277);

domestic discipline (s 278); and

excessive force generally (s 281).

7.2 PARTIES TO OFFENCES: ACCOMPLICES

The provisions of the *Interpretation Act* referred to in this section apply to all offences, including summary offences. The provisions of the *Criminal Code* are designed to apply to indictable offences.

7.2.1 General principle relating to accomplices

A person who aids, abets, counsels or procures an offence, or by an act or omission is in any way directly or indirectly concerned in the commission of an offence, is deemed to have committed the offence and is punishable accordingly: *Interpretation Act*, s 23.

7.2.2 Principal offenders

Section 7 of the *Criminal Code* extends the range of persons who may be charged with committing an offence.

> A person is deemed to have taken part in committing an offence, is deemed to be guilty of it and may be charged with actually committing it, who:
>
> - actually does the act or makes the omission which constitutes the offence;
> - does an act for the purpose of enabling or aiding another person to commit the offence;
> - aids another person in committing the offence; or
> - counsels or procures another person to commit the offence.

Involvement in any of these ways entails the same consequences.

As far as counselling or advising another person to commit an offence is concerned, if an offence is actually committed in accordance with that advice by the person to whom the advice is given, it is immaterial whether the offence actually committed by that person is the same as the one actually counselled, or whether the offence is committed in a different way from that which was counselled. All that is necessary is that the facts constituting the offence which was actually committed are the probable consequence of carrying out the counsel given to that person. The person who gave the counsel is deemed to have counselled the other person to commit the offence which that person actually committed: *CC*, s 9.

7.2.3 Common purpose

Where two or more persons form a common intention to pursue an unlawful purpose in conjunction with one another, and if an offence is committed which was a probable consequence of that purpose, each of them is deemed to have committed the offence: *CC*, s 8.

7.2.4 Accessory after the fact

A person who receives or assists another person, who is, to his or her knowledge, guilty of an offence, in order to enable him or her to escape punishment, is an accessory after the fact to the offence. Wives and husbands are excluded from this provision: *CC*, s 10.

7.3 ATTEMPTS TO COMMIT OFFENCES

A person who attempts to commit an offence against any law is guilty of an offence and is liable to trial and punishment as if the attempted offence had been committed: *Interpretation Act*, s 24. This applies to all offences.

What constitutes an offence? There are two aspects. First, it must be proved that the defendant intended to commit the full offence. Secondly, the defendant must have done some act which was a step towards the commission of the specific offence. The act must be immediately, rather than remotely, connected with the commission of the offence. Further, the doing of the act must be regarded as having no other purpose than the commission of the specific offence. Because of these rules, charges of attempting to commit a summary offence are very seldom laid.

Section 4 of the *Criminal Code* details the circumstances in which a person who intends to commit an offence, and has begun to put that intention into practice, will be guilty of attempting to commit the offence.

The elements of the offence of "attempt" are:

- The defendant intends to commit an offence.
- The defendant begins to put that intention into practice by committing an obvious act (for example, an act which is necessary to commit the intended offence).
- The intention to commit the offence is not fulfilled. If the intention is fulfilled, then the offence has been committed, and not merely attempted.

7.4 PROOF OF CRIMINAL RESPONSIBILITY: INTENTION

A presumption of innocence underpins the Papua New Guinea justice system: *Constitution*, s 37(4)(a). The burden or onus is on the prosecutor/complainant to prove every element of the offence against the defendant beyond reasonable doubt. For discussion of burden of proof and standard of proof, see Chapter 5.

Unless the statute provides otherwise, the intention of the defendant to commit the act or omission is one such element which must be proved. For most offences, the prosecution must prove not only that the defendant did the act constituting the offence, but that he or she intended to do that act. In the great majority of cases, the defendant's intention to do the act will be obvious from the facts surrounding the case. However, in some cases the defendant's intention will be an important issue in the case, and the prosecution will have to lead evidence to prove it. This is dealt with below.

Sometimes, a statute provides for a possible defence or excuse. The second part of s 37(4)(a) of the *Constitution* makes it clear that a statute "may place upon a person charged with an offence the burden of proving particular facts which are, or would with the exercise of reasonable care be, peculiarly within his/her knowledge". Section 2 of the *Summary Offences Act* puts it this way:

> "Where under the provisions of this Act, any act, if done without lawful excuse or lawful cause is an offence, the burden of proof that the act was done with lawful excuse or lawful cause, as the case may be, is on the person charged with the offence."

An example is s 14 of the *Summary Offences Act*, where paying for goods with a cheque which "bounces" (which is not paid on presentation at the bank) is an offence. However, it is a good defence if the defendant can show that he or she had reasonable grounds for believing that the cheque would be paid in full on presentation. An analysis of the more common examples of statutory justification and excuse is provided in 7.13 below.

Another type of offence is designed to make the defendant liable whether or not he or she intended to do the act complained of. This is called "strict liability", or an offence of "strict responsibility". The defendant will be convicted for the act or omission even if the prosecution cannot prove intent to commit an offence. However, such a statutory provision is rare. Also, the defence of "honest and reasonable" mistake is open to the defendant unless it is excluded by statute: *CC*, s 25; and see 7.6 below.

7.4.1 Intention

Apart from any specific intention indicated by the statute creating an offence, a person is not criminally responsible for an unintentional "act" or an accidental "event" unless the statute imposes strict responsibility.

Section 24 of the *Criminal Code* begins by saying that a person is not criminally responsible for:

- "an act or omission that occurs independently of the exercise of his will"; or
- "an event that occurs by accident".

The section goes on to say that, unless intention to cause a particular result is declared by law to be an element of the offence, "the result intended to be caused by an act or omission is immaterial".

7.4.2 Motive

Section 24 of the *Criminal Code* also states that the motive by which a person is induced to do or omit to do an act, or to form an intention, is immaterial as far as criminal responsibility is concerned.

7.4.3 Accident

It is often difficult to decide what is accidental. Generally, an event is accidental if it was not foreseen and could not reasonably have been foreseen by the person causing the event to happen.

7.4.4 Examples

If a person shoots another person with a gun, the aiming of the gun, the pulling of the trigger and discharge of the bullet would be the "act". To this point, the act has not occurred independently of the will, and is therefore intended. If it is reasonably foreseeable that the bullet might strike the complainant, then it is immaterial that the person firing the gun did not have a motive or intention to harm that person. If the victim is hospitalised with a bullet in the leg, a charge of grievous bodily harm would appear to have been made out.

In another situation, a man dashes across a city street to catch the attention of his wife whom he sees boarding a bus. In his hurry, he runs into and knocks down and kills a very frail old lady on the footpath. In this case, there was:

- the act of running;
- the event of the collision with the lady; and
- the result, namely her injury and death.

The act was clearly intentional. The event was not intended and would be treated as an event which occurred by accident, provided it was also unforeseen and not reasonably foreseeable. If the event of the collision was truly accidental, there would be no criminal responsibility for the result.

7.5 INTENTION AND AUTOMATISM

Generally, a person is blamed for having the knowledge of what he or she is doing and the intention to carry out the act. Apart from the defence of insanity, referred to in 7.10, there is the possibility that the defendant was acting without conscious mental activity – perhaps hypnotised, sleep-walking or in some other way mentally incapable of intending the act. There is no disease of the mind or insanity in such cases.

The defence of automatism has become established in Papua New Guinea, but the rules relating to proof should be examined carefully. The overriding principle remains that the state must prove every element of the offence charged, and that includes the state of mind of the defendant. Nevertheless, if that state of mind is contested, the burden is on the defendant to prove that he or she was in a state of automatism, on the balance of the probabilities. (See the cases of *The State v Hekavo* [1991] PNGLR 394 and *The State v Enakuan Salaiau* [1994] PNGLR 338. See also the cases annotated at s 24 of the *Criminal Code* in *Criminal Law Practice and Procedure*). Evidence of the defendant alone will not normally be sufficient, and the defence will fail without an expert witness who can give satisfactory evidence on the subject of automatism.

7.6 HONEST AND REASONABLE MISTAKE OF FACT

A person may do an act under an honest and reasonable, but mistaken, belief in the existence of a certain state of things. Such a person is not criminally responsible for the act to a greater extent than if the real state of things had been such as he or she believed to exist: see *CC*, s 25. Mistake is more than mere ignorance, and there must be a positive belief rather than an absence of thought on the subject. For example, if the defendant was charged with permitting an unlicensed person to drive his car, the defendant could only raise the defence of mistake by saying that he had thought about whether the driver held a licence and "honestly" believed that the driver did hold a licence (a subjective test). The belief might not be "reasonable" if the driver seemed very young (an objective test). If the defendant raises this defence in cross-examining the prosecution witnesses, it is up to the prosecution to prove that the defence does not exist in relation to the offence charged. Of course, if the defendant later goes into the witness box, claims to have been mistaken and gives evidence about the appearance of the driver which the Magistrate finds hard to believe, the defence may be negatived.

The distinction between mistakes of fact and mistakes of law is important. For example, take the case of a citizen of Fiji who has entered Papua New Guinea as a tourist without a visa and has taken employment in Waigani. She is arrested and charged with not holding the necessary employment visa. In her defence, she claims that her travel agent in Suva had told her that she would not need a work visa until she had been working in the country for over a year. This would be a mistake of law, which would not absolve her of criminal responsibility. It could be said to be "ignorance of the law": see 7.7.

7.7 IGNORANCE OF THE LAW AND HONEST CLAIM OF RIGHT

Ignorance of the law does not afford an excuse to an act that would otherwise be an offence: *CC*, s 23(1). This may be a harsh provision in parts of Papua New Guinea where people have little access to the written law and often only a poor understanding of its meaning and implications. The original common law doctrine "ignorance of the law is no excuse" assumed that the "law" referred to would be published and accessible to all citizens. Unfortunately, s 23(1) of the *Criminal Code* does not mention this assumption, and so lack of access to the laws is no excuse either. However, if the defendant can justify ignorance of the law in a particular case, the Magistrate may take this into account in passing sentence.

The defence of "claim of right" in relation to property is an extension to the law governing ignorance or mistake of law. Section 23(2) of the *Criminal Code* makes it clear that if a person "honestly" believes that he or she is entitled to property taken, and if there is no intention to defraud, that person is not criminally responsible for the property offence. The courts have applied this defence to a customary law right: see 7.16.

7.8 PRIOR CONVICTION / ACQUITTAL / SENTENCE

It is logical, and a fundamental principle of justice, that a person cannot be **charged** twice for the same offence, nor **punished** twice for the same act or omission. The citizen is entitled not to be placed in a situation of "double jeopardy".

A person may plead "already convicted" ("autrefois convict") or "already acquitted" ("autrefois acquit"). Section 37(8) of the *Constitution* makes it clear in respect of all offences – and s 15 of the *Criminal Code* makes it clear in respect of indictable offences – that it is for the defendant to prove that he or she has already been dealt with by the court for the same offence. The time to raise this defence is when the defendant is asked to plead. It should not be a plea of "not guilty", but either "already convicted" or " already acquitted". Unless the prosecutor consents, the defendant may have to summons earlier court records to satisfy the Magistrate.

Sometimes an act or omission constitutes an offence under two or more statutory provisions. In this situation, the offender is liable to be **prosecuted** and **punished** under either or any of those provisions, but is not liable to be **punished** twice for the same offence: *Interpretation Act*, s 20.

Of course, it goes without saying that a person cannot be punished twice under the provisions of any law for the same act or omission: *CC*, s 16. This section of the *Criminal Code* seems to be of wider effect than s 20 of the *Interpretation Act*. If there are two different statutory provisions – perhaps two different descriptions of an offence under the same statute – the Magistrate should look carefully at the elements of the "offence" as described by the statute, and see whether the same act or omission is the central theme or basic act in each of the offences described. The police sometimes charge an offender under two or more provisions, and if the defendant is unrepresented, it is the responsibility of the Magistrate to ensure that the defendant is punished only once for the same basic act or omission: see also 8.7.

7.9 EXTRAORDINARY EMERGENCY

Apart from the law relating to compulsion, provocation and self-defence, a person is not criminally responsible "for an act or omission done or made under such circumstances of sudden or extraordinary emergency that an ordinary person possessing ordinary powers of self-control could not reasonably be expected to act otherwise": *CC*, s 26. This section gives effect to the principle that no-one is expected (at least for the purposes of the criminal law) to be wiser or better than all mankind.

If this defence is raised as a real issue in the case, the conduct of the defendant should be judged by assuming the facts as they reasonably appeared to the defendant at the time. In *Pagawa v Mathew* [1986] PNGLR 154, a person had entered Papua New Guinea from Irian Jaya without an entry permit, and claimed, in his defence, that he was forced to cross the border in order to avoid being killed by soldiers. He gave evidence as to the emergency and as to his fear. The court held that the defence of "extraordinary emergency" had been proved in his case.

7.10 INSANITY

7.10.1 Presumption of sanity

"Every person is presumed to be of sound mind, and to have been of sound mind at any time which comes in question, until the contrary is proved": *CC*, s 27. If a defendant wishes to rebut this presumption, the defendant must prove the defence on the balance of probabilities. The question of whether a person is sane or insane is a matter of fact to be decided by the court. The court usually requires that a qualified person should give expert evidence, but this amounts to opinion evidence and the court must reach its own decision. The court may be assisted by non-experts who may give evidence as to the conduct of the defendant before and after the alleged offence.

It is important to note that the defence of insanity is a complete defence and, as a defence to a summary offence, it entitles the defendant to an acquittal and release. There is no provision for the District Courts to deal with a person who has been found to be insane. After leaving the court the person may be examined by medical practitioners and committed to a mental institution under the *Public Health Act*, but that is not the responsibility of the Magistrate. The situation is different in relation to persons acquitted of an indictable offence on the grounds of insanity, where the court is required to order the person to be kept in custody pending a decision by the Head of State, acting on advice: *CC*, s 592.

7.10.2 Insanity

Section 28 of the *Criminal Code* states:

"(1) A person is not criminally responsible for an act or omission if at the time of doing the act or making the omission he is in such a state of mental disease or natural mental infirmity as to deprive him of capacity:

(a) to understand what he is doing; or

(b) to control his actions; or

(c) to know that he ought not to do the act or make the omission.

(2) A person:

> **(a) whose mind at the time of his doing or omitting to do an act is affected by delusions on some specific matter or matters; and**
>
> **(b) who is not otherwise entitled to the benefit of the provisions of sub-section (1),**

is criminally responsible for the act or omission to the same extent as if the real state of things had been such as he had been induced by the delusions to believe to exist."

It is helpful to approach the proof of the defence of insanity in two steps.

1. At the time of the alleged offence the defendant must have been in a state of:

   mental disease; or

   natural mental infirmity, and further

2. As a result of the mental disease or natural mental infirmity, he or she was deprived of -

   the capacity to understand what he or she was doing; or

   the capacity to control his or her actions; or

   the capacity to know that he or she ought not to do the act said to constitute the offence.

An accused will sometimes claim to have been in a state of "diminished responsibility". This is not equivalent to insanity. It is not a recognised defence and is more likely to be relevant to penalty. The court should also be careful to distinguish "automatism" (7.5 above) and "intoxication" (7.11 below).

In *Goi v The State* [1991] PNGLR 161 the court said (at 169):

> "In a defence based on s 28 ..., it must be shown by the defence that the accused person's capacity to understand what he was doing or to control his actions or to know that he ought not to commit the act was taken away from him by the state of his mental disease or natural mental infirmity ... Deprivation of capacity to understand or control actions is not the same as mere impairment of such capacity."

The court, in *The State v Enakuan Salaiau* [1994] PNGLR 388, noted the drastic consequences of a finding of insanity under s 28, which obliges the court to order that the person be held at the pleasure of the government. This may mean, in effect, detention in a psychiatric hospital where there may not be a review of the person's condition for some years. On the other hand, a finding of automatism or some other state under s 24 could lead to acquittal without further consequences.

The question of whether an accused is fit to plead because of "unsoundness of mind" is a different issue: see Chapter 11.

7.11 INTOXICATION

Section 29 of the *Criminal Code* is a definitive and exhaustive statement of all defences of intoxication which may be raised. As in the case of insanity, intoxication is raised in order to negative intention on the part of the accused. Section 29 refers back to s 28 on insanity: see 7.10.

Section 29 says:

"(1) Section 28 applies to the case of a person whose mind is disordered by intoxication or stupefaction caused, without intention on his part, by drugs or intoxicating liquor or by any other means.

(2) Section 28 does not apply to the case of a person who has intentionally caused himself to become intoxicated or stupefied.

(3) When an intention to cause a specific result is an element of an offence, intoxication, whether complete or partial, and whether intention or unintentional, may be regarded for the purpose of ascertaining whether such an intention in fact existed."

Intoxication and stupefaction mean a condition graver and more extreme than is conveyed by the words "drunk" or "under the influence of drink". Sections 3-5 of the *Summary Offences Act* provide for offences of "drunkenness", which may be based upon non-expert opinion. "Drunkenness", in the *Summary Offences Act* sense of the word, will often be insufficient as a defence to excuse the commission of other offences.

Section 18 of the *Motor Traffic Act* provides for the offence of driving "under the influence of intoxicating liquor or a drug". Section 19 gives the police power to stop a person from driving who is, "by reason of physical or mental condition, incapable of having proper control of a vehicle". Again, such a person may not be so intoxicated as to give rise to an excuse which would provide a defence to the commission of other offences.

"Intoxication" is the stupefied condition of a person, for example, who has imbibed alcoholic liquor in sufficient quantity to make him or her lose, totally or partially, the use of his or her mental or nervous faculties. The person no longer has his or her normal intellectual or physical control, nor his or her powers of judgment.

With regard to s 29(2) of the *Criminal Code*, it is often difficult to decide whether a person who has gone drinking, and has consumed more liquor than originally intended, has "intentionally caused himself to become intoxicated". Once the defence has established that s 29(1) applies, on the balance of the probabilities, it seems that if the prosecution wants to negative the defence it must establish that the accused intentionally caused himself or herself to become intoxicated.

With regard to s 29(3), there are several offences under the *Summary Offences Act* which require proof of intention to cause a "specific result". For example, ss 7, 13, 17, 18, 19 and 23 all require proof of intention, and it seems that the question of whether the accused was intoxicated may be relevant in determining whether an offence was committed.

7.12 IMMATURE AGE

In the case of a person under the age of seven years, there is a presumption of law that cannot be rebutted that the person is not criminally responsible for an act or omission: *CC*, s 30(1).

In the case of a person under the age of 14 years, the question is whether the person knew the difference between "right and wrong". Section 30(2) provides that such a person is not criminally responsible unless it is proved that at the time of doing the act or making the omission the person "had capacity to know that he/she ought not to do the act or make the omission". The capacity of a child to know must be considered in the light of the child's maturity and in the light of social, parental and other pressures on the child. The capacity to know should be proved by the prosecution beyond reasonable doubt.

Section 30(3) provides that a male under the age of 14 years is presumed to be incapable of having carnal knowledge, but that this presumption is rebuttable.

In respect of children of 14 years and over, the question of the jurisdiction of the court becomes relevant, and reference should be made to 6.8.

7.13 JUSTIFICATION AND EXCUSE

As indicated in 7.4 above, a number of separate statutory provisions offer possible defences or excuses. It has been pointed out that the burden of proving that an act was done with lawful excuse is on the defendant: *Summary Offences Act*, s 4. The more common lawful excuses are set out here.

7.13.1 Justification

7.13.1.1 Execution of the law

A person is not criminally responsible for doing an act in execution of the law, such as carrying out a sentence of the court: *CC*, s 32(1)(a).

7.13.1.2 Obedience to an order

Similarly, a person is not criminally responsible for doing an act in obedience to the order of a competent authority which he or she is bound by law to obey, unless the order is manifestly unlawful: *CC*, s 32(1)(b).

7.13.1.3 Judicial officers

Except as expressly provided in the *Criminal Code*, a judicial officer is not criminally responsible for anything done in the exercise of his or her judicial functions. This applies even if the act done is in excess of his or her judicial authority, and whether or not he or she is bound to do the act: *CC*, s 31. However, Magistrates who act oppressively and maliciously may be subject to discipline and may be removed from office by the Legal and Judicial Services Commission: see Chapter 1. Also, there is a penal section relating to Magistrates requiring excessive bail and acting in their personal interest: *CC*, s 132. This section provides for defences such as "reasonable excuse".

7.13.1.4 Domestic discipline

It is lawful for a parent, or a person in the place of a parent, or for a school master, to use, by way of correction, towards a child, pupil, or apprentice under his or her care, such force as is reasonable under the circumstances: *CC*, s 278. The question of what is reasonable involves the age, physique and mentality of the child, and the punishment must be carried out with reasonable means or with a reasonable instrument. Even where the use of force by one person on another is lawful, the use of more force than is justified by law under the circumstances is unlawful: *CC*, s 281.

7.13.2 Compulsion/duress

7.13.2.1 Compelled to commit offence

Section 32(1)(d) of the *Criminal Code* absolves a person of criminal responsibility if he or she commits what would otherwise be an offence, under compulsion of threats and fear of personal harm.

In order for a defendant to succeed under this defence, there must be some evidence to show that the defendant did the act when:

- he or she was under threat of immediate death or of receiving grievous bodily harm; and
- the threat came from a person who was:
  - actually present and
  - in a position to carry out the threats; and
- he or she believed the only way to escape those threats was to do the act.

While the defendant must believe that obeying the threats is the only way to save himself or herself from immediate death or grievous bodily harm, this belief is subjective. Thus, even if there was a reasonable opportunity for the defendant to escape, the defence would still be available to him or her if he or she genuinely believed that escape was impossible.

This excuse does not protect the threatened person from liability if the act he or she carries out is so serious that it would constitute the offence of grievous bodily harm: s 32(1) proviso.

7.13.2.2 Compulsion by husband

A married woman is not free from criminal responsibility for doing an act merely because the act takes place in the presence of her husband. However, a married woman is not criminally responsible for doing an act which she is actually compelled by her husband to do, and which is done in his presence. An exception to this protection applies if the act which the married woman was compelled to do was such a serious offence that it amounted to grievous bodily harm, or intention to cause such harm. In that case, the presence of her husband is immaterial: *CC*, s 33.

7.13.3 Offences to property between husband and wife

When a husband and wife are living together neither of them incurs any criminal responsibility for doing any act with respect to the property of the other, except in the case of an act of which an intention to injure or defraud some other person is an element. This protection does not apply in the case of an act done by either of them when leaving or deserting, or about to leave or desert, the other. Also, neither of them can institute criminal proceedings against the other while they are living together: *CC*, s 36.

7.14 DEFENCE OF SELF OR PROPERTY

The use of force to defend oneself or protect one's property may be excused if it is reasonably necessary and not excessive. This section looks at the different circumstances in which self-defence may arise and the rules governing how self-defence may remove criminal responsibility for such use of force.

7.14.1 Self-defence

7.14.1.1 Justifiable assault

Assault is unlawful unless justified: *CC*, s 244 and *SOA*, s 6. Assault committed by a person in self-defence will not be unlawful where the act of assault is reasonably necessary by that person in order to resist actual and unlawful violence threatened to him or her, or to another person in his or her presence (*CC*, s 32(1)(c)), and provided the use of force is not more than is justified by law under the circumstances (*CC*, s 281).

Once self-defence is raised, the prosecution must exclude beyond reasonable doubt any of the elements of the defence. The onus is never on the defendant to establish a plea of self-defence. Throughout the whole of the trial the onus remains on the prosecution. Finally, self-defence is a complete defence. If the prosecution cannot prove beyond reasonable doubt that one of the conditions for self-defence does not exist, then the defendant must be acquitted.

7.14.1.2 Self-defence against unprovoked and provoked assault

The detailed provisions contained in ss 269 and 270 of the *Criminal Code* set out rules for determining whether self-defence is available, making the distinction between provoked and unprovoked assault.

7.14.1.3 Aiding in self-defence

Where it is lawful for a person to use force of any degree for the purpose of defending himself or herself against an assault, it is lawful for any other person acting in good faith in his or her aid to use force of a like degree for the purpose of defending him or her: *CC*, s 271.

7.14.2 Defence of property

It is usually unlawful, as a matter of legal policy reflected in the *Criminal Code*, for a person to take something by force, even if he or she has the right to possession of it. If the person cannot obtain possession of it without disturbing the peace or forcibly entering the land of another, he or she should make application to the appropriate court. Magistrates should note the provisions under the *District Courts Act* and the *Village Courts Act* which empower them to help conciliate such differences between people.

If forcible entry is made, then the person doing it could be charged with an offence under s 71 of the *Criminal Code*.

The legal policy is that generally a person in possession of property may defend that possession. However, there are limits on how far he or she can go in doing so. This is because the criminal law is not so much concerned with rights to property in these circumstances as with the need to discourage aggression and to ensure that disputes are settled according to law. Thus, the criminal law will often excuse a person defending property under a claim of right, even against the rightful owner, and will usually support a person already in possession.

7.14.2.1 Defence of dwelling-house

It is lawful for any person who is in peaceable possession of a dwelling-house, and for any person lawfully assisting him or her or acting by his or her authority, to use such force as that person believes, on reasonable grounds, to be necessary in order to prevent the forcible breaking and entering of the dwelling-house, either by night or day. Such force can be used against any person whom he or she believes, on reasonable grounds, to be attempting to break and enter the dwelling-house with intent to commit any indictable offence: *CC*, s 265.

7.14.2.2 Defence against trespass

It is lawful for a person who is:

- in peaceable possession of any land, structure, vessel or place; or
- entitled to the control or management of any land, structure, vessel or place.

It is also lawful for any person acting by the authority of such a person:

to use such force as is reasonably necessary in order:

- to prevent any person from wrongfully entering on the land, structure, vessel or place; or
- to remove from it a person who wrongfully remains on it:

if he or she does not do bodily harm to that person.

It is similarly lawful to use force in order to remove any person who conducts himself or herself in a disorderly manner, but, again, without doing bodily harm: *CC*, s 275.

7.15 PROVOCATION

7.15.1 Statutory basis

If a person is provoked into assaulting another person, or is provoked into committing an offence which involves an assault, he or she may be excused from criminal responsibility as a result of that provocation, provided that ss 266 and 267 of the *Criminal Code* are complied with. Section 266 defines provocation and s 267 states the conditions which must be met for the defence to succeed. Provocation is also available to a charge of unlawful assault under s 6 of the *Summary Offences Act*: see *Supreme Court Reference No 6 of 1984; Re Provocation and Summary Offences Act 1977, Section 6* [1985] PNGLR 31.

The detailed provisions of ss 266 and 267 should be referred to, and the following analysis may be helpful.

1. Provocation under the *Criminal Code* means a wrongful act or insult which is:

done to the defendant or done in his or her presence to:

(i)a person under the defendant's immediate care;

(ii)the defendant's husband, wife, child, parent, brother or sister; or

(iii)the defendant's employer or employee;

of such a nature as to be likely, in the circumstances, to deprive an ordinary person in the defendant's position of the power of self-control; and

of such a nature as to be likely, in the circumstances, to induce an ordinary person in the defendant's position to assault the person by whom the act is done or the insult offered.

2. The person who has been provoked will not be criminally responsible for the assault if all of the following conditions are met:

the assault was upon the person who gave provocation;

the provocation did in fact deprive the defendant of the power of self-control;

the assault was sudden and before there was time for the defendant's passion to cool;

the force used in the assault was not disproportionate to the provocation;

the force used was not intended or likely to cause death or grievous bodily harm.

7.15.2 Wrongful act or insult

A lawful act on its own can never be provocation that will excuse an assault. "Wrongful" applies to the "act" but not to the "insult": *R v Zariai-Gavene* [1963] PNGLR 203. In extreme circumstances, insult alone may be sufficient.

Words alone have been accepted in Papua New Guinea as amounting to provocation, as where a wife or husband has boasted in explicit terms to a spouse of an adulterous affair. Further, the discovery of an adulterous affair can be sufficient to ground provocation, but there will be no provocation unless the accused has acted in the heat of passion. In *R v Moses-Robert* [1965-1966] PNGLR 180, the accused heard about his wife's adultery but wilfully killed the man some time later, and the defence was not sustained. Civil trespass to personal property may be a wrongful act grounding provocation, and this should be compared with the "defence against trespass" referred to in 7.14.2.2.

7.15.3 Sorcery

Section 16 of the *Sorcery Act* provides that an act of sorcery may amount to a wrongful act or insult within the meaning of s 266 of the *Criminal Code*, and it is immaterial that the act of sorcery did not occur in the presence of the person provoked, or that it was directed at someone else. However, the mere presence of a sorcerer is not enough to amount to provocation. In order for s 16 of the *Sorcery Act* to operate, the act of sorcery relied upon must have actually commenced. The fact that it may be intended that such an act may commence some time in the future is not enough.

In sorcery cases, much turns on the state of mind or belief of the defendant. In the leading case of *R v KJ* [1973] PNGLR 93, the question was whether the defendant could also rely on s 25 of the *Criminal Code* on the ground that, although the person he attacked had not committed an act of sorcery, he honestly and reasonably, but mistakenly, believed that his victim had done so: see 7.6 above, as to mistaken belief.

When it comes to sentencing, the Supreme Court has made it absolutely clear that a customary belief in the power of sorcery is available as a mitigating factor, and that the *Sorcery Act* is entirely consistent with such an approach to sentencing: *Kwayawako v The State* [1990] PNGLR 6, and see 13.5.7.6.

7.15.4 Relative or other person in close relationship

The defendant may be provoked by a wrongful act or insult to a person described in s 266 of the *Criminal Code* as being in his or her immediate care, or to whom he or she stands in a "conjugal, parental, filial or fraternal relation, or in the relation of master or servant": see the box in 7.15.1 above and the analysis there in point 1. It has been accepted that, in Papua New Guinea, the relationship is not necessarily a direct and specific blood relationship. The words in s 266 are often used to describe relationships falling outside any strict definition. For example, the word "fraternal" has a wider meaning in common use than could be derived from a reference to a full blood brother. The expression "conjugal" of course goes outside any blood relationship. Also, the reference to the relationship of master and servant (employer and employee) gives the impression that the text is intended to include many recognised relationships where, in the normal course of experience, one would expect a person to assume some responsibility for the safety of the other, and therefore tend to lose self-control in the face of that other person being suddenly attacked or insulted: *R v Yanda-Piana* [1967-1968] PNGLR 482.

7.15.5 Loss of power of self-control

For the defence of provocation to succeed, there must be evidence that an ordinary person would have been deprived of his or her self-control in the circumstances. The "ordinary person" in this context is the ordinary Papua New Guinean living in the same cultural environment as the defendant. The test, while objective to a degree, will vary from the reaction of the ordinary rural villager living at a lower standard, to the reaction of the educated sophisticated urban dweller: *R v Gamumu* [1963] PNGLR 1.

In the case of an act of sorcery, s 16 of the *Sorcery Act* provides:

> "The likely effect of an act of sorcery relied on by virtue of this section shall be judged by reference, amongst other things, to the traditional beliefs of any social group of which the person provoked is a member."

Two further points should be noted. The "loss of self-control" is not an absolute loss of all control, but a loss related both to the degree of provocation and to the degree and form of retaliation. Further, the test is objective, so as to take into account the environment and culture of the defendant, but care must be taken that it does not become subjective and that it does not take account of facts personal to the accused: *R v Hand* [1963] PNGLR 9.

7.15.6 Before there is time for passion to cool

The defendant must have reacted quickly: see *R v Moses-Robert* [1965-1966] PNGLR 180, cited in 7.15.2.

7.15.7 Force not disproportionate to the provocation

A punch on the nose would not justify a murderous retaliation. However, because it is assumed that the defendant has, in fact, lost his or her self-control, it cannot be expected that the defendant will always have kept the retaliation in exact proportion to the provocation.

7.15.8 Provocation and mistake

It has been held that s 25 of the *Criminal Code* may operate in conjunction with s 266 to provide a defence. That is to say, if the defendant honestly and reasonably thought that a person had done something that would amount to provocation, even if he or she had not, this could be "provocation sufficient to excuse an assault": see *R v KJ* [1973] PNGLR 93 at 7.15.3.

7.15.9 Prevention of repetition of the insult

When an act or insult which is likely to amount to provocation is committed or offered, the person to whom it could be provocation may lawfully use such force as is reasonably necessary to prevent repetition of the act or insult: *CC*, s 268.

7.15.10 Burden of proof of provocation

Once the defence has raised provocation in its evidence, the onus is on the prosecution to prove, beyond reasonable doubt, the absence of provocation and of its alleged effects in the case.

7.16 CUSTOM

7.16.1 Custom in criminal matters

As discussed in 2.4, custom has wide effect outside the formal legal system and is also one of the main sources of law. However, until the underlying law is developed and declared under the *Constitution* and the *Underlying Law Act*, the application of custom in Papua New Guinea is limited by legislation such as the *Customs Recognition Act*. The effect of this Act is to exclude custom generally in criminal cases, both as to prosecution and defence, but some very significant exceptions remain: see 2.4.2.2. These exceptions provide headings under which custom may be considered, particularly where defences and penalties are concerned.

Section 4 of the *Customs Recognition Act* provides that:

Custom may be taken into account for the purpose of:

- **ascertaining the existence or otherwise of a state of mind of a person; or**
- **deciding the reasonableness or otherwise of an act, default or omission by a person; or**
- **deciding the reasonableness or otherwise of an excuse; or**
- **deciding, in accordance with any other law, whether to proceed to the conviction of a guilty party; or**
- **determining the penalty, if any, to be imposed on a guilty party,**

or where the court thinks that, by not taking the custom into account, injustice will or may be done to a person.

As to the importance of proving custom, see 5.13, but also note the responsibilities placed on the court to apply custom and develop the underlying law (2.3.8 and 2.4).

7.16.2 Ascertaining a state of mind

In some circumstances the court needs to be very aware of the particular custom setting within which the defendant's belief system operates. Without this knowledge the court may not be able to ascertain whether a particular state of mind existed at the time of the alleged offence: see 7.4.1.

7.16.3 Honest claim of right

In *Tidden v Tokavanamur-Topaparik* [1967-1968] PNGLR 231, a person accused of stealing was found not guilty on the ground that he honestly believed that he had a right under custom to take the coconuts from a plantation: see 7.7.

7.16.4 Justification and excuse

Custom may have relevance in deciding the reasonableness or otherwise of an excuse: *Customs Recognition Act*, s 4; see also 7.13 above. Custom may be particularly relevant with regard to situations of compulsion or duress.

7.16.5 Defence of self or property

The question of whether it is reasonable to take action to defend self or property, and the reasonableness of the force used, are matters in which custom may be taken into account.

7.16.6 Provocation

Similarly, custom may be relevant in answering questions about reasonableness in relation to the defence of provocation. Sorcery has been mentioned, but that is only one example which might arise in this area.

7.16.7 Injustice

The court is given discretion, which should be exercised judicially, as to whether custom should be taken into account in any particular case where, by not doing so, "injustice will or may be done to a person": *Customs Recognition Act*, s 4.

Chapter 8 – Informations

8.1 COMMENCEMENT OF CRIMINAL PROCEEDINGS

Criminal proceedings are commenced by an information in the District Court for simple/summary offences and for indictable offences triable summarily. Informations may be laid by an informant or legal representative or by a police officer or other official authorised for the purpose: *District Courts Act* (*DCA*), s 28.

8.2 FORM

An information is in writing, and is required to be in writing and on oath if a warrant is to issue: *DCA*, s 35. It is an important record of the commencement of proceedings which the Magistrate should always check. The principle is that the defendant is entitled to read an accurate statement of the allegations against him or her.

8.3 ESSENTIAL INGREDIENTS

In order to begin to exercise their jurisdiction, Magistrates of the District Courts must have before them an information which has the following ingredients:

- It should be in writing.
- It must allege all the elements of a criminal offence. Without these, the Magistrate has no jurisdiction to hear and determine the matter. The basis of this requirement is constitutional and statutory. "Nobody may be convicted of an offence that is not defined by … a written law": *Constitution*, s 37(2).
- It should describe an offence using the words which appear in the Act or other statutory instrument which has created the offence, or similar words: *District Courts Act* (*DCA*), s 30.
- It must allege the absence of justification or excuse if this is made part of the offence by the section creating it: For example, s 45 of the *Summary Offences Act* makes it an offence, without reasonable excuse, to interfere with or cast adrift any boat. The information must allege that lack of reasonable excuse.

8.4 PARTICULARS

Every person must be informed, as soon as possible and in a language that he or she understands, and in detail, of the nature of the offence with which he or she is charged: *Constitution*, s 37(4)(b). The information should refer to the time and place of the alleged offence. Details will depend on the nature of the offence. For example, the time of day may be important, while, in other circumstances, the precise date may not be essential and it may be sufficient to allege that the offence took place "on or about" the date in question. Of course, the date becomes essential if the time limit between the commission of an alleged offence and the issue of proceedings is relevant: see the discussion in 6.6. It should be noted that the six months' limitation on laying charges under the *Summary Offences Act* is an absolute requirement: *Summary Offences Act* (*SOA*), s 69.

A defendant is entitled to be informed not only of the legal nature of the offence with which he or she is charged, but also of the particular act, matter or thing which is alleged as the foundation of the charge. Nevertheless, this right to be given particulars does not entitle a defendant to ask for facts and circumstances that probe for evidence. It is a material fact, not the evidence to establish it, which must be indicated to the defendant.

The court has power to order that particulars be given to the defendant if it thinks it appropriate to do so, and the hearing of the case may be adjourned for that purpose: *DCA*, s 31.

8.5 CONSIDERATION BY THE MAGISTRATE

When an information is presented to the Magistrate, he or she has a duty to bring the judicial mind to bear, and to decide whether or not, on the information before him or her, the issue of a summons is justified. The function of the Magistrate is to protect the citizen against criminal proceedings which are substantially contrary to law or technically incorrect.

This means, that, at the very least, the Magistrate should find out if:

- the information specifies an offence known to written law;
- prima facie the essential ingredients of the offence appear to be present;
- the offence alleged is "out of time";
- the court has jurisdiction; and
- the informant has the necessary capacity or authority to lay or bring the information.

There may be the further question of whether the allegation in the information is of a trivial or vexatious nature. Where it is intended to issue a warrant in the first instance, the Magistrate will require that the information be in writing and on oath, which emphasises the judicial nature of the Magistrate's discretion to decide whether or not the proceedings should go ahead.

8.6 AMENDMENT

At the stage of the laying of charges and service on the defendant the court is not permitted to take notice of any objection to an information, summons or warrant, where the objection relates to:

- an alleged defect in the information in substance or form; or
- a "variance" between it and the evidence in support of the information.

Any such variance may be amended later by order of the court at the hearing: *DCA*, s 32. If such a variance between the information and the evidence called in support of it requires an amendment of the information, the court should consider whether the variance is such that the defendant has been deceived or misled by it. The court may, and at the request of the defendant must, adjourn the hearing of the case to some future day, on such terms as it thinks just: *DCA*, s 33.

There is the further question of how much "variance" can reasonably be amended. If the facts proved do not establish the charge as laid, but do establish an offence under the same section which is virtually the same as that charged, the information should be amended. On the other hand, where the offence disclosed by the evidence as called is really a different offence from that which is charged, the defendant is entitled to be acquitted. The Magistrate does not have power to amend an information so that it alleges a different offence. Of course, before the defendant leaves the court, or at a later date, it is open to the prosecution to lay fresh information against the defendant for the offence which is supported by the evidence. The Magistrate should adjourn the case to give the defendant more time to prepare in relation to the newly laid offence.

It should be noted that if an information does not disclose an offence as set out in a statute, the court has no jurisdiction and the Magistrate should decline to proceed: *Ganta v Nandi* [1973] PNGLR 61. However, in practice, if the insufficiency of the information escapes the Magistrate's eye, the effect of s 32 of the *District Courts Act* is to defer the jurisdictional issue to the hearing.

8.7 DUPLICITY AND UNCERTAINTY

Section 29 of the *District Courts Act* requires that an information should normally be for one matter only. However, more than one matter may be joined in the same information if:

- in the case of indictable offences, the matters of the information are such that they may be charged in one indictment (see *Criminal Code*, s 531); and
- in other cases, if the matters of the information relate to substantially the same act or omission on the part of the defendant.

The policy behind this section is that defendants should be called upon to answer only one charge at a time so that they will clearly know what they have to answer. If this policy is adhered to, the proceedings of the courts will be kept simple and the issues clear-cut. If Magistrates hear more than one charge at a time, the proceedings may become complicated by procedural rules and by questions of the relevance of evidence in relation to one charge as against another. Defending more than one charge at a time can put a defendant at great disadvantage and result in the defendant being denied a fair hearing.

Generally speaking, a single information offends the rule against duplicity if it alleges two or more offences. It will offend the rule against uncertainty if it alleges two or more offences in the alternative. For example, part of s 37 of the *Summary Offences Act* provides that a person commits an offence who, without reasonable excuse, obstructs or diverts from its channel, any public sewer, public drain, creek or other water course. An information would be bad for duplicity if a person was charged that he or she obstructed "a public sewer *and* a creek". Obstructing either would be an offence, so there would be two offences. If the information charged that he or she obstructed "a public sewer *or* a creek" it would be bad for uncertainty because it would be uncertain which of the two possible offences is alleged.

When such an information has mixed charges and is bad for duplicity or uncertainty, the Magistrate should require that the prosecution elect which charge is to be proceeded with and amend the information by striking out the words indicating the additional or alternative charge.

Section 29 of the *District Courts Act* allows the joining together in the same information of more than one charge or "count" which are based on substantially the same act or omission on the part of the defendant. On the other hand, if the nature and purpose of the two charges appear to be the same, the defendant may be in "double jeopardy": see 7.8.

Difficulties created by the laying of multiple charges in this way can be overcome if the defendant consents to the charges being heard together. In the case of a defendant who is unrepresented, it may be unwise for the Magistrate to allow the matter to proceed in circumstances where it is difficult for the Magistrate to be sure an injustice will not be done.

8.8 JOINT ACCUSED

Where an offence has been committed by two or more persons jointly, the charges may be heard together, but first the defendants must be told of their rights to separate trials and must clearly express a preference for a joint trial: *Kereku v Dodd* [1969-1970] PNGLR 176. For further discussion of joint parties and the severance of parties, see 4.5.

Chapter 9 – Summonses and Warrants

9.1 BRINGING THE DEFENDANT TO COURT

A person who is alleged to have committed an offence may be brought before the court, in the first instance, in one of three ways:

- after criminal proceedings have been commenced by the laying of informations:

  (i) in response to a summons served on the defendant; or

  (ii) on arrest under a warrant issued by the court; or

- after having been arrested without warrant.

Although the defendant is suspected of having committed an offence, it is fundamental to the system of justice in Papua New Guinea that, during the summons or arrest stages, and until found guilty by the court, the defendant is entitled to claim to be innocent until proved guilty according to law: *Constitution*, s 37(4)(a).

As in Chapter 8, this chapter will deal with summonses and warrants generally in relation to the Magistrates' Courts.

9.2 SUMMONSES

9.2.1 Form and content

A summons is a document addressed to the defendant and signed by a Magistrate or Clerk of the Court. The provisions of ss 41-48 of the *District Courts Act* (*DCA*) apply.

The *Constitution* requires that the defendant "shall be informed promptly in a language which he understands, and in detail, of the nature of the offence with which he is charged": s 37(4)(b).

A summons is required to state shortly the offence or matter of the information. As the summons has followed the laying of an information which should contain the details of the charges, as set out in Chapter 8 above, the same details should be written in the summons. As a matter of practice, a police informant should prepare the summons at the same time as the information and submit both for signature by the Magistrate or Court Clerk: *DCA*, ss 44 and 45.

The summons must state the date on which the defendant must come to court (the "return date"). In deciding on the date, it should be remembered that the summons must be served on the defendant at least 72 hours before the time appointed in the summons for the hearing. The return date may be extended: *DCA*, s 46. The summons itself must also be dated, and that date will be its date of issue.

The Magistrate has responsibility to oversee the laying of informations in the court (see Chapter 8), and shares with the clerk the responsibility for issuing summonses.

9.2.2 Service of summons and proof of service

A summons must be served on the defendant (within the time referred to above) by delivering a copy to him or her personally. If the defendant cannot be found, a copy of the summons may be left with some person, apparently not less than 16 years of age, who appears to be living at the place where the defendant was last known to have lived. For service on companies, and for substituted service, reference should be made to the specific rules contained in ss 47(1) and 48 of the *District Courts Act.*

The person serving a summons must prove that service has occurred, or the court cannot deal with the matter. Proof is by sworn affidavit. The person who served the summons should take the original summons (a copy of which has been left with the defendant) and write on the back of it a statement that he or she has served the summons in a certain way at a certain place and time. He or she must state on oath before a Magistrate, or other person duly authorised to take affidavits, that the endorsed statement is true. This is an affidavit. It must be duly signed by the server and by the Magistrate or other person before whom it was made, within seven days after service of the summons. After it has been sworn it should be returned immediately to the clerk: *DCA*, s 47(2).

At the hearing, the affidavit will be prima facie evidence of the service of the summons. This proof may be important if the summons is disobeyed and if the court has to consider an application for a warrant for the arrest of a defendant.

9.3 ARREST GENERALLY

9.3.1 Constitutional requirements

The action of the state (through courts and police officers) in arresting persons and holding them against their will would be in breach of the constitutional "Right to Liberty" were it not for certain specific exceptions and conditions. Under the heading "Rights of All Persons", s 42 of the *Constitution* sets out exceptions and conditions. Those relevant to this chapter are below.

CONDITIONS RELATING TO ARREST

Section 42 of the Constitution provides:

1. No person shall be deprived of his personal liberty except:

...

(d) upon reasonable suspicion of his having committed, or being about to commit, an offence; or

(e) for the purpose of bringing him before a court in execution of the order of a court; or ... .

2. A person who is arrested or detained:

(a) shall be informed promptly, in a language that he understands, of the reasons for his arrest or detention and of any charge against him; and

(b) shall be permitted whenever practicable to communicate without delay and in private with a member of his family or a personal friend, and with a lawyer of his choice (including the Public Solicitor if he is entitled to legal aid); and

(c) shall be given adequate opportunity to give instructions to a lawyer of his choice in the place in which he is detained, and shall be informed immediately on his arrest of his rights under this sub-section.

3. A person who is arrested or detained:

(a) for the purpose of being brought before a court in execution of an order of a court; or

(b) upon reasonable suspicion of his having committed, or being about to commit, an offence

shall, unless he is released, be brought without delay before a court or a judicial officer, and, in a case referred to in paragraph (b), shall not be further be held in custody in connection with the offence except by order of a court or judicial officer.

9.3.2 The Arrest Act

Generally speaking, the *Arrest Act* (*AA*) gives effect to the constitutional requirements, and goes further with detailed instructions covering:

how police officers should carry out their duties with regard to arrest without warrant (*AA*, s 3);

warrants issued by the court (*AA*, ss 8 and 10-13);

the manner of carrying out an arrest (*AA*, s 14); and

duties after arrest and at the police station (*AA*, ss 17-22).

It is strongly recommended that Magistrates should be fully aware of these provisions.

Three further aspects of the *Arrest Act* should be noted:

1. It abolishes all common law powers and duties in relation to arrest.

2. The Act is a more recent statute than the *District Courts Act* and takes precedence over it if there is any clear conflict. However, in most situations the Acts can be read side by side without conflict. If there is conflict, the more detailed provisions of the *Arrest Act* will apply: *The State v Kiap Bonga* [1989] PNGLR 359.

3. The *Arrest Act* provides a civil remedy for the wrongful exercise of powers conferred by the Act: ss 26-29. A person who breaches the Act in making an

arrest or carrying out other powers under the Act, or who fails to perform a duty imposed by the Act, may be liable to pay damages to the person aggrieved by that breach. Such an action may be brought in the District Court, within the jurisdiction limits provided for in s 21 of the *District Courts Act*. It should be noted that the court has the power to award exemplary damages, which means that, in addition to compensating the aggrieved plaintiff, the court may order the payment of additional damages as a punishment to the person who has breached the Act. See also Chapter 22 regarding the liability and protection of Magistrates.

9.4 ARREST WITHOUT WARRANT, AND POLICE POWERS AND DUTIES

The provisions of the *Arrest Act* relating to arrest without warrant, the manner of arrest, police duties to be performed after arrest, and questions of fingerprinting and medical examination are important and should be known by the Magistrate. Sometimes the conduct of the police will subsequently be relevant to the validity of the proceedings, to the prosecution's case or to defences raised. For example, if the statute requires that a warrant be issued in the circumstances of the case, then an arrest without warrant is illegal, any admissions made by the defendant are inadmissible, and subsequent proceedings can have no effect. The defendant should be discharged: *The State v Kiap Bonga* [1989] PNGLR 359 and *The State v Natpalau Tulong* [1995] PNGLR 329.

9.5 ARREST WARRANTS ISSUED BY THE COURT

9.5.1 The two Acts

As stated (9.3.2), the more detailed provisions of s 8 of the *Arrest Act* should be read into the sections of the *District Courts Act* relating to the issue of warrants for arrest (*DCA*, ss 49-56).

9.5.2 Issue of warrant in the first instance

Where an information has been laid before a Magistrate stating that a person is suspected of having committed an indictable offence or a simple offence, ss 49 and 50 of the *District Courts Act* give the Magistrate power to issue either a warrant for arrest or a summons against that person. Even after a summons has been issued, a warrant may also be issued at any time: *DCA*, s 49. The Magistrate must have before him or her evidence on oath "substantiating the matter of the information to his satisfaction" (*DCA*, s 50), and only then can he or she issue a warrant of arrest. This is consistent with s 35, which requires that, where it is intended to issue a warrant in the first instance, the information must be in writing and on oath: see 8.2.

Before issuing a warrant, the Magistrate must be satisfied regarding the following matters:

1. At the time the information was laid, appropriate decisions were made as to the elements of the alleged offence, the time of the offence and the court's jurisdiction, as discussed in 8.1-8.5.

2. There are reasonable grounds for believing:

(a) that an offence has been committed; and

(b) that it would not be practicable or desirable to proceed against the person by summons, because a warrant for arrest is necessary in order:

- **to ensure his or her appearance in court to answer a charge for the offence;**
- **to prevent:**

  (i) the continuation or repetition of the offence; or

  (ii) the commission of a further offence; or

  (iii) to preserve the safety or welfare of a member of the public or of the person to be arrested: AA, s 8.

9.5.3 Warrant for failure to attend on summons

The issue of a summons does not preclude the subsequent issue of a warrant at any time before the return date specified in the summons. If, on the other hand, a defendant who has been served with a summons fails to attend court on the return date specified, the Magistrate may issue a warrant for arrest. In indictable matters not to be tried summarily, authority is provided by s 93 of the *District Courts Act*. In cases of simple offences and indictable offences to be tried summarily, see s 125(b) of that Act.

Note: The provisions of s 125(a) of the *District Courts Act,* which purport to give the Magistrate the power to proceed ex parte and determine the case in the absence of a defendant who fails to appear on a summons, have been declared unconstitutional and void as a breach of a defendant's right to be heard on the charge: *Supreme Court Reference No 1A* [1981-1982] PNGLR 122.

Before issuing a warrant for failure to appear, the Magistrate must be satisfied that:

- **the summons has been duly served (see 9.2.2); and**
- **the matter of the information has been substantiated on oath (see 9.5.2).**

Also, a warrant is required to contain:

- **details of the alleged offence;**
- **the name and description of the person against whom it is issued;**
- **the name of the police officer to whom it is directed; and**
- **a direction to apprehend the defendant and bring him or her before the court: *DCA*, s 53.**

A person arrested and taken into custody for an offence must be brought before the court as soon as practicable after he or she is taken into custody: *DCA*, s 55. The person may be dealt with immediately if the prosecution is ready, and provided that the defendant has had adequate time to prepare his or her defence. It is more usual for the defendant to be released on bail: *DCA*, s 56, and see Chapter 10.

9.6 OTHER OCCASIONS FOR ARREST WARRANTS

9.6.1 Breach of bail

Where a defendant has been released on bail before the hearing takes place, or during any adjournment, and fails to appear at the time and place specified in the recognisance, the Magistrate may adjourn the hearing and issue a warrant for the defendant's arrest. If sureties have been required for the defendant's appearance, the Magistrate should check whether they have appeared at court and, if they have, examine them as to their responsibilities: see Chapter 10.

9.6.2 Indictable offences

Where a person is charged with an indictable offence which is to be dealt with under Pt VI of the *District Courts Act* and not tried summarily, the District Court has powers to issue a warrant similar to those mentioned above: *DCA*, s 93.

9.7 ATTENDANCE OF WITNESSES

The Magistrate's role in relation to witnesses has been discussed in 3.7. In order to secure the attendance of a witness, the Magistrate may issue a summons to the witness to attend at the time and place fixed for the hearing. The same rules regarding service apply as in the case of a defendant: *DCA*, ss 47, 66 and 67. If the witness fails to appear, he or she may be fined, but not until the Magistrate has considered any "just excuse" for the non-appearance.

With regard to a witness who is summonsed to attend in the case of an indictable offence and fails to appear, s 68 of the *District Courts Act* requires that proof must be given on oath by the server of the summons that a reasonable sum was paid or offered to the witness for costs and expenses of attendance. It is noted that, in many parts of Papua New Guinea, this requirement is not practicable.

When a witness appears to give evidence or to produce documents, but, without lawful excuse:

- refuses to be examined on oath;
- refuses to answer a question concerning the matter that is put to him or her; or
- refuses or neglects to produce a document specified in the summons, without sufficient excuse,

the court may adjourn the proceedings for not more than eight days, and may, in the meantime, issue a warrant committing the witness to a place where the witness will be held secure. If the witness, on being brought to an adjourned hearing, again refuses or neglects, the court may again adjourn the proceedings and commit the person for a specified period, and so again from time to time until he or she consents to be sworn or to give evidence or to produce the documents, as the case may be: *DCA*, s 70.

The Magistrate also has power to discharge such a witness on bail on recognisance, and the same conditions with regard to responding to bail and the issue of a warrant for non-appearance would apply to the witness as would apply to a defendant in similar circumstances: *DCA*, ss 79-83.

9.8 SEARCH WARRANTS

9.8.1 Constitutional requirements

In carrying out investigations and searches, the police force does not have any general power to search people, nor to enter premises to search for people or property. This is constitutionally recognised in the "Right to Privacy" (s 49) and the "Freedom from Arbitrary Search and Entry" (s 44) provisions of the *Constitution*. Nevertheless, Parliament is permitted under the *Constitution* to make reasonable provision for search and entry, which it has done by means of the *Search Act* (*SA*). Requirements that the police must observe in exercising their powers should be noted.

9.8.2 Searches of the person without warrant

Such searches, without warrant, of the person, clothing and immediate belongings must be:

- **based on a belief on reasonable grounds that the person has stolen goods, weapons, etc (*SA*, s 3); and**
- **conducted with due regard to decency and with only such force as is reasonable in the circumstances (*SA*, s 4).**

9.8.3 Searches of vehicle or premises without warrant

These searches require belief on reasonable grounds regarding theft, or entry in immediate pursuit of suspects: *SA*, s 5. Where a search of premises is carried out without a warrant and the search is not "in immediate pursuit" of a suspect, the search is unlawful and any evidence obtained in the search is unlawfully obtained and may be rejected: *The State v James Bero Popo* [1987] PNGLR 286.

9.8.4 Search warrants issued by a court

Except as described above, the police must apply to the court for the issue of a search warrant.

The Magistrate must be satisfied that there are reasonable grounds for suspecting that there is on any premises, craft, vehicle or other place:

- **any thing in respect to which any offence has been, or is believed on reasonable grounds to have been, committed; or**
- **any thing as to which there are reasonable grounds for believing it is likely to afford evidence of the commission of any such offence; or**
- **any thing as to which there are reasonable grounds for believing it is intended to be used to commit any such offence: *SA*, s 6.**

An affidavit is generally required from a senior police officer stating:

- what offence or offences it is alleged have occurred or might occur;
- the type of thing or object, document or property that the police are looking for; and
- the address or name of the premises, craft or vehicle to be searched.

In order to protect the secrecy of police operations, the police application should be heard in the Magistrate's chambers or other place from which all persons other than the Magistrate, the police officer and the clerk are excluded.

The *Search Act* spells out the powers and duties of police in relation to searches of premises. The power to enter must not involve the use of force that is greater than is reasonable in the circumstances: *SA*, ss 6(4) and 9. Within a reasonable time after the search the police must restore the place as nearly as possible to the same state of cleanliness and neatness that existed before the search: s 9.

As in the case of powers of arrest (9.3.2), a civil remedy is provided which enables a person aggrieved by a breach of the *Search Act* to bring an action for damages, and possibly exemplary damages (see 9.3.2 for an explanation), against the person who is in breach of the Act: s 17. See also Chapter 22, which deals with the liability and protection of Magistrates.

9.8.5 Respect for village custom and leadership

The *Search Act* makes special provision for the searching of a village or village garden. In this case, a search warrant requires evidence to be given to the court on oath by a commissioned police officer that there are reasonable grounds for searching any building in a village or in any part of a village or a village garden. If a warrant is issued, the police officer to whom the warrant is directed shall, where it is practicable to do so, before executing the warrant:

> "endeavour to obtain the co-operation of those persons who, by custom, are regarded as the leaders of the village in respect of which the warrant has been issued": *SA*, s 6(2) and (3).

It has been pointed out that the intention of the statute was to lay down very careful requirements where a search warrant is sought in relation to a village, where the police officer should endeavour to obtain the co-operation of the village leaders. Parliament clearly wanted searches in a village situation to be carefully dealt with by senior police officers: *The State v James Bero Popo* [1987] PNGLR 286 and *Acting Public Prosecutor v Richard Saronduo* [1988-1989] PNGLR 17.

Chapter 10 – Bail

10.1 THE PRESUMPTION OF THE RIGHT TO BAIL

10.1.1 The Constitution

Section 42 of the *Constitution* provides a number of rights to all persons who are arrested or detained. The right to bail is set out in the following words:

> **6. "A person arrested or detained for an offence (other than treason or wilful murder as defined by an Act of the Parliament) is entitled to bail at all times from arrest or detention to acquittal or conviction unless the interests of justice otherwise require."**

The right to bail is a *qualified* constitutional right. It is significant that the qualified constitutional right created by s 42(6) is subject to the "interests of justice". It is this qualification that reduces the "right" to a *presumption* in any particular case. The legislative provisions and the task of Magistrates in relation to bail are, in large measure, a means of testing this presumption to determine whether it applies in individual cases.

The *Constitution* also confers rights to those who are *refused* bail.

> **7. "Where a person to whom Subsection (6) applies is refused bail:**
>
> **(a) the court or person refusing bail shall, on request by the person concerned or his representative, state in writing the reason for the refusal; and**
>
> **(b) the person or his representative may apply to the Supreme Court or the National Court in a summary manner for his release."**

All other provisions relating to bail have their source in these constitutional provisions and must be interpreted in light of them.

10.1.2 The Bail Act

The most significant legislation relating to bail is the *Bail Act*. Section 3 of the *Bail Act* follows upon s 42(6) of the *Constitution*.

> **"The object of this Part is to give effect to Section 42(6) (liberty of the person) of the *Constitution* which provides that a person arrested or detained for an offence (other than treason or wilful murder as defined by an Act of the Parliament) is entitled to bail at all times from arrest or detention and to acquittal or conviction unless the interests of justice otherwise require."**

Again, we see the expression "interests of justice". It indicates that a decision about whether any individual who has been arrested or detained for an offence is entitled to bail is to be determined in accordance with the interests of justice.

The *Bail Act* is very comprehensive and covers nearly all the matters that affect how Magistrates deal with this issue in the District Courts. However, it is important to recognise that this Act does not codify the law of bail in Papua New Guinea. The *District Courts Act* also contains provisions that relate to bail.

10.1.3 Limits on the presumption

The expression "unless the interests of justice otherwise require" in s 42(6) of the *Constitution* and s 3 of the *Bail Act* means that the presumption of entitlement to bail *may be rebutted.* In order to rebut the presumption, it is necessary to show that the interests of justice require that an applicant for bail be denied bail. Because the presumption operates in favour of a defendant (except in cases where the defendant is charged with treason or wilful murder), it is up to the prosecution to rebut the presumption: see 5.26.

10.2 JURISDICTION TO GRANT BAIL

10.2.1 National and Supreme Courts

The National and Supreme Courts, as superior courts of inherent jurisdiction, can deal with any application for bail. However, in practice, the Supreme and National Courts only determine bail in cases where, by statute, the District Court has no jurisdiction.

Section 4(1) of the *Bail Act* limits the jurisdiction of the District Court in cases of:

- wilful murder
- murder
- an offence punishable by death
- rape
- abduction
- piracy
- burglary
- stealing with violence
- robbery
- kidnapping
- assault with intent to steal
- breaking and entering a dwelling-house where a firearm is involved (regardless of intent to use)

Bail in respect of these charges can only be granted by the National Court.

In cases where an information contains several charges, and one or more of them are within the scope of in s 4(1) of the *Bail Act*, a Magistrate must not determine bail in relation to any of the charges.

10.2.2 Bail Act

Section 26 of the *Bail Act* abolishes any common law powers or duties that govern bail in Papua New Guinea. This means that all Magistrates' jurisdiction in relation to bail must be traced to a statutory or constitutional provision.

10.2.3 District Courts Act

Sections 104-110 of the *District Courts Act* apply to the granting of bail in the District Court. These provisions regulate the exercise of that jurisdiction in the District Court. They do not enlarge the jurisdiction of a District Court Magistrate.

10.2.4 Police

Section 5 of the *Bail Act* requires an officer in charge of a police station to consider the issue of bail in some circumstances. Where a person is being held in a police station and the officer in charge is of the opinion that it is not practicable to bring the person before a court within a reasonable time, the question of bail must be considered by the officer in charge. When this happens, the officer in charge must apply the same criteria that a Magistrate applies in considering bail.

There is nothing in the *Bail Act* that specifies what "practicable" or "reasonable time" is. Police commonly interpret these terms widely, with the result that nearly all bail hearings take place before Magistrates.

10.3 APPLICATIONS IN DISTRICT COURTS

10.3.1 Onus of proof

The onus in a bail application before a Magistrate is on the prosecution: see 5.4. The prosecutor must satisfy the Magistrate that "the interests of justice" do not favour the granting of bail. The defendant need only make the application. In some circumstances, the Magistrate must consider the issue of bail even though the defendant makes no application.

10.3.2 The commencement of the period for considering bail

A Magistrate has jurisdiction to consider bail at any time after arrest or detention. A Magistrate must exercise that jurisdiction whenever a defendant makes an application for bail. An *unrepresented* defendant who appears in custody should be asked if he of she wishes to make such an application.

10.3.3 The time when a Magistrate's jurisdiction ends

The jurisdiction to consider bail normally ends when a defendant is acquitted or is sentenced after a conviction.

Where a Magistrate sentences a defendant to a period of imprisonment, the jurisdiction to hear an application for bail pending appeal continues.

In indictable cases that result in committals for trial or sentence in the National Court, bail may be considered by a Magistrate up until the first day of the National Court sitting at which the defendant is to be tried or sentenced: *District Courts Act*, s 106.

In some circumstances, a person may apply for bail before the informant or prosecutor has been advised or given an opportunity to be present. Section 6(2) of the *Bail Act* requires that an adjournment be considered to allow a prosecutor to prepare for a bail application. An adjournment for this purpose should be short and no longer than is necessary.

10.3.4 When a Magistrate must exercise jurisdiction to consider bail

During the period in which a Magistrate has jurisdiction to consider the issue of bail, there are certain times when the Magistrate *must* exercise that jurisdiction. These are whenever:

- **a person who is in custody makes an application for bail (*Bail Act*, s 6(1));**
- **the case of a person who is in custody is adjourned prior to conviction (*Bail Act*, s 7); or**
- **a person who is in custody is committed to the National Court for trial or sentence (*Bail Act*, s 8).**

10.4 ISSUES RELATING TO THE EXERCISE OF DISCRETION

In any bail hearing, the main question is whether the defendant ought to be released from custody pending trial. The secondary questions are whether conditions should apply to the release of the defendant, and if so, what those conditions should be. The issue of guilt or innocence is *not* the issue. However, the strength of the prosecution case against the defendant may be indirectly relevant to the issue of "interests of justice" which are discussed below.

The main issue of whether the defendant ought to be released breaks down into a number of subsidiary considerations that are considered below.

10.4.1 Section 9: Considerations for the Magistrate

Section 9 of the *Bail Act* provides a detailed list of considerations that a Magistrate *must* refer to whenever bail is considered prior to sentencing the defendant. It makes no difference whether an application is made by a defendant or whether, even in the absence of an application, a Magistrate considers bail pursuant to s 7 after a matter has been adjourned.

These considerations are that:

(a) the person in custody is unlikely to appear at his or her trial if granted bail; or

(b) the offence with which the person has been charged was committed whilst the person was on bail; or

(c) the alleged act or any of the alleged acts constituting the offence in respect of which the person is in custody consists of:

(i) a serious assault; or

(ii) a threat of violence to another person; or

(iii) having or possessing a firearm, imitation firearm, other offensive weapon or explosive; or

(d) the person is likely to commit an indictable offence if he or she is not in custody; or

(e) it is necessary for the person's own protection to be in custody; or

(f) the person is likely to interfere with witnesses or the person who instituted the proceedings; or

(g) the alleged offence involves property of substantial value that has not been recovered, and the person, if released, would make efforts to conceal or otherwise deal with the property; or

(h) there are, in progress or pending, extradition proceedings made under the *Extradition Act* against the person in custody; or

(i) the alleged offence involves the possession, importation or exportation of a narcotic drug other than for the personal medical use under prescription only of the person in custody; or

(j) the alleged offence is one of breach of parole.

If at least one of the above considerations is present, bail is normally refused: *Bail Act*, s 9(1). The presence or absence of one or more of these factors accounts for the determination of the vast majority of bail applications. However, see 10.4.5.

10.4.2 Meaning of "likely" in s 9(1)

The word "likely" appears in several places in s 9(1) of the *Bail Act*. In normal use, the word "likely" means that the chances of a thing happening outweigh the chances of the thing not happening. However, a slightly different judicial interpretation has been given to the word "likely" as it appears in s 9(1).

In the case of *Kysely v The State* [1980] PNGLR 36 at 30, the court considered the meaning of "likely" in relation to s 9(1)(f) of the *Bail Act*. The court held that (at 39):

> "the word 'likely' in the phrase 'likely to interfere with witnesses' in s 9(1)(f) means *likely in the sense of a tendency or real possibility*. It does not mean 'more likely than not', 'probably', or 'very likely.'" (emphasis added).

In considering s 9(1)(e) or (f), a Magistrate should interpret "likely" in accordance with the meaning given in *Kysely v The State*. In considering s 9(1)(a), a corresponding meaning should be given to the word "unlikely".

10.4.3 "Interests of justice"

Section 9(1) of the *Bail Act* appears, on its face, to include all possible considerations for deciding whether or not a defendant should be granted bail. It seems to say that unless one of the considerations set out is satisfied, the defendant must be granted bail. However, s 9 must be interpreted in light of s 42(6) of the *Constitution*, the preamble to the *Bail Act* and s 3 of the *Bail Act* which stipulates that "a person is ... entitled to bail ... unless the interests of justice otherwise require".

These provisions give a discretion to Magistrates to refuse bail, even in the absence of one of the considerations set out in s 9(1), and to grant bail, even when one of the considerations set out in s 9(1) does apply. The exercise of this discretion must be carefully guided by judicial authority.

10.4.4 Discretion to refuse bail in interests of justice

This is a discretion to refuse bail, even when *none* of the considerations of s 9(1) of the *Bail Act* apply but where it is in the interests of justice to refuse the application.

In *Re Fred Keating* [1983] PNGLR 133, Kidu CJ considered this question and said (at 135):

> "I hold the view that s 9 of the *Bail Act* 1977 does not contain all considerations that are relevant as to whether bail should be refused 'in the interests of justice'. Section 42(6) of the *Constitution* does not say that the phrase 'interests of justice' may be defined by an Act. There are two reasons why the phrase must be given a very wide meaning and application:
>
> (a) It says 'interests' – ie the plural of the word 'interest' is used; and
>
> (b) Section sch 1.5(2) says that 'All provisions of, and all words, expressions and propositions in, a Constitutional Law shall be given their fair and liberal meaning'.
>
> 'Justice' is a two-edged sword and cannot possibly be confined to mean those considerations enumerated in s 9(1) ... For instance, in my opinion, it

> would be in the interests of justice to refuse bail to a person known to be a habitual criminal, although s 9(1) does not say so."

In the same case Andrew J concurred (at 139).

The considerations of "the interests of justice" in *Re Fred Keating* did not form a necessary part of the decision in that case and were obiter dicta: see Chapter 25. Kapi DCJ dissented on the interpretation of the meaning of "interests of justice" and the discretion it afforded Judges and Magistrates to go outside a strict application of s 9(1). Nevertheless, the judgments of Kidu CJ and Andrew J provide authority for Judges and Magistrates to exercise their discretion to deny bail even when none of the considerations set out in s 9(1) apply.

Their judgments refer to several possible considerations that might give rise to the exercise of this discretion to refuse bail, such as where:

- **the prosecution has very strong evidence against the defendant;**
- **the probability of a conviction is very high; or**
- **the defendant is an habitual criminal.**

Neither Judge attempts to exhaustively list the circumstances that could provide a basis for the exercise of discretion to refuse bail even where none of the s 9(1) considerations apply.

The case of *The State v Beko Job Paul* [1986] PNGLR 97 provides further authority for the proposition that there is a discretion to refuse bail even when none of the s 9(1) considerations apply. The nature of the offence was held to be such that it justified the denial of bail in the "interests of justice". Wilson J said (at 99):

> "I consider that the offence the nature of which involves the clear intent to secure arms negates that presumption and that the interests of justice are not served by failing to give special significance to this type of crime and the consequences that flow, or could flow from it. On the basis of this reasoning I refuse bail, there being nothing in the application which convinces me that the continued detention is not justified."

Individual cases might arise where other considerations merit the exercise of discretion to deny bail. However, any consideration must be referable to the "interests of justice" used in the *Constitution* and in s 3 of the *Bail Act*.

10.4.5 Discretion to grant bail in interests of justice

A related question is whether, if one or more of the considerations set out in s 9(1) of the *Bail Act* apply, a Magistrate or Judge has the discretion to grant bail. The answer to this question also depends on the interpretation of the phrase "the interests of justice".

In *Re Fred Keating*, Andrew J (at 140) held that there is jurisdiction to grant bail in every case:

> "When one or more of the considerations in s 9(1) is shown to exist then there is a ground for refusing bail. The use of the word 'shall' does not mean, in my opinion, that bail must as a matter of course be refused when those matters are proved. To read it that way would be contrary to the whole scheme and intent of the *Constitution* and the *Bail Act*. Whether or not bail is refused is a matter of discretion."

This is authority for a Magistrate to exercise discretion to grant bail "in the interests of justice" even if one or more of the considerations of s 9(1) of the *Bail Act* does apply. The existence of this authority is supported by s 42(6) of the *Constitution*. The exercise of this discretion would arise only in rare cases and should be clearly linked by a Magistrate, in his or her reasons, to "the interests of justice" as they apply in the particular case.

10.4.6 Applications after conviction

The provisions of s 9(1) of the *Bail Act* do not specifically apply to applications for bail that are made *after* conviction but prior to sentencing or appeal. Applications for bail in those instances are made pursuant to ss 10 and 11 of the *Bail Act* respectively. Those sections provide only for bail to be granted in the court's discretion. They do not provide specific factors for the guidance of the court in exercising that discretion.

A defendant must demonstrate to the court that there are *exceptional circumstances* that justify the release on bail of a convicted person. Case law has provided some guidance:

- In *Smedley v The State* [1978] PNGLR 452, the desire of the applicant to be released from custody to instruct counsel was found *not* to be an exceptional circumstance. Nor was the applicant's desire to assist his wife in establishing a new business, to perform duties as executor of an estate, to assist his wife in finding new accommodation or to engage in a business venture.
- In *Jaminen v The State* [1983] PNGLR 122, the desire to perform duties as a member of Parliament was *not* an exceptional circumstance.
- In *Yaki v The State* SCA No 74 of 1990, the Supreme Court found that the desire of the applicant, who was a member of Parliament, to attend to his political duties and specifically to account for government funds was *not* an exceptional circumstance. The desire to be released in order to instruct counsel was similarly rejected.

These judgments suggest that a very strong prospect of success on appeal could form an exceptional circumstance.

10.5 PROCEDURE AT A BAIL HEARING

10.5.1 The issue and the burden of proof – before conviction

In a bail application prior to conviction the onus of proof is on the prosecution. If a prosecutor opposes bail, he or she must adduce evidence to satisfy the Magistrate that one of the considerations of s 9(1) of the *Bail Act* applies, or that, even where none of the considerations applies, it is in the interests of justice to order the detention of the defendant in custody: see 10.4.4.

The wording of the *Bail Act* indicates that the standard of proof required of a prosecutor who opposes the grant of bail is *less* than the criminal standard of proof. Section 9(1) begins with the words:

> "Where a bail authority is considering the question of granting or refusing bail under this Part, it shall not refuse bail unless *satisfied on reasonable grounds* as to one or more of the following considerations".

Re Fred Keating (at 140) clearly indicates that a prosecutor who opposes bail in a case where s 9 applies, must only demonstrate that *there are substantial grounds* for believing that one of the s 9(1) factors applies.

10.5.2 The issue and burden of proof – after conviction

Where an application for bail is made after conviction but before sentence or pending appeal, the constitutional right to bail does not apply. A person is not constitutionally presumed to be entitled to bail. The presumption of innocence no longer applies. The onus of proof is on the person applying for bail and not the prosecutor.

10.5.3 Evidence

Section 9(2) of the *Bail Act* provides that:

> "In considering a matter under this section a court is not bound to apply the technical rules of evidence but may act on such information as is available to it."

The effect of this section that *any relevant evidence may be admitted*, regardless of whether it complies with the strict rules of admissibility.

Hearsay: Hearsay evidence is normally admitted at a bail hearing. This gives a prosecutor, lawyer or any other witness the opportunity to make submissions that include facts that have been reported to them. For instance, bail hearings usually include submissions that are prefaced by such expressions as "My client instructs me that …" or "According to police records …".

Another form of hearsay evidence that is admissible at a bail hearing is that which is found in documents. A defendant might adduce evidence in the form of a letter from an employer, a wantok, a priest, a minister or anyone else who can offer relevant evidence for consideration by a Magistrate in deciding the issue of bail: see 5.17.

Opinion: Another form of evidence that is routinely admitted at a bail hearing, but which may be contrary to the technical rules of evidence, is opinion. For example, a witness may offer an opinion about the trustworthiness of the defendant. A prosecutor might advance an opinion about the chances of the defendant showing up for trial or the attitude of the defendant towards the victim of the alleged offence. These opinions would normally be inadmissible at a trial but may be admitted by a Magistrate at a bail hearing if they are relevant to the issue: see 5.25.

Character: Another form of evidence that may be technically against the rules of evidence is that of character. A defendant may have character traits, the evidence of which might well be inadmissible at a trial of the charges he or she faces. However, the evidence may be relevant and admitted by a Magistrate at a bail application: see 5.5.

10.5.4 Natural justice

Bail applications can be less formal than a trial. The *Bail Act* does not prescribe any formal procedure. However, it is important that at every stage of a bail application fairness prevails. Normally, when the issue of bail arises, either by way of an application made by the defendant or automatically pursuant to s 7 of the *Bail Act*, a Magistrate will ask the prosecutor what position he or she takes in connection with bail. If the prosecutor takes the position that the defendant should not be granted bail, he or she is then offered an opportunity to adduce evidence in support of that position.

Once the prosecutor has presented evidence, the defendant may adduce evidence. It is important where a defendant is unrepresented to ensure that the nature of the application, and particularly the issue, is clearly understood by the defendant.

The fundamental rules of natural justice must be adhered to in a bail hearing as they are in any other type of judicial hearing. Each side must be given an opportunity to present its case and each side must be given a chance to respond to the other side's case.

One of the rules of natural justice is that each side be given an opportunity to question those who adduce evidence against them. In hearings such as a bail application where the rule against hearsay is not routinely enforced, it may not be possible to give each side an opportunity to question the person making prejudicial assertions. Magistrates are therefore faced with a balancing of interests. On the one hand, there is an interest in keeping a bail hearing as informal, inexpensive to the parties and efficient as possible. On the other hand, natural justice applies. A Magistrate must be aware of these sometimes-conflicting priorities when determining what rules of evidence to apply.

Although the defendant may make repeated applications for bail, a prosecutor does not have the same ability to make repeated applications to refuse bail. Once bail has been granted, a prosecutor may apply to vary or revoke bail, but only on the basis of some change in circumstances since the original bail order was made.

Section 14 of the *Bail Act* allows for a person to be granted bail even though he or she is not present when it is granted.

10.5.5 Where prosecutor does not oppose bail absolutely

In some cases, the prosecution will not take the position that bail should be refused, but that it should only be granted with conditions imposed. The prosecutor may outline the conditions he or she is seeking. In these cases, Magistrates should bear in mind two matters.

1. *Understanding of defendant:* A defendant, especially one who is unrepresented, may be desperate to be released from custody and might be inclined to immediately agree to the conditions proposed by the prosecutor, even though these might be very difficult or even impossible to fulfil. Accordingly, a Magistrate should be careful to ensure that a defendant understands the conditions that he or she is agreeing to and understands what is required to fulfil them.
2. *Whether conditions required:* A further duty of a Magistrate in these circumstances is to satisfy himself or herself that the conditions are *required* in view of the provisions of the *Bail Act*. In other words, just because the prosecutor considers the grant of bail on proposed conditions that to be appropriate, it does not relieve a Magistrate of the duty to ensure that these are consistent with the interests of justice.

10.5.6 Giving reasons for decision

Section 16 of the *Bail Act* requires that reasons for a Magistrate's refusal to grant bail be delivered and recorded. However, it is a good idea to give reasons for a decision in all cases. This assists when a Magistrate or Judge is called upon to make a further decision with respect to the issue of bail. This situation can arise where variation of the conditions of bail is sought, where an application is made to revoke bail or where there is an appeal of the decision to grant bail: see Chapter 25.

10.6 THE BAIL CERTIFICATE

Section 15 of the *Bail Act* provides that a defendant is required to have a copy of the certificate in his or her possession at all times, unless it is required by his or her lawyer, or where the defendant is in custody pending the satisfaction of a condition that has been imposed in the grant of bail.

Where a person is granted bail but must satisfy conditions *prior* to release, a copy of the bail certificate is to be attached to the warrant of committal.

10.7 CONDITIONS ATTACHING TO BAIL

The *Bail Act* does not provide a finite list of possible conditions that may be imposed. Different cases will require different conditions, and some conditions might be completely unique to the application being considered. A Magistrate's job is to balance the presumption of entitlement to bail with the "interests of justice" in such a way that the conditions imposed (if any) are reasonable and fair in all the circumstances.

However, the discretion to impose conditions when granting bail is not unfettered.

Section 18 of the *Bail Act* requires Magistrates to consider what effect a particular condition may have in relation to the defendant's:

- **employment;**
- **domestic life; or**
- **political freedom.**

In deciding what conditions are appropriate, a Magistrate must remember that the issue is not guilt or innocence. For instance, it would not be appropriate to impose a condition that the defendant compensates the victim, provides the name of a person who acted jointly in the commission of the offence or makes an apology. These conditions are all *inconsistent* with the presumption of innocence.

10.7.1 Automatic condition to appear

Section 17 of the *Bail Act* requires an automatic condition, namely that the defendant appear at every time and place to which the proceedings are adjourned from time to time. This eliminates the need to attach a new bail condition each time the matter is adjourned to a new date.

This condition should be clearly brought to the attention of a person granted bail, as it may not be clear from a reading of a standard bail certificate in Form 2.

10.7 2 Conditions to be satisfied before release

Section 18 of the *Bail Act* provides a wide discretion to a Magistrate to attach appropriate conditions to a grant of bail. It may be necessary for a person granted bail to satisfy them *before* being released.

Examples of such conditions are:

- Surrender of passport: This condition may require that the passport be surrendered to the officer in charge of a particular police station or to the clerk or registrar of a court.
- Deposit of money: This must of course be in a reasonable sum given the resources of the defendant and s 18(1)(d) of the *Bail Act*. In ordering the deposit of a sum of money to secure bail, a Magistrate should be careful to explain to the defendant that this sum is not an indication of the size of any fine that might be imposed if and when the defendant is either found guilty or pleads guilty to the offence or offences with which he or she has been charged.

It is not uncommon for defendants to be under the misapprehension that once a sum of money is deposited as a precondition to bail, they have a legitimate choice of showing up for trial or not showing up and having the bail forfeited as a fine. The forfeiture of the deposit of money is an entirely separate consideration from the matter of sentence, and is also separate from any consideration governing the issue of an arrest warrant if the defendant fails to appear in court.

- Obtaining a guarantor: One of the most common conditions that are imposed is that the person granted bail secures a guarantor. This condition is referred to in greater detail below.

10.7.3 Conditions to be satisfied after release

There is a wide range of conditions that are to be satisfied after a person is released on bail.

Examples of the most common ones are:

- Reporting: This condition usually requires the defendant to report to the police at a specific place and at specific times. The purpose of this condition is usually to become aware of whether the defendant has absconded. Police are familiar with this condition and should be equipped to make records of reporting and to take steps if reporting does not take place.

However, in some cases, it may be appropriate for a reporting condition to require that the person report to a party other than the police.

- Residing: The requirement that a person resides at a particular place is often imposed to ensure that the person, by maintaining a fixed residence, is less likely to abscond. This ensures that the police or other authority is able to locate the defendant if and when it is appropriate to do so.

- Non-contact: The allegations relating to a specific charge may make this type of condition appropriate. Where an alleged victim or potential prosecution witnesses are or may feel threatened by the release of a person on bail, a condition of non-contact order may be appropriate. This non-contact order is likely to prohibit both direct and indirect contact (such as by telephone, the mail or some intermediary to contact the person).
- Non-attendance: This type of condition is similar to a condition of non-contact and may be imposed in conjunction with it. For instance, if the alleged offence occurred at a hotel, a business or at some other public or private place and, if there is a concern that the defendant might attend there for improper reasons or for reasons which, while not improper, might have a detrimental impact on other persons at the place, this condition might be appropriate. However, this type of condition might need to be tailored to address the possibility of the defendant having a legitimate or even necessary reason for attending to the place. For instance, if a condition was imposed preventing the defendant from attending within 100 meters from the Port Moresby Hospital, it would be appropriate to exempt occasions when the defendant might require treatment or might be accompanying someone else who does.
- Attendance: Apart from a condition that requires a defendant to report at a police station or some other place at regular intervals to ensure that he or she has not absconded, it might be appropriate to impose a condition that the person attend at some other place. This might be to ensure that the person continues to undergo some treatment or assessment that has been commenced or proposed. Such attendance may have to do with a defendant obtaining counselling from a pastor or other counsellor, undergoing treatment for alcohol abuse or for some other reason. This sort of condition should be as specific as circumstances permit in order that a possible breach can be clearly identified.
- Maintain employment: If a defendant is employed at the time of the charge, it is likely that the potential loss of his or her employment (if bail is denied) will be argued as a factor in favour of bail. If bail is granted in such a case, it is not unreasonable to impose a condition that the person continues to attend regularly for work. The condition should be specific enough regarding time, place and the name of the employer so that a possible breach may be clearly identified.
- Abstinence: During a bail hearing, evidence may be adduced by either the defendant or the prosecutor to the effect that alcohol or some other drug played a significant role in the commission of the alleged offences. In such cases, a condition that the defendant abstains from the consumption of alcohol or a drug may be appropriate.

10.7.4 Guarantors

A guarantor is a person who, pursuant to s 19 of the *Bail Act*, gives an undertaking to ensure that a defendant who is granted bail will appear at his or her trial and will comply with other conditions imposed.

Section 19(2) of the *Bail Act* provides that a guarantor may only be required where it is considered that without one a defendant will not appear at court or will not comply with other conditions that are imposed.

The requirement that an applicant for bail secure a guarantor is often imposed in cases where it is felt that a financial consequence should follow on non-compliance with conditions, but the defendant does not have an ability to deposit money in an appropriate amount.

Guarantors may be required to either pay money into court to secure the release of the defendant on bail *or* to undertake to pay the state a specified sum if the defendant does not comply with the conditions of bail. The former requirement is the most stringent and avoids collection proceedings and possible non-payment in the event that the state is obliged to pursue a guarantor. Therefore, when imposing an undertaking, a Magistrate should feel confident that enforcement of a guarantor's obligations, should that be required, would be successful.

Section 19(6) requires that the financial means of a guarantor be taken into account. A Magistrate, in deciding on a sum of money that will be appropriate, should also consider other factors such as the minimum amount which will provide an incentive for the guarantor to ensure that the defendant appears and abides by all bail conditions. The seriousness of the offence and the circumstances of the defendant are usually legitimate considerations in making this determination.

In many cases, the identity and suitability of a guarantor can be determined by a Magistrate in the course of a bail hearing. However, a Magistrate is able to delegate this matter to a member of the police pursuant to s 19(3) of the *Bail Act*.

In any case, no more than two guarantors may be required.

Section 21(3) provides that once a guarantor has either given an undertaking or made a deposit of money, he or she is entitled to be heard on any subsequent occasion where the terms of bail are being varied in a manner that makes the guarantor's obligations more onerous.

10.8 VARIATION AND REVOCATION

10.8.1 Variation

Between the initial grant of bail by a Magistrate and the conclusion of the case, changing circumstances may make it appropriate to change the bail status of a defendant. Section 20 of the *Bail Act* allows either the defendant or the prosecutor to apply for a variation in the terms and conditions of bail.

A successful application for variation might result in bail conditions more favourable to a defendant or more stringent conditions. Some applications for variations are relatively non-contentious. For instance, where a defendant is required to change residences or place of employment for legitimate reasons, and existing conditions prevent this, a change is appropriate.

10.8.2 Revocation

Between the time of the original bail order and the disposition of the defendant's case, a change in circumstances may come to the attention of the prosecutor. The prosecutor may consider that these changes warrant more than simply a variation of the terms of a bail order. If so, the prosecutor may apply for an order revoking bail pursuant to s 21 of the *Bail Act*. This section does not set out specific considerations for a Magistrate in relation to such an application. The section simply says that an order revoking bail may be made where there are reasonable grounds for doing so.

Reasonable grounds might consist of:

- **serious breaches of the existing terms of bail;**
- **the alleged commission of a further offence while the current bail conditions were still in operation; or**
- **other circumstances relating to any of the considerations in s 9(1) of the *Bail Act*.**

If a defendant pleads guilty and is likely to be sentenced to a period of imprisonment, this might constitute a reasonable ground for revoking bail.

A Magistrate, in considering an application to revoke bail pursuant to s 21, may, instead of revoking bail, vary the conditions of bail. This outcome would be appropriate where the prosecutor has raised legitimate concerns in relation to the existing terms of bail but these concerns are not serious enough to revoke bail altogether.

10.8.3 Forfeiture

Where a defendant fails to abide by a condition of bail, s 22 of the *Bail Act* provides that a court may make an order forfeiting any sum of money that the *defendant* has deposited or undertaken to pay. This section does not refer to money paid as security by a guarantor.

The most common circumstance in which such orders are made is where a defendant fails to appear in court on a date to which the proceedings have been adjourned. In such a case, it is not possible to hear from the defendant as to why such an order should not be made. However, s 22(3) of the *Bail Act* provides that within 14 days of the making of an order *a person affected* by the order may apply to the court making the order for variation or revocation of the order. At the very least, "a person affected" would be the defendant. However, another person who is able to demonstrate that they are "affected" by the order might also apply.

After the expiry of 14 days from the making of a revocation order, a Magistrate has no jurisdiction to extend the time for making an application pursuant to s 22(3). The Supreme Court, in *Supreme Court Reference No 12 of 1984; Re Joe Parakas v The State* [1985] PNGLR 224, held that although the defendant's non-appearance which gave rise to the forfeiture order, and his subsequent inability to apply to vary or revoke the order, were both caused by circumstances beyond his control, there is no jurisdiction (in any level of court) to entertain an application outside the 14 days.

Chapter 11 – Committal Proceedings

11.1 CRIMINAL HEARINGS GENERALLY

Hearings within the criminal jurisdiction of the District Court are partially provided for in Pt V of the *District Courts Act* (*DCA*), but relevant provisions are to be found throughout the statute. In many respects, the same provisions apply to both criminal and civil matters. In this manual, hearings in general, and criminal cases in particular, are dealt with in Chapter 4. Such issues as the conduct of court matters, witnesses and representation are to be found in Chapter 3. The primary focus of this chapter is the committal procedure.

11.2 NATURE AND PURPOSE OF COMMITTAL PROCEEDINGS

11.2.1 Background

Because of the seriousness of presenting a person for trial before a Judge in the National Court, the law requires that a preliminary examination be conducted by a Magistrate to assess the strength of the accusation that the person has committed an indictable offence. It serves the interests of both the state and the citizen in seeking to prevent weak or misconceived prosecutions from proceeding to trial. The primary objective of a committal proceeding is to determine whether there is sufficient evidence to warrant a person accused of an indictable crime being sent for trial before a Judge for the offence charged (or any other indictable offence).

11.2.2 Consequences of the committal hearing

A Magistrate who concludes that the evidence is insufficient to put the defendant on trial for an indictable offence must order that the defendant be discharged. However, if the Magistrate is of the opinion that the evidence presented is of sufficient weight, he or she must commit the defendant to stand trial, and must either remand the person in custody or grant bail until trial. The trial will be held in the National Court. If there is evidence sufficient to justify committal, a Magistrate cannot refuse to commit the person for trial because he or she regards the prosecution as oppressive or unjust. Committal proceedings are not a trial, and the Magistrate has no power to stop them, nor any proceedings which may follow, because of any concerns which the Magistrate might have about the case which is brought against the defendant.

11.2.3 A judicial act, but not an adjudication of the matter

A committal proceeding is an investigation into the strength of the case being mounted by the prosecution, and it is not an act of adjudication. Its function is not to determine whether or not the person accused is guilty of the offence charged. The proceedings are of an investigatory, tentative and non-conclusive nature. The statutory test to be applied by the Magistrate asks whether the evidence is sufficient to put the defendant on trial for an indictable offence: see *DCA*, s 95. That measure of sufficiency is less than the trial standard of "proof beyond reasonable doubt". Nor does the result of the proceeding bind the prosecution to either proceed with or to withdraw the charges. Whether the defendant is directed to stand trial or is discharged, the prosecutorial discretion not to proceed further or to continue by way of direct indictment remains intact.

Nevertheless, the Magistrate's decision is a judicial act, requiring that proper consideration be given to the matters required by the statute.

11.2.4 Benefits to the accused and to the prosecution

Traditionally, the committal proceeding gives the accused person an opportunity to obtain more precise details of the charges laid and the supporting evidence. It compels the pre-trial disclosure or discovery of the essence of the case for the prosecution. This assists in the formulation of defence strategy for those committed to stand trial. The evidence provides an opportunity for the accused's legal adviser to evaluate the merits of the evidence of the witnesses whose statements form part of the prosecution case. Any discrepancies between evidence on key issues sworn to in statements in the committal proceeding and evidence given later by the same witnesses at the trial can be used in an effort to discredit the prosecution case at a contested trial, or if a plea of guilty is to be entered, to set the foundations for a plea in mitigation.

The benefits to the prosecution are two-fold. The procedure allows for the public disposal of a weak case, saving the time and cost of a trial that will likely lead to an acquittal. Secondly, if the disclosed prosecution case is strong, it encourages the accused to plead guilty, thus saving the state the cost of a trial.

11.3 COMMITTAL JURISDICTION IN PAPUA NEW GUINEA

11.3.1 Procedural changes

Committal proceedings are conducted by a Magistrate in accordance with the procedures found in Pt VI of the *District Courts Act*. Changes were made to the procedures in 1980, the most significant of which was the change:

- **from** proceedings in which prosecution witnesses were called to give oral testimony
- **to** proceedings which rely primarily on written witness statements (often called "depositions"), other documentation and exhibits, in order to present the prosecution case.

If a committal order is made, the documents are passed to the National Court as a "hand-up brief". It should be noted, however, that, although such "paper committals" largely remove the need for prosecution witnesses to be subjected to cross-examination on two occasions (both committal and trial), they also reduce the opportunity for defence counsel to test, by cross-examination, the quality of the witness evidence.

A further change in procedure has created a short-cut which, if the defendant is legally represented and waives the right to a committal hearing, permits the "brief" of depositions to be passed direct to the National Court without a hearing. This means that, if the police and prosecution do their work conscientiously and fairly, and if the Magistrate carries out the required testing of the written statements, the defence may permit the committal stage to be reduced to a formality.

11.3.2 Jurisdiction of the District Court under Pt VI of the District Courts Act

11.3.2.1 Responsibility for indictable committals

Generally speaking, this responsibility of the District Court for committals applies to indictable offences under the *Criminal Code* (*CC*) (offences punishable by imprisonment for more than 12 months). There is one important exception.

11.3.2.2 Schedule 2 offences and the Public Prosecutor's election

The exception is the category of indictable offences listed in Sch 2 of the *Criminal Code* (known as "Schedule 2 offences"), which, under s 420 of the *Criminal Code*, may be tried summarily by a Principal Magistrate if the Public Prosecutor has elected to have the case dealt with summarily. Because the Public Prosecutor has the choice of whether:

- a Schedule 2 offence should go through the committal stage like any other indictable matter; or
- it should be tried summarily by a Principal Magistrate,

certain arrangements ("Schedule 2 arrangements") have been made to permit the Public Prosecutor to make that election at the commencement of committal proceedings. These Schedule 2 arrangements were suggested by the Supreme Court in *The State v The Principal Magistrate, District Court, Port Moresby; Ex parte The Public Prosecutor* [1983] PNGLR 43. They overcome some inconsistencies between the *District Courts Act* and the *Criminal Code*, and give effect to s 4(1)(ga) of the *Public Prosecutor (Office and Functions) Act*.

11.3.2.3 Schedule 2 arrangements

In the case of Schedule 2 offences, after the charge has been determined and before the information and documents are served on the defendant under s 94 of the *District Courts Act* (see 11.3.2), the Public Prosecutor must make the election whether or not to prosecute Schedule 2 indictable offences within the summary jurisdiction of the District Court under Pts IV, V and VII of the *District Courts Act*. It is expected that the Public Prosecutor should not delay, and should make the election within a reasonable time. If the Public Prosecutor fails to make an election in respect of a Schedule 2 offence, it will be treated as a *Criminal Code* indictable offence, and the committal provisions of Pt VI of the *District Courts Act* will apply. The service of the documents under s 94 will be deemed to be the commencement of the proceedings under Pt VI of the *District Courts Act*: see *The State v The Principal Magistrate* in 11.3.2.2 above.

If the Public Prosecutor elects to proceed summarily, the matter will be transferred to a Principal Magistrate's Court and governed by Pts IV, V and VII of the *District Courts Act*, but the Public Prosecutor will retain the power to withdraw the information: *Public Prosecutor (Office and Functions) Act*, s 4(ga).

11.4 COMMENCEMENT OF COMMITTAL PROCEEDINGS GENERALLY

11.4.1 Information and summons or warrant

Where a person is charged with an indictable offence, an information may be laid (see Chapter 8) and that person may be summonsed to appear before the District Court – and a warrant for arrest may be issued if he or she fails to appear on the summons: *DCA*, s 93. More commonly, arrest will already have occurred with or without warrant: see Chapter 9. If the relevant statute requires that a warrant be issued, then the arrest of the defendant without a warrant is illegal and will render the subsequent committal proceedings invalid: see 9.4. Accordingly, it is the responsibility of the Magistrate in committal proceedings to check that the defendant has been brought before the court in accordance with the law: *The State v Natpalan Tulong* [1995] PNGLR 329.

11.4.2 Documents to be served

Having laid an information (and subject to 11.2.2.3 above), the informant must serve on the defendant or his or her legal representative:

(a) a copy of the information;

(b) a copy of each witness statement that the informant intends to tender at the committal hearing;

(c) where a statement to be tendered at the hearing refers to documents and/or exhibits, a list of those documents and/or exhibits; and

(d) a copy of each of the documents referred to in (c).

If an exhibit cannot be adequately copied or described, the defendant must be notified where it can be inspected. The court also has power, if it considers it to be expedient in a particular case, to waive service of a document or exhibit and allow the informant or defendant to call oral evidence at a committal hearing: *DCA*, s 94(6).

11.4.3 Certificate as to truth of statement

Every witness statement (referred to in 11.4.2(b) above) must contain a certificate, signed by the maker of the statement, which certifies its truth: see *DCA*, s 94(1A) for the compulsory wording of the certificate. The certificate contains a warning as to the consequences of stating false information (which is an offence carrying a term of up to three years imprisonment – s 94A), and the statement itself is deemed to be an affidavit for the purposes of the *Evidence Act*: *DCA*, s 94(1B).

11.4.4 Service

Service of the above documentation must be made on the defendant personally at least 14 days before the date fixed for the hearing: *DCA*, s 94(2). An affidavit of service must be made within seven days and sent to the Court Clerk at least 72 hours before the hearing. Failure to comply with the time limit for service may nullify the proceedings: *The State v Rush; Ex parte Rush* [1984] PNGLR 124.

11.5 COMMITTAL WITHOUT A HEARING

11.5.1 Without consideration of the contents of the statements

As indicated above (11.3.1), a speedier procedure has been introduced, which the prosecution can use if the legally represented defendant is willing to waive the right to the conventional form of committal proceeding. The essence of the procedure under s 94B of the *District Courts Act* is that, if certain strict requirements are satisfied, the Magistrate may transmit the witness's statements and documentation to the National Court without considering their contents. The defendant will be committed for trial in the National Court without the District Court having exercised any judicial function other than the collection of the witness statements and a formal order of committal.

11.5.2 Requirements of s 94B

1. The Magistrate must be satisfied that all the evidence, whether for prosecution or defence, consists of written statements with or without exhibits. Section 94B of the *District Courts Act* does not specify what steps the Magistrate should take in order to be satisfied that the statements presented to him or her constitute all the evidence – unless the contents are examined (which the section is intended to avoid). It is suggested that the prosecutor and the defendant should be asked to confirm that they do not wish to submit any evidence other than the statements already lodged. Also, the evidence at this stage is committal evidence and the parties are not precluded from introducing further evidence at the trial, subject to the rules of the trial court.

2. The court must also be satisfied that service of the statements has occurred in accordance with s 94.

3. Committal under s 94B cannot occur where:

(a) the defendant or, if more than one, any one of the defendants does not have legal representation; or

(b) the legal representative of the defendant or of one of the defendants, as the case may be, requests the court to consider a submission that the statements do not disclose sufficient evidence to put the defendant on trial.

In other words, if the defendant has legal representation, the onus is on the defence to decide whether to challenge the form and/or content of the prosecution evidence at the committal stage. Provided reasonable time is allowed to the defence to make its decision, the Magistrate may be entitled to rely on the fact that no request has been received from a legal representative that the court should consider the submission that the witness statements do not disclose sufficient evidence.

11.6 INQUIRY INTO THE DOCUMENTATION UNDER S 94C

Where the court has not committed the defendant for trial under s 94B of the *District Courts Act*, it will proceed to the first stage of the committal hearing process. Here, the court's task is to consider the witness statements, documents and exhibits which have been served on the defendant (11.4 above) for the purpose of admitting them as evidence.

Before admitting a written statement, the court must be satisfied that the person who made the statement had read and understood it, or, if unable to read, had had it read to him or her in a language that he or she understood. Section 94C(2) establishes this requirement as a statutory test.

This is an inquiry which is independent of the trial process and one which the court must conduct in the exercise of its judicial function. In short, the Magistrate must ensure that:

- the statement was made by the maker of the statement whose name appears on the statement; and
- the maker of the statement had full knowledge of not only the contents of the statement, but also the correctness and truth of the statement: *The State v Kai Wabu* [1994] PNGLR 498.

After conducting the inquiry into the making of the witness statements, the Magistrate has a discretion to admit or reject any statement depending on his or her conclusion as to whether it satisfies the statutory test. Failure to conduct such an inquiry and to record its findings may result in the subsequent committal being voided: *The State v Kai Wabu*. A statement improperly obtained may be ruled inadmissible on appeal: *Hami Yawari v Tolimo English* [1996] PNGLR 446.

The requirements of s 94C(2) of the *District Courts Act* place a duty on the police informant, or any other person who obtains and records a statement in writing, to ensure that the maker of the statement reads the statement before he or she signs it. If the person cannot read, the statement must be read back to him or her. If the statement is to be recorded in a language different from the one used by the maker of the statement, then it must be read and translated to the person before he or she signs it. The assistance of an interpreter will often be required, and an endorsement should be made on the written statement certifying that the statement has been interpreted to its maker. In *The State v Kai Wabu* [1994] PNGLR 498 at 501, Injia AJ suggested a form of certificate that should be signed by the interpreter.

Without certificates as to the reading of a statement and/or the interpreting of it, the statement cannot be accepted, despite the fact that the maker has signed it in accordance with s 94(1A). The only way that defects in such certification requirements can be overcome is by calling the person or persons concerned to give oral evidence: *The State v Kai Wabu* [1994] PNGLR 498.

While it is clearly the responsibility of the Magistrate to be satisfied as to matters under s 94C, it is less clear whether the defendant may be heard on questions that he or she may wish to raise relating to compliance with the section. The Act is silent on the point: see also 11.7.1 and 11.7.2.

11.7 CONSIDERATION OF THE EVIDENCE

11.7.1 Sufficient evidence

Where all the written statements and oral evidence offered on the part of the prosecution have been received and tested to the Magistrate's satisfaction, the Magistrate moves on to consider, under s 95 of the *District Courts Act*, whether that evidence is sufficient to put the defendant on trial. The section heading of s 95 refers to a "prima facie case" and, in *R v McEachern* [1967-1968] PNGLR 48, the court held that the test is whether the Magistrate is of the opinion in good faith that there is a "sufficient prima facie case" against the defendant.

11.7.2 Witnesses

The Act is again silent as to whether witnesses may be called and questioned at this stage. As indicated in 11.6 above, a person who has made a written statement may have to be called in order to deal with otherwise fatal inadequacies in the statement, or the Magistrate may feel unable to understand the nature of the allegations made against the defendant without questioning one or two witnesses.

The Act is not clear as to the role of the defendant during this stage of the committal. On the one hand, the judgment of Woods J, in *Philip Nagira v Besasparis* [1986] PNGLR 199, refers to the constitutional right to examine the witnesses called by the prosecution, and to the fact that the defendant's right to question witnesses is traditionally part of the committal process. The court upheld the defendant's right to do so under the *District Courts Act*. On the other hand, there is the view that it is sufficient if the defendant's rights in relation to the prosecution evidence are protected in the course of his or her trial in the National Court: *Justin Wayne Tkatchenko v Dessy Magaru* (4 May 2000, OS 235 of 1999).

Subsection (3) of s 96, which was added to the section in 2000, states:

> "In an examination of a defendant in accordance with this Division [Div 1 – General] neither the defendant nor his legal representative shall be permitted to subject any witness to cross-examination."

This amending provision does not seem to determine the matter, because it appears to relate to the subsequent stage of the committal process, namely the examination of a defendant.

11.7.3 Outcome of decision

If the Magistrate decides that the evidence is insufficient, the Magistrate should discharge the defendant in accordance with s 95 of the *District Courts Act*. If the court is of the opinion that the evidence presented in accordance with ss 94 and 94C is sufficient to put the defendant on trial for an indictable offence, it then proceeds with the examination required by s 96: *DCA*, s 95(3).

11.8 EXAMINATION OF THE DEFENDANT

11.8.1 Explanation to the accused

Section 96 of the *District Courts Act* sets out the explanation which the Magistrate must give to the defendant after deciding that there is sufficient evidence to put the defendant on trial. Omission to give the explanation means that the subsequent proceedings are invalid and of no effect.

The court should take the following steps:

- **Read the charge to the accused.**
- **Explain its nature in ordinary language.**
- **Say to him or her the words set out in s 96, "or words to the same effect".**

Because the words in the section contain so much condensed information which might be confusing, it is recommended that the Magistrate should prepare and use his or her own words. The Magistrate should be able to explain the defendant's position more clearly, in his or her own words, "to the same effect" as the words of s 96.

Section 96 states:

"Having heard the evidence for the prosecution, do you want to be sworn and give evidence on your behalf, or do you desire to say anything in answer to the charge? You are not obliged to be sworn and give evidence, nor are you obliged to say anything, unless you desire to do so; but whatever evidence you may give upon oath, or anything you may say, will be taken down in writing and may be given in evidence upon your trial. You are clearly to understand that you have nothing to hope from any promise or favour and nothing to fear from any threat which may have been held out to you to induce you to make any admission or confession of your guilt; but whatever you now say may be given in evidence upon your trial, notwithstanding any promise or threat."

11.8.2 The Magistrate's duty to the unrepresented accused

It is accepted principle that the Magistrate's obligation to ensure that the hearing is conducted fairly, and in accordance with law, means that the Magistrate must explain to an unrepresented accused the rights and choices available to him or her in relation to the various matters which arise in court proceedings. On the other hand, the Magistrate is not obliged to recommend to the accused how to exercise those rights or what choices to make: see 3.2.2 above, for further discussion of the unrepresented accused.

The information that should be given to the accused, and the decisions the accused must make, are complex – and necessary in the interests of justice. However, if the accused is unrepresented, the warning required by s 96 of the *District Courts Act* does not seem to be enough on its own. Certainly the words of s 96 contain several explanations, some of which do inform the accused of his or her rights.

The rights may be summarised as the rights to:

- require the prosecution to prove its case without co-operation from the defendant (the presumption of innocence under s 37(4)(a) of the *Constitution*);
- silence (*Constitution*, s 37(10));
- make an unsworn statement without being questioned upon it; and
- give evidence and to call witnesses.

However, further explanation may be required. Unfortunately, the words provided for in s 96 fail to explain to the defendant the legal consequences of saying or not saying anything. Also, if the defendant chooses to say something, should he or she make a sworn statement or an unsworn statement? Unless the defendant is clearly advised as to the right of the prosecutor to cross-examine a defendant who gives sworn evidence, the defendant may not be in a position to make an informed decision on this vital point.

In *The State v Nagari Topoma* [1980] PNGLR 18, the court felt that if the defendant is not advised of the legal consequences of his or her options, the National Court may, in its discretionary power, reject the record of answers given by the defendant in response to cross-examination. Of course, it would only do so if it considered that, in all the circumstances, it was unfair to admit the answers.

11.8.3 Statement of the defendant

The explanation in s 96 of the *District Courts Act* contains a warning that any evidence that the defendant gives, or anything he or she may say in an unsworn statement, will be taken down in writing in accordance with s 96(2), read to him or her and then signed by the Magistrate. This statement of the defendant will be kept with the statements of the witnesses and transmitted to the Public Prosecutor.

It should further be noted that, if a defendant is committed for trial, a statement made by him or her under s 96 may be given in evidence without further proof at the trial, provided the statement purports to be signed by the Magistrate before whom it was made: *DCA*, s 97.

11.9 DISCHARGE OR COMMITTAL OF THE DEFENDANT

When the evidence (if any) tendered by the defendant has been considered, the court must decide whether the totality of the prosecution and defence evidence is sufficient to put the defendant on trial: *DCA*, s 100. As Akuram J said in *Backley Yarume v Sylvester Euga* (1996) N1476, the whole purpose of committal hearings is:

> "to gather evidence and assess it to see whether it is sufficient to commit the accused for trial ...This requires proper and reasonable assessment of the evidence with a view to seeing whether all the elements or ingredients of the offence are present".

This test of the sufficiency of the evidence is the same as the test required under s 95 of the *District Courts Act*: see 11.7.1 above. It is appropriate for the Magistrate to modify the earlier opinion formed under s 95 for the purpose of the decision under s 100: *R v McEachern* [1967-1968] PNGLR 48. See also *R v Wewak Resident Magistrate, Ex parte Dyer* [1967-1968] PNGLR 511 and *Arthur Gilbert Smedley v*

The State [1980] PNGLR 379.

> Having decided that the defendant should be put on trial, the court should:
>
> by warrant commit the defendant into custody until the appropriate sitting of the National Court; or
>
> admit him or her to bail (see Chapter 10).

11.10 DEFENDANT'S ADMISSION OF GUILT

If a defendant, on being asked in accordance with s 96 of the *District Courts Act* whether he or she has anything to say in answer to the charge, says that he or she is guilty of the charge, the Magistrate is required to commit the defendant to the National Court for sentence: *DCA*, s 103. Before announcing committal for sentence, the Magistrate should consider carefully whether the defendant has understood the information and explanations given under s 96, and, if necessary, question the defendant further as to his or her understanding of the significance of pleading guilty. Once satisfied, the Magistrate should announce the committal for sentence and ensure that the defendant's statement embodying the admission of guilt is taken down in writing. The statement must be signed by the Magistrate and, if he or she desires, by the defendant. As above, the defendant will be committed on warrant or released on bail.

11.11 WITNESS STATEMENTS MAY BE RELIED ON AS EVIDENCE AT TRIAL

When a person has been committed for trial or sentence, all statements tendered in evidence to the Magistrate may, with the consent of the National Court, be taken as evidence at the defendant's contested trial or sentence hearing in that court. No further proof of the statements is needed, provided that the prosecution can prove that they have been served on the defendant or his or her legal representative. This may be done by producing a certificate signed by the Magistrate to whom the statement was tendered, or by calling a witness to testify to service: *DCA*, s 102(b).

Furthermore, if at the trial a witness can be proved to have died, be insane, so ill as not to be able to travel, or "kept out of the way" by or on behalf of the defendant, the statement of that witness can be taken in evidence at the trial without further proof: *DCA*, s 102(a).

Chapter 12 – Guilty Pleas

This chapter offers a guide to the law and practice relating to taking the defendant's plea of guilty.

12.1 WHAT CONSTITUTES A GUILTY PLEA

A plea of guilty constitutes an admission of the essential ingredients of the offence charged. Collateral facts not essential to the legal definition of the offence, but which may be relevant to sentence as being matters of aggravation or mitigation, are not admitted by a plea of guilty, and may be challenged by the defendant.

Chapter 13.3 discusses the difficulty of making the important distinction between aggravating circumstances that are an actual element of the offence, and those which are not. Facts presented from the bar table and the problem of disputed facts and reliance on custom are also considered there.

A plea of not guilty of the specific offence charged, but guilty of some other alternative offence, is available only if the defendant pleads guilty to some other offence of which he or she could have been convicted by the court on facts arising out of the same circumstances.

The consequences of making such a plea are the same as if the charge to which the plea was made had actually been included on the charge sheet. There is no obligation on the prosecutor to accept such a plea and to abandon the more serious charge. However, the defendant's lawyer will often have discussed the matter with the prosecution and have advised the client to plead guilty to certain offences if the prosecution agrees not to lead any evidence in relation to the others: see 12.4.

12.2 SUMMARY OF PROCEDURE

The steps may be summarised as follows (see 4.8A):

- The charge is read to the defendant.
- If the defendant pleads guilty to the charge, the Magistrate should note the plea provisionally.
- The prosecutor reads a brief statement of the facts.
- The Magistrate asks the defendant if he or she wishes to say anything in answer to the charge.
- If not, the Magistrate may enter a plea of guilty.
- If the defendant makes a statement which raises a possible defence, the Magistrate should change the plea to not guilty and proceed to trial. An adjournment may be necessary.
- If the plea of guilty is accepted, the Magistrate proceeds to hear what the prosecution and defence have to say on the question of penalty.

12.3 SIGNIFICANCE OF GUILTY PLEA

By pleading guilty, the defendant waives the constitutional right to require the prosecution to prove the charge. Any opportunity to challenge the evidence which would establish the elements of the charge is lost.

A guilty plea does not, of itself, amount to a conviction, even though it has been accepted by the prosecution. It must also be expressly or impliedly accepted by the Magistrate. Of course, by moving on to ask about prior convictions, or asking the defendant whether he or she has anything to say before sentence is passed, the Magistrate has accepted the plea as one of guilty.

The defendant's guilty plea in committal proceedings is dealt with in 11.8 and 11.10.

12.4 SAFEGUARDS IN THE LAW AND PRACTICE

12.4.1 The unrepresented defendant

The situation of the unrepresented defendant has attracted much attention from the courts, and no area is of more concern than the decision to plead guilty or not guilty. The subject is introduced in 3.5 and 4.8A. The *Constitution* emphasises the concepts of presumption of innocence, information in detail, understanding the language and adequate time and facilities: *Constitution*, s 37(4)(a)-(d), and 6.2.3 above.

12.4.2 The Magistrate's duty

The court is not obliged to accept a plea of guilty. It is the duty of the Magistrate to make absolutely sure that the defendant understands the elements of the charges to which he or she pleads: *Moses Aikabi v Ephraim Tami* [1971] PNGLR 1550. Whenever the Magistrate is in any doubt as to whether or not the defendant is pleading guilty, the Magistrate should enter a plea of not guilty and proceed to hear the evidence against the defendant.

Appearances can be deceiving. Magistrates should take considerable care when a defendant appears to plead guilty to a charge. Magistrates have a discretion as to whether or not they accept what appears to be a guilty plea. They should check by questioning the defendant. For instance, if the defendant says, when asked to plead to a charge of assault, "Yes, I hit him, but I did it to stop him hitting me", the Magistrate should enter a plea of not guilty, because a defence of self-defence has been raised.

After the charge has been read through once, the best way is for the Magistrate then to put the elements of the offence to the defendant one at a time and note his or her replies. This may mean reading the relevant facts that relate to each element and asking the defendant whether he or she accepts those facts. This is so particularly if a question, when translated into Pisin or a local language, sounds like an accusation or a statement. It may be better to put the words into some form such as "The police say 'xxx', have they told it correctly?" and "What do you say about what the police have said?": see *Eliza v Mandina* [1971-1972] PNGLR 422.

The Magistrate should also remember that the circumstances of aggravation surrounding the alleged offence have to be proved by the prosecution, and these facts also should be put carefully to the defendant.

When dealing with an unrepresented defendant, a Magistrate should use simple language and avoid the use of words and phrases which, though well understood by Magistrates, police and lawyers, may confuse people not familiar with the courts.

The Magistrate must be cautious and not turn the taking of the plea into an interrogation of the defendant. It is up to the prosecution to prove its case against the defendant, and not for the defendant to convict himself or herself out of his or her own mouth. A lengthy interrogation, in which the defendant is encouraged to tell his or her story, could amount to breach of the defendant's right under s 37(10) of the *Constitution*, namely, "No person shall be compelled to be a witness against himself". Also, the Magistrate must avoid giving the defendant the impression that he or she is expected to admit committing the offence with which he or she is charged.

12.4.3 Improper influence to obtain a guilty plea

Before accepting a plea of guilty in any case in which a police officer is the complainant and the accused is not represented by a lawyer, the Magistrate should point out to the accused that the severity of penalties does not depend on whether he or she pleads guilty or not guilty. The Magistrate might inquire of the accused whether any police officer has suggested that the accused should plead guilty. If the Magistrate does not receive from the accused a prompt and convincing rejection of any such suggestion, the Magistrate should advise the accused to plead not guilty.

This statement was adopted as a "rule of prudence" in *R v Cervetto and Ibara, Ex parte Madaha-Rabura* [1965-1966] PNGLR 110. In that case, it was clear that a police constable had urged the defendant to plead guilty, by saying that the court would be harder on her if she denied the offence.

12.5 PLEA-BARGAINING

Prosecution and defence, for their own and often different reasons, may agree to avoid a hearing on a charge, perhaps preferring a guilty plea on a lesser charge. These agreements are often described as the process of "plea-bargaining", which may describe two different practices.

1. The first and most common practice is that of discussions between prosecution and defence to negotiate the exchange of guilty pleas to some charges for the withdrawal of other charges (sometimes known as "charge-bargaining").

2. The second practice, permitted in very few countries, involves discussions between counsel and the trial judge in relation to the sentence likely to be imposed if a guilty plea is accepted. This practice is regarded as unacceptable in Papua New Guinea. It is not the same thing as a situation which may arise after the defendant has pleaded guilty and the sentencing process has begun. The Magistrate may decide to give an advance indication of the likely sentence, or the range within which the sentence is likely to fall. Such advance indication may help to focus the minds of the prosecutor and defence counsel as to what further information might assist the Magistrate in arriving at a final decision.

Where several charges have been laid, the defendant's lawyer may discuss with the prosecution the defendant's willingness to plead guilty to some charges, provided the prosecution will agree not to proceed with those that are not admitted. Because the choice of charges that a defendant faces rests entirely with the prosecution, and does not involve the courts, Judges and Magistrates have not directly criticised such practices. However, there is potential for abuse. The police or prosecutor may "over-charge" a defendant in order to negotiate a guilty plea on a reduced, less serious charge. Also, the defendant may not understand the significance of such an arrangement and may fail to appreciate the possibility of realistic defences to the more serious charge. For these reasons, the courts have stressed the importance of ensuring that a guilty plea is not made through mistake, ignorance, or as a result of duress. This applies especially if the defendant is unrepresented. In fact, it would be considered unfair for a prosecutor to approach an unrepresented defendant with a view to conducting plea negotiations.

"Plea-bargaining" is open to abuse, particularly as it is conducted in secret. It is also very much the responsibility of the prosecution. In *The State v Jack Gola and Mopana Aure* [1990] PNGLR 206, Brunton J considered the role of the Public Prosecutor and State Prosecutor in relation to decisions about proceeding with charges following discussions with counsel for the defence. He said (at 214):

> "The essence of the system of law that has developed from English and Australian antecedents, in Papua New Guinea, is that the system of justice must be open, above board, and capable of respect by the public. While the *Constitution* and the statutes vest in the Public Prosecutor the discretion to choose the charge on which to lay an indictment, the exercise of that discretion must be such as to appear to conform with the expectations of society.
>
> It may well be that in some cases the State Prosecutors feel that the evidence and witnesses may not be sufficient to obtain a conviction on a trial, and that it is better to accept a plea to a lesser charge, rather than end up with an acquittal. But this has to be balanced against the need to maintain public confidence in the system as a whole. Certainly the appearance of having decisions made out of court between opposing counsel as to what charge is to be preferred, and what charge is to be pleaded to, should be avoided."

While this judicial concern is understandable, it is difficult to see how the courts can give effect to it. If the Magistrate becomes aware of improper practice involving prosecutor and/or defence counsel in relation to plea-bargaining, a report may be made to the office of the State or Public Prosecutor, or to the Lawyers Statutory Committee: see 3.4. The Magistrate's concern is that justice be done.

12.6 PROCEDURE ON A PLEA OF GUILTY

The procedure on a plea of guilty is the same as that which is followed in relation to a finding of guilt after a trial. The acceptance of the plea constitutes proof of the guilt of the defendant.

12.6.1 Previous convictions

Before other matters are considered, any previous convictions should be put to the defendant at this point. If the previous convictions are admitted by the defendant, or the issue of previous convictions has been dealt with, the court will administer the *allocutus*, which is the question put to the defendant calling on him or her to take the opportunity to address the court in mitigation of penalty: see 13.2.

If the defendant does not admit the previous convictions, the prosecutor may either abandon the allegations or seek an adjournment in order to produce evidence to prove them.

A previous conviction is taken to mean not only a prior conviction, but also findings of guilt by a criminal court where the defendant has been punished by some form of sanction such as a fine, adjournment of sentence, compensation order, or release on probation subject to conditions.

A person may only be lawfully dealt with as a second offender if the conviction for the first offence has been recorded before both the acts and the conviction which constitute the second offence. Subsequent offences which do not satisfy this test cannot be taken into account as "previous convictions" to increase the penalty that would otherwise be imposed for the present offence. However, subsequent offences may be relevant as part of the offender's past history.

12.6.2 Withdrawal of guilty plea

Leave to withdraw a plea of guilty after conviction is a *discretionary* matter. Once a clear plea of guilty has been entered and the court proceeds to consider sentence, the prisoner is regarded as having been convicted, and it is wholly a matter of the court's discretion as to whether the conviction should be set aside and the plea of guilty vacated. This may be regarded as part of the underlying law of Papua New Guinea. Decisions in other jurisdictions that limit the exercise of this discretion in certain ways should not be followed in this country: see *Gabriel Laku v The State* [1981] PNGLR 350.

Chapter 13 – Sentencing

13.1 PURPOSE

The primary purpose of the criminal justice system is said to be fourfold:

13.1.1 Retribution

Punishment is, in part, a form of retaliation against the offender. People in society expect that certain conduct will be punished. If it is not punished, their sense of justice will be outraged. Action by the state will discourage victims and friends from taking private revenge of a violent nature, which would be unacceptable in today's society. It has been said that retribution as a proper purpose of punishment is not foreign to the cultures of the people of this country. This is what is normally referred to as "payback": *Acting Public Prosecutor v Uname Aumane* [1980] PNGLR 510.

13.1.2 Deterrence

Penalties for certain conduct will deter people from engaging in it. The offender will be deterred from repeating it, and other potential offenders will be deterred by knowledge of the penalty. From time to time, however, statistics show that punishment for many types of crimes is not an effective deterrent, particularly where the causes of crime lie in the social and economic spheres.

The court must take general deterrence into account, despite limits on its effectiveness: *The State v Keputong Nagong (1980) N225*; *Acting Public Prosecutor v Uname Aumane* [1980] PNGLR 510. Deterrence may mark the disapproval by the law of the conduct in question, and there is the hope that other people will be deterred from like behaviour. In some cases deterrence must take priority, even in the case of young first offenders: *Luneme Meuso v Maiak Nagy* (1978) N139. However, deterrence is a proper consideration so long as it does not result in a convicted person being made the scapegoat of other people who have committed similar crimes but have not been caught and convicted. To make a person a scapegoat constitutes an unsound exercise of discretion: *Wilkeson, Stephens and Michalov v Grant* [1967-1968] PNGLR 112. There is also the question of whether a sentence that the court has in mind is likely to have a deterrent effect on the offender.

13.1.3 Restraint

Through its capacity to imprison and otherwise detain offenders, the criminal justice system can protect society from dangerous individuals.

13.1.4 Rehabilitation

If imprisoned in appropriate circumstances and able to undergo a suitable rehabilitative program, an offender may be assisted in such a way that he or she is unlikely to commit crimes in the future. On the one hand, while rehabilitation is one of the purposes for punishment, it should not be allowed to obscure the consideration of deterrence and protection of the public from the commission of crimes: *John Elipa Kalabus v The State* [1988] PNGLR 193. On the other hand, the prospects of the rehabilitation of young offenders must always be a matter of concern for the courts: see 13.5.7 and 13.5.11.

13.2 THE SENTENCING HEARING

13.2.1 Invitation to defendant and the right to be heard: allocutus

Where a defendant has pleaded guilty or has been found guilty after trial, the criminal process moves to the sentencing stage. Before this begins, or at the beginning of the sentencing hearing, the question of previous convictions is dealt with. The prosecution should put the details of these to the defendant. The nature and significance of previous convictions are discussed in 12.6.1. The sentence hearing proceeds with the court giving the defendant a clear invitation to address the court ("allocutus") before sentence is passed. Section 593 of the *Criminal Code* uses the traditional wording – "the proper officer shall ask [the defendant] if he has anything to say why sentence should not be passed on him". The Latin word "allocutus" and the wording of the Code do not explain adequately what is involved at the sentencing stage: *The State v Bafe Quati* [1990] PNGLR 57.

Frequently, the Magistrate will adjourn to allow time for preparation of plea material. The defendant may be remanded in custody or released on bail.

The courts of Papua New Guinea have accepted that the defendant must always be invited to address the court, either directly or through a lawyer, and, if he or she wishes, to call evidence on the question of penalty. Failure to give this invitation, and to provide the necessary opportunities to the defendant, is a denial of natural justice and may render any sentence pronounced a nullity: *Moses Aikaba v Tami* [1971-1972] PNGLR 155. This is an appropriate stage for the defendant to raise any allegation of breach of constitutional rights, such as police conduct affecting rights under ss 36 or 37(17) of the *Constitution*. These matters may be raised by the defendant as relevant to sentence, but they may have to be proved and the prosecution should be given a right to reply: *The State v Bafe Quati* [1990] PNGLR 57.

Natural justice in the sentencing process may also require the Magistrate to permit the offender to re-open his or her sentencing plea after it has concluded (but before sentence), if additional critical material needs to be put to the court. It is a denial of natural justice for the Magistrate to fail to obtain sufficient facts upon which to found the sentence. Such failures may render the sentencing process a nullity and give grounds for appeal.

Questions of enforcement of, and compensation for, breaches of constitutional rights would have to be referred to the National Court, if contested.

13.2.2 Role of defence counsel

Representations by defence counsel at the sentencing stage have an important impact on the sentencing outcome. Counsel's task is to confirm or, if necessary, challenge the factual basis upon which sentence is to be imposed (which is more likely to be appropriate in the case of a guilty plea) and to highlight to the court mitigating factors present in the circumstances of the offence and the offender's background. Counsel's duty to the client is to aim to obtain the least punitive sanction available for the offence which has been committed. Counsel is expected to assist the court with such options as compensation, restriction of movement and probation, which the Magistrate is required to give some thought to in many cases. The Magistrate should not hesitate to make demands on counsel in order to obtain the information that the Magistrate feels is necessary for the proper disposition of the case. In matters involving custom, counsel has a statutory duty to assist the court with evidence and information: *Underlying Law Act*, ss 15 and 16; see also 2.3.8.4 and 3.4.2.

Defence counsel has no duty to disclose anything to the Magistrate regarding the offender's prior convictions, or other information adverse to the offender's interests. Nevertheless, if counsel knows that the offender has prior convictions which appear to be unknown to, or overlooked by, the prosecution, counsel cannot make an assertion as to his or her client's absence of prior convictions. To do this would be to mislead the court.

13.2.3 Role of the prosecution

The courts acknowledge that it is the duty of the prosecutor to assist the court in the sentencing process by an adequate presentation of facts surrounding the commission of the offence, particularly where, as on a plea of guilty, the full circumstances of the offence have not been revealed by evidence before the court.

In *Acting Public Prosecutor v Uname Aumane* [1980] PNGLR 510, the court took the opportunity to note that, by 1980, the practice had developed in Papua New Guinea where the prosecution rarely made submissions on sentence, leaving the matter up to defence counsel and the court. It was pointed out that, as the Public Prosecutor has a statutory right of appeal, it also has a duty to avoid appealable error in the trial court. Furthermore, the Public Prosecutor has a duty to the court to assist in the task of passing sentence. For example, there are sentencing matters which the Magistrate usually must consider and which require input from the prosecutor – such as payment of compensation, restriction of movement and probation. The Magistrate should, therefore, urge the prosecution to address the court on sentencing matters. These may include matters of custom: *Underlying Law Act*, ss 15 and 16.

The onus of alleging and proving prior convictions, or other background information adverse to the offender, is on the prosecution, unless admitted by the defendant. If the offender's co-defendants have been convicted and sentenced earlier in other courts, the prosecutor is responsible for advising the court how they have been dealt with. The prosecutor should draw the Magistrate's attention to any principles of sentencing relevant to the present case, and the prosecutor is entitled to test the defence claims that mitigating circumstances exist.

When requested by the Magistrate, the prosecutor should assist the court by a submission on any social danger represented by the offender's conduct, or the range of sentences which might be reasonably open to the court in relation to offences of a like nature.

13.2.4 Delivery and record of decision

As indicated in 4.6 and 4.8, and discussed in Chapter 25, the Magistrate should conclude the sentencing process by delivering his or her decision in open court. The defendant must be asked to stand, and the Magistrate should address his or her remarks directly to the defendant. If necessary, they should be interpreted into the language used by the defendant. It is essential that the importance of the court's sentence upon the defendant be made clear to the defendant in this direct manner. The significance of this occasion as a judicial act within the administration of justice cannot be left to the defendant's counsel to pass on to his or her client.

Reasons for the sentence should be given to the defendant and recorded in the appropriate court records. Although the statutes do not require Magistrates to give their reasons for sentence unless an appeal is lodged, Magistrates should record their reasons while the circumstances are fresh in their minds. Of course, the record must agree with the spoken words, because the reasons announced publicly constitute the decision. In matters involving custom, the court's responsibilities regarding decisions are discussed in 2.3.8, 2.4 and 25.6.4.

13.3 SENTENCING FACTS

13.3.1 Circumstances of aggravation

Although a Magistrate must consider the circumstances of the offence, and whether any aggravating factors are present, the offender cannot be sentenced for any crime with which he or she has not been charged, or in relation to which he or she has not been found guilty. Circumstances of aggravation (such as the use of firearms in committing the offence, the seriousness of injury caused, or the quantities of drugs found) which are referred to in the statutory provision creating an offence may be either an element in the definition of the offence itself, or a factor relevant only to sentence. This is a matter of statutory interpretation.

13.3.1.1 Element of the offence

If the aggravating circumstances are an actual element in the offence, they should be alleged in the charge or indictment and proved by the prosecutor as part of the substantive offence charged.

13.3.1.2 Not an element of the offence

If the aggravating factors are relevant only to sentence, they need not be charged and it is for the Magistrate to decide whether they exist: see 13.5.12. It is important to note that circumstances of aggravation which could have been made the subject of a separate charge, or which may have warranted a conviction for a more serious offence, but were not so used, should not be relied upon as aggravating factors in fixing sentence: see *Toiona v Bryant* [1969-1970] PNGLR 201.

13.3.2 Facts on plea of guilty

13.3.2.1 From the bar table

A guilty plea itself, although admitting the essential ingredients of the offence and negativing all possible defences, does not admit any of the circumstances of aggravation which are not elements of the offence and which might be alleged or implied by the prosecution: *R v Gabai Vagi* [1973] PNGLR 30. Nor does a guilty plea negative any circumstances of mitigation. On a plea of guilty in the District Court, facts relevant to the circumstances of the offence are normally supplied by the prosecutor reading a summary of the charge and of the circumstances as agreed to by the defence. The Magistrate can also be informed from material in witness statements in the possession of the prosecution.

The Magistrate can accept supplementary and additional material raised by the defence without requiring that it be supported by evidence on oath. When a plea of guilty avoids the necessity for a trial, it is no doubt convenient for the facts relevant to sentence to be stated from the bar table to the extent to which those facts are agreed on or, not being reasonably open to challenge, remain unchallenged.

13.3.2.2 Disputed facts and custom

On the other hand, if the alleged act or circumstance is not common ground between prosecution and defence, that act or circumstance should be proved by the calling of evidence by the party on whom the evidentiary onus rests: *Acting Public Prosecutor v Uname Aumane* [1980] PNGLR 510. Where the defence relies on a custom in mitigation of sentence, it is not sufficient for the custom merely to be explained from the bar table. A custom must be proved, particularly just what the custom is and whether the defendant has complied with it. According to s 16 of the *Underlying Law Act*, custom is a question of law and not fact. A Magistrate may ascertain custom by reference to cases, books and official statements, as well as evidence adduced by the parties or on the Magistrate's own initiative. Section 15 of the Act places a duty on counsel to assist the court: see 2.3.8.4 and 3.4.2.

If, on a sentencing plea, one side or the other disputes an assertion of fact relevant to sentence, or if the Magistrate has indicated an unwillingness to act on the version of the facts tendered by the parties, admissible evidence may be adduced to establish the facts. This will normally be sworn evidence called by both parties. More frequently, where the defendant asserts facts in mitigation, the Magistrate will accept that version unless there is good reason to require sworn evidence.

13.3.3 Standard of proof

The standard of proof applicable to sentencing matters which go beyond the basic factual elements of the offence that have been established by the finding or plea of guilt, varies, according to the consequences of the facts in question. If the prosecution alleges facts detrimental to the defendant, or if the Magistrate proposes to take into account additional facts relating to the circumstances of the offence or the offender in a way that is adverse to the interests of the offender, the defendant may object. Proof of those facts is required beyond reasonable doubt: *William Norris v The State* [1979] PNGLR 605. However, where the facts proposed to be taken into account are in the offender's favour and would mitigate the penalty, the Magistrate need only be satisfied of them on the balance of probabilities. Of course, in the majority of cases, prosecution and defence do not dispute the facts relating to sentence.

13.4 SENTENCING PRINCIPLES

The only purposes for which sentences may be imposed are those stated in 13.1 above. The broad principles discussed in this section have been accepted as generally applicable to sentencing: see the cases annotated at s 596 of the *Criminal Code* (*CC*) in *Criminal Law Practice and Procedure*. Specific matters which must be considered are dealt with in 13.5.

13.4.1 Proportionality

The principle of proportionality in sentencing means that the extent and type of punishment should be in proportion to the gravity of the harm and the degree of responsibility of the offender. This principle does not permit an increase in sentence beyond that which is commensurate with the seriousness of the crime, even for the purpose of a longer prison sentence in order to protect society. The principle of proportionality is breached if the sanction is either too severe or too lenient.

In relation to persons who may be regarded as serious repeat offenders, the courts often go beyond what the offender's latest crime warrants by way of proportion of sentence in order to protect the community from future danger if these persons re-offend: *CC*, s 596.

13.4.2 Concurrent or cumulative sentences and the totality principle

Unless the court otherwise orders, a sentence of imprisonment on conviction on indictment takes effect from the first day of the sittings of the court at which the offender is convicted and, on summary conviction, takes effect from the commencement of the offender's custody under that sentence. This means that two or more sentences of imprisonment will be concurrent unless the court orders that they be cumulative so as to take effect one after the other: see *CC*, s 20. In *Mase v The State* [1991] PNGLR 88, the court observed:

> "It is clearly laid down by this Court in the cases referred to that there are three stages to go through in coming to a total sentence. [1] The first step is to consider the appropriate sentence for each offence charged, and then [2] consideration should be given as to whether they should be concurrent sentences or cumulative sentences. [3] Where the decision is made to make two or more sentences cumulative, the court is required to look at the total sentence and see if it is just and appropriate. If it is not, the court must vary one or more of the sentences to get a just total. This principle must be observed because a straightforward addition of sentences usually leads to a total sentence that is excessive in the whole circumstances."

It is clearly difficult for a Magistrate to arrive at a total sentence which is just and proportionate to the totality of the criminal behaviour involved in all the offences concerned. There is no hard and fast rule to be followed, and, of course, the maximum penalties provided by law for each offence should be taken into account. As was pointed out in *Mase v The State* [1991] PNGLR 88, although maximum sentences may be justified in the "worst type" of cases, there are many situations where cases of the "more serious type" would, if handled by way of aggregate sentences, seem to be altogether too crushing, especially on young people: *CC*, ss 20 and 596.

13.4.3 Plea of guilty

While a plea of guilty may be taken into account in the offender's favour in mitigating the penalty, the converse is not true. An offender must not receive a more severe sentence for having exercised the right to plead not guilty and contest the case.

An early guilty plea carries greater mitigatory weight than a later one. Where a guilty plea is accompanied by co-operation with the police in apprehending and convicting a principal offender, a sentence reduction may be justified: see *Kali Mari v The State* (1980) SC175 and *Elipa Kalabus v The State* [1988] PNGLR 193. A plea of guilty in order to show remorse, or a desire to save a victim the trauma or unpleasantness of appearing as a witness at the trial, may carry some weight.

13.4.4 Co-operating with authorities

A sentence discount may be offered to defendants who act as informers against fellow criminals. Disclosing other as yet uncharged offences may mitigate the penalty.

13.5 MATTERS WHICH MUST BE CONSIDERED

13.5.1 "Yes, I have considered them all"

Throughout, the Magistrate must have in mind the four primary purposes of the criminal justice system: see 13.1. There are certain matters to which Magistrates must have regard in imposing sentence. These matters are all relevant to sentence, which means that the Magistrate must be able to say – "Yes, I have considered them all". In case of the aggravating or mitigating factors, the Magistrate may in fact attach relatively little significance to some and greater weight to others: see Chalmers, Injia, Weisbrot and Andrew, *Criminal Law and Practice of Papua New Guinea*, Ch 3, s 596.

13.5.2 Statutory maximum penalty

The maximum punishment prescribed by law should be reserved for only the worse cases: see *CC*, s 19. It is a general principle of sentencing that the maximum penalty applies only to the most serious instances of an offence, the worst possible case normally encountered in practice. This is an application of the "principle of proportionality" referred to in 13.4.1.

On the other hand, the fact that a case falls into the worst type category does not mean that the maximum sentence automatically applies. For example, if the accused is 14 years of age, the maximum sentence of life imprisonment for murder would not be appropriate: *John Elipa Kalabus v The State* [1988] PNGLR 193.

A Magistrate must take all the circumstances into account. In *Pius Endari v Senior Constable Wangiwa* (1973) No 751, where a Magistrate imposed the maximum punishment in four cases of stealing, he was entitled to do so on the ground that they involved deliberately stealing from unsophisticated victims after warnings of the illegality, and no compensation was paid to the victims.

13.5.3 Statutory minimum penalty

The court should not use any minimum prescribed by law as a base figure. If the court decides that a custodial sentence is appropriate, it should consider what sentence it would impose if there was no minimum provided. If this is the same or less than the minimum, then it should impose the minimum sentence. If it is higher than the minimum, then it is appropriate to impose the higher sentence: *Boas Kuna v*

Police (1994) No 1296. For a fuller discussion of minimum penalties see *Supreme Court Reference No 1 of 1984: Re Minimum Penalties Legislation* [1984] PNGLR 314.

13.5.4 Statutory considerations

13.5.4.1 Payment of compensation

See 6.8.2.

13.5.4.2 Restriction of movement

See 6.8.3.

13.5.5 Current sentencing practices

13.5.5.1 Scale of penalties

General policies as to sentences may be set, but not by way of fixing a rigid scale of penalties. Only the Parliament may do that by way of legislation. If Magistrates were to attempt to do that, in advance, they would be abdicating their statutory duty to exercise their discretion in each case in accordance with the facts disclosed: *Guje Beng v Billey Kombel* [1975] PNGLR 49. If a rigid scale of penalties is applied, and the Magistrate does not take into account circumstances special to the offender that ought to have been weighed in his or her favour, a substantial miscarriage of justice has occurred.

13.5.5.2 Parity

As a general rule, members of the judiciary try to achieve some parity in sentencing – to ensure that, across the country, there is no gross inconsistency between sentences handed down for similar offences in similar circumstances.

13.5.5.3 Discretion in each case

It is perfectly proper for a meeting of Magistrates to agree upon a pattern of punishments from time to time, provided the pattern is not adopted rigidly and provided discretion is exercised: *Johnson Takovong v Tino Tarerea* (1975) No 837. A Magistrate cannot put aside the duty to exercise discretion in each particular case simply by relying on a general scale of penalties drawn up by himself or herself or the bench generally. An appeal from the District Court was allowed in a case where the Magistrate stated that, as a matter policy, all persons convicted on stealing charges would get a three months sentence rather than a fine, and that all repeat offenders would receive the maximum sentence. "Each case, if justice is to be done, must be considered on its own background. Every convicted person is a separate individual": *Vagi Gau v Ken Kone Eava* [1976] PNGLR 485. Because each case must be considered on its own facts, it is sometimes helpful for a Magistrate to think in terms of the balancing of the various interests. In *The State v Uname Aumane* [1980] PNGLR 510, the court considered that it had three interests to balance:

> "1. The first is the interest of the State. Collective living within a nation state demands that individuals and villagers, tribes and communities have to give up a little of their territorial and personal sovereignty.
>
> 2. But the nation and its arms of the law must also recognise the interests of the community to which the offenders belong. This second consideration – the impact of the penalty on the community to which the offender belongs – must be a foremost consideration.
>
> 3. The third consideration is the question of the prisoners themselves.": *CC*, s 596.

13.5.6 Nature and gravity of the offence

The main indication of the seriousness of an offence is seen in the maximum (and any minimum) sentence set by Parliament: see 13.5.2 and 13.5.3.

13.5.6.1 Prevalence

The court may also wish to take into account evidence as to the prevalence of a particular offence in a particular area.

13.5.6.2 Community perception

It is not wrong in principle to have regard to the prevailing community perception of the relative seriousness of offences. This perception may be reflected in the level of sentences: *Mase v The State* [1991] PNGLR 88; *CC*, s 596.

13.5.7 Culpability – how blameworthy is the offender?

13.5.7.1 Participation

The degree of participation of one offender, among others who were also involved, would not normally prevail as a mitigating factor where the criminal act depended on each offender actively playing his or her part: *Gimble v The State* [1988-1989] PNGLR 272. However, in a case where two members of a larger group are the only ones arrested, there may be justification for less than the maximum penalty on the ground of lesser participation: *The State v Peter Plesman; The State v Paul Moaina* (1997) N1657.

13.5.7.2 Course of criminal conduct

It may be relevant whether the offence was part of a course or series of criminal acts.

13.5.7.3 Ignorance of the law

While this is not a defence, it may be relevant to blameworthiness: *Ulao Amentasi v Secretary for Law* [1975] PNGLR 134.

13.5.7.4 Conduct of victim

Where the victim has offered some aggravation or provocation that does not amount to an offence, this may be taken into account in appropriate circumstances: *Ure Hane v The State* [1984] PNGLR 105.

13.5.7.5 Moral guilt

In some circumstances, the degree of moral guilt of an offender may be relevant: *The State v Panikuiaka Nope* (1979) N195, and in the Supreme Court at [1979] PNGLR 536.

13.5.7.6 Obedience to custom

Under s 4(e) of the *Customs Recognition Act*, custom is to be taken into account in determining the penalty (if any) to be imposed on a guilty party. With regard to establishing what the appropriate custom is, if any, s 16 of the *Underlying Law Act* stipulates that custom is a question of law and not fact. A Magistrate may ascertain custom by reference to cases, books and official statements, as well as evidence adduced by the parties or on the Magistrate's own initiative: see 2.3.8, 2.4, 5.13 and 25.6.4. This means that a particular custom may be taken into account to explain the offender's behaviour. For example, the offender may have committed the offence under customary pressure. Custom becomes a mitigating factor providing a cultural justification of the offender's behaviour that reduces his or her culpability or blameworthiness. In some instances, the custom may increase the seriousness of behaviour. In incest cases, the offence may be regarded in custom as particularly immoral, and custom may call for more severe punishment.

Similarly, the *Customs Recognition Act* means that the court may take into account customary punishment which the court is aware will be inflicted upon the accused regardless of any sentence the court imposes: *R v Jim Kaupa* (1973) No 765.

Genuine belief in the power of sorcery is a mitigating factor in sentence. This is related to the discussion of custom above at 7.15.3, and see s 596 of the *Criminal Code*.

It should be noted that, although the court may increase or decrease the sentence depending on custom, the court is still bound to impose an appropriate sentence as contemplated by Parliament: see 13.5.2 and *Acting Public Prosecutor v Uname Aumane* [1980] PNGLR 510 and *CC*, s 596.

13.5.7.7 Position of trust

Breach of a position of trust may warrant a heavier sentence: *Meaoa v The State* (1996) SC504; *The State v Paulus Takesi* (1996) N1468.

13.5.7.8 Youthfulness

Although the offender may be over the age of 16 (see 6.7 above), youthfulness may be an important mitigating factor: *Passingan v Beaton* [1971-1972] PNGLR 206. However, where breaking and entering has become prevalent and is normally committed by young persons, they may not receive special treatment unless there are exceptional circumstances: *Paulus Mandatititip v The State* [1978] PNGLR 128 and *Acting Public Prosecutor v Joe Kovea Mailai* [1981] PNGLR 258. There is concern that young first offenders should not be sent to jail, and Magistrates should give consideration to probation orders where possible. Punishment for young offenders should be rehabilitative. To the extent that prisons do not make separate provision for young persons, the age of a person is a circumstance which the court should consider: *Acting Public Prosecutor v Clement Maki and Tom Kasan* (1981) SC205.

A number of cases have discussed the problems of dealing with young offenders, such as (in addition to those referred to above) *Paia Lifi v Phillip Dege* (1981) N291; *Kuri Willie v The State* [1987] PNGLR 298; *The State v Nyama* [1991] PNGLR 127; and *The State v Willie Paul Songul* (1997) CR No 771 (National Court).

13.5.7.9 Lack of sophistication

It is relevant for the court to have regard to the offender's degree of sophistication and the traditional ways of the community from which he or she comes as important in arriving at an appropriate sentence. On the other hand, the courts are careful not to over-emphasise such considerations. More recent statements are to the effect that, subject to exceptional circumstances, lack of sophistication can no longer be an excuse for reduction of sentence: *Public Prosecutor v Keru and Moroi* [1985] PNGLR 78; followed in *The State v Miriam Kakun* (1997) N1673: *CC*, s 596.

13.5.7.10 Diminished responsibility

Although diminished responsibility that does not amount to insanity is no defence, justice requires that an offender's diminished responsibility should be taken into account in mitigation of sentence: *The State v Eric Gordon Berry* [1977] PNGLR 128.

13.5.7.11 Alcohol

The courts have generally not permitted the alcohol factor to have significant bearing on sentences. A person who voluntarily gets drunk must know that the capacity to control himself or herself will be impaired. Alcohol may have some relevance in certain circumstances, such as provocation or a severe case of diminished responsibility: see 7.11 and *Kesino Apo v The State* [1988] PNGLR 182; *Mase v The State* [1991] PNGLR 88; and *The State v Patrick* (1995) N1355.

13.5.8 Personal circumstances of the victim, and nature and extent of injury, loss or damage caused

It is always appropriate, and in some cases necessary, for the prosecution to inform the court of these matters.

13.5.9 Restitution made; compensation paid; traditional settlement

13.5.9.1 Restitution

In cases concerning misappropriation and stealing, guilty pleas coupled with full restitution may be significant factors in mitigation. Together, they go a long way to redressing the harm done: *The State v William Welford* (1986) N572. Full restitution may be indicative of genuine remorse and unqualified recognition of wrongdoing.

13.5.9.2 Customary compensation

The payment and acceptance of customary compensation is a mitigating factor, but mitigation will depend on the facts of each case and the relevant custom must be properly proved in court: *Acting Public Prosecutor v Nitak Mangilonde Taganis* [1982] PNGLR 299. Section 16 of the *Underlying Law Act* stipulates that custom is a question of law, and a Magistrate may ascertain custom by reference to a range of materials: see 2.3.8, 2.4, 5.13 and 25.6.4. The *Criminal Law (Compensation) Act* makes the award of compensation a punishment, and recognises that the payment of customary compensation is an honourable exercise in exchange in order to restore peace and harmony between the relatives of the parties involved: see 6.8.2; *The State v Peter Kose Weena* [1993] PNGLR 168; and *The State v Philip Susuve Raipa* [1994] N1268. Compensation is not to be considered as a way of buying one's liberty. If it is paid in accordance with custom, it amounts to an acceptance of legal and moral responsibility. Appropriately managed, it is an effective deterrent. It creates continuing obligations on the part of the offender, who has to live with the people wronged: *The State v Tendi Kalio Ulo* [1980] PNGLR 350.

13.5.9.3 Traditional settlement

Where a traditional settlement has occurred, it may be appropriate in certain cases for the court to release the offender on a good behaviour bond: *The State v Paul Pokolou* (1983) N404. It must be remembered that, while considerable weight may attach to a traditional settlement, the sentence must still be within the range determined by Parliament. In *The State v Emp Mek* [1993] PNGLR 330, the National Court was prepared to impose imprisonment of only two years for manslaughter in a situation where relatives of the victim were satisfied with a family settlement.

13.5.10 Contrition and remorse

Clear evidence of contrition and remorse will count in favour of the offender. In most cases, this would require a plea of guilty. The earlier the plea and the earlier the expression of remorse after the commission of the offence, the more favourable it will be for the offender. Such sentiments expressed at the trial for the first time may carry very little weight: *John Elipa Kalabus v The State* [1988] PNGLR 193. The offender may also gain some credit for pleading guilty in order to save embarrassment to prosecution witnesses or inconvenience to the state: *Public Prosecutor v Tom Ake* [1978] PNGLR 469 and *R v McGrath* [1971] PNGLR 247.

Voluntary restitution and compensation can also be regarded as evidence of contrition.

13.5.11 Offender's personal circumstances and previous character

In addition to the matters affecting the question of culpability (see 13.5.7), the Magistrate must take into account such factors as:

- previous convictions, if any;
- other offences that have been committed and that should be taken into account; and
- other personal circumstances and matters of character that seem relevant.

13.5.12 Aggravating or mitigating factors

13.5.12.1 Assistance to police

This may be a mitigating factor: *R v McGrath* [1971] PNGLR 247. There may be circumstances in which the offender has cooperated, or undertaken to cooperate, with the police in the investigation of the offence or other offences, or in relation to other proceedings such as those for the forfeiture and confiscation of the proceeds of crime.

13.5.12.2 Public shame

If it can be shown that the offender has suffered, or will suffer, shame in the aftermath of the offence, this may be taken into account in assessing the appropriate penalty. Shame may be less public but still involve disclosure to family, relatives and friends: *The State v Minabkali Asu* (1980) N236 and *The State v Keputong Nagong* (1980) N225.

13.5.12.3 Imposition of fines

It is sometimes said that the imposition of a fine is ineffective when it is paid by relatives rather than by the offender himself or herself. However, a burden of that sort, when imposed on relatives, is itself of deterrent effect to the extent that they will take steps to ensure that the offender does not break the law again: *The State v Keputong Nagong* (1980) N225. Accordingly, a Magistrate may be disposed to order the payment of a fine rather than imprisonment where it appears that the collective weight of family and relatives will be brought to bear on the future behaviour of the offender.

13.5.12.4 Effect of jail on the offender's family

While this is clearly relevant, the probable effect that a sentence under consideration by the Magistrate would have on an offender's family should not always be given much weight. Where offenders have planned to commit serious crimes that they knew would result in them being in jail for some time if they were caught, they cannot automatically expect a non-custodial sentence because their families need them: *The State v Waiyake Komane* [1992] PNGLR 524.

13.5.12.5 Effect of jail on offender's future prospects

Where a jail term will prejudice the offender's job, education or income to an extent that is out of proportion to the seriousness of the offence, this is a mitigating factor: *Agiru Aieni v Tahain* [1978] PNGLR 37.

13.6 SENTENCING OPTIONS

13.6.1 Types of sentences and orders

The types of sentences and orders which are open to the Magistrate have been reviewed in 6.8, particularly orders relating to:

- payment of compensation (6.8.2);
- restriction of movement (6.8.3);
- probation (6.8.4);
- recognisances for good behaviour (6.8.5);
- community work (6.8.6);
- conditional discharge (6.8.7); and
- costs (6.8.8).

All that remains is to point to the statutory provisions that regulate the imposition of imprisonment and fines.

13.6.2 Imprisonment

13.6.2.1 Jurisdiction

As outlined in 6.3, the District Court's jurisdiction is limited to the maximum sentence of imprisonment provided by the *Criminal Code*, the *Summary Offences Act* and other statutes which create offences.

13.6.2.2 Calculation of term

The *Criminal Justice (Sentences) Act* provides that a sentence of imprisonment takes effect from the beginning of the day on which it is imposed: s 3(1). The court may deduct any period which the defendant has spent in custody before sentence was imposed: s 3(2); and see *The State v Paul Jimmy Moiana* (1997) N1657. In imposing sentence, the Magistrate must do the arithmetic – that is to say, the Magistrate should specify the length of the sentence imposed, the period spent in custody before sentence and the length of the balance of the sentence to be served: s 4. It has been held that a person who chooses not to ask for bail prior to sentence, but chooses to stay in custody, may be given credit for the period of the loss of liberty: *Public Prosecutor v Posopon Salaian* [1994] PNGLR 53.

13.6.3 Fines

The *Summary Offences Act* frequently specifies a maximum fine instead of, or as an alternative to, imprisonment. In dealing with offences to which the *Criminal Code* applies (where penalties are expressed only in terms of imprisonment), s 19 of the Code allows the court to impose a fine not exceeding K2,000 instead of, or in addition to, imprisonment.

Once the Magistrate has fixed the fine having regard to the sentencing principles and considerations referred to above, the Magistrate has discretion as to the time for payment and payment by instalments: *District Courts Act*, s 165.

13.6.4 Imprisonment in default of payment

When Magistrates impose fines they must also specify a term of imprisonment in default: *District Courts Act*, s 168. If the statute appoints a term of imprisonment, that term should be specified to be served in default of payment of the fine. If the statute does not appoint a term, the court may impose such term as it thinks fit, but not exceeding the term specified in the statute with reference to the amount to be recovered.

Where the fine and any costs do not exceed K50, the maximum term of imprisonment is 14 days. Between K50 and K200, the maximum term is 28 days, and above K200 it is 60 days: *District Courts Act*, s 201. If a warrant for arrest of the offender has been issued and part of the fine is paid, the term of imprisonment is reduced by the number of days bearing, as nearly as possible, the same proportion to the total number of days in the term as the sum paid bears to the sum adjudged to be paid: *District Courts Act*, s 202.

13.7 PREVENTIVE ORDERS

The court's powers to take action to reduce the likelihood of further offending include those mentioned in Chapter 6, such as restriction of movement (6.8.3), probation (6.8.4) and recognisances (6.8.5). The detailed statutory provisions should be looked at closely to enable the court to make best use of the preventive orders available and to ensure that the specific wording of the statute is complied with: see also Chapter 19C.

PART 4

Civil, Family and Other Jurisdictions

Chapter 14 – General Matters Relating to Civil Litigation

14.1 INTRODUCTION

The purpose of this chapter is to provide guidance to Magistrates in relation to some of the more common jurisdictional and procedural issues that arise in civil matters. This chapter can be contrasted with Chapter 15, which deals with common substantive matters that arise in civil cases in the District Courts.

14.2 CONSIDERATIONS RELATING TO JURISDICTION IN THE DISTRICT COURT

Before a Magistrate presides over any civil matter in the District Court, he or she must be satisfied that the court has jurisdiction to hear the matter and make an order. Although s 9 of the *District Courts Act* creates a presumption of jurisdiction with respect to a District Court Magistrate, this is a presumption only, and does not relieve a Magistrate of the duty to ensure that he or she is acting within the jurisdiction of the District Court. The following are some of the important considerations in this regard.

14.2.1 Geographic jurisdiction

Unlike the National and Supreme Courts, which have jurisdiction throughout the entire country, the District Courts have geographical jurisdiction only over the areas specifically provided for by statute. With respect to civil cases, geographic jurisdiction is determined mainly by the residence or place of business of a defendant or the place where the cause of action arose. Sections 13(2)(a) and (b) and 21(5) of the *District Courts Act* specify limits on the geographic jurisdiction of the court in relation to these matters.

14.2.2 Limitations related to causes of action

The types of cases that may be heard in District Courts are limited by the scope of the sections that provide for their jurisdiction. Section 21 of the *District Courts Act* provides for general civil jurisdiction with specific restrictions set out in s 21(4).

These restrictions exclude the following cases from the jurisdiction of the District Court:

- **where the validity or effect of a devise or bequest or a limitation under a will or settlement, or under a document in the nature of a settlement, is in dispute;**
- **the infringement of trade names;**
- **an action for or in the nature of slander of title to land (other defamation actions are within the jurisdiction of a District Court);**
- **an action for illegal arrest, false imprisonment or malicious prosecution;**

- **an action for seduction or breach of promise to marry;**
- **when the title to land is bona fide in dispute.**

14.2.3 Monetary jurisdiction

Section 21(1) of the *District Courts Act* provides that the monetary jurisdiction in the District Court is K10,000 where the court consists of one or more Principal Magistrates, and K8,000 in other cases.

It is permissible for a plaintiff in a civil matter to bring a civil claim in excess of the monetary jurisdiction of the court. However, the amount of any order or judgment is limited by the monetary limit. It is not possible for a party to divide a claim into more than one part for the purpose of bringing each part of the claim within the jurisdiction of the court. This is sometimes referred to as *splitting a claim*. Section 38 of the *District Courts Act* prohibits the splitting of a claim.

"**38. Demands not to be divided.**

(1) A complainant shall not divide a cause of action for the purpose of making two or more complaints before a Court, but a complainant having a cause of action for more than the amount for which a complaint may be made under this Act, may:

(a) abandon the excess by so stating in his particulars of demand; and

(b) recover to an amount not exceeding the amount that the Court has jurisdiction to award.

(2) The order of the Court on the complaint is conclusive evidence of abandonment of the excess and is in full discharge of all demands in respect of the cause of action, and entry of the order of the Court shall be made accordingly."

Section 154 of the *District Courts Act* provides that in cases where a successful set-off exceeds a complaint, judgment will go to a defendant. It also provides that where a bona fide set-off exceeds the monetary jurisdiction of the District Court (and where the defendant does not abandon the excess), no order should be made on the complaint.

14.2.4 Limitations by time

There are various public policies that are served in requiring parties to exercise their rights to bring an action within a certain time after a cause of action arises. These include the fact that memories fade and evidence tends to disappear as time goes by. It is also important that potential defendants are not exposed to an indefinite threat of litigation over something that happened in the distant past.

These interests are reflected in the provisions of the *Fraud;s and Limitations Act*. Sections 16-20 provide for the limitation of actions. Once the complainant's cause of action is identified, this is generally a straightforward matter. The limitation period begins to run when the cause of action accrues.

Section 20 provides that the limitation periods for set-offs and counterclaims are considered separately from the plaintiff's action. It is therefore possible that a plaintiff's claim will be barred by the expiry of the relevant limitation period, but that a defendant in the same action will be able to proceed with the cause of action upon which the set-off or counterclaim is based.

14.2.5 Extension of limitation periods

The *Limitation Act*, at ss 21 and 22, provides for the extension of limitation periods in cases where a plaintiff is under a disability. Generally stated, the scheme of these sections is that in cases where the plaintiff is under a legal disability (due to age or otherwise) at the time that the cause of action accrues, the limitation period does not commence running until the plaintiff is no longer under a disability. In practice, these sections frequently apply to claims of persons who were infants at the time the cause of action accrued. This does not prevent an infant (or anyone else under a disability) from bringing an action while still under a disability: see also 14.3.1 below.

14.2.6 Dissolution of customary marriage

Section 22A of the *District Courts Act* now provides the District Court with jurisdiction in relation to confirmation of the dissolution of customary marriages.

It is important for Magistrates to recognise that this jurisdiction does not amount to the actual dissolution of a customary marriage. A court must hear evidence, which may or may not include a copy of an order from a Village Court with respect to the marriage, and, if satisfied that the marriage has been dissolved in accordance with custom, the court may issue a certificate accordingly.

14.2.7 Mediation

The District Court has also been vested with the jurisdiction to mediate in any civil matter. However, a particular Magistrate, in order to be qualified to mediate in the District Court, must be "approved by the Judicial and Legal Services Commission for the purpose": see 14.6.1 below.

14.2.8 Ancillary jurisdiction

Rather than attempt to set out explicitly every type of order that a Magistrate can make in a civil matter, the *District Courts Act* contains sections that provide general authority to make orders that are appropriate. The regulations add to this flexibility.

District Courts Act:

"22. General ancillary jurisdiction.

Subject to this Act, a Court as regards a cause of action for the time being within its jurisdiction, shall, in proceedings before it:

(a) grant such relief, redress or remedy, or combination of remedies, whether absolute or conditional; and

(b) give the same effect to every ground of defence or counterclaim, whether equitable or legal, as ought to be granted or given in a similar case by the National Court and in as full and ample a manner."

District Court Regulations:

"46. Supplying deficiencies in Regulation, etc.

Where in this Regulation, there is no provision, or no sufficient provision, for or in respect of any matter or thing, then the Court may supply the deficiency, or allow it to be supplied, in such manner as may be just and proper, and for that purpose regard may be had to any relevant or analogous practice, procedure or form in use by, or for the purposes of, the National Court."

14.3 PARTIES

14.3.1 Capacity

It is fundamental to the adversarial system that, except in rare circumstances, people choose for themselves whether or not to bring a civil claim to court. However, there are limitations on a person's right to bring an action. One factor relating to a person's ability to bring an action is the legal capacity of the intending claimant.

Without a statutory provision to the contrary, a person who is under a legal disability (from age or otherwise) does not have the legal capacity to bring a claim in court. However, s 39 of the *District Courts Act* eliminates this restriction in the case of infants. It provides:

> "(1) A person under the age of 21 years may sue in a Court in all respects as if he were of full age."

Similarly, s 39(3) provides that anyone over the age of 16 may be sued. This eliminates the requirement that in all cases a person under the age of 21 sues or is sued through a *next friend or a guardian ad litem* as the case may be.

However, s 39(3) of the *District Courts Act* provides Magistrates with a discretion by which they may require the appointment of a next friend or a guardian ad litem in particular cases where a person under the age of 21 brings a claim.

Factors which could affect the exercise of the discretion would include the:

- **age of the plaintiff or defendant;**
- **mental maturity, education and language of the plaintiff or defendant;**
- **complexity of the litigation; or**
- **importance of the litigation and the affect that its outcome could have on the plaintiff or defendant**

14.3.2 Standing

Although a person may have the legal capacity to bring an action in court, in order for that person to bring an action, he or she must have a sufficient relationship to the dispute or the issues that are to be decided. A sufficiently proximate relationship with these issues is often referred to as "locus standi". This is not a matter of statute, but derives from the common law. A person is said to have locus standi if that person has a *legitimate interest* or *sufficient interest* in the proceedings. The matter of locus standi has been considered in a number of cases in Papua New Guinea.

Mamun Investments Pty Ltd v Paul Ponda [1995] PNGLR 1 is authority for the proposition that a party who has no legal or equitable interest in the subject matter of a claim has no standing to bring an action in relation to that subject matter.

However, standing cannot always be determined by the strict test used in *Mamun*. If, for instance, the case involves custody of a child or damages for nuisance, there may be no legal or equitable interest in subject matter. In such cases, the test of *sufficiently proximate relationship* may be the guideline to be used. There is nothing to prevent customary relationships from being taken into consideration in relation to this question.

14.3.3 Corporations as parties

An incorporated company is a separate legal entity from its shareholders or directors. This is as true for a small closely held company as it is for a much larger company. It may bring an action or be sued as any natural person can. In the National Court case of *AGC (Pacific) Ltd v Woo International Pty Ltd* [1992] PNGLR 100, the court considered an appeal from a District Court judgment involving the liability of a company pursuant to a guarantee. The following excerpt refers to the relevant provision of the *Companies Act* and is a clear explanation of the capacity of a corporation to sue and be sued:

> "The point is further illustrated by looking closely at one of the essential attributes or characteristics of a company as a corporate entity or body. And this is its capacity to sue and liability to be sued: s 18(4) *Companies Act*. When a wrong is done to the company, the company is the proper plaintiff to maintain, in its own name, an action for redress. Members, as such, have generally no standing to sue on behalf of the company. Similarly, if a company commits a wrong or incurs a liability in the course of its operations, it (and not the members or officials) is the proper defendant. This is sometimes referred to as the 'proper plaintiff' rule or the rule in *Foss v Harbottle* (1843) 2 Hare 461, Ch 12 LJ 319. And the wrong obviously is the wrong (liability) committed by the officers and employees of the company. That a company is capable of suing and is liable to be sued in its corporate name is not merely an administrative convenience; it follows logically from the concept of separate legal entity and principles of agency. Thus, civil liability and criminal responsibility of the company arise from a myriad of situations through the acts and omissions of its servants and agents."

It is not sufficient for the proper party to bring an action. That party must be properly named on the complaint. Similarly, a defendant must also be properly named. A Magistrate may only give judgment in favour of or against the parties as they appear on the complaint. If an artificial party is improperly named, then it is not a legal entity at all. An example of this can be seen in the case of *The United States of America, on behalf of the Embassy of the United States of America, Papua New Guinea v W R Carpenters (Properties) Ltd* [1992] PNGLR 185. In that case, it was held that the Embassy of the United States of America is not a legal person or "an entity" in law and, therefore, is not a proper party to an action.

It is not necessary for a plaintiff to bring an action against all the defendants against whom the plaintiff has a cause of action. Even where a plaintiff has a cause of action against more than one defendant, it is entirely up to the plaintiff to decide which defendant or defendants to sue. Where only one or some of several jointly liable defendants are sued, and the plaintiff is successful against the defendant or defendants who are sued, those defendants may claim against the unnamed defendants for contribution for their portion of liability: see *District Courts Act*, s 149.

14.3.4 The state as a party

With respect to claims in contract and tort, the *Claims By and Against the State Act* provides a right and procedure for suing the state:

> "2. A person making a claim against the State in contract or in tort may bring a suit against the State, in respect of the claim, in any court in which such a suit may be brought as between other persons."

The Act is silent with respect to suits against the state where the cause of action arises other than in contract or tort. However, there is case authority to the effect that the state may be sued in relation to declarations and presumably other causes of action.

In all cases where the state is being sued, it is sufficient to name the defendant as "The Independent State of Papua New Guinea". It is unnecessary to name particular office holders: see *Arawe Logging Pty Ltd and Thomas Krokio v The Independent State of Papua New Guinea and Minister for Forests* [1988-1989] PNGLR 216.

The *Claims By and Against the State Act* also provides that service upon the state must be upon the Principle Legal Advisor or a person approved by the Minister to receive service. The Act also provides that "The State" may be a plaintiff in the same way as a natural person.

14.3.5 Unincorporated businesses as parties – The Business Names Act

When bringing an action in court, it is generally necessary for a plaintiff to name a proper legal entity as a defendant. This may be a natural person or some artificial legal entity. However, in some cases, where a corporation or person carries on a business, it is not easy for members of the public (including potential plaintiffs) to know the proper legal name of the entity that they are doing business with, whether it is a person or a corporation. The *Business Names Act* creates a scheme whereby anyone carrying on a business is obliged to register the name of the business. A public register is created which allows persons to learn the proper legal name of any business. Potential plaintiffs are therefore theoretically able to determine the proper legal name of any entity carrying on business in Papua New Guinea.

However, although it is an offence not to do so, not all legal entities that carry on business bother to register under the *Business Names Act.* This can make it impossible for a plaintiff to know the legal entity that is operating the business in relation to which the cause of action arose. Section 28 of the *Business Names Act* provides some relief to plaintiffs in such cases.

"28. Proceedings against persons under a business name.

(1) Subject to Subsection (2), proceedings may be taken and prosecuted in a court of competent jurisdiction against any person or persons in the business name under which the person is or the persons are carrying on business if the business name is not registered under this Act.

(2) In proceedings to which Subsection (1) applies:

(a) the name is, for the purpose of the proceedings, a sufficient designation of the person or persons referred to in that subsection in all writs, summonses, plaints and other legal documents and instruments; and

(b) a judgment obtained or order made may be enforced against that person, or against those persons or any of those persons, as the case may be.

(3) This section does not exempt a person from compliance with any provision of this Act."

14.3.6 Business groups as parties – The Business Groups Incorporation Act

The *Business Groups Incorporation Act* provides for the creation of a legal entity known as a "business group". In some ways, a business group is like an incorporated company under the *Companies Act*. Section 17 provides that a business group is a corporation and may sue and be sued in its corporate name.

14.3.7 Associations as parties – The Associations Incorporation Act

The *Associations Incorporation Act* provides that an association that is incorporated under that Act is also capable of suing and being sued in its corporate name.

14.4 COMPLAINTS AND DEFENCES

Before a civil case proceeds to hearing, a cause of action must be made out. It should be possible for both the defendant and the Magistrate to discern, before evidence is called, what the claim is about and the basic legal framework on which it rests. In cases in the District Courts, a plaintiff, especially one without representation, may be unsure of the legal basis of the cause of action. Even if the plaintiff is clear, in his or her own mind, of the basis of the claim, it is often the case that the complaint as filed does not set out clearly what the cause of action is.

The *National Court Rules* require that parties proceeding in the National Court file detailed pleadings. These pleadings ensure that both parties and the Judge understand the basic legal framework of the action and the main factual allegations supporting it.

When dealing with limitations on monetary jurisdiction of the District Court, court registry personnel should be able to explain to intending claimants the relevant limitation on jurisdiction by the amount claimed. It may also be appropriate for a Magistrate to explain to a party the relevant limitation. The options available to the party may also need to be explained. In relation to many claims (especially those that exceed K10,000 by some amount), it can be to a claimant's practical advantage to bring a claim in the District Court, before a Principal Magistrate, with full knowledge that the maximum monetary award can be no more than K10,000. This may be the case where the costs and delay entailed in bringing the claim in National Court would outweigh the amount that will be foregone by bringing the claim in the District Court.

Formal pleadings are not automatically required in the District Courts. Section 28 of the *District Courts Act* provides that civil claims are to be commenced by way of a *complaint*. A complaint, in Form 15, provides for a complainant to state the "subject matter" of the claim only. In many cases, such a statement will be sufficient to alert both the defendant and the Magistrate to the legal basis of the claim.

14.4.1 Involvement of court personnel in drafting complaints

Unrepresented persons frequently ask court personnel for advice about what should be included in a complaint. In some cases, even where no advice is requested, it will be apparent to a clerk who is asked to file a complaint that the complaint is insufficient in some respect. Court personnel sometimes assist a complainant in drafting a complaint. However, court personnel should be very cautious about their involvement in this capacity. Any involvement that could be construed as legal advice should be strictly avoided. In most cases, this will include any advice about the drafting of a complaint.

Similarly, a Magistrate should refrain from providing a party with legal advice regarding his or her claim. There are at least two reasons for this:

- **it creates an impression of bias or conflict of interest where one party is receiving advice from the court and the other party is not;**
- **any "advice" that is received may be incorrect and conflict with a later ruling by a Magistrate presiding in court.**

Legal information may be distinguished from legal advice. It is permissible for court personnel to provide legal information to complainants and defendants. Legal advice is typified by telling a person what he or she *should* do in particular circumstances. Legal information does not include advice about what *should* be done, but may provide straightforward factual information about court procedures and requirements.

One exception to the general rule is where, pursuant to s 156 of the *District Courts Act*, a clerk is asked to file a default summons. In such a case, a clerk is obliged to discern whether a claim is for a debt or other liquidated sum, advise the complainant and proceed accordingly: see 14.6.2 below.

14.4.2 Obtaining particulars from the complainant

There are steps that can be taken to provide clarification of the claim before evidence is called. Pursuant to s 135 of the *District Courts Act*, a Magistrate may require further particulars of the plaintiff's claim. The same discretion exists in relation to set-offs pursuant to s 136.

There are two technical drawbacks to s 135. The first is that the defendant must make an application for particulars. A Magistrate might deal with this drawback by informing a defendant that such an application can be made and would be favourably considered.

The second drawback is that the application may only be made at the hearing. Leaving an application for particulars to this late stage of the proceedings can result in an application for an adjournment and subsequent delay where the particulars raise allegations for which the defendant is unprepared.

The effect of the second drawback may be minimised if court personnel who review and file complaints in the first instance are alert to complaints which fall short in detail and which are likely to result in an application under s 135. Details may then be provided in the complaint at the outset of the matter.

14.4.3 Particulars from the defendant

Although greater emphasis is placed upon the particulars of a complaint than on the defence, s 140 of the *District Courts Act* provides that a Magistrate may order that the defendant, prior to evidence being taken, "give a concise statement of his defence to the complaint and of the points on which he relies". A Magistrate should make use of this provision where there is any doubt what the real outstanding issues are. Where a defendant is represented or otherwise able to provide one, a written statement should be considered rather than an oral one.

Requiring a concise statement of defence can be an effective means of highlighting the real outstanding issues between the parties. This in turn can eliminate confusion and irrelevant evidence and save time for the court and the parties.

Defendants in claims for debt have a specific obligation to notify the plaintiff of particular defences upon which they intend to rely. These defences, set out in s 153 of the *District Courts Act*, are illegality, infancy, coverture, a *Statute of Limitations* or discharge under a law relating to bankrupt or insolvent debtors. Unless notice is given in compliance with s 153, a defendant is prevented from raising any of these defences at the hearing.

14.4.4 Amendment

Where a complaint is not clear, or where allegations have changed since it was filed, an amendment of the complaint to reflect the true issues between the parties may be in order. Section 133(4) of the *District Courts Act* provides:

"The Court, at any time before an order is made, may allow either party to alter or amend the particulars of his demand or set-off on such terms as to costs, adjournment or otherwise as the Court thinks just."

Section 138 provides:

"On the hearing of a complaint, the Court may allow such amendment of the summons as it thinks just, and on such terms as it thinks just, and all such amendments shall be made as are necessary for the purpose of determining the real questions in controversy between the parties."

As is the case with particulars, an amendment can result in a defendant becoming aware of a significant change in the nature of the complaint. When this happens for the first time at a hearing, an adjournment may be appropriate to allow a defendant to prepare to meet the complaint as amended.

14.5 CIVIL HEARINGS IN THE DISTRICT COURT

14.5.1 Matters to confirm before proceeding

It is useful for a Magistrate and beneficial for parties if, before proceeding with a contested civil hearing, a Magistrate checks to ensure that matters are in order. The following checklist includes routine matters that a Magistrate should consider before proceeding. In District Courts where civil hearings are preceded by a mention at which both parties attend, these matters should be considered at that stage. Where such a preliminary appearance does not take place, these matters should be considered at the earliest opportunity in advance of the leading of evidence.

CHECKLIST

- **Has a cause of action been disclosed by the complaint and defence?**
- **Does the District Court have jurisdiction to hear the matter?**
- **Has there been proper service of documents on the defendant and necessary witnesses?**
- **Are particulars required from either the complainant or the defendant and, if so, have they been obtained?**
- **Is evidence at the hearing to be adduced by way of affidavit? If so, does either party wish to have the deponent of the affidavits produced for cross-examination? If so, has this been arranged?**

- **Have any admissions been made by either party? If so, are the admissions recorded in the Magistrate's notebook and confirmed with the party making the admission? If not, has the possibility of admissions been canvassed with the parties?**
- **Has the possibility of settlement, either by way of negotiation or by way of mediation, been discussed with the parties? Have parties been asked to advise the court as soon as possible of any settlement?**
- **Are there any orders that can be made by consent?**
- **Have there been previous applications in relation to the matter which should be taken into account at the trial?**
- **Is the trial date acceptable to all parties and to the parties' lawyers? (where an appearance is made before the hearing date)**

14.5.2 Procedure at civil hearing

The procedure for a civil hearing in the District Court is similar to that of the National Court. In a contested hearing, parties are entitled to call witnesses and to cross-examine the witnesses called against them. This is an application of the rules of natural justice. Specific application of these rules in a civil context is set out in detail in 4.8.

14.5.3 Defendant called upon to admit or deny facts

Section 139 of the *District Courts Act* requires that, at the commencement of a civil hearing, the Magistrate reviews the substance of the complaint with the defendant and asks the defendant why an order should not be made against him or her. This step, in effect, obliges a defendant to either deny facts alleged or raise a defence to meet the allegations. This step is therefore capable of bringing out the real issues in the proceedings and, like obtaining particulars or requiring a statement of defence (see 14.4.3), can be a means of simplifying the proceedings before they begin. Of course, if a defendant, on being confronted with the complaint pursuant to s 139, does not show cause why an order should not be made, a Magistrate should consider making whatever order is appropriate in favour of the plaintiff.

When a defendant answers with a denial of the plaintiff's allegations, or raises facts or a defence in his or her own favour, the defendant's points must be taken down in writing pursuant to s 145.

When allegations of the plaintiff are not admitted, or where a defence is alleged, the hearing must proceed. Section 141 provides the outline procedure that applies to the hearing. Section 142 provides that a civil hearing should accord as closely as possible with a civil hearing in the National Court.

14.5.4 Recording evidence during a civil hearing

During a hearing, the evidence of all witnesses must be taken down in writing and signed by the witnesses. As any Magistrate knows, this can be a time consuming process. However, it is necessary in order to preserve any meaningful opportunity for either party to appeal a decision following upon the evidence. All exhibits must also be marked and a list of exhibits compiled.

The central rule of evidence is that of relevance. Often a Magistrate is required to inquire into the relevance of evidence that is being adduced during a civil hearing. Irrelevant evidence should not be admitted. Section 137 of the *District Courts Act* has the effect of limiting the plaintiff's evidence to that which concerns the demand as set out in the complaint or the summons as amended. For a fuller discussion of relevance and other evidential issues, see Chapter 5.

14.5.5 Contempt etc

Occasionally, during the taking of evidence in a civil hearing, a witness (who may or may not be a party) will either refuse to be examined, deliberately speak falsely (prevaricate) or misbehave in court in a manner that disrupts proceedings or shows disrespect. The *District Courts Act* contains a number of provisions that allow a Magistrate to deal with such situations.

Section 70 provides that where a witness refuses to be examined, proceedings may be adjourned for up to eight days and the witness committed to custody. If necessary, the same procedure may be repeated when court reconvenes.

Section 277 deals with contempt of court, and makes it an offence for a person to:

- wilfully interrupt the court;
- conduct himself or herself disrespectfully to the court during the sittings of the court;
- obstruct or assault a person in attendance, or an officer of the court, in view of the court;
- wilfully disobey an order made by a court under s 63 (by which witnesses may be ordered to leave court); or
- in the opinion of the court, wilfully prevaricate,

A person in contempt may be convicted of an offence pursuant to s 277 immediately upon the offence being committed. A fine of up to K100 may follow. However, unlike other criminal convictions, where a Magistrate is functus officio upon conviction and sentencing, fines imposed under s 277 may be remitted in whole or in part by a Magistrate on the apology of the offender: see 3.1.3 for further discussion of the court's powers in relating to contempt and related matters.

When dealing with troublesome witnesses, a Magistrate must be restrained. It does not assist matters to react with anger, and to some extent often plays into the hands of the troublesome witness. An even-tempered but firm response works best. It is usually advisable to give witnesses a warning that a repetition or continuation of their conduct will not be tolerated, and to point out that repetition or continuation will be met with specific consequences. In a worst case scenario, where a person in court, whether a witness or not, threatens or uses violence, the provisions of the *Arrest Act*, the *Criminal Code* or the *Summary Offences Act* are available to deal with the circumstances.

14.5.6 Discontinuation to avoid dismissal

Section 147 of the *District Courts Act* serves as a means for a plaintiff (or defendant advancing a set-off) to avoid the dismissal of a case where evidence at a hearing falls short of what is required to succeed. It allows the plaintiff to discontinue at any stage of the hearing (before judgment) and reserve the right to "sue afresh in respect of the same matter." Such a step may cause considerable inconvenience and expense to the opposing party and expose the other party to the threat of ongoing litigation. Section 147 provides that a Magistrate may redress this by making an order for the *immediate payment* of reasonable costs in this event.

If a plaintiff (or defendant, in relation to a set-off) does not discontinue in accordance with s 147, a Magistrate is free to dismiss the claim (or set-off) as the merits of the case on the evidence adduced requires. This is simply part of a Magistrate's duty to make an order after the parties have completed adducing evidence and have made their submissions.

14.6 DISPOSITION WITHOUT CONTESTED HEARING

14.6.1 Mediation

As mentioned in 14.2.7, a Magistrate may attempt to resolve a dispute by acting in the capacity of a mediator. Such a practice should be encouraged where resources allow.

In considering the exercise of discretion to act as a mediator, a Magistrate should consider the:

- **ability of a Magistrate to mediate a dispute;**
- **availability of another person qualified to act as a mediator pursuant to s 22B of the *District Courts Act*;**
- **attitude of the parties and the perceived likelihood that mediation in a particular case would be successful;**

- **extent to which a reference to mediation would affect case management, either positively or negatively, and thereby affect the interests of other members of the public (for instance, where the only available Magistrate would have to disqualify himself or herself in the event of an unsuccessful mediation); and**
- **extent to which mediation would affect the costs of the parties either positively or negatively.**

Although s 22B of the *District Courts Act* provides for specific persons to act as mediators, it should be remembered that just as parties are free to settle a dispute by themselves out of court through a process of negotiation, so they are free to engage anyone else who they both consent to act as a mediator, arbitrator or in some other capacity in relation to the settlement of their dispute. A Magistrate should encourage such attempts when they do not create difficulties in accommodating last minute requests for adjournments that adversely affect the orderly flow of other cases through the court.

For more information on mediation and out-of-court settlement of disputes, see Chapter 24.

14.6.2 Where defendant does not appear

Section 143 of the *District Courts Act* provides options to a District Court Magistrate where a defendant does not appear. If there is evidence on oath:

(a) that the defendant has been served 72 hours before the time of the hearing, or otherwise in accordance with an order for substituted service; and

(b) it appears that there is no sufficient ground for an adjournment,

the court may either proceed to hear the claim ex parte or adjourn the hearing.

If grounds for an adjournment are apparent, a Magistrate should reset the hearing date far enough in the future so that service may be effected on the defendant at least 72 hours in advance of that date.

14.6.3 Default summons

The determination of disputes should not require more time, expense or use of judicial resources than necessary. Complainants are entitled to the speediest possible justice. The *District Courts Act* provides for an accelerated procedure where a claim is made for repayment of a debt or for a liquidated sum of money. In such cases, a greater onus is placed upon a defendant to take immediate steps to defend, in the absence of which a complainant may seek judgment without a court hearing. Sections 155-159 of the *District Courts Act* provide for default judgments. The provisions contained in these sections seek to balance the need for speedy justice with the procedural requirements of natural justice.

14.6.4 Liquidated claims

Default judgments only apply where a complaint is for a liquidated amount of money. A claim in debt is for a specific amount, and is an example of a liquidated claim. So is any other claim where the amount claimed is able to be made certain by mathematical calculations from factors which are in the possession or knowledge of the party from whom the demand is being made. For example, a claim for arrears of rent pursuant to a lease would, in most cases, be a liquidated amount. However, if the claim includes a component for an amount that requires assessment at trial, such as loss of opportunity or general damages, the claim is not a liquidated one.

Unliquidated damages are sometimes considered to be liquidated claims and therefore mistakenly made the subject of a default summons. Claims brought by way of a default summons that do not involve a liquidated claim should not be allowed to proceed. Similarly, court personnel, as well as Magistrates, should be alert to other cases where a default summons is the appropriate means of proceeding, and should provide appropriate information to members of the public whose claims are obviously liquidated ones.

Even where a claim is for a liquidated sum, a Magistrate, in processing a default judgment, should be mindful that, although neither party may be present, he or she is performing a judicial act. Magistrates should be particularly mindful of two matters in particular.

An example of a claim that could be mistaken for a liquidated claim could occur in relation to damages to a vehicle. The amount claimed may be based on a repair estimate obtained by the plaintiff. While this may result in a specific amount being claimed, that specific amount is based on an opinion and has not been incurred as an expense. The basis of the calculation might not be available to the defendant. Even if it is, it is a matter of opinion and not fact until the damages are actually completed and paid for.

A Magistrate, in dealing with a default summons, should also be careful to ensure that the requirements of service have been complied with. These requirements are set out in s 157 of the *District Courts Act*. Although a defendant may apply to set aside a judgment based on a default summons, he or she is only able to do so if there has been proper service. Otherwise, it may not be until enforcement of the judgment has commenced that the defendant becomes aware of the judgment. At such an advanced stage, an application to set aside a default judgment entails a great deal of wasted time and effort, and it creates added stress and conflict for the parties.

14.6.5 Procedure in relation to default summons

A default summons must be served at least six days before the return date. Service must be in accordance with s 157 of the *District Courts Act* and be supported by an affidavit. A defendant who wishes to dispute the claim in the default summons must respond at least two days before the return date. A defendant is provided with a form of defence in the default summons itself. Where a defendant files a defence and serves it in accordance with s 157, the defendant is entitled to a contested hearing.

Where a defendant does not file a defence, judgment may be entered in favour of the complainant on the return date. No hearing is necessary and the complainant need not attend. However, a Magistrate, in considering whether to enter judgment in this way, must be mindful that he or she is performing a judicial role.

A Magistrate, before granting an order in relation to the default summons, should check that:

- **the amount claimed is a debt or a liquidated sum;**
- **service has been effected properly;**
- **no defence has been filed; and**
- **the required times for service have elapsed.**

14.6.6 Where defendant attends in response to default summons

A defendant may appear at the return date for the default summons *without* having first filed a defence in accordance with the provisions of s 157 of the *District Courts Act*. When this occurs, a Magistrate has the discretion, but is *not* obliged, to grant a hearing to the defendant. The onus should be placed on a defendant to satisfy the court that he or she should be granted an opportunity to defend the claim: see s 159; see also 14.6.8 where relevant considerations for setting aside a default judgment are considered.

Where a Magistrate allows a defendant an opportunity to defend, an adjournment may be appropriate and, where a complainant is not present, would certainly be granted. Terms and conditions, including an order for costs may also be appropriate.

14.6.7 Ex parte hearings

Section 143 of the *District Courts Act* provides that a hearing may proceed in the absence of a defendant where a defendant does not appear in response to a summons or at a time to which the matter has been adjourned.

Before proceeding ex parte, a Magistrate must ensure that the following criteria are satisfied:

Section 143

"(a) it appears to the Court on oath that:

> **(i) the summons was duly served at least 72 hours before the time appointed in the summons for appearing; or**
>
> **(ii) an order for substituted or other service or for the substitution for service of notice by advertisement or otherwise was duly complied with; and**
>
> **(b) no sufficient grounds are shown for an adjournment."**

Experience on the bench teaches that, in nearly all contested cases, there are "two sides to the story". An ex parte hearing is, by its very nature, a departure from the normal adversarial process. Although ex parte hearings nearly always occur as a result of a choice made by a defendant, and even though an ex parte order can be set aside, it is necessary for a Magistrate to treat evidence adduced at an ex parte hearing with care. The plaintiff must prove the case on the basis of evidence adduced. A Magistrate in an ex parte hearing, as in a contested hearing, must remain neutral and unbiased.

14.6.8 Setting aside ex parte orders

If at an ex parte hearing an order is made in favour of a plaintiff, a defendant may make an application to set aside the order.

> "25. A conviction or order made when one party does not appear may be set aside on application to the Court on such terms as to costs or otherwise as the Court thinks just, and the Court, on service on the other party of such reasonable notice as the Court directs, may:
>
> (a) proceed to hear and determine the information or complaint in respect of which the conviction or order was made; or
>
> (b) adjourn the hearing and determination of the hearing to such time and place as it thinks fit and direct such notice of the adjourned hearing as it thinks fit to be given to a party."

The National Court case of *Commodity Development Pty Ltd v Peter Karai* [1994] PNGLR 463 provides guidance for the exercise of discretion in relation to an application to set aside an ex parte order. The principles that guide Magistrates are the same as those that guide Judges of the National Court in similar applications:

1. There must be an affidavit stating facts showing a defence on the merits.
2. There must be a reasonable explanation of why judgment was allowed to go by default.
3. The application must be made promptly and within a reasonable time.

The fact that in the first instance a defendant is not automatically required by the *District Courts Act* to file a defence, unless required to do so pursuant to s 138, does not relieve a defendant from demonstrating a defence on the merits.

Where an ex parte order is set aside, a District Court Magistrate has the option of making a final determination of the case on its merits at the time the ex parte order is set aside, or adjourning the case for a hearing. This decision will be guided in most cases by the readiness of both parties to proceed with a contested hearing at the time the ex parte order is set aside and the availability of court time for the hearing.

14.7 ORDERS

Chapter 25 provides guidance for Magistrates in making orders and giving reasons for orders. Further considerations relating to orders and judgments in civil matters are set out below.

14.7.1 Lump sum or payments by instalments

The most common type of order for compensation or damages is an order for the payment of a lump sum of money. Once this type of order is made, the entire sum becomes due and payable immediately. This is how the common law has developed. The National Court has departed from this on occasion using its inherent powers: *Aundak Kupil and Kauke Kensi v Independent State of Papua New Guinea* [1983] PNGLR 350. However, the District Court has specific jurisdiction to make an order for compensation by instalments.

> "**165. Time for payment or payment by instalments.**
>
> (1) Where, by a conviction or order, a fine or sum of money or costs is or are ordered to be paid, the Court may do all or any of the following things:
>
> (a) allow time for the payment; and
>
> (b) direct the payment to be made by instalments; and
>
> (c) direct that the person liable to pay is at liberty to give security for the payment.
>
> (2) Where a fine or sum of money or costs is or are directed to be paid by instalments, the instalments shall be paid to the Clerk or to such other person as the Court orders and, if default is made in the payment of an instalment, the same proceedings may be taken to recover the amount then remaining due as if an order for payment by instalments had not been made."

When making orders pursuant to s 165 of the *District Courts Act*, a Magistrate should consider whether the ability of a defendant to pay compensation over time may be diminished or impaired and thereby prejudice the ability of a plaintiff to recover.

Further, the terms of an order pursuant to these sections should be spelled out very clearly in order that a defendant will not be able to frustrate the intention of the order.

Chapter 15 – Key Concepts in Some Civil Matters

This chapter outlines some of the more common civil causes of action. It is not possible in one chapter to deal exhaustively with all types of civil cases that come before a District Court Magistrate. Therefore, this chapter restricts itself to contract, negligence and defamation, together with some related concepts. It is intended to assist Magistrates, especially those who do not have ready access to a law library. However, it is *not* intended to serve as a substitute for texts, case authority or the Papua New Guinean legislation to which it makes reference.

Parties, particularly those without a lawyer, often do not have a clear idea of the issues or the legal basis (if any) for their claim or defence. Because detailed pleadings are not always required in the District Court, it is up to the presiding Magistrate in such circumstances to listen to the evidence and at the *same time* understand how (or whether) the claim fits within any cause of action or defence that is known to the law. At the conclusion of evidence, submissions from unrepresented parties (and sometimes lawyers) are unhelpful in revealing the applicable law. This chapter may be used as a handy guide for Magistrates in these circumstances, especially where the case falls within the scope of contract or tort law. Magistrates should be aware that the causes of action and remedies outlined in this chapter are not the *only* ones within the jurisdiction of the District Court: see 14.2.2.

15.1 CONTRACTS AND THEIR ELEMENTS

Contracts are widespread in contemporary Papua New Guinean society, and are therefore commonly the basis of disputes that come before Magistrates of the District Courts. The essence of a contract is an agreement between two or more parties. All contracts consist of several essential elements. If an essential element of a contract is missing, then it cannot provide a basis for enforcing rights and obligations. In such cases, there may be an alternative cause of action or defence that is available.

The essential elements of a contract considered below are:

- **Offer**
- **Acceptance**
- **Certainty of offer and acceptance**
- **Intention to create legal obligations**
- **Consideration**

15.1.1 Offer

An offer may be oral, written or even result from conduct or a gesture by a party. The essential feature of an offer is that there must be an intention by the person (the offeror) to be bound by the terms that are contained in the offer if the offer is accepted. An offer can be made to a single person or to the whole world.

Sometimes an offer is preceded by two-way communications in the form of negotiations. It is important to distinguish an offer from an invitation to treat, which is an indication by a party that he, she or it is in the market to sell goods or services and is prepared to consider offers. A shop that displays goods for sale at an indicated price is inviting a party to make an offer. A party that places an advertisement in a newspaper to sell a vehicle at a particular price is making an invitation to treat. The person who *responds* to the invitation to treat may do so by means of an offer.

An offer maybe withdrawn at any time before it is accepted. It does not matter how this is communicated to the offeree (the person to whom the offer is made). As long as the offeree has knowledge that the offer has been withdrawn (revoked), then a purported acceptance has no legal significance.

15.1.2 Acceptance

An offeree may accept the offer. At the moment the offer is accepted, a contract comes into existence (provided the other essential elements are present).

Unless the person who makes an offer stipulates how an acceptance is to be communicated, or a statute (such as the *Statute of Frauds and Limitations* or *Goods Act*) imposes certain requirements, an acceptance may take the form of words, writing or conduct.

Sometimes it is not necessary for acceptance of an offer to be communicated. For example, if the owner of a lost dog makes an offer to pay a reward to anyone who returns the dog, then a person to whom the offer was made may find the dog and present it to the owner (thereby having performed contractual obligations) without previously having communicated to the owner that the offer was accepted.

The *Goods Act* is an important statute that governs the law regarding the sale of goods in a number of respects.

Section 6 contains provisions that relate to offer and acceptance:

> "6(1) A contract for the sale of goods of the value of K20.00 or more is not enforceable by action unless:
>
> (a) the buyer:
>
> (i) accepts part of the goods sold and actually receives them; or
>
> (ii) gives something in earnest to bind the contract or in part payment; or
>
> (b) a written note or memorandum of the contract is made and signed by the party to be charged or his agent for the purpose.
>
> (2) This section applies to every contract referred to in Subsection (1) notwithstanding that:

(a) the goods:

(i) may be intended to be delivered at a future time; or

(ii) are not made, procured, provided or fit or ready for delivery at the time when the contract is actually made; or

(b) some act is required for making or completing the goods or making them fit for delivery.

(3) There is an acceptance of goods within the meaning of this section when the buyer does an act in relation to the goods that recognizes a pre-existing contract of sale, whether or not there is an acceptance in performance of the contract."

15.1.3 Certainty of offer and acceptance

Even where parties exchange offer and acceptance in matching terms, a contract may not be enforceable if there is uncertainty about what is agreed to or if the parties have left too much to be decided at a later date. For example, an agreement to make an agreement is uncertain and therefore not enforceable.

15.1.4 Intention to create legal obligations

In order for a contract to exist, the parties must have intended to bind themselves in a *legally enforceable* way. This is seldom stated explicitly but may be inferred from the circumstances. On the other hand, it may be possible to infer from circumstances that, although there is an agreement, there is no intention to make it legally binding. For instance, if a husband tells his wife that if they save their money he will take her for dinner at a restaurant, it is unlikely that a court would infer that there was an intention to be legally bound.

Sometimes parties expressly state an intention that their agreement is *not* legally binding. Words such as "memorandum of understanding" or "agreement in principle" may be evidence of this intention.

15.1.5 Consideration

In order for a contract to exist, there must be consideration. Consideration is what one party gives or promises in exchange for what the other party is giving or promising. Without consideration flowing in both directions, there is no contract. Courts do not look at the adequacy of consideration or judge whether a contract makes good business sense. Therefore, if a person agreed to sell his or her car for K500, the contract is enforceable even though the car might be worth K10,000. However, other issues, such as fraud, misrepresentation or duress, might exist as defences and therefore render such a contract unenforceable.

Consideration can sometimes take the form of an agreement *not* to do something. For instance, an employee might agree not to enter into competition with his or her employer. This type of consideration might be in either express or implied terms.

Consideration can take the form of a promise to do or not do something at some time in the future. This is known as *executory* consideration. When both sides give consideration in the form of promises to do something in the future, the contract is known as an *executory* contract.

The act of doing something or refraining from doing something may be in the past when an agreement is made. That is, the so-called consideration has passed between the parties before there is any agreement. Generally, this past consideration is not sufficient to form the basis of a contract.

15.2 OTHER CONTRACTUAL TERMS

15.2.1 Contents of the contract

Contracts consist of promises between the parties. These are often referred to as terms of a contract. A term may be *express* or *implied*. Some terms are automatically incorporated into the contract by statute: see the *Goods Act*.

Simple contracts contain few terms, for example, the contract between a seller of petrol and the motor vehicle driver who stops to buy petrol. Other contracts, usually written, contain many terms.

Some terms of a contract are more important than others. They are said to go to the heart of a contract. These terms are sometimes called *conditions*.

If a person breaches a condition of a contract, the other party is entitled to treat the contract as at an end.

The *Goods Act* provides for the operation of conditions in contracts to which the *Goods Act* applies.

"**12. Conditions of contracts of sale.**

(1) Subject to this section, where a contract of sale is subject to a condition to be fulfilled by the seller, the buyer may:

(a) waive the condition; or

(b) elect to treat the breach of the condition as a breach of warranty and not as a ground for treating the contract as repudiated.

(2) Whether a stipulation in a contract of sale is:

(a) a condition the breach of which may give rise to a right to treat the contract as repudiated; or

> (b) a warranty the breach of which may give rise to a claim for damages but not to a right to reject the goods and treat the contract as repudiated,
>
> depends in each case on the construction of the contract."

Terms that are part of a contract but do not go to the heart of the contract are sometimes called *warranties*. When a party breaches a warranty, it does not give the other party the automatic right to treat a contract as being at an end. Section 1 of the *Goods Act* defines warranty, in relation to contracts for the sale of goods, as follows:

> **"'warranty' means an agreement with reference to goods that are the subject of a contract of sale:**
>
> **(a) that is collateral to the main purpose of the contract; and**
>
> **(b) the breach of which:**
>
> **(i) gives rise to a claim for damages; but**
>
> **(ii) does not give a right to reject the goods and treat the contract as repudiated."**

It is not always obvious whether a term is a condition or a warranty. The provisions of the *Goods Act* may be a useful guide in making this distinction, even in relation to other types of contracts.

15.2.2 Express terms

Promises that are expressly stated in a contract are called express terms. An express term may be written or oral. These terms are easy to identify (subject to issues of credibility in the proof of what express terms exist in an oral contract).

15.2.3 Implied and statutory terms

Express terms in a contract seldom cover every detail of the intention of the parties. Every contract is likely to have one or more implied terms. An implied term is a term that parties have not expressly dealt with, but that may be presumed to be part of the contract, judging from the circumstances.

For instance, if one party got into a taxi and told the driver to drive to the airport, the taxi driver might say nothing but simply drive off. The express terms in this contract are few. However, there might be a number of implied terms. In this example, an implied term might be that the taxi would not pick up another passenger on the way to the airport. Another implied term might be that the taxi would take a direct route to the airport.

As is demonstrated above, terms may also be incorporated into a contract by statute. The *Goods Act* sets out a number of terms that are incorporated into certain types of contracts, whether the parties have actually directed their minds to these terms or not.

The *Employment Act* includes a number of statutory terms that are automatically incorporated in various types of employment contracts. Statutory terms bind parties to a contract whether or not they directed their minds to the provisions of the statute at the time that the contract was made.

15.2.4 "Standard form" – exemption clauses

A party entering into a contract may be given a ticket or asked to sign a standard form that has been prepared by the other party. Either of these types of documents frequently contains some "fine print". The party that is given the written form contract has no real opportunity to negotiate its terms. The question might arise whether these terms form part of the contract. This issue sometimes arises when the party that provided the standard form seeks to rely on one of the terms set out. Often the term in question is one exempting or limiting the liability of the party.

Where a party signs a contract, he or she is taken to have agreed to the terms of the contract. Where a printed form contains terms and a party is not asked to sign the "contract", then reasonableness governs whether the printed terms form part of the contract. The question becomes whether the party who seeks to rely on the terms on the document did all that was reasonably necessary to bring the terms of the printed document to the attention of the party before the contract was entered into. If a person has an opportunity to read the terms of a contract drafted by the other party, but has not done so, it does not exempt the person from the terms that were not read.

One issue that can arise is how a standard term on a written contract should be interpreted by a court where there is some *ambiguity*, that is, where the term might have more than one possible meaning. One possible interpretation could favour the party who provided the contract, while another interpretation could be more favourable to the other party. The principle, known as the *contra proferentem* rule, holds that any ambiguity is resolved in favour of the party against whom the term would be enforced.

15.3 PARTIES TO THE CONTRACT

The general rule is that everyone has the legal capacity to enter into a contract. However, there are several important exceptions.

15.3.1 Children and persons under disability

Persons under a legal disability are not automatically bound by the terms of all contracts, even where the essential elements are otherwise present. Pursuant to s 21 of the *Frauds and Limitations Act*, a person is deemed to be under a disability if that person is under 21 years of age or is of unsound mind within the meaning of Pt VIII of the *Public Health Act*.

15.3.2 Children or incompetent persons – contracts for necessaries

The *Goods Act* contains provisions for the sale of necessaries to persons under 21 years of age and to other legally incompetent persons.

> "**4. Capacity to buy and sell.**
>
> (1) In this section, 'necessaries', in relation to a person, means goods suitable to:
>
> (a) the condition in life of the person; and
>
> (b) his actual requirements at the time of the sale and delivery.
>
> (2) Subject to Subsection (3), capacity to buy and sell is regulated by the general law concerning capacity to contract and to transfer and acquire property.
>
> (3) Where necessaries are sold and delivered to:
>
> (a) an infant; or
>
> (b) a person who by reason of mental incapacity or drunkenness is incompetent to contract,
>
> he shall pay a reasonable price for them."

The word "necessaries" has been interpreted to include things such as food, clothing and shelter. Note that the *price* agreed to by the person buying necessaries may not be binding. The section says that the buyer is bound only to pay a *reasonable* price.

15.3.3 Young persons – contracts for employment

Contracts of employment with persons under the age of 16 are not permissible in some circumstances and are restricted in others. Section 103 of the *Employment Act* contains provisions relating to the employment of young persons.

> "(1) Subject to Subsections (2) and (3), a person under 16 years of age shall not be employed.
>
> (2) Subject to Subsection (3), a person over 11 years of age but under 16 years of age may be employed if the employer first obtains:
>
> (a) at the employer's own expense, a certificate from a medical practitioner indicating that the person is fit for the type of employment proposed; and
>
> (b) the written consent of his parent or guardian to the employment.

> (3) Where the employment:
>
> (a) is not prejudicial to attendance at school; and
>
> (b) is outside the hours prescribed for attendance at school,
>
> and the employer has complied with Subsection (2), a person:
>
> (c) who is over 11 years of age but under 16 years of age may be employed in an undertaking in which only members of his family are employed; and
>
> (d) of 14 or 15 years of age may be employed in any industry other than an industrial undertaking or the fishing industry.
>
> (4) Notwithstanding Subsection (3), a person of 14 or 15 years of age may be employed during the hours prescribed for attendance at school where the employer is satisfied that the person no longer attends school."

While an infant is not bound by the terms of a contract entered into before the infant is of an age of majority, the infant may ratify a contract when he or she reaches 21 years of age. Section 14 of the *Frauds and Limitations Act* sets out specifics in relation to this matter.

15.3.4 Agency and assignments of contracts

Agency is a relationship between a principal and an agent. An agent may bind a principal in a contractual arrangement – in almost any case where the principal could bind himself or herself. Agencies can arise by express appointment (which in most cases is either oral or written) or implied authority (which in some circumstances arises out of circumstances between parties, such as husband and wife, employer and employee etc). An agency relationship may be created when the principal ratifies an arrangement entered into by an agent. An agent is not automatically personally bound by the terms of a contract entered into on behalf of a principal, but *may* be bound, especially where the name of the principal, or even the fact that there is a principal, is not disclosed to the other contracting party.

Assignment of a contract is where a third party accepts the benefits and obligations of one of the parties to an existing contract and becomes bound by its terms. This can happen by operation of law, as is the case when a party dies or becomes bankrupt. It may also happen by means of agreement of the original parties to the contract. In some other circumstances, equity will recognise an assignment of a contract where fairness requires it, even though it has not been legally assigned.

15.4 DEFECTS IN CONTRACTS AND ELEMENTS THAT MAKE CONTRACTS INVALID (VITIATING ELEMENTS)

15.4.1 Misrepresentation

A misrepresentation that is relied upon by a party may affect the range of rights and obligations that exist between the parties pursuant to a contract. A misrepresentation may be innocent, negligent or fraudulent. It might be a misrepresentation that induces a party to enter into a contract but is not a term of the contract itself. A misrepresentation may also be a term of the contract, or it may be a statement that induces a party to enter into a contract.

For a misrepresentation to have an effect on the relationship of the parties to a contract, it has to be a misrepresentation of fact.

If the misrepresentation is serious and goes to the root of the contract, it can give the party who relied upon it the right to treat the contract as being at an end. For instance, if the vendor of a vehicle made a representation that the vehicle was a 1999 Pajero when in fact the vehicle was a 1989 Mazda sedan, the misrepresentation would go to the root of the contract and the purchaser could treat the contract as at an end (rescind the contract). The purchaser would not be obliged to go through with the deal and would be entitled to the return of any monies already paid.

Other misrepresentations may form part of a contract but may not go to the root of the contract. In such a case, the other party does not have a right to treat the contract as being at an end, but may be entitled to damages instead. For instance, if a person was purchasing a car and the vendor made a misrepresentation to the effect that the radio in the car was working when in fact the radio was defective, damages in an amount required to replace or repair the radio would likely be appropriate.

A fraudulent or negligent misrepresentation that is *not* a term of a contract may still give a party a right to damages or rescission. However, if the misrepresentation is innocent (that is not deliberately made to deceive) and is not a term of the contract, the party who relied upon it may not have any recourse. This falls within the general meaning of the term "caveat emptor" or "buyer beware".

15.4.2 Illegal contracts

An illegal contract or a contract made for an illegal purpose is, in most cases, of no force and effect. It may involve potential criminal sanctions. An example would be a contract to rent premises for the purpose of prostitution or illegal gambling. An agreement to buy and sell illegal drugs would be unenforceable for the same reason.

15.4.3 Breach

A breach of contract is an event or statement that is inconsistent with, or repudiates one or more terms of, the contract. It may take a number of forms. A party may verbally tell another party that it will not perform its contractual obligations. Alternatively, a party may do something or omit to do something that is an obligation under the contract. In either circumstance, a party is said to have repudiated the contract.

Repudiation may occur at any time between the time the contract is entered into and when it is fully performed. When an innocent party learns that the other party has repudiated a contract by words to that effect, he or she may take action immediately by accepting the repudiation, or may continue to act as if the contract will be performed and then, when it is not, take action.

A breach of contract may be a breach of *warranty* or a breach of *condition*. A breach of warranty does not discharge a contract. A breach of condition does not necessarily discharge a contract, that is, it does not give the innocent party the automatic right to treat the contract as at an end. It is a matter for a court to decide. However, at the least, it does give the innocent party a right to be compensated for unavoidable damages suffered as a result of the breach.

If a contract is *divisible* then a breach will not normally have the result of discharging the entire contract. For example, if a party in Port Moresby hires a company in Mount Hagen to supply potatoes every month for a year, and the company in Mount Hagen is several days late in supplying potatoes in the sixth month, a court would be unlikely to allow the first party to treat the entire contract as at an end (unless the parties had previously agreed that the first party could do so). It is more likely that the first party would be entitled to damages suffered as a result of the breach, and the remainder of the contract would remain in place.

15.4.4 Frustration

Frustration of a contract happens when some event that could not be foreseen at the time a contract was entered into makes it impossible for one or both parties to perform their obligations. The event may occur as a result of the destruction of the subject matter (for example, where a stadium is struck by lightening and burns down, thereby preventing a concert from taking place). Frustration may occur where an expected event, on which the contract depends, does not take place in circumstances that make it unforeseeable. It may also occur where a person with a unique or particular skill, and upon whom the performance of the contract depends, is somehow incapacitated (for instance, when a person who has been contracted to play the piano is unexpectedly hospitalised for burns to the hands). It can occur when intervening events make the performance of the contract illegal (for example, if a new law was passed banning possession of baui, thereby frustrating an executory contract for the sale of buai).

If the event that makes it impossible to perform the contract is something that a party caused, or if it could reasonably have been foreseen when the contract was made, then it is unlikely to amount to frustration.

When a contract is frustrated, the contract is discharged at the date of the frustrating event. The parties' obligations under the contract cease at this time, but the contract is fully enforceable up until that date. Although case law provides guidance, courts generally attempt to make an order that is fair to both parties in the circumstances. In some circumstances it might be fair for the parties to retain the benefits they have received under the contract and be excused from performing any further obligations. For example, if a contract provides for the hire of a stadium for a concert, and the party who hired the stadium was not obliged to pay until the day of the concert, but the stadium collapses a week before the contract, the status quo may be the fairest result. In other circumstances fairness may require an order for payment of money or return of property by one party. For instance, if a party has paid in advance for a service to be rendered in the future, and the contract is frustrated in a way that makes it impossible to perform the services, a court might order the return of the money to the party who paid for the services.

15.4.5 Discharge

A contract that is discharged is no longer operative. Frustration may lead to discharge. A serious breach that gives another party the right to treat the contract as at an end (rescind the contract) is another way that a contract may be discharged. Fortunately, the majority of contracts are discharged by the parties performing all of their obligations in accordance with the terms of a contract. Magistrates seldom hear about these contracts. Contracts that are discharged by either breach or frustration are more likely to find their way into a District Court.

15.5 REMEDIES FOR BREACH OF CONTRACT

When a contract is breached, a complainant is entitled to a remedy. The general objective is to put a complainant in the position he or she would have been in if the contract in question had been performed. In addition to damages, the law recognises alternative remedies in the form of specific performance, injunction or restitution. The most common remedy for breach of contract is damages. There are several types of damages.

15.5.1 Liquidated damages

Liquidated damages are damages that are capable of exact arithmetic calculation. An illustration of this is where a guest at a hotel runs up a bill for food and accommodation and fails to pay. The amount of damages suffered by the hotel can be easily calculated and is known to both parties. It is an amount equal to what the guest would have paid if he or she had not breached the contract. Another example would be a loan of money at a specified rate of interest. If the money is not repaid according to the terms of the contract, damages are usually a matter of arithmetical calculation. Sometimes parties agree in advance what the damages will be in the event of certain breaches, and include a specific clause setting out the damages payable on breach. They represent a sum that the parties agree would be reasonable compensation in the event of a breach. An example would be where a car rental contract stipulates that there will be a specified charge for each hour or each day that the rental car is overdue. Regardless of the actual loss suffered by the rental company, the parties agree that the contractual charges are a reasonable pre-estimate.

15.5.2 Penalties and liquidated damages

Courts are careful to distinguish liquidated damages from penalties. A contract may stipulate an amount of liquidated damages that will result in the event of a particular breach, but the amount might be excessive, unconscionable and extravagant in relation to the actual loss. In this case, the amount is characterised as a penalty. A court will not enforce a penalty clause in a contract. If the car rental company in the above example stipulated in the contract that damages of K3,500 per day would be payable for each day that the car was overdue, it would clearly be more than a reasonable pre-estimate of damages for breach of the contract, and the court would likely consider it to be a penalty. As such, it would be unenforceable.

15.5.3 General damages

Some losses do not lend themselves to exact arithmetic calculation, but must be assessed by a Judge or Magistrate. General damages in contract cases usually take the form of compensation for some financial loss that a plaintiff has suffered. They may include (but are not limited to) the cost of making right what the defendant has done improperly, finding another, more expensive source of goods or services that a defendant had agreed to supply, and lost profit or lost income that is a result of a defendant's breach of contract. A court must take into account all of the relevant facts and circumstances in making an award of damages.

The main objective in assessing damages for breach of a contract is to put the plaintiff in the position he or she would have been in if the contract had not been breached. Sometimes, where this approach results in excessive or wasteful damages, an alternative approach is employed. This is a calculation of the difference in value between what the innocent party bargained for and what they actually received. For instance, if a builder agreed to build a swimming pool for a buyer, a term of the contract might stipulate that the pool is to be 240 cm deep at the deep end. Suppose the pool is built in complete conformity with the terms of the contract except that it is only 235 cm deep at the deep end. Suppose also that altering the pool to the correct depth would require the replacement of the entire pool. A court would be likely to approach the assessment of damages on the principle that the buyer should be compensated in damages that are equal to the difference between a pool that is 240 cm deep and a pool that is 235 cm deep.

The common law has only recently allowed damages for distress, frustration and hurt feelings arising from a breach of contract, particularly in the context of the breach of an employment contract. Courts in Papua New Guinea have allowed damages to compensate for these things: see *Harding v Teperoi Timbers Pty Ltd* [1988] PNGLR 128; *Rooney v Forest Council of PNG* [1990] PNGLR 406. However, for a case where this head of damages was not compensated, see *Jessey Lapon v Dobel Farming & Yrading Pty Ltd* [1992] PNGLR 215.

15.5.4 Remoteness of damage

Damages are limited to losses that can reasonably be foreseen to have arisen from the breach or that can reasonably be supposed to have been in the minds of the parties at the time they made the contract. Any damages that fall outside the scope are too remote. In the famous case of *Hadley v Baxendale*, a carrier took a piece of equipment from a mill to be repaired. There was a delay in returning the equipment. This delay amounted to a breach of the contract. The delay resulted in the mill closing for a week and the consequent loss of profits for that week. It was held that these damages, although caused by the breach, were not known to the carrier and could not reasonably have been expected to result from the breach. They were too remote and therefore the carrier was not liable for these losses.

In cases for wrongful dismissal, even a plaintiff who is wrongfully dismissed, and who is unsuccessful in finding other employment before trial, may not be entitled to damages equal to lost income for an indefinite period. A reasonable period of notice, by which an employer could dismiss an employee for no reason, must be found in the contract. It may be an express term but is often an implied term: see *Christopher Appa v Peter Wama, Secretary Department of Western Highlands and the State* [1992] PNGLR 395.

15.5.5 Mitigation

A party who suffers damages as the result of another party's breach of contract has a duty to take reasonable steps to minimise the loss. For instance, if a term of a contract provides that goods are to be delivered to a party, but they are not delivered, the party who suffers the loss would be expected to purchase goods elsewhere if there is an available source. An award of damages is reduced by an amount representing the value of any failure to take reasonable steps to mitigate the loss: see *Kopen v Independent State of Papua New Guinea* [1998-1989] PNGLR 659.

An example of the duty to mitigate commonly arises in employment cases, where a wrongfully dismissed plaintiff has a duty to look for alternative employment. This duty arises immediately on the occurrence of the breach.

15.5.6 Quantum meruit

Quantum meruit means "as much as the thing is worth". It is an award of compensation that may be used where fairness requires it. Strictly speaking, quantum meruit does not arise out of a contract. It arises where a party provides goods or services to another party, believing there is an agreement, and the other party accepts them. When the first party seeks to be compensated for the goods or services, there is no contract to rely upon and therefore no breach. However, in circumstances where fairness requires, a court will compensate the party in an equal amount to that by which the other party was enriched by the goods or services. This amount may be different from the damages that would be awarded if a contract had existed.

15.5.7 Specific performance

Specific performance is an order that a party to a contract carry out his or her obligations pursuant to the terms of the contract. Generally speaking, specific performance is *discretionary* and is ordered only when damages will not adequately compensate an innocent party to a breached contract. A party who contracts to purchase a unique or rare item could be in such a position. Land is often regarded as unique, and specific performance is often ordered in relation to contracts for sale of land that are breached by the vendor. In such cases, a vendor may be ordered to sell the thing in accordance with the contract. Specific performance is often ordered where damages in the form of money will not provide the plaintiff with an adequate remedy. For instance, suppose a company required a particular type of aircraft for use in its operations. The availability of this type of aircraft might be quite limited, and in Papua New Guinea there might only be one aircraft that suits the needs of the company. As another example, suppose a person entered into a contract to purchase a specific artefact, and the vendor breached the contract by refusing to sell the artefact. Suppose further that the artefact was unique and there was nothing available that could be purchased as a substitute. In such a case, damages might not be adequate as they would not provide the plaintiff with the ability to put himself or herself in the position he or she would have been if the contract had been performed. A court might consider specific performance (forcing the vendor to sell) to be appropriate in such circumstances: see *Woodward v Woodward* [1987] PNGLR 92.

Because specific performance is an equitable remedy, courts have been careful to order it only where the plaintiff has not delayed unreasonably in seeking the remedy, and where it is just and equitable to do so under all the circumstances.

The common law has always been reluctant to award specific performance in contracts that require a party to perform personal services for another party, either as an employee or as a contractor: *Christopher Appa v Peter Wama and The State* [1992] PNGLR 395.

15.5.8 Injunction

An injunction is another equitable remedy that is awarded only in the court's discretion. It is an order that obliges a party to do or to refrain from engaging in specific conduct or acts. An injunction may be ordered to preserve the status quo where, in the circumstances, a defendant is likely to cause continuing damage to the plaintiff's interests before a final order can be made at trial, and where damages are not suitable. Courts in Papua New Guinea have been reluctant to order an injunction when another remedy is available: see *Ume More v UPNG* [1985] PNGLR 401.

Interim injunctions are sometimes awarded to maintain the status quo between the parties. A particular type of interim injunction, sometimes referred to as a Mareva injunction, is made to prevent a defendant from disposing of assets or removing them from the court's jurisdiction in order to frustrate the enforcement of any judgment that the plaintiff might obtain at trial. However, courts have held that the authority to make such an order comes from s 155(4) of the *Constitution*: see *Mauga Logging Company Pty Ltd v South Pacific Oil Palm* [1977] PNGLR 80; *Wawa Trading v Lie Tat Swie Lie and Bank of New South Wales* [1982] PNGLR 375.

15.6 TORTS

The law of tort cannot be accurately or concisely defined. It is an area of the law that allocates responsibility for behaviour that has an injurious effect on other people. It is based on the notion of fault. The wrong might be deliberate, such as assault and battery, some types of nuisance or defamation. It might be inadvertent, such as negligence. This section examines two of the most common types of tort that come before the District Court; negligence and defamation.

15.6.1 Negligence – the duty of care

The tort of negligence is based on a *duty of care* that is owed either to a particular person or to a group of people. The test for the existence of a duty is whether a person can *reasonably foresee* that his or her behaviour will cause injury to somebody. If so, then a duty of care exists towards that person or all people falling within that description.

Although criminal liability and civil liability for negligence overlap in some cases, they are not identical. For instance, a person who causes an accident while driving may be liable civilly but not criminally. Also, the different standards of proof in civil and criminal cases can affect an outcome, even where the defendant's actions are alleged to be wrong in both a criminal and civil sense: see 5.35.

Negligence does not account for all damages that are caused by someone's inadvertence. For instance, suppose a person who is carefully driving a vehicle has a sudden heart attack while driving and as a result causes an accident. Others may suffer damages as a result. However, the driver may not have been negligent if he or she could not have reasonably foreseen that his or her behaviour would cause injuries to others. There would be no fault on the part of the driver in such a case, and therefore no negligence.

A determination of whether a duty of care exists has often made use of the concept of the "reasonable man". This term is widespread and, although not gender neutral, is applicable to both men and women. Determining whether a duty of care exists, therefore, turns on whether a reasonable person would recognise a risk and take care to avoid injuring someone. In this sense, the test for negligence is objective and it does not matter what a defendant *actually* thought about the possibility of his or her behaviour causing injury to someone.

In another sense, the "reasonable man" does incorporate some recognition of the characteristics of the actual defendant. For instance, a 10 year old would not be likely to be judged by the same standard as a reasonable adult in determining whether particular conduct is negligent. The behaviour of a 10 year old defendant would be measured against that of a reasonable 10 year old. Similarly, the conduct of a professional, such as a doctor acting within the scope of his or her professional duties, would be judged in accordance with the conduct of a reasonable doctor with the same qualifications.

The existence of a duty of care is associated with the risk involved in a person's behaviour. If the risk is a reasonable one and a reasonable person would take precautions to guard against it, then a person who does not take these precautions and causes damages to another will probably be negligent. The greater the potential harm, the greater the precautions that are required.

It is not necessary that a reasonable person would foresee the *exact type* of damage that a plaintiff would suffer or the degree of seriousness of that damage. What matters is that a reasonable person would recognise the risk of *some* damages resulting from his or her behaviour. A particular plaintiff's susceptibility to a greater-than-normal amount of damage, does not relieve the defendant from liability for the actual damages suffered.

15.6.2 Negligence – causation

In order for a person's conduct to amount to negligence, a breach of a duty of care must be the direct cause of the injury to the plaintiff. One test sometimes used to assist in determining whether the defendant's conduct is the cause of the plaintiff's injury is the "but for" test. If the injury would not have occurred but for the defendant's conduct, then causation is established (subject to apportionment for other causes, such as contributory negligence: see 15.6.3).

15.6.3 Contributory negligence – Wrongs Miscellaneous Provisions Act

More than one party's negligence might be the cause of the damages suffered by a plaintiff. When the plaintiff has been negligent, and that negligence has, together with the negligence of a defendant, caused the plaintiff's damage, we say that the plaintiff is guilty of contributory negligence. Contributory negligence is usually expressed as a percentage. For instance, we might say in a claim by a pedestrian who was not careful in crossing the road and was injured, that there is 30 per cent contributory negligence. Of course the exact percentage would depend on the circumstances of any particular case.

At common law, even the slightest amount of contributory negligence was enough to forfeit the plaintiff's claim. However, the *Wrongs Miscellaneous Provisions Act* provides that a plaintiff is entitled to recover a portion of the damages that is equal to the portion that is caused by the defendant.

Sections 40 and 41 of the *Wrongs Miscellaneous Provisions Act* provides that where the total damages suffered may exceed the jurisdiction of the court, damages based on contributory negligence may be awarded up to the limit of the court's monetary jurisdiction.

In addition, these sections deal with particular situations involving contributory negligence in relation to:

- employers;
- deceased persons; and
- third parties who suffer damages.

15.7 STATUTORY SOURCES OF LIABILITY FOR FAULT

15.7.1 Occupiers' liability

Part XII of the *Wrongs Miscellaneous Provisions Act* replaces the common law relating to the liability of occupiers for damages that are suffered on premises.

An occupier is not necessarily the owner of premises. The occupier may be a tenant or someone else. The key concept in determining who is an occupier is that of *control*. The control to admit persons to premises or exclude persons from premises is what determines who is an occupier. Premises may have more than one occupier, for instance, a contractor and an owner may both be occupiers in certain circumstances.

Section 52 of the *Wrongs Miscellaneous Provisions Act* sets out the extent of an occupier's liability in ordinary circumstances:

> "(1) An occupier of premises owes the same duty (in this section referred to as 'the common duty of care') to all his visitors, except so far as

he is free to, and does, extend, restrict, modify or exclude his duty to a visitor by agreement or otherwise.

(2) The common duty of care is a duty to take such care as in all the circumstances of the case is reasonable to see that the visitor will be reasonably safe in using the premises for the purposes for which he is invited or permitted by the occupier to be there.

(3) The relevant circumstances for the purposes of this section include the degree of care, and of want of care, that would ordinarily be looked for in such a visitor, so that, amongst other things, in proper cases:

(a) an occupier must be prepared for children to be less careful than adults; and

(b) an occupier may expect that a person, in the exercise of his calling, will appreciate and guard against any special risks ordinarily incident to it, so far as the occupier leaves him free to do so."

The section goes on to deal with the effect of warnings that occupiers are obliged to give to visitors about the condition of premises. It also deals with occupiers' liability where dangerous premises are the result of faulty work by a contractor.

Sections 53 and 54 refer to the relationships between a landlord and tenant, occupiers and third parties. Even where a landlord is not an occupier, he or she may owe a duty in some circumstances as if he or she was an occupier.

15.7.2 Claims by dependants of deceased persons

Although compensation for death is widespread in the customs of Papua New Guinean society, at common law a person whose negligence resulted in the death of a person was *not* liable in tort to pay compensation to the dependants of the deceased for losses arising out of the death. However, Pt IV of the *Wrongs Miscellaneous Provisions Act* changes this. It creates a statutory basis for *some* dependants to claim against the person who wrongfully caused the death of the person upon whom they were dependent.

Section 25 is the key section that creates the right to sue for damages arising from death:

> "Where the death of a person is caused by a wrongful act, neglect or default and the act, neglect or default is such as would (if death had not ensued) have entitled the party injured to maintain an action and recover damages in respect of it, the person who would have been liable if death had not ensued is liable to an action for damages notwithstanding the death of the person injured and notwithstanding that the death has been caused under such circumstances as amount in law to an offence."

Section 26 defines the range of people on whose behalf an action may be brought:

> "**26. Actions under Section 25.**
>
> (1) An action referred to in Section 25 shall be for the benefit of the wife, husband, parent and child of the deceased person, and a person who is, or is the issue of, a brother, sister, uncle or aunt of the deceased person, and shall be brought by and in the name of the executor or administrator of the person deceased."

Section 24(1) provides a non-inclusive definition of child and parent:

> "'child' includes son, daughter, grandson, granddaughter, stepson and stepdaughter;
>
> 'parent' includes father, mother, grandfather, grandmother, stepfather and stepmother"

The amount of damages to be awarded is assessed in accordance with s 28:

> "(1) In an action referred to in Section 25, the court may award such damages as it thinks proportioned to the injury resulting from the death to the respective parties for whom and for whose benefit the action is brought, and the amount so recovered, after deducting the costs not recovered from the defendant, shall be divided amongst those parties in such shares as the court directs.
>
> (2) In an action referred to in Section 25, damages may be awarded in respect of medical expenses incurred as a result of the injury causing the death, together with reasonable expenses of the funeral or cremation of the deceased person (including the cost of erecting a headstone or tombstone over the grave of the deceased person), if those expenses have been incurred by one or more of the parties for whose benefit the action is brought."

Section 29 provides for an award for solatium to a parent for the loss of a child. Solatium is compensation for grief over the loss of a child. This award is limited to K600, but may be in addition to other damages which might fall within s 28.

Section 31 prescribes a limitation period of three years.

15.7.3 Claims against the Motor Vehicles Insurance Trust

At common law an action could be brought against the negligent driver or negligent owner of a motor vehicle for damages. The *Motor Vehicle Insurance Trust (Third Party) Insurance Act* changes that in respect of claims involving death or bodily injury arising out of the use of:

- a motor vehicle insured under the *Motor Vehicle Insurance Trust (Third Party) Insurance Act*;

- an uninsured motor vehicle in a public street; or
- a motor vehicle on a public street where the identity of the motor vehicle cannot, after due inquiry and search, be established.

Pursuant to s 54, these types of claims are brought against the Motor Vehicle Insurance Trust as defendant, and not against the owner or driver of the vehicle.

Section 54(3) provides that a claim may proceed even if the owner or driver is:

(a) dead;

(b) cannot be found; or

(c) is the spouse of the person whose death or whose bodily injury has been caused.

> **Notice:** Section 54 also imposes an obligation on a person who wishes to bring an action pursuant to s 54 to give a written notice of the claim to the Trust within a period of six months of the occurrence that gives rise to the claim. The Commissioner of the Trust or a court has the discretion to extend the six-month period on *sufficient cause* being shown. There are numerous cases that deal with the exercise of this discretion: see for instance *Motor Vehicles Insurance Trust v Viel Kampu* [1996] SC587; *Carol Laime an infant by her next friend Willie Laime v Motor Vehicles Insurance Trust* [1995] PNGLR 224.

15.7.4 Defamation

The *Defamation Act* consolidates the common law of defamation. A defamatory matter is defined in s 2 of the Act as:

> "(1) an imputation concerning a person or a member of his family, whether living or dead, by which:
>
> (a) the reputation of that person is likely to be injured; or
>
> (b) he is likely to be injured in his profession or trade, or
>
> (c) other persons are likely to be induced to shun, avoid, ridicule or despise him".

Defamatory matter that is oral is commonly referred to as slander. Defamatory material that is written is commonly referred to as libel. However, this distinction is unimportant under the *Defamation Act*. Defamatory material may be *published* in a written or oral form or by means of signs or gestures.

The *Defamation Act* provides for a number of *protections* that serve as defences in actions for defamation. These include protection relating to:

- petitions to Parliament;
- official reports;
- matters of public interest; and
- fair comment.

These are set out between ss 6-11 of the Act. Defences are also provided to innocent sellers of periodicals and books who are without knowledge of the defamatory nature of the publication.

15.8 REMEDIES FOR TORTIOUS WRONGS

Where liability is established in a claim for negligence or some other wrongful conduct, a Magistrate will be called upon to assess damages. Damages are not presumed, and the legal burden is on the plaintiff to prove damages. Damages break down into several widely recognised categories.

15.8.1 General damages

General damages refer to losses suffered that are not capable of exact arithmetic computation. General damages break down into a number of categories (which are not exact, and overlap to some extent).

Loss or damage to part of the body: This may be serious, such as loss of a limb or paralysis, or may be less serious, such as a scar.

Loss of function or use of the body: This may take the form of an inability to walk, climb stairs, the inability to have sexual intercourse, brain damage or loss of sight.

Pain and suffering: This takes many forms, for example, muscle pain, back pain, arthritis, headaches etc.

Psychological injury: Compensation for this form of general damage is available pursuant to s 36 of the *Wrongs Miscellaneous Provisions Act.*

Loss of amenities: This refers to a diminishment in one's ability to enjoy life. It can take many forms, for instance, the inability to sleep through the night, the inability to enjoy a hobby, the loss of the enjoyment of playing a sport or the inability to drive a car because of the effects of an injury.

Loss of expectation of life: Where an injury results in the loss of expectation of life, that may be taken into account in awarding general damages.

Future loss of income or ability to earn an income: This is something that commonly results from physical injuries that leave a permanent disability. Even a partial diminishment of an ability to earn an income is compensable. This type of loss may result from business or employment.

Other losses which will be incurred in the future: This may include the cost of rehabilitation, medical care or other expenses which the plaintiff will incur in the future as a result of the defendant's wrong. In *Simin Dingi v Motor Vehicle Insurance Trust* [1994] PNGLR 385, a claim pursuant to the *Wrongs Miscellaneous Provisions Act* by parents for the wrongful death of their daughter, included an award for loss of expected bride price according to custom.

Awards of general damages can be assessed with guidance from other cases where similar damages have been assessed. General damages include losses that will be suffered in the future and which must be estimated at the time of trial. With its limited monetary jurisdiction, a District Court is not required to hear claims with major general damage components. However, the above principles, as elucidated in the case law of the National and Supreme Courts, are applicable to the assessment of general damages in District Courts. As written reasons for judgments in the District Courts are compiled and made available, this further valuable source of precedent will provide guidance to Magistrates.

15.8.2 Special damages

Special damages refer to items of damage capable of precise calculation: see 15.5.1. These include expenses incurred by a plaintiff up to the time of the trial. For example, if a plaintiff is seeking damages in a civil claim as a result of being punched in the face by a defendant, the plaintiff may have had his or her glasses broken in the assault. If the glasses have been replaced by the time of the trial, the cost of the replacement glasses would be an item of special damage. Medical expenses incurred as a result of the assault would also fall within special damages that would be claimed. In this example, general damages would also probably be awarded.

15.8.3 Exemplary damages

Both general damages and special damages are intended to put a plaintiff in a position that he or she would have been in if the wrong in question had not been committed. Exemplary damages depart from this general principle. In common law, the three possible bases of exemplary damages are:

(1) where actions by servants of a government have been oppressive, arbitrary or unconstitutional;

(2) where a defendant's conduct has been calculated to make a profit for the defendant that exceeds the compensatory damages he or she would suffer; and

(3) where they are specifically provided for by statute. In Papua New Guinea, the *Arrest Act* and *Search Act* specifically provide for exemplary damages in civil actions for unlawful search or arrest.

In Papua New Guinea, cases that involve claims for damages arising out of illegal police raids on villages frequently entail a consideration of exemplary damages. These cases fall within the first category. An example is the case of *Pike Dambe v Augustine Peri and Independent State of Papua New Guinea* [1993] PNGLR 4. In that case, an award of K30,000 in exemplary damages was made. Although exemplary damages are primarily used to make an example of a defendant in appropriate circumstances and deter the type of behaviour that attracted the liability, this case suggests that exemplary damages in Papua New Guinea may include a compensatory element. See also *Helen Jack v Marius Kavani and The State* [1992] PNGLR 391 and *Kofowei v Siviri* [1983] PNGLR 449.

Recent cases have established that, in respect of claims for exemplary damages arising out of police raids, exemplary damages may not be awarded against the state, although, in appropriate circumstances, they may be awarded against individual members of the police force: see *Abel Tomba v The State* (1997) SC518; *Andate More and Manis Andale v Henry Tokam and The State* (1997) N1645.

15.8.4 Aggravated damages

Aggravated damages, although seldom awarded, may be used to compensate for fear, indignity, humiliation or public disgrace. These may be awarded, for instance, where the actions of a defendant amount to an unprovoked assault. An example of this is the case of *Alex Lathan v Henry Peni; Kathleen Lathan v Henry Peni* (1995) N1463. A Magistrate who considers an award for aggravated damages must ensure that he or she does not duplicate elements of compensation contained in general damages.

15.8.5 Mitigation

In an action for damages arising out of a defendant's wrong, a plaintiff has a duty to take *reasonable* steps to minimise the damage he or she suffers. If a plaintiff acts unreasonably and the damages become greater because of this, the excess damages are not laid at the feet of the defendant. What is reasonable varies from case to case. In *Motor Vehicle Insurance Trust (PNG) v Pupune* [1993] PNGLR 370, the Supreme Court held that a failure by a plaintiff to undergo plastic surgery to reduce scarring amounted to a failure to mitigate. Damages were awarded for the scarring at the level that they would have been if the plaintiff had acted reasonably and undergone the surgery. The duty to mitigate is not restricted to personal injury cases. A plaintiff has a duty to take reasonable steps to minimise economic or business losses that result from a defendant's wrongdoing: See *Kopen v Independent State of Papua New Guinea* [1988-1989] PNGLR 659; see also 15.5.5.

Chapter 16 – Family and Children's Matters in Magistrates' Courts

16.1 INTRODUCTION

A great deal of Magistrates' work concerns family matters. Judges of the National and Supreme Courts have an inherent jurisdiction in relation to children. This jurisdiction is known as *parens patriae.* The literal meaning of this term is "parent of the country". It gives Judges a residual role as guardians of persons (including infants) who cannot look after themselves. Magistrates, on the other hand, have only the express powers given to them by statute, and are therefore without this residual power. Therefore, when exercising their jurisdiction, Magistrates must be careful that they are utilising only powers that are expressly given by statute.

This chapter focuses on the most common family matters that arise in the District Courts and Children's Courts. It covers the types of family orders that can be made by Magistrates. It goes on to consider provisions for the enforcement of maintenance orders. Enforcement in non-family civil matters is considered in detail in Chapter 20.

The jurisdiction of Magistrates in relation to family matters derives primarily from the following statutes:

- *Deserted Wives and Children Act*
- *Adultery and Enticement Act*
- *Child Welfare Act*
- *Juvenile Courts Act*
- *Local Courts Act*
- *Maintenance Orders Enforcement Act*
- *Customs Recognition Act*

16.2 DETERMINATION OF PATERNITY: CHILD WELFARE ACT

Part IX of the *Child Welfare Act* provides Magistrates with the jurisdiction to determine paternity. A finding of paternity may, in turn, give rise to liability of a father to provide support. Such an order may only be made in relation to single mothers or illegitimate children. Neither married women nor legitimate children are entitled to relief pursuant to Pt IX of this Act. An application for such an order may be made either before or after the birth of a child.

An application that is made pursuant to s 50, before the birth of a child, may, on a finding that the defendant is the father of the unborn child, result in an order that the defendant pay confinement expenses in connection with the birth of the child. However, such an order cannot exceed K150: *Child Welfare Act*, s 53.

An application may also be made for a finding of paternity after the birth of a child pursuant to s 51. A man, who is found, pursuant to this section of the Act, to be the father of a child, may be ordered to pay maintenance for the support of the child.

This obligation continues, unless discharged or varied, until the child reaches the age of 16.

16.2.1 The court

Paternity applications may be heard by a Children's Court and, in some other instances, by a District Court.

A Children's Court must be properly constituted in order to make a valid order. The requirements are set out at s 28 of the *Child Welfare Act*. A Magistrate may not sit alone but must have another member present. Further, pursuant to s 28(2), one member of the Children's Court must be a woman. A Children's Court that is improperly constituted cannot make a valid order. This was confirmed in the case of *Kanai Pineri v Lina Balus* [1993] PNGLR 475, where an order made by a Magistrate sitting alone was held to be invalid and the case was resubmitted to the Children's Court for rehearing.

The District Court also has jurisdiction to hear applications pursuant to Pt XI of the *Child Welfare Act* where there is no Children's Court established for the particular area pursuant to s 33(3) of the Act.

16.2.2 The applicant

In most cases an application will be made by the mother or, in the case of confinement expenses of an unborn child, by an expectant mother. However, a mother or expectant mother may consent to an application being made by the Director of Child Welfare or a person authorised in writing by the Director to make an application. A Magistrate should ensure before commencing a hearing that the applicant has standing.

16.2.3 Prerequisites for an application

- In any application for an order pursuant to Pt XI of the *Child Welfare Act*, an application must be made in writing *on oath*. In the case of *Charlie Kipit v Elizabeth Chonghahan* [1994] PNGLR 274, this requirement was confirmed. However, in that case, the appeal Judge held that, since no objection was raised at the hearing, this technical defect should not be allowed to defeat an otherwise meritorious claim.
- The complaint must state (ss 50 and 51):
    - the name of the complainant;
    - the name of the defendant;
    - that the defendant is over the age of 16;

and either:

- that the woman is pregnant; or
- that the defendant is the father of the child and has left the child without means of support.

- A complainant must, prior to issuance of a summons or warrant, produce, on oath, either in writing or orally, evidence that *corroborates*, in some material way, the paternity of the child. Evidence of sexual intercourse with the defendant at the relevant time, or evidence of an admission by the defendant that he is the father, are examples of evidence that can constitute corroboration. Such an admission may be explicit or implicit from the behaviour of the defendant towards the child.

16.2.4 Compelling attendance of the defendant

A Magistrate, on being satisfied that the prerequisites set out above have been satisfied, may compel the attendance of the defendant by means of the issue of a summons or, "if satisfied that the circumstances of the case require it", by the issuance of a warrant: *Child Welfare Act*, s 52. Such circumstances would amount to a reasonable conclusion on the part of a Magistrate that a summons, for whatever reason, would not be effective in compelling attendance of the defendant at court.

Pursuant to s 27, a summons may be served on the defendant personally, "or if he cannot be found", then at his last or most usual known place of residence. The case of *Eric Siam v Lamus Lom* (1981) NZ84 dealt with the right of a defendant to be heard, and the discretion of a Magistrate to hear an application ex parte where the voluntary non-attendance of a defendant may be presumed to be voluntary.

16.2.5 Paternity hearing

Although there is no prescribed procedure for a hearing pursuant to Pt XI of the *Child Welfare Act*, the rules of natural justice apply. It is, therefore, necessary that the defendant be given an opportunity to be present. He must have an opportunity to give evidence and call witnesses if he wishes. Further, he is entitled to a full cross-examination of the complainant and her witnesses.

16.2.6 Defence – common prostitute

It is a defence to an application under Pt XI of the *Child Welfare Act* that the mother is a common prostitute. The meaning of this expression has not been judicially clarified. However, taking money from only one person for sexual intercourse, even repeatedly, does not automatically make a person a common prostitute: see *Raukisa v Leahy* [1967-1968] PNGLR 153; *L v M* [1987] PNGLR 365. Where this defence is successfully raised, it effectively precludes a child of a common prostitute, even one whose paternity is admitted, from the benefit of an order for maintenance.

16.2.7 Standard of proof

The standard of proof in hearings to establish paternity is the civil burden of *balance of probabilities*. This is not explicitly set out, but can be inferred from the various provisions. In relation to confinement expenses, ss 53(2)(c) and 55(2)(c) of the *Child*

Welfare Act are both consistent with this in preventing any order being made where the evidence establishes that it is "impossible or unlikely" that the defendant is the father of the child.

In situations where a man admits sexual intercourse with the complainant "in circumstances where he may possibly be the father", the court may make an order. Similarly, where sexual intercourse is not admitted but is proved to have taken place in circumstances that make it possible that the respondent may be the father, the court may make an order: see ss 58(1) and (3).

16.2.8 Mediation

Where a court hears an application under Pt XI of the *Child Welfare Act*, it may proceed initially by way of mediation pursuant to s 22B of the *District Courts Act*. Mediation may also be conducted at any stage of the hearing: see Chapter 24. In relation to matters of disputed paternity, mediation may be inappropriate. Mediation is likely to be more appropriate where paternity is not in dispute and the only issue is an appropriate amount of maintenance, or, where disputed, the court has determined paternity and the hearing proceeds to the next issue, namely the quantum of maintenance. A Magistrate should be sensitive to possible disparity in the respective bargaining position of the parties, which might result in one party capitulating.

16.2.9 Limitation period

There is National Court authority that the *Frauds and Limitations Act* applies to applications pursuant to Pt XI of the *Child Welfare Act*. The limitation period is six years from the date that the cause of action arose: see *Gone v Alick* [1994] PNGLR 545, which was followed in *Morgan v Faith* [1995] PNGLR 273. This means that, in effect, no application may be brought more than six years after the birth of the child in question.

16.2.10 Finding against more than one person

The *Child Welfare Act* creates the possibility of more than one person being ordered to pay maintenance. Section 58 provides that where a male person, apparently over the age of 16, admits to sexual intercourse with the mother of the child in question, then if the court is satisfied that he "may possibly be the father of the child", it may order that male to pay maintenance. This section diminishes the burden upon a complainant from that of proof of paternity on a balance of probabilities to one of possibility.

Because more than one male may possibly be the father of a child, it is possible that more than one male may be the subject of an order under s 58. This possibility reflects an apparent intent on the part of Parliament to give priority to the needs of children over the need for a high degree of proof that a person is the father of the child. It appears that orders against more than one person under s 58 are rarely, if ever, made. Such orders, however, might be appropriate where a pregnancy arises from a pack rape.

It should also be noted, in relation to s 58, that no application is required in order to make an order against a person. This appears to mean that a Magistrate could make an order against a witness who makes an admission that he had sexual intercourse at the relevant time with the mother of the child.

16.2.11 Evidence

Evidence in support of a finding of paternity will normally include medical opinion about the time of conception. This would be especially true in a case where a mother had sexual intercourse with more than one person at or close to the approximate date of conception. A Magistrate may also take judicial notice of the fact that the normal gestation period is approximately nine months. In some cases, however, where there is more than one act of sexual intercourse around the expected period of conception, or where there is no evidence that the gestation period in question was normal, this may be insufficient to make a determination of paternity.

As a trier of fact, a Magistrate may also draw inferences as to paternity from a physical resemblance between the defendant and a child in relation to whom an application is being made: see *DD v PK* (1991) SC423.

Medical opinion may be in the form of an affidavit pursuant to s 37 of the *Evidence Act*: see Chapter 5. Care should be taken to avoid a party being prejudiced by the sudden production of an affidavit containing medical opinion, where the party against whom it is produced wishes to cross-examine the deponent or at least have an opportunity to examine the document and make submissions on whether an adjournment is warranted.

Presumption regarding age: Section 51(3) of the *Child Welfare Act* creates a rebuttable presumption regarding the age of a person against whom a complaint is made. The effect of this presumption is to place the burden of proof regarding age on a person who maintains that he is under the age of 16. If a person upon whom this burden rests is not able to discharge it, then a court must find that the person is over the age of 16.

16.2.12 Corroboration

A Magistrate must ensure that the evidence of a complainant in a paternity application is corroborated "in some material particular" before making a finding of paternity. This does not require evidence by an eyewitness to the act of sexual intercourse. It may be satisfied if evidence is given of meetings between the mother and the defendant at the presumed time of conception, where there was an opportunity for the parties to have sexual intercourse. A court may infer from such an opportunity that sexual intercourse took place, and this may constitute corroboration:

see *Charlie Kipit v Elizabeth Chonghahan* [1994] PNGLR 274. A false denial by a defendant of a material matter in relation to allegations of paternity may also amount to corroboration: see *Bob Lightbody v Lilly Maiban* [1987] PNGLR 365. Also, in relation to corroboration, see *PK v DD* (1990) N843 (4 May).

16.2.13 Without any means of support

Before a court can make an order for maintenance under Pt XI of the *Child Welfare Act*, it must be satisfied that the defendant "has left the child without any means of support". This expression is contained in ss 51 and 53 of the Act. The meaning of this expression does not appear to have been subjected to judicial interpretation. However, it is submitted that if a defendant is already making financial provision for the maintenance of a child, a court would not find that he "has left the child without any means of support".

16.2.14 Orders for maintenance

The determination of the amount of maintenance or the amount of confinement expenses in any case depends upon a finding of paternity, and is conceptually separate and follows upon a finding of paternity.

Sections 54 and 55 of the *Child Welfare Act* provide little guidance to how a Magistrate should calculate the amount of maintenance in any given case. Both sections only provide for maintenance in an amount that "the court thinks proper".

It is useful to keep in mind four factors when hearing evidence regarding the amount of maintenance. These factors are the:

- **amount of support that the child gets from other sources;**
- **amount of money required by the child in order to be reasonably supported;**
- **amount of income received or likely to be received by the defendant; and**
- **financial obligations of the defendant apart from the obligation to maintain the child.**

None of the above factors alone may indicate what amount of maintenance is appropriate. They should be considered together and carefully balanced off against each other: see *X v Y* [1977] PNGLR 34.

16.2.15 Payment of maintenance

Where orders for maintenance are made against two or more males pursuant to ss 58(2) or 59(4) of the *Child Welfare Act*, the total amount of maintenance ordered must not exceed what would have been ordered if the application had been made against one male under s 51: see ss 58(5) and 59(7).

Except under s 54 (where an maintenance order is incidental to an application for confinement expenses), maintenance must be ordered to be paid on a weekly basis.

Section 56(b) provides that an order for maintenance under ss 54 or 55 (and, in accordance with the deeming provisions of ss 58(4) and 59(5), orders made under those sections) apply to "maintenance of the child from the date of birth of the child". It is not clear whether this means that every maintenance order must provide for payments commencing at the child's birth regardless of when the application is brought.

Orders continue in effect until a child reaches the age of 16, dies or until the order is discharged, whichever first occurs.

Orders for maintenance and confinement expenses made pursuant to Pt XI of the *Child Welfare Act* must direct that payments of maintenance be made to the Director of Child Welfare. A Magistrate need not be concerned in the first instance with particulars of the payment of money to the Director or the payment of money by the Director. However, if either the Director or the mother of the child makes an application, a court may give directions as to the disposal of the money: *Child Welfare Act*, s 57(2).

16.2.16 Variation

Section 100 of the *Child Welfare Act* provides that an order for maintenance may be varied on the application of either the Director, the mother of the child in question or the person liable to pay money under the order. Where an application is made to vary maintenance, a Magistrate may summon to court all persons stated in the complaint to be liable for maintenance of the child. Section 59(6) also provides for variation of orders that have already been varied.

Section 100(2) sets out the requirements of an application for variation. A Magistrate who hears an application for variation need not be the same Magistrate who made the original order: s 100(4).

On hearing an order for variation, a court may "alter, vary, suspend or discharge the order or make a new order as it thinks just in light of fresh evidence adduced". Where a finding of paternity is made and evidence supports an award of maintenance, an order will be made for maintenance: s 100(5).

16.3 ORDERS FOR MAINTENANCE: DESERTED WIVES AND CHILDREN ACT

The *Deserted Wives and Children Act* provides a means for dealing with the maintenance of wives who have been left without support by their husbands, and for children who have been left without support by their fathers.

The Act also provides for awards of custody of children where a father has deserted his child or left the child without means of support.

16.3.1 Grounds for bringing complaint

Section 2 of the *Deserted Wives and Children Act* provides a basis for bringing a complaint pursuant to the Act.

A claim may be brought against a husband where the he has:

- unlawfully deserted his wife;
- left his wife without means of support; or
- is about to leave the country without making adequate provision for his wife.

A claim may be brought against a father where he has:

- deserted his child;
- left the child without means of support; or
- is about to leave the country without making adequate provision for the support of the child.

Note that the grounds for bringing a complaint against a father or husband only differ in that, where desertion is a ground, in the case of a wife the desertion must be "unlawful". The significance of this difference is not clear, and does not appear to have been subjected to judicial interpretation.

There is nothing to prevent a single application being made collectively on the behalf of a wife and child or children. However, where this happens, a Magistrate must allocate sums of maintenance to each person rather than making an order for a single amount: s 13.

An application may be made on behalf of a child whether that child is born to married parents or out of wedlock: *PR v SC* [1986] PNGLR 69.

A complaint must be made on oath. Where a complaint is not made on oath, any order that is made by a Magistrate pursuant to that complaint will be invalid.

Where a marriage has been dissolved, no further order may be made on behalf of a wife. This applies to both a statutory marriage and to a marriage that has dissolved in accordance with custom: *Martha Aeava v Oa Ikupu* [1986] PNGLR 65.

A husband who has been deserted by his wife cannot make an application pursuant to the *Deserted Wives and Children Act*: *Agua Bepi v Aiyu Simon* [1986] PNGLR 233. The principle of this case is presumably wide enough to prevent an application from being made on behalf of a child who has been deserted or left without support by his or her mother.

16.3.2 The hearing

It is important to note that, unlike many other proceedings in the District Courts, a hearing under s 3 of the *Deserted Wives and Children Act* is in the nature of an inquiry. Section 3 says that "a Court shall inquire into the matter". The significance of this is that a court has a much more active role to play in an inquiry than it does in a traditional adversarial hearing in the nature of a trial. In an inquiry, a Magistrate is at liberty to ask more questions of witnesses, and to summon witnesses to a greater extent than does a Magistrate in a trial situation (particularly a criminal trial). Where parties are not able to articulate questions clearly and are not familiar with the requirements of the statute, a Magistrate's role includes ensuring that the issues are defined and the relevant evidence is adduced both in support of, and in opposition to, the claim. However, where parties are represented, or where they are able to take a lead in the proceedings, a Magistrate should take a less active role than he or she otherwise would.

16.3.3 Evidence

At all times, a Magistrate must ensure that the requirements of natural justice are complied with in the proceedings. This means that each side must be given an opportunity to call witness in support of their case, and must have an opportunity to cross-examine the opposing party and witnesses called by that party.

In all proceedings under the *Deserted Wives and Children Act*, both spouses are competent and compellable: s 18. This includes proceedings pursuant to ss 22 and 23, which create offences for unlawfully and unreasonably deserting a wife and child. The effect of this is to remove the privilege that otherwise attaches to an accused in a criminal proceeding, and which prevents a court from drawing an adverse inference from the failure of a defendant to testify. An adverse inference may be drawn from the voluntary failure of a father or husband to testify. It is also possible for a party to summon a husband, wife or father to give evidence. However, if this occurs, the party calling the witness must treat the witness as their own, and, subject to a declaration that the witness is hostile (see Chapter 5), may not engage in unfettered cross-examination of the witness.

16.3.4 Meaning of desertion

As mentioned above, unlawful desertion is a ground for an application for maintenance for a wife. Desertion is a ground for an application on behalf of a child. The meaning of desertion in relation to a wife has been considered in a number of cases.

The physical departure of a husband or father from the family home is the most common form of desertion. However, where a wife leaves a family home, her departure may amount to desertion *by the husband*. This is known as *constructive desertion*. Constructive desertion results from a state of affairs, created by a husband, which makes it intolerable for a wife to remain in the family home, with the result that she is compelled to leave. Section 20 of the *Deserted Wives and Children Act* provides that:

> "a wife who has been compelled to leave her husband's residence under reasonable apprehension of danger to her person or under other circumstances that reasonably justify her withdrawal from that residence shall be deemed to have been deserted without reasonable cause".

Frequently, constructive desertion results from repeated threatened or actual physical abuse inflicted on the wife by the husband. The departure of a wife due to the husband bringing another woman into the home in a spousal relationship may also amount to constructive desertion: *Kunjil v Monpi* [1995] PNGLR 281.

Section 21 of the Act creates a presumption of desertion where a husband or father has abandoned a wife or child for a period in excess of 80 days, during 14 of which the wife or child has been left without means of support. Other evidence may lead to a finding of desertion where abandonment of fewer than 80 days exists.

16.3.5 Proof of marriage

Although most facts in an application for maintenance by a wife are provable by viva voce evidence, s 19 of the *Deserted Wives and Children Act* creates a special requirement for proof of marriage. Direct evidence of a marriage is required, and if no direct evidence is available, then the wife must produce an affidavit setting out the time, place and circumstances of the marriage. The meaning of direct evidence does not appear to have been subjected to scrutiny in the National or Supreme Court. However, it would appear to require the production of a marriage certificate in the case of a statutory marriage: see *Evidence Act*, s 57.

16.3.6 Defences

Reasonable grounds for desertion: A husband who has deserted his wife, left her without reasonable support, or is about to leave the country, may defend himself against a claim by a wife on any of these grounds if he has *reasonable* grounds for his actions. Where reasonable grounds are demonstrated, a Magistrate *may* decline to make an order in favour of a wife. The court is left with some discretion in the matter. This applies to applications on behalf of both wives and children. What the term "reasonable" contemplates is not clear, and it does not seem to have been subjected to interpretation in any National or Supreme Court case. Clearly, what is reasonable is a matter of fact to be decided in any particular case where the defence is raised.

Elias Tokom v Luisa Tokum [1985] PNGLR 195 is authority for the proposition that a husband will only have reasonable cause for leaving his wife if her misconduct is so weighty and grave as to make married life quite impossible. Mere unhappiness or incompatibility is not sufficient to provide a husband with a reasonable excuse for deserting his wife or leaving her without any means of support.

Adultery or drunken habits: A more specific defence is available to a husband under s 3(4) of the *Deserted Wives and Children Act*. This section provides that a wife who has committed adultery or is of drunken habits is not entitled to an order for maintenance pursuant to the Act. Subject to s 3(5), a Magistrate is left with no discretion where this defence is raised. The burden of proving the existence of this defence is on the husband who alleges it. A Magistrate, after hearing all the evidence, must be prepared to determine whether, on the evidence, the husband has established that the wife is either of drunken habits or has committed adultery.

However, pursuant to s 3(4), such a defence is not available to a husband who has "conduced or connived at the adultery or, by his cruelty, wilful neglect or misconduct, conduced to the adultery or drunken habits". A Magistrate must therefore, where the wife is either of drunken habits or has committed adultery, be prepared to determine, on the evidence, whether the husband has condoned or connived at the adultery or, by cruelty, wilful neglect or misconduct, whether he has conduced to the adultery or drunken habits.

Condonation: To condone means to voluntarily overlook or forgive adultery, and to treat a wife as if it had never happened: *Black's Law Dictionary* (6th ed).

Connivance: To connive, pursuant to s 3(4), is to co-operate secretly with, or to have a secret or clandestine understanding with, one's wife in relation to her adultery. It implies knowledge of and consent to the adultery of the wife: *Black's Law Dictionary* (6th ed).

Conduce: To conduce means to contribute to the adultery or drunken habits. In *Billy Tau Noi v Irong Noi* [1990] PNGLR 335, the court adopted *Halsbury's Laws of England*, Vol 13, para 1318, where it states that "misconduct conducing to adultery or desertion is conduct which in itself constitutes the true cause of the adultery or desertion". In that case, the husband's failure to fulfil his obligations to maintain his family, together with his brutality towards his wife, amounted to misconduct that conduced to the adultery of the wife.

Whether a husband has connived, conduced or condoned the wife's behaviour is a matter of fact for a Magistrate to determine based on the evidence in a particular case. The onus of proving the existence of these would be on the wife who is seeking to bar a husband from relying upon her adultery or drunken habits as a defence.

Where a Magistrate is of the opinion that a husband has conduced to the adultery or drunken habits of a wife, it is important that the Magistrate "expressly state to that effect and also give the reasons for such refusal [to discharge an order]": *Jubilee v Ealo* [1991] PNGLR 98 at 103.

16.3.7 Quantum of maintenance

The only guidance that the *Deserted Wives and Children Act* provides to Magistrates, in relation to the quantum of maintenance, is that it should be in such amount as the Magistrate considers reasonable for the use of the wife or support of the child as the case may be: s 3(1)(a)(iii) and (v).

It should be noted that the earnings of the wife cannot be taken into account in determining whether a husband has left a wife without means of support. However, a wife's income may be considered in determining what is a reasonable amount of maintenance to order for the use of the wife: *Elias Tokom v Luisa Tokom* [1985] PNGLR 195.

The lifestyle and level of affluence enjoyed by a wife and child prior to the desertion of the husband or father are relevant considerations in determining a reasonable amount of maintenance: *P v P* (1990) N931 (7 December).

In addition to the income and reasonable expenses of a wife or child recipient of a maintenance order, the financial circumstances of the husband (both income and expenditures) should be considered in the determination of a proper award of maintenance. See *Jacobs v Jacobs* [1976] PNGLR 532 for a consideration of how a husband's subsequent obligations to a mistress and her children should be taken into account.

Where the reasonable need of a recipient exceeds the ability of a father or husband to pay, careful attention should be paid to the expenditures of both parties in order to ensure that an award of maintenance identifies and distinguishes the essential expenditures of a husband or father from those which may require compromise in favour of his obligations to a wife or child. In making an award which will result in a husband or father having to compromise on expenses for himself or others who he is not legally or morally bound to support, an explanation of reasons should be given.

16.3.8 Structure of a maintenance order

Magistrates have some discretion in determining how an order for maintenance should be structured. Unlike Pt XI of the *Child Welfare Act* (paternity applications) where maintenance orders must be structured on a weekly basis, the *Deserted Wives and Children Act*, at s 3(2), provides that a Magistrate may order that payments pursuant to an order for maintenance shall be paid weekly, fortnightly or monthly, and to such person as the court orders. Where a defendant father or husband is in receipt of a regular income (from employment or otherwise), this allows for maintenance payments to be made at the same intervals as the income.

An order for the support of a child does not extend beyond the child's 16th birthday: *Deserted Wives and Children Act*, s 3(2). In making an order for maintenance of a child, a Magistrate should ensure that this limitation is expressed in the order.

However, any arrears that are unpaid beyond a child's 16th birthday continue to be recoverable.

A Magistrate is given a wide discretion in determining the recipient of an order for maintenance made for the benefit of a wife or child. Section 3(2) provides that payments may be ordered to be made to "such person and in such manner as the Court orders".

Factors which will influence a Magistrate's discretion in this regard are likely to include:

- **the need for certainty in the accounting of maintenance payments;**
- **the desirability in some cases of limiting direct contact between a husband or father and the wife or children on whose behalf an order is made; and**
- **the responsibility of available persons who may be entrusted with applying child maintenance payments to the welfare of the child.**

In cases where the court registry is able to deal with the administration of maintenance payments, it should be considered as a recipient of child maintenance payments.

16.3.9 Variation

After an order for maintenance or custody has been made, circumstances of either party can change in ways that are relevant to the order. Section 11 of the *Deserted Wives and Children Act* provides for the variation of an order for custody or maintenance. An application may be made by or on behalf of a wife, child, husband or parent of a child.

An application may only be made at a court that satisfies the geographical requirements of s 11(2) and (3).

A court hearing an application for variation of maintenance may hear evidence of circumstances of the parties both after and before the making of the original order. However, in relation to circumstances before the original order, only evidence that was not available at the time of the original order is admissible. The meaning of the expression "not available" is not clear, and may refer to the fact that it was not adduced at the original hearing. Alternatively, it may refer to evidence which, even with due diligence on the part of the party, could not have been adduced at the time of the application for the original order.

16.3.10 Discharge

An application, pursuant to s 11 of the *Deserted Wives and Children Act*, may be made to discharge the order, or an application to vary may result in the discharge of the order. The discharge of an order should only be made where it is clear that circumstances will not change in a way that would merit the continuation of the order. In circumstances where a temporary lapse would be more appropriate than a discharge, the reduction of a maintenance order to a token amount (perhaps K1) is warranted.

An example of circumstances that would warrant the discharge of an order would be the death of the beneficiary of the maintenance order. Another would be the remarriage of a recipient spouse. However, remarriage of a mother should not automatically result in the discharge or variance of maintenance for children. A further ground for the discharge of a maintenance order in favour of a wife would be her adultery in circumstances where there is no "defence" for the adultery: see s 11(7).

The discharge of an order for maintenance does not amount to the quashing of the original order. Therefore, although a discharge may be made retroactively, payments made pursuant to the original order are not automatically refundable, even where ground for discharging the order existed for some time prior to the order itself. Where a customary marriage is dissolved in accordance with native custom, it will provide a ground for the discharge of an order for spousal maintenance. See *Igua Nou v Karoho Vagi* [1986] PNGLR 1, which considered this issue under the provisions of the *Maintenance Orders Enforcement Act*. See also *Martha Aeava v Oa Ikupu* [1986] PNGLR 65.

16.4 CHILD CUSTODY UNDER THE DESERTED WIVES AND CHILDREN ACT

Section 3(1)(a)(iii) of the *Deserted Wives and Children Act* provides for a custody order to be made by a Magistrate. The custody order may be made in favour of the wife or "some other person". The *Deserted Wives and Children Act* cannot be used as a means of deciding the custody of a child or children unless the father has deserted the child, left him or her without means of support or is about to leave the country: *Raymond Mura v Dan Gigmai* (1997) N1573.

In contested claims for custody in the National Court pursuant to the *Matrimonial Causes Act* or the *Infant Act*, the best interests of the child in question are the paramount consideration. Magistrates do not hear applications under these statutes, but should be guided by the same principle. This is consistent with s 14 of the *Deserted Wives and Children Act*, which states that "the welfare of the child" should be the primary criterion.

In *RG v MG* [1984] PNGLR 413, the National Court set forth some considerations that might be relevant in relation to the best interests of the child. These are:

- **the claim of the mother and her preferred role;**
- **the relative circumstances in which it is intended to raise the child;**
- **the ability of the competing claimants to provide for the child in question, including their ability to provide for the child's advancement in life;**
- **the age of the child; and**
- **the need to maintain existing relationships.**

Relevant custom may also play a role in the determination of contested custody claims. However, consideration of custom should be made in light of the child's best interests. Also, where custom is considered, a Magistrate must be aware of the limitations in the application of custom as set out in Sch 2.1 of the *Constitution* and in s 3 of the *Custom Recognition Act.*

In *Wan v Koman* [1990] PNGLR 322 (decided under the *Infants Act*), it was held that where a child is from an area where custom governs social structure, decisions about custody should take into account the child's social security as part of a larger group according to custom.

16.5 AWARDS OF COMPENSATION FOR ADULTERY AND ENTICEMENT

The *Adultery and Enticement Act* eliminates any pre-existing common law right to compensation for adultery or enticement of a spouse, and creates a statutory entitlement to damages. The District Court has jurisdiction over this statutory remedy.

In most respects, an action under the *Adultery and Enticement Act* is a civil proceeding. The statute does not provide particulars about the form of complaint or service of the complaint on a defendant. Magistrates should be guided by the provisions of the *District Courts Act* in relation to filing of complaints, the issuance of a summons or warrant and service of process.

16.5.1 Limitation period

The time for bringing an action for damages for adultery or enticement is restricted by s 8 of the *Adultery and Enticement Act*. Rather than a limitation period measured in years, which is usual for civil claims, the limitation for bringing a claim under the Act is six months from the date of the adultery or enticement that is complained of. A Magistrate is given the discretion under s 8(2) to extend the period for up to three months where a complainant has a "reasonable cause for not bringing an action" within the six-month period.

The Act does not specify what constitutes reasonable cause, and there appears to be no reported authority. However, it might be reasonable to extend the period in cases where the complaining party does not learn about the alleged act of adultery or enticement until more than six months from its alleged commission.

16.5.2 Parties to an action for adultery or enticement

The spouse of a party may bring an action under the *Adultery and Enticement Act*. A spouse is defined in s 1 as "a party to a relationship between a man and a woman which can be reasonably considered as a subsisting relationship having the status of a marriage". This definition leaves several questions, none of which appear to have been resolved by judicial authority. It is not clear whether "status" has a legal meaning or a non-legal objective meaning. In other words, does a relationship have to have the status of a legal or customary marriage for a spouse to bring an action? The answer is not clear.

A spouse may give permission to a relative to bring an action on his or her behalf. The degree of relationship required is not clear. Degrees of relationship may conceivably extend beyond a sibling, parent or child relationship to more distant ones. It may also extend to relationships of marriage rather than blood. Some guidance may be found in the notion of standing: see 14.3.2.

If a spouse is unable or incapable of giving consent, a relative may do so pursuant to s 6(b)(ii). A complaint brought by a relative should set out the basis of the authority for bringing the complaint. This includes the relationship of the complainant to the person entitled under ss 4 or 5 of the Act, and the basis of the authority for bringing the complaint. In any event, this should be clarified under oath when the proceeding commences. If a relative does not establish grounds for bringing the action, it should be dismissed.

A party named as a defendant may be the spouse of the complainant or the person who has allegedly committed adultery with or enticed the spouse.

16.5.3 Consolidation of proceedings

Under s 8 of the *Adultery and Enticement Act*, where more than one separate complaint is made under the Act, they may be consolidated in certain circumstances. This may occur where more than one complaint is brought for enticement or adultery against the same person. It may also happen where two actions are brought in relation to the same alleged act of adultery or enticement, one against the spouse and one against the person who enticed the spouse or who allegedly committed adultery with the spouse.

A consolidation of actions pursuant to s 8 may be accomplished on the initiative of a Magistrate, without application of a party and without additional documents being filed. However, an order for consolidation should be clearly made and recorded. Also, court staff should be instructed in advance to be alert to cases that may be consolidated, so that when an order is made, a single court date can be set and unnecessary adjournments can be avoided.

16.5.4 Mediation

Mediation plays an important role in the resolution of disputes under the *Adultery and Enticement Act*. Section 10 requires that a Magistrate endeavour to have the matter settled by mediation. A Magistrate who is approved by the Legal and Judicial Services Commission may attempt this. Magistrates who involve themselves as mediators should disqualify themselves from presided at a hearing of the case when mediation fails, unless both parties expressly consent to the Magistrate presiding at a contested hearing. In any event, the matter may be referred to whoever is available and appropriate to act as a mediator in the community. In many cases, there is nobody available with formal qualifications, but pastors, elders and others who have the confidence of both parties may serve as mediators: see Chapter 24.

16.5.5 Hearing

A hearing pursuant to the *Adultery and Enticement Act* is essentially civil in nature. Accordingly, a Magistrate has the discretion to allow a proceeding to take place on an ex parte basis (provided that mediation has already been canvassed) where the absence of the defendant or defendants can be presumed to be voluntary.

The rules of natural justice apply to hearings. This involves the right of a party to call and give evidence, and the right to cross-examine witnesses called for the opposing side. Each side should be provided with an opportunity to make submissions at the conclusion of the evidence, and should be prevented from making submissions (except on ancillary matters that arise during the hearing) before that time. The burden of proof is on the balance of probabilities.

16.5.6 Defences

Section 9 of the *Adultery and Enticement Act* provides defendants with specific defences that may be advanced alone or in combination.

A defendant may avoid liability by showing that:

- the person entitled to bring the action consented to the act of adultery or enticement prior to its commission;
- the person entitled to bring the action has forgiven the defendant. This may be either the spouse or the person who enticed or committed adultery with the spouse of the person entitled to bring the action; or
- the defendant believed, on reasonable grounds, that the person they enticed or committed adultery with was not married.

The onus of proof in relation to these defences is on the defendant who advances the defence, and the standard would be on a balance of probabilities.

16.5.7 Determination of compensation

The *Adultery and Enticement Act* places a ceiling on the amount of damages that may be awarded for adultery and enticement. The limitations in this regard may be found in ss 12 and 13.

Where an action is brought against two defendants for an act of adultery, the total amount of compensation must not exceed K1,000. Where an order is made against two or more defendants for enticement, the total compensation must not exceed K500. Where a person entices and commits adultery with a spouse, a claimant is not entitled to more than a total of K1,000 for both the adultery and the enticement.

In *John Gawi and Diana Apes v Mary Gawi* (1997) N1584, it was held that repeated acts of adultery between the same partner are to be treated as one act of adultery. There cannot be a repetition of actions for continuing acts of adultery between the same partners. According to this decision, "[i]t cannot be intended that where there is a continuous adulterous relationship, there can be a repetition of actions." The court held that to allow repeated actions for repeated acts of adultery would, in effect, amount to forcing a marriage to continue against the will of one of the spouses. In such cases, the proper forum for relief is the National Court, where proceedings pursuant to the *Matrimonial Causes Act* may be brought.

Where an award for compensation is made in respect of more than one defendant, the order must, pursuant to s 15, clearly state how liability for compensation is apportioned between or among defendants.

Compensation may be ordered to be made in cash or in goods or in a combination of the two. This allows for appropriate compensation in some cases where a defendant is not able to make a cash payment. Compensation may be ordered to take place in a lump sum or by way of periodic instalments.

The amount of compensation takes into account the defendant's ability to pay. Section 16 of the *Adultery and Enticement Act* requires a Magistrate to take into account a defendant's earning capacity and "any other financial hardship likely to be suffered from the making of the order". This section distinguishes awards of compensation for adultery and enticement from most other forms of civil damages. In most civil cases, damages are based solely on the amount required to compensate a victim. The quantum is geared towards placing the victim in the position that he or she was in prior to the cause of action. A defendant's ability to pay compensation is irrelevant in most (non-family) civil cases, but, pursuant to s 16 of the *Adultery and Enticement Act*, it becomes a relevant consideration.

Magistrates are also directed by s 16 to take into account any other matters that are relevant, including any compensation that has already been paid by custom.

Care should be taken in framing orders in order to avoid ambiguity or vagueness, especially where an order departs from a lump sum award in money.

16.6 CERTIFYING THE DISSOLUTION OF CUSTOMARY MARRIAGES

16.6.1 Customary marriage and dissolution

The formation and dissolution of a customary marriage takes place without the interference or participation of a court or any government regulatory body. A customary marriage ends in a similar way. However, when a customary marriage ends, parties to the marriage may wish to obtain conclusive proof that their marriage has been dissolved. Section 22A of the *District Courts Act* provides that a Magistrate, on being satisfied that a customary marriage has been dissolved in accordance with custom, may grant a certificate of dissolution. The Magistrate does not actually dissolve the marriage, but merely provides official recognition of the dissolution.

There are two questions in deciding upon whether a certificate of dissolution of a customary marriage should be granted:

1. Have the parties been married in accordance with custom?
2. If the parties have been married in accordance with custom, have they been divorced (has their marriage been dissolved) in accordance with custom?

One or both parties may assume that the relationship they have had is a customary marriage, when in fact it is not. If it is not, then no hearing pursuant to s 22A of the *District Courts Act* needs to be concluded, and no certificate of dissolution of marriage is required.

In relation to the formation of a customary marriage, s 3 of the *Marriage Act* provides:

> "(1) Notwithstanding the provisions of this Act or of any other law, a native, other than a native who is a party to a subsisting marriage under Part V, may enter, and shall be deemed always to have been capable of entering, into a customary marriage in accordance with the custom prevailing in the tribe or group to which the parties to the marriage or either of them belong or belongs.
>
> (2) Subject to this Act, a customary marriage is valid and effectual for all purposes."

The determination of whether a customary marriage has taken place entails the question of what is the relevant custom in relation to the marriage of the parties. According to s 16 of the *Underlying Law Act*, custom is a question of law and not fact. A Magistrate may ascertain custom by reference to cases, books and official statements, as well as evidence adduced by the parties or on the Magistrate's own initiative. For further discussion of the effect of this Act, see 2.3.8, 2.4, 3.4.2, 5.13 and 25.6.4.

Schedule 2.1 of the *Constitution* should also be borne in mind in the determination of whether a customary marriage exists. It prevents the recognition of custom that is inconsistent with the general principles of humanity.

In *Re Maip* [1991] PNGLR 82, the National Court held that a de facto relationship does not automatically give rise to a customary marriage, even in the face of a recognition that custom is changing in Papua New Guinea.

Similar considerations are involved in the determination of whether a customary marriage has been dissolved. The relevant custom must be considered as a question of fact, bearing in mind Sch 2.1 of the *Constitution*. Evidence of the dissolution of a customary marriage may take the form of viva voce evidence of the parties. Evidence may also take the form of a certificate of dissolution of customary marriage, issued by a Village Court. The determination of this issue remains, however, a question of fact to be decided upon the evidence. In some cases, a party may be seeking a certificate of dissolution in order to be legally remarried. In such cases, the parties may not have gone through the necessary customary steps to dissolve the marriage.

A marriage that has been solemnised by statute is not a customary marriage and cannot be dissolved by the District Court: *The State v Floyd Robinson* [1992] PNGLR 205.

16.6.2 Consequential orders

A number of consequences may follow upon recognition by the court of the dissolution of a customary marriage. One of these may be the return of the bride price payment made pursuant to custom by the husband's family at the time of the marriage. An application for the return of such a payment may be heard as part of the same proceeding in which a certificate of dissolution is sought.

Custom must be applied in applications for the return of bride price payments on dissolution of marriage. Fault also plays a part in deciding how much, if any, of a bride price payment must be repaid on the dissolution of a customary marriage. For instance, if a husband makes life intolerable for a wife and in effect precipitates the dissolution of the marriage, it would be likely that less (or perhaps none) of the bride price payment will be ordered to be returned: *Kere v Timon* [1990] PNGLR 103.

The same case stands for the proposition that, where the customs of the husband and the wife's people conflict, "[i]t is a question of fairness whether one custom should be applied in an area where there is a different custom in existence and accepted and practised by people in that area." In the absence of strict statutory guidelines or a large body of written decisions to guide Magistrates, the concept of basic fairness will continue to be an important guiding principle.

16.7 ENFORCEMENT OF MAINTENANCE ORDERS: MAINTENANCE ORDERS ENFORCEMENT ACT

The *Maintenance Orders Enforcement Act* applies to all orders for maintenance made pursuant to the *Deserted Wives and Children Act*, the *Child Welfare Act* (including orders for the payment of confinement expenses and for payment of the funeral expenses of a ward) and all orders of maintenance made by a Local Court. It does not apply to orders for maintenance pursuant to the *Matrimonial Causes Act*.

All applications under the *Maintenance Orders Enforcement Act* must be made in the District Court.

16.7.1 Hearings and evidence under the Maintenance Orders Enforcement Act

Proceedings under the *Maintenance Orders Enforcement Act* are commenced by way of complaint. The complaint must be made under oath: s 65(1). Upon the filing of a complaint, the Clerk of Court may issue a summons or, if the whereabouts of the defendant are unknown, may issue a warrant: s 65(3). Where a defendant does not appear after being served with a summons, a court may proceed ex parte (if it is satisfied that service of the summons was effected or, if after "strict inquiry", service has not been possible), or it may issue a warrant and adjourn the proceedings. However, if a warrant is issued, a court may still proceed ex parte, then or later: s 66(5).

Where a person makes an application on behalf of another person pursuant to the *Maintenance Orders Enforcement Act*, the authority of the person to make the application is presumed, pursuant to s 69, and does not require proof.

Where an issue arises about whether a payment has been made or money has been received, and court records, in the form of books of account, purport to disclose the relevant information, those books are admissible to prove the information contained in them. This is a specific exception to the hearsay rule that eliminates the need, in most cases, to call witnesses who made the entries, or witnesses who provided the information upon which the entry is based: s 70.

Section 71 provides a means of supplementing an original enforcement order with further directions or changes in the order. This would be appropriate where a defendant changes employers between the time an attachment order is made and the completion of payment of arrears. Another instance would be where an order for seizure and sale of property is frustrated in some technical way that can be alleviated by the giving of further directions.

A defendant, in whose absence a hearing has taken place pursuant to s 66 (where the defendant was not served), may apply to set aside the order within 21 days of learning of the existence of the order. If the original order is set aside, a new hearing takes place: s 72(2).

A defendant is compellable and may be cross-examined about his means and ability to comply with any order made against him under the Act. Further, a defendant may be compelled to provide, in the form of a signed statement, information pertaining to his employer, his income and any other relevant matters the court requires: s 74. The same section provides that a person who is alleged to be indebted to the defendant may also be required to provide a signed statement that sets out relevant information: s 74(2).

Statements provided under s 74, and purporting to be such, may be introduced into evidence and are deemed to prove their contents.

Section 47 of the *District Courts Act* governs the rules of service of documents under the *Maintenance Orders Enforcement Act*. In addition, substituted service may be ordered under s 75(2) of the *Maintenance Orders Enforcement Act*. Section 75(4) provides rules for service on infants.

Service must be effected 10 clear days prior to the hearing to which service relates: s 75(6). However, proceedings are not invalidated by failure to give this much notice. In order to preserve the elements of natural justice, however, an adjournment should be considered for a person who has had fewer than ten days notice and feels prejudiced by this: s 75(8).

16.7.2 Types of orders available

The *Maintenance Orders Enforcement Act* sets out the following main types of orders that may be employed to ensure the payment of maintenance and enforce the payment of arrears of maintenance:

1. Order a defendant in arrears to go to prison. This includes orders that impose conditions for payment of arrears and automatic imprisonment where those conditions are not met. Sections 4-6 of the Act deal with this.
2. Provide for a person, in whose favour a maintenance order has been made, to proceed to the National Court for enforcement pursuant to the jurisdiction of that court. Magistrates are not directly involved in this procedure.
3. Order that a defendant enter into a recognisance, either at the time that a maintenance order is made or subsequently.
4. Order the seizure and sale of property belonging to a defendant who is in arrears in respect of a maintenance order.
5. Order that earnings, or a portion of the earnings, of a defendant in arrears be attached and paid towards the satisfaction of the outstanding maintenance.

Each of these types of orders is considered in greater detail below.

16.7.3 Prison

The problem with prison is that it does not automatically result in the payment of any money pursuant to a maintenance order. At best, it works as an inducement to pay. The powers in ss 4-6 of the *Maintenance Orders Enforcement Act* provide a Magistrate with several means of utilising this inducement. They include ways of applying the inducement in the form of a threat of imprisonment and, where this is considered sufficient to secure the desired result, it should be considered in preference to automatic imprisonment.

The power to enforce a maintenance order by imprisonment may only be used against a male person. The application is brought by or on behalf of the person who is the beneficiary of the maintenance order. The application may be brought ex parte in some circumstances: s 66.

A Magistrate may sentence a defendant to prison for up to one year. Magistrates should bear in mind the nature of an order for commitment pursuant to s 4. It is not a criminal sentence. The term of imprisonment that is imposed should be calculated on the basis of what it would take to secure payment, and not on the basis that it is a punishment for failure to pay maintenance.

16.7.4 Defences to an application for commitment to prison

A defendant may not be committed to imprisonment more than once in relation to the same arrears of maintenance.

Section 5 of the *Maintenance Orders Enforcement Act* also provides a defendant with further defences based on his inability to pay the arrears. The principle underlying this section is that only those defendants who wilfully fail to pay arrears of maintenance should be committed to prison.

Particular attention must be paid to a defendant who has previously appeared in court in relation to arrears of maintenance and *not* been committed to prison for a particular amount of arrears. A Magistrate, pursuant to s 5(2), must only commit a defendant to prison in relation to his arrears if satisfied that circumstances "have so altered as to make it reasonable for him to be committed to prison for its non-payment".

Section 26 provides a defence to an application for imprisonment (or any other proceeding in relation to arrears of maintenance). If a defendant, who is in arrears in relation to an order for maintenance, provides adequate support to the person for whose benefit the order was made, during the period to which the arrears relate, no order for imprisonment may be made.

16.7.5 Partial payment after committal order

A defendant who is committed to prison may make partial payment of the outstanding arrears in relation to which the order has been made. The period of imprisonment is accordingly reduced in proportion to the amount of arrears paid.

Sections 202 and 203 of the *District Courts Act* are incorporated by s 4(6) of the *Maintenance Orders Enforcement Act* in this regard. Section 6(2) of the *Maintenance Orders Enforcement Act* provides for a similar pro-rationing of the arrears where partial payment has been made between the time of an order and the time that a warrant of committal is issued or executed.

Section 4(7)-(10) contains further particulars in relation to orders for imprisonment.

Section 6 provides a Magistrate with some flexibility in committing a defendant to prison. This flexibility may be directed toward the goal of using the threat of prison, rather than imprisonment itself, as an effective inducement to pay. This flexibility arises from the power to delay the issue or execution of a warrant of committal. Section 6(1)(c) provides for an order that payments be made by instalments, and that failure to make such payments will result in the issue or execution of the order of committal.

16.7.6 Wording of the order

It is very important that Magistrates carefully consider the wording of an order. It is advisable to adjourn a case briefly after the conclusion of evidence and submissions. During the adjournment, a Magistrate can carefully consider the terms of the order and how they can be concisely and accurately expressed in a manner that allows the parties, the collector, and any other authority that comes into contact with the order, a payment or the defendant to interpret it correctly.

An example of the sort of order where such care is required is where a Magistrate imposes conditions pursuant to s 6 of the *Maintenance Orders Enforcement Act*, and the order for committal applies to a portion of arrears only.

16.7.7 Recovery of arrears in National Court

Section 7 of the *Maintenance Orders Enforcement Act* deals with enforcement of arrears of maintenance in the National Court. This does not directly involve Magistrates.

16.7.8 Recognisances

A recognisance is an acknowledgment made by a defendant of the amount of arrears due, together with a promise by the defendant to pay the maintenance. Although the *Maintenance Orders Enforcement Act* does not specifically indicate that an order that a defendant enter into a recognisance may be conditioned by a deposit of money in a specified sum, s 8(5) implies that this is the case.

A Magistrate may order a defendant to enter into such a recognisance at the time of making the original maintenance order or at any other time on application. A recognisance may therefore apply to maintenance as it becomes due, or to arrears that have already accrued: s 8.

A surety may be required as a condition of the recognisance. The *Maintenance Orders Enforcement Act* does not provide specific guidance about considerations relating to a surety. A Magistrate, in deciding whether the requirement of a surety should be imposed, should be guided by two considerations. One is whether a surety is necessary to ensure that the recognisance is complied with. The other is whether the defendant can realistically be expected to secure a surety who will satisfy conditions imposed.

An order that a defendant enter into a recognisance may not be made unless the defendant has shown, by past conduct, that he is unlikely to comply with a maintenance order, or has persistently failed in the past to comply: s 8(2).

Where a defendant fails to enter in to a recognisance when ordered to do so, he may be committed to prison under s 8(3). Further, under s 8(4), where the terms of a recognisance are not complied with, a recognisance may be cancelled, and moneys secured under the terms of the recognisance may be forfeited.

There is no provision under s 8 that provides for the automatic or discretionary imprisonment of a defendant who fails to comply with the terms of a recognisance. However, an application may be made under s 4(2), with the possible result that a defendant is committed to imprisonment.

16.7.9 Execution against property

An application pursuant to s 10 of the *Maintenance Orders Enforcement Act* may be made for an order that property belonging to a defendant who has failed to satisfy the terms of a maintenance order be seized and sold. A Magistrate before whom such an application is made, on being satisfied that there is property to be seized and sold, may direct "a specified person [to] seize and sell any goods, chattels and securities belonging to the defendant". An order may also state that the specified person may "demand and receive any annuity, rents or other income".

16.7.10 Attachment of earnings

Sections 11-25 of the *Maintenance Orders Enforcement Act* deal with the attachment of earnings of a defendant whose maintenance payments are in arrears. These sections provide for the interception of moneys that are payable to the defendant, and for their payment to the benefit of the person on whose behalf the maintenance order was made instead. In this way, moneys are paid towards the satisfaction of maintenance arrears without the defendant receiving them in the first place.

In most cases, moneys secured by an attachment of earnings order would be the wages payable to a defendant by an employer. However, the definition of "earnings" in s 11 is wide enough to include pension benefits and annuities in relation to loss of employment benefits.

Not all moneys owed to a defendant are attachable. In making an attachment order, a Magistrate is obliged to specify a normal deduction rate and a specified earnings rate. This ensures that the amount deducted is sufficient to provide for the payment of the arrears, while at the same time ensuring that the defendant is left with a reasonable income upon which to live. The fact that many defendants will be earning modest incomes creates a challenge for Magistrates in reaching a fair division between protected earnings and non-protected earnings.

There is always a third party involved when an attachment of earnings order is made. Section 13(2)(b) restricts the third party to the defendant's employer. The section does not specify whether this includes a former employer, although the wording suggests that it does not.

Section 15 provides that an attachment of earnings order need not be initiated by an application for that purpose. It may take place in the context of other proceedings.

Section 15(2) provides that an attachment of earnings order puts a stop to any other enforcement orders unless the court otherwise directs. This requires a Magistrate to clearly state if any other enforcement order (for instance, seizure and sale of assets) is to continue during the time that an attachment of earnings order is in effect.

Section 16 provides for an attachment of earnings order to be varied, suspended or discharged on application by the defendant, the person for whose benefit the maintenance order was made or someone on behalf of that person.

An attachment of earnings order ceases to have effect if any subsequent process is commenced, or order is made, in relation to the maintenance to which the attachment order applies: s 17. It also ceases to have effect upon the discharge of the attachment order or upon the discharge or variation of the maintenance order to which the attachment order relates.

In some cases, an employer to whom an attachment order is directed will have some question about whether certain moneys, or a portion of them, are payable pursuant to the terms of an attachment order. Section 22 provides a means for such questions to be answered and for the moneys to be dealt with accordingly.

16.7.11 Reciprocal enforcement of maintenance orders

Part III of the *Maintenance Orders Enforcement Act* deals with the registration and enforcement, within Papua New Guinea, of maintenance orders made in reciprocating states. Its provisions are relatively self-contained. This part of the Act is applied rarely. It serves the interests of persons who have obtained a maintenance order in a foreign jurisdiction and wish to enforce it against a respondent who is in Papua New Guinea.

16.8 ENFORCEMENT OF MAINTENANCE ORDERS: CHILD WELFARE ACT

Sections 56(a), 61 and 101 of the *Child Welfare Act* also contain provisions relevant to the enforcement of orders for maintenance.

Section 56(a) provides that an order for maintenance pursuant to ss 54 or 55 (orders for maintenance made upon a finding of paternity) is not enforceable until notice of the date of birth of the child is served on the defendant. This curious provision is understandable in the context of maintenance orders made before birth. However, it applies to all maintenance orders under both ss 54 and 55 and is, therefore, a technical defence that may be available to a defendant in some cases.

Section 61 of the *Child Welfare Act* contains provisions that overlap with some of the provisions of the *Maintenance Orders Enforcement Act*. Under this section, the Director of Child Welfare, or someone on his or her behalf, may make application in the case of a defendant who has allegedly failed to comply with the terms of a maintenance order, or who is thought to be attempting to leave the country without making satisfactory arrangements. This section provides for a Magistrate to make an order of committal to prison for up to one year, or an order that the defendant provide suitable security in such cases.

Section 101 provides a means of having arrears of maintenance enforced in the same way that the *District Courts Act* provides for the enforcement of other civil judgments: see Chapter 20. The Director, or person authorised by the Director, obtains a certificate of arrears from the court and files it in the District Court as a judgment.

16.9 ENFORCEMENT OF MAINTENANCE ORDERS: DESERTED WIVES AND CHILDREN ACT

16.9.1 Jurisdiction

The *Deserted Wives and Children Act* gives wide powers to Magistrates to include terms in maintenance orders that help ensure that the orders will be complied with. One of these is to order a defendant husband or father to enter into a recognisance with or without sureties. The powers of a Magistrate to make such an order, and the procedure, are set out at s 4 of the Act. The power is wide enough that such a condition may be imposed at the original application for maintenance or at any time afterwards on such notice as the court directs.

There is no National or Supreme Court authority on this section of the Act. Whether or not a recognisance is necessary is determined by a show cause hearing: s 4. This means that the onus is on the defendant to satisfy the court that *no* recognisance or surety is necessary. It is not up to an applicant to show that either of these things *are* necessary. However, the rules of natural justice must be complied with. An order would not be made in the absence of a defendant, and a surety would not have obligations imposed without the surety's consent to those conditions. Parties must have an opportunity to call evidence and to cross-examine witnesses called by the opposing party.

16.9.2 Attaching funds owed to a defendant or held in trust by a third party

Section 5 of the *Deserted Wives and Children Act* provides for the attachment of income of the defendant father or husband. This includes all forms of periodic income, including employment income and any other money held in trust on behalf of a defendant. This includes money on deposit in banks, security deposits payable to a defendant (power, water etc) and refunds that a defendant is entitled to receive. Care must be taken in cases where the defendant is associated in some way with a limited company, to ensure that money that is attached under s 5 is money that the defendant is entitled to personally, and not money that a limited company is entitled to receive: see also *Maintenance Orders Enforcement Act*, ss 11-26.

In making an order under s 5 of the *Deserted Wives and Children Act*, a third party is necessarily brought into the proceedings. The third party may not be present at the hearing where an attachment order is made. For instance, if a defendant is employed, the evidence of the employment and the basis for the order attaching wages under s 5 may be heard without benefit of evidence from the employer.

Where circumstances require it, directions may be given to clarify the particulars of the order. A question may arise on the part of a third party who is obliged to pay money owed to the recipient of the maintenance. This may relate to whether the money in question is owed, when it accrues to the benefit of the defendant, when it should be paid, how much should be paid etc. A defendant who takes the position that money that is being paid or is about to be paid is not owed to him might make an application. A beneficiary of an order might apply for particulars where money is not being paid and it is arguable that it should be paid pursuant to the terms of an existing attachment order.

The wording of an attachment order should be clear and concise with specific names of parties, dates, where the money from the third party should be paid, how it should be paid and how often such payments should be made. These measures prevent some of the potential problems that might otherwise arise later on.

Chapter 17 – The Land Courts

17.1 INTRODUCTION

The *Land Disputes Settlement Act* deals with the resolution of disputes in relation to interests in, or boundaries of, customary land. Section 1 of the Act sets out the purpose of the legislation and the general approach to be employed in achieving that purpose.

> "1. The purpose of this Act is to provide a just, efficient and effective machinery for the settlement of disputes in relation to interests in customary land by:
>
> (a) encouraging self-reliance through the involvement of the people in the settlement of their own disputes; and
>
> (b) the use of the principles underlying traditional dispute settlement processes."

District Court Magistrates may be involved with Land Court matters, either as a Local Land Court Magistrate or a Provincial Land Court Magistrate. This chapter examines these roles and the duties they entail. It also offers guidance to Magistrates in the discharge of their duties in relation to the *Land Disputes Settlement Act*.

17.2 MEDIATION

Mediation is given priority as a means of dispute settlement in the *Land Disputes Settlement Act*. Land Mediation Areas may be declared and, within these, Land Mediation Divisions. Land Mediators are primarily responsible for conducting mediations. They are appointed from among Village Magistrates or others within each of these divisions. Local Land Court Magistrates and Provincial Land Court Magistrates must be familiar with the duties and procedures of mediation.

Under s 15, the *primary function* of a Land Mediator is to assist in the attainment of peace and harmony by mediating in, and attempting to obtain the just and amicable settlement of, disputes. More than one Land Mediator may jointly attempt to bring about the resolution of a dispute through joint mediation. A Land Mediator may also seek the assistance of some other person with customary authority to assist in the mediation process.

Where, in the opinion of a Local Land Court Magistrate, a person other than an existing Land Mediator might be best suited to a particular mediation, then, pursuant to s 16, such a person may be appointed by the Local Land Court Magistrate to conduct a mediation. A Local Land Court Magistrate may consider such an ad hoc appointment where no Land Magistrate is available, or where those who are available have been involved in the dispute in one way or another, which creates a conflict of interest or the *perception* of a serious conflict of interest.

When Land Mediator *may* mediate: A Land Mediator has a discretion to mediate a dispute where he or she is of the opinion that it may be successful, provided that no other Land Mediator has been appointed or commenced to act as a mediator.

When Land Mediator *must* mediate: A Land Mediator must mediate where he or she has been requested to do so by, among others, a Magistrate of a District Court, Local Land Court or Provincial Land Court: *Land Disputes Settlement Act*, s 17(2). Normally the Land Mediator who is appointed will be from the Land Mediation Division where the dispute exists. However, occasionally, for reasons including those set out in s 17(5), a Magistrate may appoint a mediator from outside the division. In any event, where a Land Mediator is requested to act, a record of such a request must be forwarded to the Local Land Court Magistrate located nearest to the land in question.

Where more than one Land Mediator has commenced a mediation in relation to the same dispute, a Local Land Court Magistrate has the responsibility to resolve the issue of who will continue with the mediation. During an ongoing mediation, a Land Magistrate may replace one mediator with another.

Times and places for mediation: Mediation may take place at any time and place appointed by the Land Mediator or other person acting in that capacity. A mediator may adjourn the proceedings from time to time and request the presence of any persons or group of persons at the mediation.

The process of mediation: The *Land Disputes Settlement Act* does not set out any specific procedure. The objective of mediation is to achieve a clear and voluntary settlement of the dispute and thereby achieve the overall objectives of the Act. A mediator must remain neutral throughout the process and must not prescribe a settlement. Any settlement must be reached by the parties themselves. A good mediator will facilitate communication between parties, keep discussions focused and provide support to the parties. The principles, stages and skills of mediation are described in greater detail in Chapter 24. A particular issue that Land Mediators should always be mindful of is whether there are other potential parties to a dispute, who are not engaged in the mediation, but who might come forward after the matter has been settled. It is important that all parties to a dispute be involved at the initial stages where possible. This enhances the prospect of the mediation being truly successful and not later being challenged.

When mediation is successful: Where a mediation results in a settlement of the dispute, a Land Mediator has several obligations. He or she must make a record of the agreement and forward a copy to the nearest Local Land Court Magistrate. The Land Mediator shall also, as far as practicable, walk the boundary with the parties to the dispute, taking notice of prominent features and marking the boundary of the land as appropriate.

A Local Land Court Magistrate who receives a record of settlement must forward a copy to the Provincial Land Court for the province and, if requested to do so, to the

Local Government Council and the parties to the settlement: *Land Disputes Settlement Act*, s 18.

When mediation is not successful: An unsuccessful mediation may be partially successful if even some of the outstanding issues are settled. A Land Mediator should attempt, where possible, to get the parties to agree to any disputed facts, even if they are unable to agree on a final settlement. Such a partial agreement should be reduced to writing, so that when and if the matter proceeds to a Local Land Court, the parties may be asked to admit the particular facts and thereby shorten and focus the proceedings.

Parties to an unsuccessful mediation have a right to proceed to the Local Land Court to have their dispute adjudicated.

17.2.1 Effect of mediated settlements

A mediated settlement can have one of two effects, depending on whether it is approved by a Local Land Court Magistrate or not.

Where agreement approved: If the parties to a mediated agreement apply to a Local Land Court to have the agreement *approved* under s 19(1) of the *Land Disputes Settlement Act*, it is the duty of a Magistrate to ensure that:

- the terms of the agreement are fully understood by the parties;
- where a party consists of a group of people, that "a substantial majority of the persons comprising the group concur in the terms of the agreement"; and
- the agreement is not in breach of any law or contrary to natural justice or public policy.

A Local Land Court Magistrate should *not* approve a settlement where:

- one or more parties were not present at the mediation or did not agree to the settlement; or
- the mediation itself was not conducted properly.

Specifically, it must be clear that no party was intimidated or otherwise forced to agree.

A Magistrate who is satisfied that the prerequisites have been fulfilled, may approve the agreement.

An agreement that is approved has effect as an order of the District Court: *Land Disputes Settlement Act*, s 19(6).

Where agreement is not approved: Unless and until a mediated agreement is approved pursuant to s 19 of the *Land Disputes Settlement Act*, it does not have the effect of a court order, but is, in any legal proceedings, "evidence of the interests of the parties at the date of the agreement". However, it is not like a contract and is not binding on a party or a party's heirs, successors or assigns.

Where a Magistrate is not satisfied regarding any of the above criteria, he or she may mediate, or direct the Land Mediator who has been involved in the matter to conduct further mediation, with a view to reaching an agreement that satisfies the criteria. However, parties should be informed that they have a right to proceed to a court hearing of their dispute. Further mediation should not be imposed, or even recommended, where it is unlikely that it would succeed. Further mediation should never be used as a means of simply deferring a matter in the Local Land Court.

17.3 LOCAL LAND COURTS

17.3.1 Make-up of the Local Land Court

Where a process of mediation does not settle a land dispute, the Local Land Court is the appropriate forum for the resolution of the dispute. A Local Land Court comprises a Local Land Court Magistrate and either two or four Land Mediators. If possible, one of the mediators should be the one who attempted to resolve the matter by means of mediation. Clerks may or may not be appointed. The duties of clerks are set out in s 24 of the *Land Disputes Settlement Act*. If there is no clerk, the Magistrate may perform the clerk's duties in the Local Land Court.

The proceedings of a Local Land Court are subject to transfer to another Local Land Court, either on the motion of the court where the application is instituted, or at the instance of a Provincial Land Court. The effect of a transfer is that any further proceedings in the court from which the matter has been transferred are of no effect.

The membership of a Local Land Court may change, in accordance with the provisions of s 34, where the original Magistrate is unable to continue to preside.

17.3.2 Applications to the Local Land Court

Applications to the Local Land Court are commenced by application to a District Court Magistrate, who shall forward the application to the Local Land Court with apparent jurisdiction, or to a Local Land Court Magistrate.

A range of individuals or institutions may make applications (*Land Disputes Settlement Act*, s 31):

- A party to the dispute;
- A Village Court;
- A Land Mediator;
- A Local Land Court Magistrate or Local Land Court, other than the Magistrate or court before whom the application is made;
- A District Court Magistrate;

- A Provincial Land Court Magistrate or Provincial Land Court;
- A Provincial Commissioner, a Deputy Provincial Commissioner, a District Officer (Lands) or an officer in charge of a Subdistrict, Patrol Post or Base Camp.

Standing: In order to have standing, a party need not establish ownership of an interest in the land in question. A claim, based on custom, is sufficient to provide a party with standing: *Kuberi Epi v Turama Forest Industries Ltd, National Court* (1998) N1761.

Application: An application may be made orally or in writing, but if made orally must be reduced to writing before the hearing commences. The application must contain a general description of the land in question.

Notice of Application: A Local Land Court, to which an application is made, shall give notice of the application in accordance with ss 31(5) and 71 of the *Land Disputes Settlement Act*. Section 71 sets out several steps that are *required*:

giving notice to the parties;

publishing notice at the office of a Local Government Council and notifying the Local Government Council at its next meeting;

publishing notice by radio in the province in which the land is situated.

Further steps to bring the application to the attention of the parties and others in the community *may* be utilised:

posting a copy of the notice in a conspicuous place on the land concerned;

informing all concerned, or possibly concerned, parties on the land or in the surrounding land;

notifying appropriate meetings in the area;

using any customary means of transmitting orders to bring people notice of the application.

It is important that these measures are used to ensure that the hearing, and any subsequent order made, does not come as a surprise to any person who may have had an interest in the subject matter of the hearing.

17.3.3 Jurisdiction

Before proceeding with a hearing, a Local Land Court Magistrate must be satisfied that the court actually has jurisdiction to hear the application. Where two or more Local Land Courts have jurisdiction, the court that will proceed to hear the matter is determined by agreement or by a Provincial Land Court.

The main precondition to the jurisdiction of a Local Land Court is that there is a dispute. A Local Land Court does not have jurisdiction to respond to an application in the form of a "reference", nor may it make a declaratory order in the absence of a genuine dispute. In *The Application of Rimbo Susu on Behalf of Himself and Other Finschhafen Landowners* [1992] PNGLR 37, a party took issue with an agreement to sell customary land in a manner contrary to custom. This was held to constitute a dispute.

Where a dispute relates to land wholly or partly within a Land Mediation Area, the certification of a Land Mediator that he or she has acted in relation to the dispute, is a necessary prerequisite to jurisdiction and the requirements of s 27(1) of the *Land Disputes Settlement Act*. If the land is not within a Land Mediation Area, certification is still required of a Magistrate.

A dispute involving an interest to customary land may be inextricably involved with some other dispute or criminal proceeding. Where this is the case, a Local Land Court Magistrate may decide not to proceed with the hearing in a Local Land Court until the other dispute is resolved, either in the District Court or elsewhere.

17.3.4 Preventative jurisdiction

Where a dispute is unlikely to come before a Local Land Court for hearing within a month and, in the meantime, action is needed to preserve the peace, a temporary order may be made pursuant to s 30 of the *Land Disputes Settlement Act*. Temporary orders may:

authorise the use or occupation of land;

prohibit the use or occupation of land; or

restrain a party from interfering with the use or occupation of land.

Where a temporary order is made, the Local Land Court must commence hearing the dispute relating to the land within three months of the temporary order.

Magistrates should be aware of the jurisdiction of a Village Court, pursuant to s 43 of the *Village Courts Act*, to make a temporary order in respect of the use or occupation of customary land. While the existence of such a Village Court Order does not preclude the exercise of jurisdiction by a Local Land Court Magistrate, the terms of an order should not be inconsistent with that of a Village Court.

17.3.5 Hearings

The *Land Disputes Settlement Act* does not set out a formal procedure for the hearing of disputes. The conduct of hearings, however, must comply with the requirements of natural justice: see 4.1.

In addition, s 36 of the Act places an obligation on a Local Land Court to inspect the land in dispute, with the parties, before making an order. This sometimes creates a situation of great tension, and members of a Local Land Court may occasionally require the assistance of members of the police force to accompany them on an inspection.

A Local Land Court may call witnesses. An order compelling a witness to appear before the court may be oral or written, and may be enforced by a direction to a member of the police force or a Village Peace Officer to arrest the witness and bring him or her before the court.

A finding that a party has exercised an interest in the disputed land for more than 12 years creates a *presumption* that the party has a vested interest in the land, even if no other party has given permission for the exercise of that interest. See Chapter 5 for a discussion of the evidential significance of a presumption.

A Local Land Court is *obliged*, pursuant to s 68 of the *Land Disputes Settlement Act*, to determine all relevant customs of any group which appears or is represented in the court. The provisions of the *Customs Recognition Act* do not restrict the court in the determination or application of customs.

At a hearing, a party may be represented by anyone other than a lawyer.

17.3.6 Records

A Local Land Court is obliged to keep records of proceedings before it.

These records should be a complete record of proceedings before the court, and should include:

- the names of the parties;
- a description of the land in dispute;
- the names of all witnesses and minutes of the evidence given by the witnesses;
- the relevant dates of all proceedings;
- the wording of any orders made in the proceedings; and
- a copy of the application and, if possible, copies of all relevant documents produced or filed at the hearing of a matter.

In *Siamon Riri and Dei Riri v Simion Usai, Wasaf Musas, Musai Mamas, Fiu Gaus* (1995) N1377, the National Court, pursuant to s 155 of the *Constitution*, reviewed the decision of a Local Land Court. In the process, the record keeping of the Local Land Court was scrutinised and found to be "just not good enough". Records should indicate which of the s 39 factors were taken into account in reaching a decision. A failure to do so is not within the "spirit or intent of the Act".

17.3.7 Orders of a Local Land Court

A Local Land Court is given flexible powers in the terms that it may include in an order. These are set out in s 39 of the *Land Disputes Settlement Act*. The range of possibilities is wider than that which could be made in a court with only legal or equitable powers. The terms of an order made by a Local Land Court may pertain to any customary interests, and may include a feast, customary tribute or compensation.

Orders must not include terms that concern an interest in the land in question that is not in dispute, or persons or groups that are not parties to the dispute. However, where an unnamed party is present at a hearing and takes part, and where no named party objects to the participation of that party, an order may be made which does affect the interest of the unnamed party: see *Tony Vagi Heni and Guba Idau Maima and Lohia Tolana* (1992) N1201.

Reasons for an order must be given as soon as practicable after the conclusion of a hearing. These reasons must be given in the presence of the parties: *Land Disputes Settlement Act*, s 41. A Magistrate, in formulating reasons, must ensure that the terms of any orders are clear and unequivocal. Parties should not be able to misinterpret any order, either genuinely or deliberately. Further guidance on the formulation and delivery of orders and reasons is contained in Chapter 25.

In addition, s 42 of the Act provides that, where an order affects the boundary to customary land, as far as is practicable, the court shall walk the boundary with the parties, mark the boundary and record the boundary in an appropriate manner. The names of five witnesses who are prepared to testify to the position of the boundary must also be recorded.

Although an order made by a Local Land Court is conclusive evidence and establishes a right in relation to the interests in the land specified in the order, any interest that is not specified in an order of a Local Land Court may be the subject of a future claim.

An order of a Local Land Court may be varied in certain circumstances that are set out in s 44 of the Act. However, an application to vary may only be brought by a party to the original dispute on the basis that the original order is causing hardship. Further, an application to vary an order may not be brought within 12 years of the order that is to be varied.

17.4 PROVINCIAL LAND COURTS

The main function of Provincial Land Courts is to deal with appeals from decisions of the Local Land Court. Section 60 of the *Land Disputes Settlement Act* purports to make decisions of the Provincial Land Court final and not subject to review. However, this limitation has been found to be unconstitutional. In *Siamon Riri and Dei Riri v Simion Usai, Wasaf Musas, Musai Mamas, Fiu Gaus* (1995) N1377, it was held, pursuant to s 155(3) of the *Constitution*, that s 60 is not a bar to constitutional relief. This follows upon earlier decisions to the same effect.

17.4.1 Make-up of Provincial Land Courts

A Provincial Land Court is made up of one Principal Magistrate who may, pursuant to s 47 of the *Land Disputes Settlement Act*, request that one or more Land Mediators sit on the case as advisers. Section 48 of the Act also provides for clerks "as are necessary". In some circumstances, *necessity* may be defined by availability. In any event, where no clerk is present, a Magistrate will assume the functions that would otherwise be assumed by a clerk.

17.4.2 Jurisdiction

A Provincial Land Court may sit at such times and places as are convenient and necessary, but where *practicable*, must sit on or near the land in dispute.

An appeal must *only* be in relation to land that is wholly or partly within the area for which the court is established.

An appeal may be brought within three months of the date of the order appealed against, but a Provincial Land Court has the discretion to extend that period for up to 12 months from the date of the order appealed against. In *Abel Ameng v Mathew Poia* (1996) N1765, the National Court confirmed that a Provincial Land Court has no jurisdiction to extend the period for appeal beyond the 12-month limit set out in s 54 of the *Land Disputes Settlement Act.*

Sections 55 and 56 of the Act set out the requirements in relation to the filing of an appeal and service of the appeal on the respondent. Non-compliance with these statutory requirements would render any further proceedings in relation to the case invalid.

Section 58 of the Act sets out the only grounds upon which an appeal may be made.

These grounds may be summarised as follows:

- The Local Land Court exceeded or refused to exercise its jurisdiction.
- The decision of the Local Land Court was made in a manner contrary to natural justice.
- No court doing justice could have made the order that is appealed against.
- The order made was not supported by the facts.

A Provincial Land Court may do one of two things. It may either affirm the order appealed against or quash it. Where the order is quashed, the Provincial Land Court may make an order in substitution for the original order, or may remit the matter to the Local Land Court, where necessary with instructions as to how the matter should be dealt with.

A Provincial Land Court cannot affirm an order of a Local Land Court *and* amend it. This was confirmed in the National Court case of *Keberi Epi v Turama Forest Industries Ltd and The State* (1998) N1761, where it was stated:

> "The question of whether a District or Provincial Land Court on appeal can affirm an order and change it has been considered in *The State v District Land Court, ex parte Nuli* [1981] PNGLR 192. Section 59(1)(a) was held to limit a Provincial Land Court to affirming the order. It cannot go outside the four corners of the order and amend it. It can only make further orders when it quashes an appeal. It, therefore, cannot uphold and amend."

17.4.3 Practice and procedure

Provincial Land Courts must endeavour, pursuant to s 50 of the *Land Disputes Settlement Act*, to do "substantial justice between all persons interested in accordance with ... relevant custom". In seeking to achieve this goal, Provincial Land Courts are not bound by any "rule of law, evidence, practice or procedure", other than that set out in the Act itself: s 50. Any proceedings of a Provincial Land Court must be conducted in accordance with the rules of natural justice: see 4.2.

A Provincial Land Court may call and examine witnesses or "inform itself on any question before it in such manner as it thinks proper". Either before or during a hearing, a Provincial Land Court may inspect the land in question.

In relation to custom and presumptions of interest in customary land, the same provisions of the Act apply to Provincial Land Courts as apply to Local Land Courts: see 17.3.5 above. A party in a Provincial Land Court may be represented by anyone other than a lawyer.

17.4.4 Orders and records

As mentioned above, a range of orders is available to a Provincial Land Court: *Land Disputes Settlement Act*, s 59. A Provincial Land Court Magistrate should fully explain to the parties the terms of a decision and the reasons for it. The considerations set out in 17.3.4 above are relevant to a Provincial Land Court Magistrate.

Section 52 provides that the records of a Provincial Land Court should include reasons for decisions made. Other matters which should be included in the records of a Provincial Land Court are those set out above in relation to the Local Land Court.

17.5 INSPECTIONS

Section 73 of the *Land Disputes Settlement Act* provides that Provincial Land Court Magistrates may be called upon to conduct inspections of the Local Land Courts and of the Land Mediators within a province. There are two main functions involved in inspections:

1. A Provincial Land Court Magistrate should point out to the Local Land Courts and Land Mediators any shortcomings in practice or procedure. In

doing so, it is helpful to be as constructive as possible. The matters set out above in 17.2 and 17.3 would be relevant in conducting an inspection, as would any written directions or guidelines that the Land Mediators or Local Court Magistrates have received. Although informal discussions are a good way to learn and communicate, any recommendations or advice should be provided to the recipient in writing, with a copy kept by the Provincial Land Court Magistrate for reference in relation to future inspections.

2. A Provincial Land Court Magistrate should encourage uniform practices in Local Land Courts and by Land Mediators throughout the province. This objective helps to ensure a perception of fairness. Written guidelines and checklists for use by all Local Land Courts are helpful in establishing uniformity throughout a province.

Chapter 18 – The Village Courts

18.1 INTRODUCTION

The Village Courts of Papua New Guinea fall within s 172 of the *Constitution*. Since their inception, the Village Courts have played a vital role in the justice system of Papua New Guinea, providing access to justice for a significant portion of the population. The more formal courts of the country are inaccessible to many Papua New Guineans and, in many cases, are inappropriate to the types of disputes that go before Village Courts. Although most Village Courts are located in outlying rural areas, they are also found in and around cities and settlements.

There are approximately 1,000 Village Courts across Papua New Guinea. These courts place the administration of justice largely in the hands of people in the communities in which the disputes arise.

The Village Courts, like the District Courts, are courts of statutory jurisdiction. They exist only pursuant to statute, and have only those powers that are expressly granted by statute. The primary source of statutory jurisdiction is the *Village Courts Act*. The *Constitution* also imposes important limitations on the jurisdiction of the Village Courts, just as it does on other courts in Papua New Guinea.

Decisions made in the Village Courts may substantiate a plea of *autrefois convict, autrefois acquit or res judicata*, both in higher courts and in other Village Courts. In other words, a final decision in a Village Court represents the completion of a matter and precludes someone from later raising the same dispute in another court. The only exception to this is where an indictable offence is charged and is brought in another court after the same subject matter has been adjudicated upon in a Village Court. An earlier decision in a Village Court with respect to the same matter is *not* a bar to it proceeding in a higher court.

This chapter contains a brief description of some of the important features that distinguish the Village Courts from other courts in Papua New Guinea. This is followed by an examination of the ways that Magistrates of the District Courts are likely to come into contact with the Village Courts. This includes some suggestions and guidelines for how Magistrates should discharge their duties in relation to the Village Courts.

18.2 UNIQUE CHARACTERISTICS OF VILLAGE COURTS

18.2.1 Community orientation

It could be said that the primary role of formal courts is to provide for the adjudication of disputes in accordance with the laws of the country. However, the primary role of the Village Courts has a different emphasis. The primary role of the Village Courts is to ensure *peace and harmony* in the communities in which they operate: *Village Courts Act*, s 57. This is significant, in that it moves the emphasis of the role of Village Courts away from a winner/loser determination of disputes, and allows Village Court Magistrates to take account of a larger group of people. This may involve compromise in a way that is acceptable, not just to the parties to a dispute, but also to the wider community.

18.2.2 Custom

Another important feature of the Village Courts is the extent to which they are given jurisdiction over matters of custom. Section 57 of the *Village Courts Act* provides:

> "(1) Subject to Subsections (2) and (3), in all matters before it a Village Court shall apply any relevant custom as determined in accordance with Sections 2, 3 and 7 of the *Customs (Recognition) Act* (Chapter 19).
>
> (2) Custom shall be applied in accordance with Subsection (1) whether or not it is inconsistent with any Act.
>
> (3) The power conferred on a Local Level Government body by the *Local Government Act* (Chapter 57) or an Act of a Provincial Legislature to make rules, extends to making rules declaring what is to be taken as the custom relating to any matter, and such a declaration is binding on Village Courts."

Other references to custom in the *Village Courts Act* include the following:

- Section 43: A Village Court may, in relation to disputes over customary land, make orders regarding the use or occupation of the land. Orders relating to the ownership of the land are not within the jurisdiction of the Village Court, but are dealt with by Land Courts: see Chapter 17.
- Section 46: A Village Court may make orders in relation to bride price, custody of children and death. Section 47 confines the jurisdiction over custody of children to children whose parents were married under customary law or who are illegitimate.
- Section 89: Magistrates conducting reviews and appeals of Village Court matters must appoint two or more Village Court Magistrates to assist by advising on custom and other relevant matters in relation to the appeal or review.

- Section 100: Where a group order is made, it may be restricted to particular members of a group who are recognised as being liable in accordance with local custom.
- Regulations: The *Village Courts Regulations* prescribe the offences that are within the jurisdiction of the Village Courts. These include, in s 3(n), "[f]ailure to perform customary duties or to meet customary obligations after having been informed of them by a Village Magistrate."

18.2.3 No lawyers

In the Village Courts, lawyers are *not* allowed to represent parties. This is in contrast to most other courts in Papua New Guinea, where parties are entitled to be represented by a lawyer if they wish. It might be viewed as a way to keep the formal justice system at a distance and allow the Village Courts to be conducted as *people's courts*.

18.2.4 Court personnel

Village Court personnel are likely to be well acquainted with the customary practices of the community in which they perform their duties. They generally come from the areas in which particular courts are located. They are appointed taking into account their recognised roles as prominent members of their communities and their knowledge of local customs and traditions. It is unusual for Village Court Magistrates to have a great deal of formal legal training. They are *not* judicial officers as defined by the *Constitution*. This contrasts with Judges and Magistrates in other courts who do have formal legal training but may not have extensive knowledge of local custom. However, Village Court personnel *are* subject to prosecution for offences relating to their office, as are persons who hold judicial office: *Village Courts Act*, s 102. Village Peace Officers and Village Court Clerks are liable for prosecution for offences relating to members of the police force and members of the public service respectively.

The lack of legal training of Village Court personnel might serve to promote the operation of the Village Courts as village-based and custom-oriented institutions, responsive to the circumstances of the village and free from many of the formal practices of other courts. It does *not* excuse a Village Court from conducting its proceedings in accordance with the principles of fairness and natural justice.

18.2.5 Evidence and procedure

The rules of evidence and procedure in Village Courts are flexible. Section 59 of the *Village Courts Act* provides:

> "(1) Subject to Subsection (2), in any proceedings before it a Village Court shall not apply technical rules of evidence but shall admit and consider such information as is available.
>
> (2) The powers and procedures of a Village Court shall be exercised in accordance with the principles of natural justice."

18.2.6 Mediation

Village Courts are obliged to attempt the resolution of disputes first by way of mediation. The requirement is mandatory. Section 53 of the *Village Courts Act* provides:

> "(1) The mediatory jurisdiction of a Village Court may be exercised by a single Village Court Magistrate.
>
> (2) In all matters before it relating to a dispute, a Village Court:
>
> (a) shall, before exercising its jurisdiction under Division 3 or 4, attempt to reach a settlement by mediation; and
>
> (b) may, if it thinks that by doing so a just and amicable settlement may be reached, adjourn any proceedings in which it is exercising jurisdiction under those Divisions."

It is arguable that a Village Court that proceeds directly to a contested hearing, without attempting mediation, acts without jurisdiction. This does not appear to have been tested.

Although mediation may be attempted in relation to disputes in the District, National or Supreme Courts (mediation is *required* in relation to some matters, for instance, matters under the *Adultery and Enticement Act*), mediation in the Village Courts is integral to their existence, and its application is wider than in other courts.

18.2.7 Group orders

Groups of people who would otherwise have no legal personality, and therefore would have no standing as parties in another court, may be recognised as parties in the Village Court. Section 98 of the *Village Courts Act* provides that a Village Court Magistrate may, for the purpose of determining who may be a party, recognise a number of persons who have a common interest. Further, a Village Court Magistrate may determine in what manner the group should be represented in the Village Court. However, such a group may *not* be the subject of a criminal conviction in the Village Court.

An order against a recognised group has effect (s 100) as an order against *each* member of that group, except where the Village Court orders otherwise or where it would be contrary to recognised custom.

18.2.8 Joint sittings

In particular circumstances, two Village Courts may join forces and hold a joint sitting where the dispute or parties in question cover more than one Village Court area. A decision to hold a joint sitting must be made by agreement of the Chairpersons of the respective courts or, if there are no Chairpersons, by the Village Court Magistrates. Also, a joint sitting may be initiated on the directions of a Supervising Magistrate or at the request of a Peace and Good Order Committee.

18.2.9 Uniformity of civil and criminal proceedings

The Village Courts have been given the ability to mix criminal and civil proceedings in ways that other courts cannot. Section 78 of the *Village Courts Act* provides that, subject to any published procedures to the contrary, a Village Court, in any proceeding, may make orders pursuant to its criminal or civil jurisdiction. This gives a Village Court a degree of flexibility in the way it disposes of matters that come before it, and in the procedure for dealing with these matters. However, this flexibility is subject to the overall requirements of natural justice and compliance with the *Constitution*.

18.3 VILLAGE COURT ORDERS

The Village Courts retain the powers to make orders in relation to:

(a) compensation, debts and damages to a maximum of K1,000 (*Village Courts Act*, s 45);

(b) temporary use or occupation of customary land (s 43);

(c) preventative orders in relation to anticipated breaches of the peace (s 51);

(d) custody of children born of couples who are married by custom, or of illegitimate children (s 47);

(e) compensation in relation to bride price (s 46);

(f) divorce in relation to customary marriages (certification of which is within the jurisdiction of the District Court – see 16.6); and

(g) criminal offences within its jurisdiction (s 41).

The *Village Courts Act* restricts the powers of a Village Court in several important respects.

A Village Court may not make an order in relation to disputes involving:

(a) a motor vehicle; or

(b) the ownership of land,

and may not impose a term of imprisonment.

However, the *Village Courts (Amendment) Act* 2000 gives the power to impose a community work order in a wide range of circumstances.

In addition, the power to impose a fine has now been *restricted*: see 18.3.3.

18.3.1 Community work orders

A community work order is defined in s 1 of the *Village Courts Act*. The work that a person may be ordered to perform may be for a period not exceeding:

(a) eight hours in a day;

(b) six days in a week; or

(c) a total period of six months.

Conditions, including supervision, may be included in a community work order. A community work order should specify the work to be done and, if possible, the work should benefit a person who is aggrieved in relation to the original matter.

Failure to comply with a community work order is an offence pursuant to s 63.

18.3.2 When a community work order may be imposed

Where a person disobeys a Village Court order in relation to any of the following, he or she may be liable to a community work order.

1. Obstruction of the Village Court or a Village Court official: *Village Courts Act*, s 60.
2. Failure to obey an order of the Village Court in relation to:

   (a) an ancillary order;

   (b) the temporary use or occupation of customary land;

   (c) the custody of a child or children; or

   (d) a summons that is issued by a Village Court to compel the attendance of a witness before the Village Court.
3. Wilful failure, without reasonable excuse, to comply with an order to pay compensation, debt or damages.

18.3.3 Consequences of failure to comply with a community work order

Failure to comply with a community work order is an offence. A person convicted of an offence may be fined a sum not exceeding K50 for each week of work not performed: *Village Courts Act*, s 63.

A fine *must be endorsed* by a District Court Magistrate, pursuant to s 64, for it to have any effect: see 18.5.

18.3.4 Failure to obey order for payment of compensation, debt or damages

Where a community work order is made for failure to obey an order for the payment of compensation, debts or damages (see above), the order does not operate as a satisfaction of the compensation, debts or damages that are owed. Where a failure to pay an order for compensation, debts or damages is wilful and without reasonable excuse, it may result in a community work order: *Village Courts Act*, s 62(2).

However, it is always open to a person in whose favour an order for payment of compensation, debt or damages is made to take steps to enforce the order, regardless of whether non-payment is made wilfully and without reasonable excuse, or whether a community work order has been made. The way for such a person (judgment creditor) to proceed is to apply for an order for execution under s 62(2).

An order for execution is of no force and effect unless and until a District Court Magistrate *endorses* it.

18.3.5 Giving effect to orders for execution and fines

For an order for payment of a fine or an order for execution to have any effect, it must be endorsed by a Magistrate. Section 64 of the *Village Courts Act* provides the criteria for a Magistrate to consider in relation to the endorsement of a fine. Section 65 provides identical criteria in relation to an order for execution.

18.4 RELATIONSHIP OF MAGISTRATES WITH THE VILLAGE COURTS

The role of District Court Magistrates in the affairs of the Village Courts is limited, but is important to the effective functioning of the Village Courts.

When approaching their duties in relation to the Village Courts, Magistrates should be aware of the balance that the Village Courts are required to maintain. On the one hand, they are expected to adhere to custom, work towards the peace and harmony of the community, remain flexible and apply mediation. On the other hand, Village Courts are subject to the *Constitution* and must (particularly in cases where mediation fails) adhere to the principles of natural justice.

Each party must be afforded the right to a full hearing, including:

- the right to call witnesses;
- the right to cross-examine the witnesses of the opposing party; and
- the protection of the principles of natural justice, in particular, a hearing where no presiding Magistrate has (or may reasonably be seen to have) an interest in the case over which he or she is presiding.

In practice, cross-examination is often conducted indirectly through the presiding Magistrate. Instead of asking an opposing witness questions directly, a party may ask the Magistrate to ask the question. This practice preserves parties' rights, while at the same time minimising the potential for flare-ups between parties, and interminable cross-examination.

18.5 ENDORSEMENT OF VILLAGE COURT ORDERS – FINES AND ORDERS FOR EXECUTION

A District Court Magistrate is given the responsibility of deciding whether or not to endorse a Village Court order for payment of a fine (*Village Courts Act*, s 64) or for execution (s 65).

It is necessary for that Magistrate to carefully consider the background of the order.

This consideration must be directed at the following question:

Is there any reason to believe that the Village Court, in making the order for fine or execution, acted without jurisdiction or acted beyond its powers?

Since every valid order for execution or a fine in the Village Court always follows on an *earlier* order (which is allegedly not complied with), it is also necessary, in answering the above question, to look at the validity of not one, but two orders. These are:

(1) the order for fine or execution; and

(2) the first order made, either for compensation or performance of community work, which has resulted in the order for a fine or for execution.

The fairness of the Village Court proceedings that resulted in each of the above orders is an important consideration: see 18.4. For instance, a party being subjected to the order must have been given the opportunity to prove that he or she had a reasonable excuse for not complying with the original order.

The jurisdiction to make the original order is also an important consideration. For instance, in the case of an order for compensation or repayment of debt or damages, a consideration of s 45 (which incorporates s 46 orders) is required. These sections limit the scope of an order for compensation, damages or the repayment of a debt, to an amount not exceeding, in cash or in value, the sum of K1,000, or to compensation relating to bride price, custody of children or death in such amount as the Village Court considers just: see 18.3.

Although Village Courts are no longer able to make orders for imprisonment, two National Court cases, in relation to the endorsement of Village Court orders for imprisonment, are illustrative of matters that District Court Magistrates ought to be mindful of in considering whether to endorse a Village Court order for imprisonment. These cases demonstrate the effects of endorsing a Village Court order *without* ensuring that the orders made by a Village Court were within its jurisdiction.

In the case of *In the Matter of Kabia Maris and in the Matter of Nalik Village Court* [1994] PNGLR 314, a Village Court issued orders for imprisonment of a man for a civil debt. In that case, two warrants for imprisonment were endorsed, despite the fact that there were serious defects in relation to each. The first warrant was defective because the defendant was not given an opportunity to deal with the issue of whether failure to pay the fine was without reasonable cause. Further, the imprisonment did not take into account part payment of the fine that had been made by the defendant. The second warrant was ostensibly made in relation to compensation. It was defective because no amount of compensation was specified in the original order. The Village Court had acted without jurisdiction in relation to both orders, and the orders should not have been endorsed.

In the case of *Lina Mark* [1995] PNGLR 234, a woman was ordered to be imprisoned, despite the fact that no hearing had been held to determine whether the original compensation order had been complied with. The woman had not been given an opportunity to explain whether she had reasonable cause for not paying the order for compensation. The Village Court had, therefore, acted without jurisdiction. Its order should not have been endorsed.

If a District Court Magistrate, in considering a Village Court order for payment of a fine or an order for execution, finds that it should not be endorsed, then the Magistrate is obliged, by s 75(4) of the *Village Courts Act*, to exercise the power of review: see below.

18.6 ENFORCEMENT OF FINES AND ORDERS FOR EXECUTION

Where a District Court Magistrate endorses an order imposing a fine or an order for execution, the order takes effect and may be enforced. The enforcement of these orders is no longer a matter for the Village Courts. Section 64 of the *Village Courts Act* stipulates that the provisions of the *District Courts Act* apply with respect to fines, and s 65 of the *Village Courts Act* provides that the provisions of the *District Courts Act* apply in relation to orders for execution: see Chapter 20.

18.7 APPEALS AND REVIEWS

18.7.1 Time for appeal

Appeals from Village Court decisions are made to the District Court. An appeal can be commenced within three months of the date of the order being appealed against. A District Court Magistrate has a discretion to allow an extension of the time to appeal up to 12 months from the date of the order that is being appealed.

The *Village Courts Act* does not set out any specific considerations in relation to an application to extend the time for an appeal.

The following questions might be relevant to an application for extension:

- Would the extension of time prejudice the party being appealed against as a result of the destruction or loss of relevant evidence?
- Has the party being appealed against, after three months from the date of the order, conducted his or her affairs in a way that either implicitly or explicitly relies upon the existence of the original Village Court order in relation to which the application for extension is being made?
- Are there any other factors that make it unfair to allow the extension of time to appeal?

18.7.2 Involvement of Village Court Magistrates

Section 89 of the *Village Courts Act* requires that the Magistrate who is hearing the appeal against, or making the review of, a Village Court decision, must appoint two or more Village Court Magistrates to preside with him or her at the appeal or review. The Village Court Magistrate who made the original order is eligible for this role. Where the appointed Village Court Magistrates, for whatever reason, fail to sit on the appeal or review, the District Court Magistrate conducting the appeal or review *may* proceed alone: s 90.

Where the appointed Village Court Magistrates *do* preside at an appeal or review, their role is to advise the Magistrate hearing the matter on custom and other relevant matters. They have no power to make a decision or govern the conduct of the appeal or review.

18.7.3 Procedure

The procedure for conducting an appeal or review is similar to that for a hearing in the Village Court. Lawyers are not permitted to represent parties at an appeal. Section 90 of the *Village Courts Act* provides that a Magistrate conducting an appeal, or hearing a review, may "receive such evidence (if any) and make such enquiries" as he or she considers necessary. Parties have a right to be present and to call evidence and make submissions. Relevant custom is to be applied in the determination of the appeal.

18.7.4 Types of orders

Section 92 of the *Village Courts Act* gives three options to a Magistrate hearing an appeal:

1. **Confirm original order:** One option is to confirm the original order being appealed against. This must be done unless the Magistrate is satisfied that:

   (a) the Village Court that made the order was not properly constituted;

   (b) a party was absent at the original hearing, and the party's absence is not excused under s 79 of the *Village Courts Act*;

   (c) a party was not given a reasonable opportunity to present his or her case;

   (d) the Village Court exceeded its jurisdiction or powers; or

   (e) a Village Court Magistrate who presided at the original hearing had a substantial interest in the matter such that there was a miscarriage of justice: s 92(2).

   In any event, where the lapse of time (from the events constituting the subject matter of the original complaint or chargc) or failurc of an aggricvcd party to appeal earlier would result in injustice, a Magistrate conducting the appeal or review shall confirm the original order.

2. **Quash the original order:** This would be appropriate where, on appeal, it is established that the Village Court that made the original order acted without jurisdiction or beyond its jurisdiction.

3. **Order that Village Court rehear matter:** Where a Magistrate conducting a review or hearing an appeal does not confirm or quash the original order, that Magistrate may order that the matter be dealt with again by the Village Court. When a matter is remitted to the Village Court, a Magistrate may provide directions to the Village Court to assist the Village Court in curing

any defect which marred the earlier proceedings: s 92(1)(c). The option of ordering that the Village Court rehear a matter would be appropriate where the Village Court hearing was not conducted in accordance with the principles of natural justice, to the prejudice of the appealing party.

18.7.5 Records and further review

A Magistrate who conducts a review or hears an appeal must make a record of his or her decision and reasons, and forward the record to the Provincial Supervising Magistrate. The Provincial Supervising Magistrate may, in turn, conduct a further review of the matter. The Provincial Supervising Magistrate has the same powers as the Magistrate who heard the appeal or conducted the initial review.

18.8 SUPERVISION OF VILLAGE COURTS

A District Court Magistrate may be appointed as a Provincial Supervising Magistrate or a Deputy Provincial Supervising Magistrate: *Village Courts Act*, s 15. In such a role, a Magistrate will be called upon to take a supervisory role in relation to the Village Courts.

Effective supervision will bring to light difficulties or problems in the operation of the Village Courts. It is also an opportunity to informally provide guidance and instruction to Village Court personnel where it is needed. There is no formal procedure for supervision, and different circumstances may call for different approaches. However, it is necessary that, in all dealings with the Village Court in a supervisory role, a Supervising Magistrate maintains a professional detachment from the people and matters that are being supervised, while at the same time attempting to be as constructive as possible in dealing with the Village Court and its personnel.

The respect of the community is essential for the effective operation of a Village Court. Therefore, in supervising, a Magistrate should be mindful of ways that the particular Village Court enhances or diminishes the respect of the community by the way it operates, and should advise accordingly.

There is no closed list of matters that come within the scope of a Supervising Magistrate's or Deputy Supervising Magistrate's duties. When supervising a Village Court, one should be familiar with all the provisions of the *Village Courts Act*. In addition to the *Village Courts Act*, a Supervising Magistrate should be familiar with the personnel and infrastructure of the Village Court or courts being supervised. The following headings outline some specific matters that should be considered by a Supervising Magistrate.

18.8.1 Constitutional rights

Village Courts must operate in accordance with the *Constitution*.

It is important, in exercising supervisory duties, to be particularly alert to ways in which the Village Courts may have acted inconsistently with constitutional provisions. The following is a basic checklist of some of provisions of the *Constitution* that a supervising Magistrate ought to have in mind when supervising a Village Court:

- Section 37: Rights on arrest, detention and charge by a Village Court;
- Section 42: Right to liberty;
- Section 43: Freedom from forced labour;
- Section 44: Freedom from arbitrary search and seizure;
- Section 45: Freedom of conscience, thought and religion;
- Section 46: Freedom of expression;
- Section 47: Freedom of assembly and association;
- Section 48: Freedom of employment;
- Section 49: Right to privacy;
- Section 51: Freedom of information;
- Section 52: Freedom of movement;
- Section 53: Protection from unjust deprivation of property.

18.8.2 Rules of natural justice and procedure generally

Section 59 of the *Constitution* incorporates the rules of natural justice into the underlying law of Papua New Guinea. Since the *Underlying Law Act* came into force in 2000, these rules must be applied only in accordance with the provisions of that Act. See 25.6.4 for an explanation of how this statute must be referred to in judgments. In any event, where appropriate in accordance with the *Underlying Law Act*, the rules of natural justice comprise the following basic rules of fairness:

- the right to be informed of a claim or charge;
- the right to be given an opportunity to make an answer to the claim or charge;
- the right to question an opposing witness; and
- the right to be judged by a person with no interest in the outcome of a case.

Section 79 of the *Village Courts Act* provides further statutory precision to these principles in respect of the entitlement of parties *to be present* at Village Court proceedings.

18.8.3 Records

Section 84 of the *Village Courts Act* requires that, as far as practicable, a Village Court shall keep records of its proceedings. A Village Court Magistrate, Village Court Clerk or a Deputy Village Court Clerk must certify the records as correct, and when so certified, those records are prima facie evidence of the matters set out in them.

A Supervising Magistrate must be aware of the practical difficulties that Village Court personnel sometimes face in relation to record keeping. In many Village Courts, protection of records from the weather and from possible theft or destruction by parties or others is a real concern. A locked room or container should be made available for Village Court records. Unless circumstances require otherwise, records should always be kept in the same place. More than one person should be aware of where the Village Court records are kept at all times.

Many Village Court procedures have forms associated with them. Village Courts sometimes do not have a ready supply of the required forms. In such circumstances, a photocopy of a form may be used. If there are no photocopies, an *unofficial form*, containing all the required information and drafted by Village Court officials, may be used. Village Court officials should be made aware that the forms are important, not because of the stationery on which they are printed, but because of the information they contain about the parties and proceedings to which they relate.

A Supervising Magistrate should be aware of the needs of a Village Court in relation to records and forms, and should do everything possible to supply Village Courts with proper forms or photocopies of forms.

Section 110 of the *Village Courts Act* makes it an offence to alter the records of a Village Court or to wilfully damage or record information incorrectly in Village Court records.

18.8.4 Custom

In addition to the formal records that are required by statute, a Village Court can assist in the overall development of the underlying law of Papua New Guinea by recording customs that affect its decisions. The *Underlying Law Act* requires Magistrates to address the particular matters relating to the application of the underlying law when rendering a judgment: see 25.6.4.

18.8.5 Women

Although the equal rights of women are covered in the *Constitution*, a Supervising Magistrate should take special care to determine whether women are treated differently from men. If so, the question of whether there has been a breach of the *Constitution* arises. A Supervising Magistrate should be sensitive to the sometimes-conflicting need to maintain local custom, and the need to ensure that everyone who comes into contact with the Village Courts is treated in accordance with their constitutional rights. Where custom and the *Constitution* conflict, the *Constitution* takes priority. For instance, although it may be consistent with local custom to order that a woman returns to her husband against her will, such an order is unconstitutional.

18.8.6 Children

While it is common for Children's Court and District Court hearings involving the interests of children to be held *in camera*, many Village Court hearings involving the custody of children are held in *open court*, often before the entire village. A Supervising Magistrate should be mindful of the adverse effects that a fully public hearing can have on the wellbeing of a child, and should advise a Village Court accordingly.

18.8.7 Conflict of interest

The right to be judged by a person who has no conflict of interest in the outcome of the case is a basic right falling within the principles of natural justice. Section 82(2) of the *Village Courts Act* states that a Village Court Magistrate who has a *substantial interest* in the subject matter of a dispute is *not* eligible to sit as a member of the Village Court. Section 82(2) does not say that the Village Court Magistrate should have *no* interest. The fact that Village Court disputes are adjudicated within a village setting, where collective as well as individual interests are recognised, and where it is to be expected that interests will be tightly woven together, makes it impractical to expect that a Village Court Magistrate will have no interest whatsoever.

18.8.8 Case flow

A Supervising Magistrate should, in addition to talking with Village Court officials, examine the records of the Village Court. These records should reveal whether the cases that come before the court are being heard within a reasonable time after the complaint is made or the charge is laid in the Village Court. Also, cases must not be dealt with so quickly that parties do not have an adequate opportunity to prepare or to arrange for the attendance of witnesses.

18.8.9 Referring matters from Village Court to another court

A Supervising Magistrate should also be mindful of s 97 of the *Village Courts Act*, which provides for the transfer of proceedings (which may be within the jurisdiction of a Village Court) from one Village Court to another court (either District or Village). This may be appropriate where the issues in dispute are technical, or where the Village Court Magistrates do not have the confidence or expertise to deal with a particular matter. It may also be appropriate where the Village Court Magistrates have a substantial interest in the outcome of a case or where one or more of them should be available as witnesses rather than as judges of a matter. A transfer should normally not take place until after mediation has been attempted pursuant to s 53.

18.8.10 Conduct of Magistrates

There have been instances where Village Court Magistrates take enforcement matters into their own hands. This has involved improperly selling the property of a judgment debtor (see Chapter 20) and purchasing that property at less than fair market price. While this practice may not be widespread, a Supervising Magistrate should be mindful of the potential for it and related practices to take place.

Chapter 19 – Coroners, Elections and Other Jurisdictions

Chapter 19A – Coroners' Inquests

Chapter 19B – Elections

19A – CORONERS' INQUESTS

19A.1 THE CORONER'S JURISDICTION

19A.1.1 Coroners Act

Coroners' hearings into the causes of deaths and fires have a long history in the United Kingdom and Australia where the law has been developed and reformed. The jurisdiction is based on statute, and, in Papua New Guinea, the current legislation is the *Coroners Act*, which is likely to be replaced by new legislation. A brief summary of the jurisdiction is provided here.

19A.1.2 Administration

Coroners must be appointed by the Judicial and Legal Services Commission, and District Court Magistrates are frequently appointed as Coroners for the provinces within which they act as Magistrates: *Coroners Act*, s 2.

Coroners are required to work closely with the police and the office of the Attorney-General. The police submit their investigations and reports to the Coroner under the *Coroners Act*, and assist the Coroner during inquests. The police officer working with the Coroner is the "officer assisting the Coroner", and is frequently a police prosecutor.

19A.1.3 Functions

The Coroner has responsibility for inquiring into three types of matters:

1. **Deaths** – the "manner and cause" of the death of a person in any of the circumstances set out in s 7 of the *Coroners Act*, which are often summed up as "sudden, suspicious or unusual" deaths.
2. **Fires** – the "cause and origin" of any fire which has destroyed or damaged property: s 17.
3. **Missing persons** – the "cause and circumstances" of the disappearance of a missing person: s 20.

As the jurisdiction is entirely statutory, a Coroner has no power to inquire into any other matters.

19A.1.4 Procedural stages

There are two stages:

Stage I: In the case of each of the three types of matters above, the Coroner's duties begin with an initial investigation into the report of death, fire or missing person that the Coroner has received: 19A.2.1. This task ends with the Coroner's decision on whether or not to hold a formal inquiry, called an "inquest": 19A.2.2.

Stage II: If an inquest is to be held, further procedural rules apply: 19A.3.

19A.2 STAGE I – INITIAL INVESTIGATIONS

19A.2.1 Notices, reports and examinations

On receiving notices and reports from doctors, police officers and members of the public, as required under the *Coroners Act*, the Coroner may request the police to carry out further inquiries, and may, if appropriate, direct the post-mortem of a deceased person or issue a warrant for the exhumation of a buried body.

19A.2.2 Decision whether to hold an inquest

After considering all the information received, the Coroner is required to decide whether or not to hold an inquest. In the case of death or fire, if the Coroner considers that "no good purpose would be served" by holding an inquest, the Coroner must report the decision to the Attorney-General: *Coroners Act*, s 7 in the case of deaths, and s 17 in the case of fires. Where a missing person is concerned, the Coroner may be called upon to decide whether, "in the opinion" of the Coroner, an inquest should be held: s 20.

In every such case, the decision of the Coroner is a judicial act that must be carried out on the basis of the evidence available, in good faith, and having regard to the purposes of the Act (which include the public's interest in having satisfactory explanations of deaths, fires and disappearances).

19A.2.3 Directions by Attorney-General and requests by other persons

Independently of the Coroner's decision, the Attorney-General is empowered to direct that an inquest be held. In prescribed circumstances, persons recognised by the Act may request an inquest, in which case the Coroner is obliged to conduct one.

19A.3 STAGE II – INQUESTS

19A.3.1 Purposes of the findings of an inquest

The purposes for which the Coroner is required to make findings are linked to the Coroner's three main functions: see 19A.1.3 above. The Coroner is required to ascertain, so far as the evidence may establish, and certify findings as to:

- **Deaths** –
  - the identity of the deceased;
  - how, when and where the deceased came by his or her death; and
  - whether the cause of death was through wilful murder, murder or manslaughter, and, if so, the person responsible: *Coroners Act*, s 10.
- **Fires** –
  - the time when, and the place where, the fire occurred;
  - the cause of the fire; and
  - where the offence of arson has been committed, the person (if any) whom the Coroner finds to have been guilty of the offence: s 17.
- **Missing persons** –
  - whether the missing person is alive or dead; and
  - if the person is alive, or likely to be alive, his or her whereabouts at the time of the inquest: s 20.

19A.3.2 Inquest procedure generally

The Coroner's inquest is normally held in a courthouse open to the public, and with much the same procedures and formalities as those of a criminal hearing. For example, the Coroner has all the powers of a Magistrate conferred under the *District Courts Act* in respect of the preliminary hearing of an indictable offence (*Coroners Act*, s 22): see Chapter 11.

Because the functions of a Coroner are not the same as those of a Magistrate, Coroners are addressed as "Sir" or "Madam", and not "Your Worship". At the beginning of the inquest, the officer assisting the Coroner opens the proceedings by announcing "The inquest concerning the death of the late ... [name] ... is now in session".

19A.3.3 Coroner's control of the evidence

In order to perform his or her functions, the Coroner is required to examine on oath all persons:

whom he or she thinks fit to examine;

who tender their evidence; or

who, in the opinion of the Coroner, are able to give relevant evidence respecting the facts: *Coroners Act*, ss 10, 17 and 20.

Note that the Coroner is required by the Act to examine all witnesses who fall within the above categories.

The Coroner may issue summonses and warrants in order to secure attendance of witnesses: ss 25 and 26. The Coroner's control of inquest proceedings is supported by the power to impose fines for contempt: s 28.

19A.3.4 Difference between inquest and prosecution

The Coroner's inquest is not intended to be a process that determines criminal responsibility or civil liability. Accordingly, no person who claims to be interested in the proceedings has the absolute right to call or cross-examine witnesses. The Coroner will call the witnesses, and will usually allow cross-examination by, or on behalf of, persons who are recognised as having a sufficient interest: see 19A.3.7.

Natural justice requires the Coroner to protect the procedural interests of any person who it seems may be found to have caused the death or fire. Such a person must be allowed to cross-examine witnesses, and the Coroner should consider carefully whether to call those witnesses whom the suspect person wishes to give evidence at the inquest.

Furthermore, witnesses who claim that they might incriminate themselves if required to answer particular questions, may request to have the benefit of the rule against self-incrimination: see Chapter 5.

19A.3.5 Prosecutions

If, after initial investigations have been carried out by the Coroner (Stage I – 19A.2) and the police, the latter decide to prosecute the person they consider responsible for the death or fire, the Coroner will usually suspend or adjourn the inquest until after the criminal proceedings have been concluded.

19A.3.6 Charge and committal by the Coroner

The Coroner is also given power to charge a person with the offence of wilful murder, murder, manslaughter or arson: *Coroners Act*, s 19. This power is seldom used, because it is desirable to keep the inquest and prosecution functions separate and, in any case, the police are usually in a better position than the Coroner's staff to conduct a prosecution.

If a person is charged under s 19, the Coroner is required to read the charge and explain its nature in ordinary language to the effect of the words set out in s 19. The Coroner must put into writing whatever the charged person says, and commit that person for trial in the National Court. The accused will be detained, and all witnesses examined at the inquest will be bound by recognisance to appear at the trial. The Coroner must transmit the charges, depositions and statements to the Registrar of the National Court without delay.

19A.3.7 Presence at inquests and publication of proceedings

Witnesses are not normally permitted to be present at the inquest except during and after the giving of their evidence. However, any person, whether summonsed as a witness or not, whom the Coroner considers:

- has a particular interest in the proceedings, or
- is responsible for any conduct or act which is material to the subject matter of the inquest,

may be permitted to be present throughout the inquest. Such a person is entitled to examine and cross-examine witnesses and to be represented by a lawyer: *Coroners Act*, s 29.

Subject to the above, a Coroner may exclude a person from the inquest in the interests of public morality: s 30(1). Lawyers and representatives of newspapers may not be excluded, but the Coroner may forbid the publication of any report or the account of the evidence or other proceedings in the inquest: s 30(2) and (3).

19A.3.8 Depositions, findings and reasons

The Coroner must put into writing all evidence given before him or her, and such depositions of witnesses must be read to or by the witness and signed by the witness and the Coroner. On the trial of a person, the depositions and any statement of the person charged taken under s 19 are admissible in evidence at the trial.

At the conclusion of every inquest, the Coroner must record his or her findings as to the death or fire (ss 10 and 17 – see 19A.3.1), complete the required certificate and forward it to the Attorney-General: *Coroners Act*, s 23. The findings should arise directly out of the relevant evidence, and, before making a particular finding, the Coroner should be satisfied on the balance of the probabilities (except where considering whether to commit a person for trial, when the Coroner must be satisfied that there is a prima facie case). Of course, it is particularly important that the Coroner should give reasons for his or her findings, so that these may assist in the prevention of deaths and fires in the future.

The Coroner is also required to prepare an abstract of the proceedings, and his or her findings, that refers to the names of all the witnesses examined, the costs and the amount of time taken for the inquest. This abstract must also be forwarded to the Attorney-General: s 34.

19A.3.9 Reopening the inquest

If a Coroner considers that an inquest should be re-opened, or is requested to do so by a person authorised under s 21(5) of the *Coroners Act*, the Coroner may, as a judicial act, re-open an inquest that was previously closed by him or her or by another Coroner. The Attorney-General has final authority to require that an inquest be held or re-opened: s 21(1).

19A.3.10 Changing demands on today's Coroners

Many coronial inquests are now broad in their scope, and a finding that a person caused or contributed to the death of another person (or to a major fire) will lead not only to criminal prosecution and the possibility of civil action, but also to significant media attention. Indeed, whether or not there is such a finding, public attention is often attracted to the inquest. While the inquest is technically an inquisitorial proceeding, there are often, in practice, a number of "parties" with fundamentally opposed objectives. Because of the increasing recognition of the potential impact of coronial findings following notorious crimes or major disasters, proceedings in Coroners' Courts are often aggressively contested before the Coroner in an adversarial manner. Consequently, the Coroner needs to be aware of the importance of the findings and recommendations of the inquest. During the course of the hearing, the Coroner will need to pay special attention to such matters as the appearance of witnesses as "parties", the level of proof required, suppression (if desirable) of publication of parts of the proceedings, the privilege against self-incrimination, and the function of the police with regard to prosecutions.

19B – ELECTIONS

In a democratic society, the courts play a vital role in ruling on disputes associated with the electoral process. In the interests of speedy and certain outcomes in elections, the courts are called upon to hear the parties and deliver reasoned decisions without delay. In Papua New Guinea, the relevant law is contained in the *Organic Law on National and Local-level Government Elections* ("*Organic Law on Elections*"), as supplemented by decisions of the courts.

In Papua New Guinea, Magistrates may be involved in three aspects of the election process:

- **enrolment appeals:** national and local-level elections;
- **petitions:** disputed elections or returns (local-level elections); and
- **references:** disputed qualifications or vacancies (local-level elections).

This chapter will deal with each of these.

19B.1 ENROLMENT APPEALS (NATIONAL AND LOCAL-LEVEL ELECTIONS)

19B.1.1 Objections to enrolment

In both national and local-level elections, the right to vote is dependent upon the citizen's name being on the correct electoral roll at the time of the election. The Returning Officer decides persons' claims to be enrolled or to have their enrolment transferred, and also decides questions of objections to names on a roll and removal of names from a roll. Any elector on the same roll can object to a name, and the Returning Officer is obliged to object to a name that he or she believes ought not to be on the roll. When an objection has been lodged and served, the Returning Officer makes a determination on the objection and advises the parties.

19B.1.2 Appeal to the District Court

Under two identical sections of the *Organic Law on Elections* (s 72 for national elections and s 270 for local-level elections), the decisions of Returning Officers can be appealed to the District Court.

There are two likely situations:

- One situation is where a person's claim for enrolment or transfer has been rejected on the initiative of the Returning Officer. The aggrieved person may apply to a District Court for an order that the name be enrolled or reinstated, as the case requires: *Organic Law on Elections*, ss 72(1) and 270(1).
- Another situation is where the Returning Officer has removed a person's name from a roll after an objection by another party. Where the Returning Officer has determined an objection adversely to a person objecting, that person may apply to a District Court for an order sustaining the original objection: ss 72(2) and 270(2).

The application is to be made to the District Court in the prescribed manner. Regulation 12 of the *National and Local-level Government Regulation* 1997 provides that the application must be in writing, lodged within two months after receipt of notice of the rejection or after determination of the objection, as the case may be. A notice of the application must be served on the objector or the person objected to, as the case requires.

19B.1.3 The hearing

Sections 72 or 270 of the *Organic Law on Elections* (depending on the level of the election) confers jurisdiction on the District Court to "hear and determine" such an application, and to make such order regarding the costs of the application as it thinks fit. The *Organic Law on Elections* provides no other guidance as to how the court should proceed to deal with the matter. These applications to the District Court are in the nature of civil actions to test and/or enforce the right to be enrolled for the purpose of elections, and they are served on other parties to enable them to appear at the hearing.

For the above reasons:

- the hearing should be conducted in open court as a civil matter;
- the parties should be required to prove their respective cases from the outset (for example, a Returning Officer would be required to establish the grounds which led him or her to make the removal order. It would not be sufficient for the Returning Officer merely to produce the order of removal);
- where the facts are disputed, the burden of proof rests on the applicant, and the standard of proof is the civil test of a finding on the balance of the probabilities;
- the calling of witnesses and production of documents should proceed in accordance with the *District Courts Act*;

- the right of parties to be represented by lawyers applies as in the District Court; and
- at the close of the case, the Magistrate should announce a short adjournment during which he or she will consider the court's decision.

19B.1.4 Determination of the court

In the process of reaching a decision on the merits of the case, it may be useful for the court to:

- review the history or background of the matter;
- examine relevant words and phrases used in the *Organic Law on Elections* in relation to the roll of electors, the statutory conditions surrounding enrolment and the powers and duties of the Returning Officer – and make a check for National Court decisions on any of those words and phrases;
- review the evidence and find the facts upon which the determination will rest;
- summarise the legal issues and apply them to the facts; and
- write a decision which records the court's findings of fact, interpretation of the law and awarding of costs.

The clerk of the court is required to send a certified copy of the court's order to the Returning Officer, who must make such entries in the roll as are necessary to give effect to the order: *Organic Law on Elections*, ss 70(6) and 270(6).

19B.2 PETITIONS: DISPUTED ELECTIONS OR RETURNS (LOCAL-LEVEL)

19B.2.1 Disputed elections and returns under the Organic Law on Elections

19B.2.1.1 Court of disputed elections and returns

It is the responsibility of the court system to deal with disputes, irregularities and illegalities that occur during general elections at national and local levels. An efficient electoral process requires the just and prompt resolution of such matters in the public interest. A special jurisdiction is conferred on National and District Courts by the *Organic Law on Elections*. It is conferred on National Courts for national elections, and on District Courts for local-level elections, and such courts sit as courts of "Disputed Elections and Returns".

It is well established, in countries with parliamentary systems similar to that of Papua New Guinea, that the Court of Disputed Elections and Returns takes full responsibility for these matters, and that, in the interests of disposing of electoral challenges early, and to achieve finality following an election, there is no appeal from the court's decision. Such a decision "shall not be questioned in any way": *Organic Law on Elections*, ss 220 and 287.

19B.2.1.2 Scheme of the Organic Law on Elections

The *Organic Law on Elections* is a code of the law relating to elections at both levels, supplemented only by the *Criminal Code*. Most of the *Organic Law on Elections* is taken up with elections generally and national-level elections. Part XIX deals with local-level elections in particular. As far as disputed elections and returns are concerned, the *Organic Law on Elections* spells out the law governing the role of the National Court (Pt XVIII), and declares that most, but not all, of that law shall also apply, with modifications, to the role of the District Court in local-level elections: see Pt XIX and the important provisions of s 287. It must be remembered that the *Organic Law on Elections* applies to local-level elections only to the extent authorised by Pt XIX: s 3.

19B.2.1.3 Electoral rights

The constitutional guarantees of the rights to vote and stand for public office, freedom of expression, freedom of assembly and freedom of information are essential to the notion of "free and democratic elections". The courts are the guardians of these rights. The *Organic Law on Elections* may restrict these rights only to the extent necessary to give effect to the public interest in public safety, public order and public welfare: s 1.

19B.2.1.4 Electoral process in local-level elections

The *Organic Law on Elections* provides for the entire process, beginning with the issue of writs for the elections (Pt XIX, Div 8), nominations, voting (or "polling") on election day, scrutiny of votes cast, return of the writs, illegal practices and disputed elections and returns (Pt XIX, Divs 9-14).

19B.2.1.5 Disputes and offences in local-level elections

The requirements of free and democratic elections at the local-level are re-enforced by procedures laid down in the *Organic Law on Elections* for:

(a) **petitions** disputing the validity of an election or return on the ground of irregularities, illegal practices, bribery or undue influence; and

(b) **prosecution** of persons alleged to have committed:

  (i) illegal practices defined in s 286;

(ii) breaches of Pt III, Div 3 of the *Criminal Code*; or

(iii) other breaches of provisions of the *Organic Law on Elections*.

This chapter (19B) is concerned only with petitions, and not with prosecutions.

19B.2.2 Jurisdiction of the District Court

19B.2.2.1 The court's powers

Subject to specific modifications that are spelled out, Pt XVII, Div 3 of the *Organic Law on Elections*, which confers powers on the National Court, is deemed to apply also to the District Court in the case of local-level elections.

In proceedings brought by petition (see 19B.2.3 below), the District Court has powers that fall into three categories:

1. **Verdict on the election itself:** The court may:
   (a) declare that a person who was returned as elected was not duly elected;
   (b) declare a candidate duly elected who was not returned as elected; or
   (c) declare an election absolutely void: *Organic Law on Elections*, s 212(1).
2. **Inquiry into the voting and the Returning Officer's return:** The court may:
   (a) inquire into the identity of persons and whether their votes were improperly admitted or rejected, assuming the roll of electors to be correct (The court must not inquire into the correctness of the roll: s 214; see also *In re Election Petition for Lufa Open Electorate National Court* (1998) N1679 (Sawong J)); or
   (b) order a re-count of ballot papers in a ward: s 212(1).
3 **Procedural powers:** The court may:
   (a) compel the attendance of witnesses and the production of documents;
   (b) examine witnesses on oath;
   (c) grant parties leave to inspect the roll of voters; and
   (d) adjourn proceedings, award costs and punish for contempt by fine or imprisonment: s 212(1).

19B.2.2.2 Grounds on which court may exercise powers

The *Organic Law on Elections* declares that the District Court may exercise all or any of the above powers on such grounds as it, "in its discretion, thinks just and sufficient": s 212(3). Although subsequent sections introduce some limitations on the discretion, it remains a very wide discretion which imposes a duty on the court to familiarise itself with the *Organic Law on Elections*, to ensure that the statutory procedures are strictly complied with and to develop its reasoning carefully.

19B.2.2.3 Bribery, undue influence and illegal practices

If a successful candidate is found to have committed bribery or undue influence (see *Criminal Code*, ss 102 and 103), or to have attempted to commit either of them, the District Court must declare the election void: *Organic Law on Elections*, s 215(1). It is also clear that proof that illegal practices were committed in connection with an election may be sufficient ground for the court to declare a person not duly elected or to declare an election void: s 212(4).

However, this is subject to an important safeguard. The court has no power to declare a person not duly elected, or to declare an election void:

- on the ground of an illegal practice committed by a person other than the candidate and without the candidate's knowledge or authority; or
- on the ground of an illegal practice other than bribery or undue influence,

unless the court is satisfied that:

- the result of the election was likely to be affected; and
- it is just that the candidate should be declared not to be duly elected, or that the election should be declared void: *Organic Law on Elections*, s 215(3).

Section 286 of the *Organic Law on Elections* lists 22 illegal practices, each of which is also an offence punishable by fine or imprisonment. In addition, "illegal practice" is defined (s 235) to include offences under the *Criminal Code*, such as undue influence, bribery and illegal practices: *Criminal Code*, ss 102, 103,105 and 106.

19B.2.2.4 Residence, irregularities and other grounds

Lack of residential qualification to be elected as a head or member of a local-level government, or councillor of a ward, may be a ground for action against a candidate, bearing in mind the constitutional requirement of residence: *Constitution*, s 103, and *Organic Law on Elections*, s 253 in relation to wards. See *In re Disputed Return for Moresby North-West Electorate* (1998) N1670 (Woods J); *Joel McRay Aka v Dinah Patiliu (Ward 8 in Kimbe Town Local-level Government)* [1998] PNGDC 17 (Manuhu, Principal Magistrate); and *Vitus Noah v Gilson Leslie (Wards 1 and 2 in Mosa Local-level Government)* [1998] PNGDC 16 (Lenalia, Principal Magistrate).

Residence is described as a "threshold question", which, although it is not specifically mentioned in the *Organic Law on Elections*, falls to be decided by the Court of Disputed Elections and Returns: *In re Election for Enga Provincial Electorate* (1997) N1701 (Sakora J).

Failures on the part of a Returning Officer, Presiding Officer or other officials to administer an election strictly in accordance with the *Organic Law on Elections* may result in grounds for relief in the court: see examples of such failures in *In re Election for Enga Provincial Electorate* (1997) N1701 (Sakora J); and *In re Election for Kainantu Open Electorate* (1997) N1752 (Sakora J). The *National and Local-level Government Electoral Regulation* 1997 also sets out several specific procedures to be followed by officials.

However, immaterial errors will not be allowed to upset an election. The test is whether delay on the part of an officer, or absence, error or omission, affected the result of the election. Further, if an elector is prevented from voting for such a reason, the court is not permitted to admit evidence of which way the elector intended to vote at the election: *Organic Law on Elections*, s 218.

Subject to the specific restrictions and limitations imposed by the *Organic Law on Elections*, the court is given wide discretion as to the grounds on which it may rely in reaching its decision: see 19B.2.2.1.

19B.2.3 Procedure

19B.2.3.1 Petition

The only procedure by which a local-level election or return can be disputed is by petition to the District Court. It is to be heard and dealt with by a single Magistrate: *Organic Law on Elections*, ss 206 and 207. There is no prescribed form for an election petition, but it must:

set out the facts relied upon to invalidate the election or return; and

specify the relief to which the petitioner claims to be entitled: s 208(a) and (b).

Compliance with these requirements is strict, and failure to comply can result in the petition being struck out or dismissed at a preliminary stage of the proceedings. In the case of *In re West New Britain Provincial Electorate, Greg Mongi v Bernard Vogae and Electoral Commission* (1997) N1635, the petition was struck out by Injia J because insufficient facts were set out to support the grounds alleged and the petition failed to seek the correct relief. See also *In re Election for Kairuki-Hiri Open Electorate* (1997) N1676; and *In re Election for Enga Provincial Electorate* (1997) N1701.

Further, the petition must be signed by a candidate at the election or by a person qualified to vote: *Organic Law on Elections*, s 208(c) and (d). The court must itself inquire whether the petition is duly signed: s 214. The petition must also be attested by two witnesses whose occupations and addresses are stated: s 208(d).

19B.2.3.2 Filing petition and security for costs

A petition to dispute a local-level election must be filed at the District Court in the town containing the headquarters of the provincial government, which includes the area of the local-level government in respect of which the election was held: *Organic Law on Elections*, s 287(3). The time for filing a petition is not specified. Section 208(e), which requires national-level petitions to be filed within 40 days after the declaration of the result of the election, does not apply to local-level elections (s 287(1)), and practice directions may be made on the subject: see 19B.2.4.

Where there is a time limit fixed for filing a petition, it will be strictly applied by the courts (*In re Election for Central Bougainville Open Electorate* (1997) N1694 (Sawong J)), and no amended petition can be filed after that time (*In re Namatanai Open Electorate* (1997) N1627 (Injia J)).

Security for costs in the sum of K50 must be deposited with the clerk of the District Court: *Organic Law on Elections*, s 287(4).

19B.2.3.3 Strict compliance

In addition to the approach taken by the courts referred to above, it should be noted that the provisions of the *Organic Law on Elections* are such that the District Court is powerless to hear proceedings on a petition unless the above-mentioned requirements under ss 208 (a)-(d) and 214 have been complied with.

19B.2.4 Service of petition and compulsory conference

19B.2.4.1 Practice directions

In 1997, the National Court issued "Practice Directions for Presentation and Conduct of Election Petitions". It is likely that these will apply to local-level government elections in future, with suitable modifications to conform to the *Organic Law on Elections* on such elections and to make them applicable to the District Court. The following sections are written with these practice directions in mind, but Magistrates should check whether they, or subsequent practice directions, are current and applicable.

19B.2.4.2 Service of petition

The 1997 practice directions require that, within 14 days of filing, the petition must be served personally on the respondent, together with notification of a compulsory conference. A copy of the petition must also be sent promptly to the clerk of the local-level government (*Organic Law on Elections*, s 221), and a copy should be sent to the Electoral Commission, which is entitled to be represented at the hearing: s 211.

Proof of service on the respondent must be filed in the District Court within 14 days of service. A respondent who intends to appear on the hearing of the petition must file a notice to that effect in the court and serve a copy on the petitioner. The practice directions also deal with the place of trial and production of documents.

19B.2.4.3 Compulsory conference

It is always desirable (and is required by the practice directions) that a compulsory conference of the parties be held before a Magistrate, to determine such matters as:

representation by counsel;

possibility of settlement;

simplification of issues and streamlining of pleadings;

necessity to direct electoral records to be produced;

estimation of length of hearing; and

date of hearing.

19B.2.5 Hearing and decision

19B.2.5.1 Hearing and representation

An election petition should be heard in the same manner as a civil claim: see Chapter 4 as to hearing procedure. No party is entitled to be represented by a lawyer unless all parties consent or the court gives leave – and in no case may more than one lawyer appear for a party: *Organic Law on Elections*, s 222. Woods J, in the case of *In re Election for Lufa Open Electorate* (1997) N1617, pointed out that it greatly assists the court if a person with knowledge of the statute and procedure, preferably a lawyer, has drafted the petition.

19B.2.5.2 Evidence and "substantial merits of the case"

The onus of proof of the allegations made in the petition is on the petitioner throughout. The standard of proof required is the civil standard, but it is raised to take into account the seriousness of the issue at stake. Frost CJ, in the case of *In re Moresby North East Parliamentary Election (No2)* [1977] PNGLR 448 at 450, observed that "an election is a serious and expensive matter and is not lightly to be set aside", and stated the test adopted, namely:

> "in a case such as the present where the issues are of real gravity, the Court should require clear and cogent proof so as to induce, on a balance of the probabilities, an actual persuasion of the mind that the candidate did in fact lack the required qualifications".

In the case of *In re Election for Kairuki-Hiri Open Electorate* (1997) N1676, Sakora J referred to the heavy obligation on the petitioner to plead and prove his or her case: see also *In re Return for Moresby North West Electorate* (1998) N1670; *In re West New Britain Provincial Electorate, Greg Mongi v Bernard Vogae and Electoral Commission* (1997) N1635; and *Joel McRay Aka v Dinah Patiliu (Ward 8 in Kimbe Town Local-level Government)* [1998] PNGDC 17.

This test of proof adopted by the courts must be read together with the broad discretion as to evidence conferred by the *Organic Law on Elections*. Section 217 states that the court:

> **"shall be guided by the substantial merits and good conscience of each case without regard to legal forms or technicalities, or whether the evidence before it is in accordance with the law of evidence or not".**

There is certain evidence that the court is not permitted to hear in relation to a witness claiming that he or she was not permitted to vote: *Organic Law on Elections*, s 219. Also, although the court can inquire into whether votes were improperly admitted or rejected, it cannot hear evidence as to the correctness of the electoral roll: s 214. As to the weight to be attached to evidence of immaterial errors committed by officials, see 19B.2.2.4 above.

Finally, the "substantial merits" test, referred to above, may lead to the need for a common-sense approach. For example, Woods J, in the case of *In re Election for Eastern Highlands Regional Electorate* (1998) N1690, found that the undue influence and false statements complained of "was no more than tough political campaigning", and that "what had happened in PNG over the past year was bound to lead to tough criticism and campaigning".

19B.2.5.3 Decision and finality

Having read the documents, heard the evidence and listened to argument from both sides, the Magistrate is advised to adjourn for several days in order to prepare the decision and the reasoning that supports it. In view of the urgency of electoral matters, an adjournment of more than a week might be regarded as unacceptable.

In preparing the decision, the Magistrate should go back through the provisions of the *Organic Law on Elections* that confer jurisdiction, and carefully examine the court's powers: see 19B.2.2 above, particularly 19B.2.2.1 on "verdict" and 19B.2.2.2 on "grounds – just and sufficient". In a case of bribery, undue influence or illegal practices, it is useful to refer to 19B.2.2.3, and to note where the court is bound by law to declare the election void (s 215(1)) and where the court's powers are limited (s 215(3)).

The court should also be aware of the effect that a particular decision will have. This is spelled out, in s 226 of the *Organic Law on Elections*, as follows:

- **If a person who has been returned as elected is then declared by the court not to have been elected, that person shall cease to be a member.**
- **If a person who has not been returned as elected is then declared by the court to have been duly elected, that person may take his or her seat accordingly.**
- **If an election is declared to be absolutely void, then a new election shall be held.**

Costs may be awarded against an unsuccessful party and, if it is the petitioner who is unsuccessful, the deposit of security for costs will be paid as part of the other party's costs. A successful petitioner recovers his or her deposit: *Organic Law on Elections*, ss 223 and 224.

The decision on the petition should be announced in open court, and a copy of the court's order must be forwarded promptly to the clerk of the local-level government.

In keeping with the function and purpose of a Court of Disputed Elections and Returns, its decision is **"final and conclusive and without appeal"** and **"shall not be questioned in any way"**: *Organic Law on Elections*, s 220. **Thus, the weight of the court's responsibility to reach a decision that is correct in law, while also fair and just, is heavy indeed.**

19B.3 REFERENCES: DISPUTED QUALIFICATIONS OR VACANCIES (LOCAL-LEVEL)

19B.3.1 Jurisdiction

19B.3.1.1 Questions referred by local-level government

At any time during the life of a local-level government, and most commonly during or after an election, a question may arise as to whether:

a member of a local-level government is qualified to be a member;

a person is capable of being chosen or of sitting as a member; or

there is a vacancy in the government.

Such a question may be referred to the District Court by the local-level government: *Organic Law on Elections*, s 228.

19B.3.1.2 Statement of the question

If the local-level government decides, by resolution, to refer a question to the District Court, the head of the government should transmit to the court a statement of the question upon which the determination of the court is desired, together with any proceedings, papers, reports or documents, in the possession of the government, that relate to the question: *Organic Law on Elections*, s 229.

19B.3.2 The hearing

19B.3.2.1 Parties and representation

To establish who will be parties to contest the question before the District Court, the court may allow persons who, in the court's opinion, are interested in the determination of the question, to be heard at the hearing of the reference, and may direct notice of the reference to be served on any person whom the court considers could assist the court. Persons allowed to be heard or served with notice are deemed to be parties to the reference: *Organic Law on Elections*, s 230.

The position with regard to lawyers appearing in court is the same as for the hearing of disputed petitions: s 222; and see 19B.2.5.1.

19B.3.2.2 Hearing of the reference

Since the responsibility lies upon the District Court to answer the question referred to it, the court should proceed to conduct an inquiry and utilise its powers under the *Organic Law on Elections* to compel the attendance of witnesses for examination by the court and the production of documents: *Organic Law on Elections*, ss 212 and 231. At the same time, it is likely that certain parties will be interested in establishing certain facts (for example, a member of government may seek to establish that he or she is qualified to be a member, while another candidate may have evidence to the contrary). It is recommended that the court should hold a compulsory conference of the parties before the hearing, in order to determine on which party, if any, a burden of proof should lie. The court may also deal with such of the matters set out in 19B.2.4.3 as are relevant to the hearing of the reference.

Once commenced, the hearing must proceed in open court (s 231), and may be adjourned from time to time to enable further evidence to be obtained: s 212(1)(a). The court is to be guided by the "substantial merits and good conscience of each case without regard to legal forms or technicalities, or whether the evidence before it is in accordance with the law of evidence or not": ss 217 and 233.

The provision relating to immaterial errors in petition hearings also applies: ss 218 and 233.

19B.3.3 The determination

19B.3.3.1 The court's powers

In answering the question referred to it, the District Court has all the powers relevant to petitions as listed in s 212 of the *Organic Law on Elections* (see 19B.2.2.1), together with the power to determine three further matters (provided in s 231 and set out in 19B.3.1.1 above) relating to references.

19B.3.3.2 Declarations and finality

The court should take time for consideration, but not more than is strictly necessary. It is important to note that the law and practice set out in 19B.2.5.3 above, with regard to forwarding the court's declarations to the local-level government, and with regard to the finality of the court's decision, also apply to this jurisdiction.

19C – SURETY OF THE PEACE AND GOOD BEHAVIOUR

19C.1 PART X OF THE DISTRICT COURTS ACT

19C.1.1 Causing fear in others

Members of society sometimes act in a fashion that falls short of criminal behaviour (or criminal behaviour that is likely to result in a prosecution) and yet which causes fear in others. Part X (ss 209-218) of the *District Courts Act* provides Magistrates with a jurisdiction to deal with such behaviour and impose orders designed to alleviate the fears that it causes.

19C.1.2 Jurisdiction

Part X of the *District Courts Act* empowers Magistrates to compel persons before the court to answer complaints about their behaviour or intentions. Specifically, it may be alleged that a person has threatened, or indicated an intention to cause, a breach of the peace. Where grounds are made out to support these allegations, the person (the defendant) may either be required to enter into a recognisance to keep the peace or, if this is refused, be committed to prison for up to six months. A Magistrate's jurisdiction under Pt X is, strictly speaking, neither criminal nor civil in nature. It is a special statutory jurisdiction that may be utilised in a variety of contexts, often where no other available remedies or sanctions are appropriate.

A recognisance is a promise that is made by a defendant to the court to keep the peace. The expression "keep the peace" is not defined in the *District Courts Act*. It is an expression that has a long history in the common law. Some guidance may be found in the meaning of "peace" as it has been found in other common law jurisdictions. It has been interpreted to mean "the King's peace in its widest sense, the general peace and order of the realm as provided for by law": *Stephens History of the Criminal Law*, Vol 1, p 185. It may also be considered to connote "a quiet and harmless behaviour towards the King and his people": *R (Wilbur) v Magee* [1923] 3 WWR 55. When this meaning is applied in a Papua New Guinean context, a wide range of behaviour may amount to a breach of the peace.

A recognisance to keep the peace may require the defendant to pay a sum of money to the court. It may also require third parties, known as *sureties*, to come forward and either promise to pay, or actually deposit a sum of money with, the court on condition that the money will be payable or forfeited (as the case may be) to the court in the event that the defendant does not comply with his or her obligations during the term of the recognisance.

19C.2 GROUNDS FOR INVOKING THE COURT'S JURISDICTION

The grounds for invoking the jurisdiction of the District Court pursuant to Pt X of the *District Courts Act* are:

- Threat of bodily injury to the complainant, his wife, child or a person under the care of the complainant. (It does not appear that a wife may make a complaint on behalf of a husband who has been threatened, unless he is under her care).
- Threat to burn or injure the house of a complainant.
- Threat to commit a breach of the peace towards the complainant, his wife or a person under the complaint's care.
- Allegation that a person is of evil fame. (The meaning of this archaic expression is unclear).

The *District Courts Act* does not provide that a threat must be communicated in any specific manner. It is therefore possible to invoke the jurisdiction of the court where a threat consists of spoken words, written words or gestures, or a combination of these. The Act does state that using language that indicates intention to do any of the above acts is sufficient. A threat may be communicated directly or indirectly to the informant.

An information under Pt X is essential. In the absence of an information, a Magistrate has no power to make an order under Pt X, even where the Magistrate becomes aware of a threat to a person in the course of some other proceedings.

19C.3 THE PROCEDURE

A proceeding under Pt X of the *District Courts Act* is initiated by way of an information pursuant to s 209 or 210. The information must be in writing and may be on oath in every case, except where the defendant is alleged to be of evil fame, in which case the information must bc on oath.

If an information is on oath, a Magistrate has a choice of compelling the attendance of the person named in the information by means of a warrant. If the information is not on oath, a summons is used. If a summons is used and the defendant does not appear, a warrant may be issued pursuant to s 212(1)(a), in the same way it would be if a defendant charged with a simple offence failed to appear. In such cases, a Magistrate must ensure that service of the summons has been effected on the defendant.

If a Magistrate is satisfied that an information is laid only as a result of malice or vexation, he or she may refuse to issue any process to compel the attendance of the defendant. This effectively puts a stop to the proceedings. Reasons should be given to the complainant in such a case.

A hearing under Pt X of the *District Courts Act* is conducted in the same manner as a hearing for a simple criminal offence. The rules of natural justice are observed. A Magistrate must provide a defendant with an opportunity to answer the information and the evidence adduced against him or her. It is not clear whether a defendant has a right to cross-examine the makers of affidavits supporting the allegation in the information. If evidence against a defendant is adduced *orally*, a defendant will certainly have that right.

19C.4 EVIDENCE

19C.4.1 Affidavits

Section 211 of the *District Courts Act* establishes a statutory exception to the hearsay rule, in providing that the information may be supported by affidavits from third parties. This does not rule out the more usual manner of admitting sworn oral evidence.

19C.4.2 Standard of proof

The burden of proof required in a proceeding under Pt X of the *District Courts Act* is not specified. However, it appears that the burden is something *less* than beyond a reasonable doubt, the usual criminal standard.

19C.5 RECOGNISANCE

Section 214 of the *District Courts Act* provides that after hearing and considering evidence in relation to the information, a Magistrate may:

(a) dismiss the case;

(b) require the defendant immediately, or at some time to be specified by the court, to enter into an oral or written recognisance, with or without sureties, in such reasonable amount as the court thinks fit, to keep the peace or be of good behaviour, as the case may be, for such time as it thinks fit; or

(c) in default, commit the defendant to a corrective institution or police lock-up for such time as the court thinks fit, not exceeding six months, unless in the meantime the required recognisance is given.

If a recognisance is conditioned on the defendant *keeping the peace*, the commission of a criminal offence will not automatically result in a breach of a recognisance. This is because some offences do not amount to a breach of the peace. However, a criminal offence will automatically result in a breach of a recognisance that is conditioned on *good behaviour*, as the commission of any offence is, by its nature, bad behaviour.

The main benefit of an order requiring a defendant to enter into a recognisance is the deterrent effect that comes with the risk of forfeiting money if the terms of the recognisance are not complied with. This deterrent effect is presumably enhanced where sureties are involved and the amount of money in question is, in the eyes of the defendant and the sureties, substantial.

Another benefit may stem from a simple recognition on the part of a defendant that the justice system is capable of dealing with a threatened breach of the peace. When a defendant has been brought to court pursuant to Pt X of the *District Courts Act*, a Magistrate has an opportunity to speak directly to the defendant and warn him or her of the seriousness of the matter and the consequences of breaching a recognisance.

19C.6 FORFEITURE OF RECOGNISANCE

A Magistrate may declare a recognisance forfeited on application. Section 217 of the *District Courts Act* imposes no restrictions on who may apply. However, in order for an application to succeed, it must be proved that:

the person bound by the recognisance has committed an offence that amounts to a breach of the recognisance; and

notice of the application has been personally served or left at the usual or last known residence of the person at least seven days before the application.

The realities of the investigation and successful prosecution mean that a defendant, in many cases, will be able to delay any possible conviction until after an existing recognisance has expired. Further, behaviour that amounts to a breach of the peace or bad behaviour, and thereby breaches a recognisance but does not amount to a criminal offence, cannot result in a forfeiture. The result is that, under the present law, few recognisances are likely to be forfeited.

19D – MOTOR VEHICLE DEATHS COMPENSATION

19D.1 THE MOTOR VEHICLES (THIRD PARTY INSURANCE) (BASIC PROTECTION COMPENSATION) ACT

19D.1.1 Purpose of the Act

The *Motor Vehicles (Third Party Insurance) (Basic Protection Compensation) Act* is intended to provide for the speedy payment of a limited amount of compensation to the dependants of persons whose deaths are directly or indirectly attributable to the use of motor vehicles, without regard to the issue of negligence: preamble to the Act. The underlying purpose of the scheme is to use the prompt payment of some compensation to the deceased's dependants as a means of discouraging violent retributive action on their part, and also to contribute towards their expenses arising out of the death.

19D.1.2 Assessment Officers and assessors

Magistrates of the District Courts and Coroners are, by virtue of their office, Assessment Officers, and have jurisdiction, power and authority throughout the country: s 6. An Assessment Officer ("AO") may appoint up to three persons to assist him or her with a particular inquiry, and such assessors will carry out the functions and duties directed by the AO, but will not take part in the making of a determination under the Act: s 7. The *Motor Vehicles (Third Party Insurance) (Basic Protection Compensation) Regulation* suggests the type of work assessors should carry out: reg 2.

19D.2 THE INQUIRY

19D.2.1 Two-stage process

In brief, the *Motor Vehicles (Third Party Insurance) (Basic Protection Compensation) Act* requires two stages, the second dependant on the first. If, in the first stage, the AO finds that the death of the person under inquiry was not directly or indirectly attributable to the use of a motor vehicle, that is the end of the matter. If, on the other hand, the death was found to be so attributable, the AO must go to the second stage in order to determine three questions – by whom compensation should be paid, to whom and how much.

19D.2.2 Initiating the inquiry

An AO is required to conduct a full inquiry into the cause of death of a person if the AO has reasonable cause to believe that the death of the person was directly or indirectly attributable to the use of a motor vehicle: see definition of "motor vehicle" in s 1 of the Act. The AO may initiate the inquiry himself or herself, but, in any case, must do so as soon as practicable after receiving a request to do so from:

a person likely to be entitled to compensation;

a member of the police force; or

the Minister: s 8(1).

The request may be oral or written: reg 3.

If the AO is unable to conclude an inquiry within two weeks of receiving a request from any of the above, the AO must report to the Minister the reasons for being unable to do so: s 8(2). That report must be sent to the Minister within 21 days after the request to conduct the inquiry was received by the AO: reg 4. It is clear that speed is a major factor in carrying out the purpose of this legislation.

19D.2.3 Conducting the inquiry

The AO's inquiry under this Act is similar, in many respects, to a Coroner's inquest. It has the characteristics of a judicial function, requiring all those attributes of impartiality, fairness and a just outcome that the public expect of judicial officers. Magistrates and Coroners are appointed as AOs because they are members of the judiciary. AOs are indemnified against liability for their conduct in office in good faith, in the same manner as Magistrates sitting in court (s 28), and judicial notice must be taken of their official signatures (s 26).

The main difference between the AO's inquiry and that of the Coroner is that the AO's inquiry does not require the AO to conduct a public hearing as such. The AO's inquiry under this Act is to be conducted without regard to legal forms and solemnities. The AO is not bound to apply technical rules of evidence, but is obliged to admit and consider such relevant information as is available, including hearsay: s 9. It should be noted that, because the purpose of the coronial inquiry is different, the Act does not affect the operation of the *Coroner's Act*: s 4.

Nevertheless, the AO's inquiry becomes a hearing whenever witnesses are called to give evidence and oral argument is presented. This is clear from s 11 of the Act, which allows an entitled person (see below) to be represented before an AO by any person other than a lawyer. The importance of the AO's function as a judicial officer requires that such a hearing be held in a separate room provided for the purpose.

Persons may be summonsed before the AO to give evidence or produce documents: s 10. It is an offence for a person to fail to attend when summonsed, to refuse or fail to give evidence or answer lawful questions put by the AO, or wilfully to interrupt proceedings or obstruct an AO acting under the Act: s 12.

In short, the AO's inquiry under this Act may be a combination of hearing oral evidence and argument, and obtaining and reading documentation. The AO should keep a careful record of the facts of the accident and the evidence given at the inquiry, as these must be summarised for the AO's "Record of Inquiry": see reg 5, Sch – Form1.

19D.3 DETERMINATIONS

19D.3.1 Cause of death and related determinations

As indicated above, the first determination is whether or not the death was directly or indirectly attributable to the use of a motor vehicle: *Motor Vehicles (Third Party Insurance) (Basic Protection Compensation) Act*, s 15. If the death was attributable to such use, the AO must inquire into and determine by whom compensation should be paid, to whom and how much.

19D.3.2 By whom compensation is to be paid

In the course of the AO's inquiry into the death, the AO is required to determine:

whether the deceased was an occupant of a motor vehicle;

if not, where it is possible to do so, the identity of the motor vehicle(s) "most closely associated with the death" (s 16(1)); and

whether the motor vehicle was a government vehicle (s 20).

If the motor vehicle was a government vehicle, compensation is payable by the state. In the case of a vehicle other than a government one, the compensation is payable by the "successor company" in relation to the vehicle, as nominated under s 65 of the *Motor Vehicles (Third Party Insurance) Act.* In any other case, the Minister may determine the proportion of compensation payable by each of the successor company and the state: *Motor Vehicles (Third Party Insurance) (Basic Protection Compensation) Act*, s 20. The AO must provide full details of the vehicle, its registration number, owner, driver and third party insurance in the "Record of Inquiry" form: 19D.2.3 above.

19D.3.3 To whom compensation is to be paid

If the deceased died leaving a dependant wife or dependant child, compensation is payable to the wife or child. In any other case, compensation is payable to the head of the deceased's immediate customary kinship group as agent for all members of that group: s 17. In the latter situation, the AO must, as part of the AO's inquiry into the facts, determine which person is, for the time being, the head of that kinship group: s 16.

A person to whom compensation is payable under s 17 of the Act is an "entitled person": s 1.

> **Note:** As drafted, s 17 allows only one person to be an "entitled person" in respect of the deceased. Either that person is the dependant wife or dependant child, or that person is the head of the kinship group. This is consistent with the fact that the "immediate customary kinship group", which is represented by one "entitled person", seems to be defined in s 1 to include everyone other than dependant wife and dependant child. On the other hand, s 19 and the "Record of Inquiry" form clearly contemplate the possibility that there will be more than one "entitled person". One explanation for this inconsistency in the Act may be that, although the Act does not say so, Parliament intended each member of the kinship group to be an "entitled person".

19D.3.4 How much compensation

Subject to the maximum figures fixed in s 18 (K5,000 for dependant wife or dependant child or both, and K2,500 in any other case), the AO has full discretion to assess the amount of compensation, provided that the AO takes into account:

any customary disposition of property on death;

any economic loss suffered by any or all of the entitled persons; and

any other factor the AO thinks relevant: s 19.

The AO may also assess the proportionate amount payable to each entitled person, and may impose such conditions on an award as he or she chooses to specify: s 19.

It should be noted that an award of compensation under this Act does not affect the right to claim damages for the deceased's death, provided allowance is made for compensation recovered: s 25.

In carrying out this assessment aspect of the AO's function, it is again clear that the AO has a duty to make the assessments in the manner of a judicial task – with fairness and impartiality directed towards a just outcome.

19D.4 AWARD AND ENFORCEMENT

The AO makes an award under s 19 of the *Motor Vehicles (Third Party Insurance) (Basic Protection Compensation) Act*, and certified copies of the document are sent "as soon as practicable" to the Minister, the Minister for Justice, entitled person(s) named in the award and, where relevant, the successor company: s 21. The "Record of Inquiry" required by reg 5 must be lodged, with a copy of the award, in the District Court for the area in which the inquiry was conducted. The award operates as an order for the payment of a sum of money under the *District Courts Act* (s 22), and the AO may issue an "Order for Payment" against the person liable to make payment under the award: reg 8, Sch – Form 2.

A person liable to make payment under an award must, within seven days after service of a copy of the award under s 21 (and an order under reg 8), deposit the whole of the moneys payable with the District Court. Failure to do so is an offence (reg 7), and unpaid compensation will accrue interest at five per cent per annum: s 20.

PART 5

Enforcement and Costs

Chapter 20 – Enforcement

20.1 INTRODUCTION

Making a court order does not guarantee that the order will be complied with. Sometimes a person who is the subject of a court order will comply with the order. In many cases it is necessary to take further steps to enforce an order. This chapter deals primarily with the enforcement of orders that are made for the payment of money, either in the form of a fine or as compensation in a civil matter. It does not deal with the enforcement of family maintenance orders, which are dealt with in Chapter 16.

In addition to the enforcement of orders for the payment of money, this chapter also deals with the enforcement of fines against a corporation. Finally, the chapter deals briefly with the subject of contempt of court, the powers that a District Court Magistrate has in this regard, and how they may be exercised.

Part IX of the *District Courts Act* sets out a procedure for the enforcement of court orders. This part of the Act is complex, and uses terminology that is archaic in any other context. Although orders that may be enforced by means of Pt IX usually originate in the District Court, it may, in some circumstances, also be utilised to enforce orders that originate elsewhere, for instance, orders of a Village Court that have been endorsed by a District Court Magistrate.

20.2 ENFORCEMENT OF CIVIL JUDGMENTS

Enforcement orders for the payment of money that have been made in order to compensate a person or persons, result from orders made in civil proceedings either in the District Court or pursuant to an order for execution made under s 65 of the *Village Courts Act* and endorsed by a District Court Magistrate: see 18.5 and 18.6. An order for compensation made under the *Adultery and Enticement Act* that is not complied with may also be enforced as a civil order using the provisions of the *District Courts Act*.

Enforcement of orders for the payment of a fine is dealt with below at 20.6.

All enforcement proceedings in relation to orders to pay money originate from a minute or memorandum that is made by a Magistrate when the order is made. Section 160(2) of the *District Courts Act* provides that, while the minute does not form part of a subsequent warrant of execution, it is prima facie evidence for all purposes of the making of the order. The Act does not require a formal order to be drawn up pursuant to s 161 in order to commence enforcement proceedings.

20.2.1 Lump sum and instalments

Most orders made for compensation in civil proceedings provide that compensation be made in a lump sum of money. However, an order may provide for payment of compensation by instalments. Regulations 14 and 15 of the *District Courts Regulations* provide record-keeping procedures to be followed by the clerk of a

District Court where such an order is made. Where a person who is subject to an order to pay instalments does not make an instalment payment, the entire remaining amount becomes due and may be enforced as a lump sum: *District Courts Act*, s 165.

20.2.2 Orders against more than one defendant or partner

Regulations 22 and 23 of the *District Courts Regulations* provide that where an order is made jointly against more than one defendant, the order may be fully enforced against any one of the jointly named defendants. This may include partners where they are named as co-defendants in an action and where an order is jointly made against them. Where an order is enforced against one of the jointly named defendants, it is open to that defendant to seek indemnity from other jointly liable defendants. However, this does not affect the right of a person in whose favour an order is made to fully enforce the order against any one of the defendants. This allows a person in whose favour an order is made to enforce the order against whichever defendant provides the easiest target for enforcement of the order.

20.2.3 Place of enforcement

The District Court that made the original order retains the jurisdiction to enforce the order and, in most circumstances, this will suit the circumstances of the person in whose favour the order is made. However, enforcement proceedings may be "delegated" to another District Court for enforcement where the clerk is of the opinion that it would be "more convenient" to do so. Section 166 of the *District Courts Act* provides procedures for the transfer of enforcement proceedings to another District Court. However, the original District Court remains involved with the enforcement proceedings. It is sent an acknowledgment of receipt of the file by the court to which the matter is transferred. Any steps taken by the court to which the matter is transferred must be reported to the original District Court. Any moneys recovered must be sent to the original District Court.

Section 166 also provides for the further transfer of the file to a third court or back to the original court. Such transfers are governed by convenience. Only one court may engage in enforcement proceedings at any one time.

20.2.4 Oral examination of debtor

A person who is entitled to enforce an order for the payment of money is sometimes hampered by a lack of knowledge about what, if any, assets or entitlement to money the judgment debtor has. Without this knowledge, it is difficult for the judgment creditor to know whether or how the order may be enforced. The determination of this matter is often the first step towards enforcement of an order. Regulation 43 of the *District Courts Regulations* provides that, immediately upon the making of an order for payment of money, a Magistrate may cause the person who is liable to make the payment to be examined. At a subsequent time, an examination may take place on application under s 181 of the *District Courts Act*. A summons is issued in order to bring the person who is liable to make payment before the court.

The oral examination of a person under reg 43 or s 181 may be directed towards the determination of whether the person has any property that may be used to satisfy the order, whether there are any debts owing to the person that may be used to satisfy the order, or whether there are any other means of satisfying the order. Questioning may take the form of cross-examination. Where the party in whose favour the order is made is represented, their lawyer may conduct the examination. Where a party is unrepresented and unable to conduct an effective examination, the Magistrate should conduct the examination.

The examination of a judgment debtor may yield information that results in a warrant of execution.

20.2.5 Warrant of execution

A warrant of execution is an order that has the effect of ordering a person (usually a police officer) to seize and sell assets that belong to a judgment debtor. The procedure is designed to ensure that the sale of assets is at, or close to, the fair market price. The proceeds of sale are then used to satisfy the costs of the execution proceedings and the judgment debt. There is no punitive element to a warrant of execution. Any surplus moneys realised by a successful warrant of execution are paid to the judgment debtor.

Warrants of execution issued in the District Court normally arise from judgments made in the District Court. However, warrants of execution may also be issued in a Village Court. If a District Court Magistrate endorses a Village Court order for execution, the proceedings that govern the execution are those of the District Court: see 18.6.

20.2.6 Procedure on warrant of execution

The *District Courts Act* does not specifically state that a judgment creditor shall make an application for a warrant of execution, but this is implicit in the other provisions. In any event, no notice to the judgment debtor is required before initiation of proceedings for the issue of a warrant of execution.

A Magistrate, on hearing an application for a warrant of execution, may include terms in the warrant of execution as seem just in the circumstances. One condition may be that the warrant does not take effect until a given date: s 172.

The police officer or other person to whom a warrant of execution is directed may delegate the power to another person. Section 174 sets out the procedure that is to be followed by the person acting under authority of the warrant for execution. It provides for certain possessions of a judgment creditor to be exempt from seizure. Goods seized are to be sold by public auction. Except with respect to the sale of perishable goods, a public notice must be made at least five days before the sale of the goods. A sale must take place within 14 days of the seizure.

A person authorised to carry out the seizure and sale of goods under a warrant of execution may also "seize" money belonging to the judgment debtor, and may assume the rights of the judgment debtor in relation to cheques and other financial instruments. These rights include the right to demand payment and sue in the place of the judgment debtor: see s 175.

20.3 THIRD PARTY CLAIMS AGAINST PROPERTY

Sometimes, in the course of enforcement by a judgment creditor, either by seizure of property or attachment of debts, a third party may claim that he or she has a right to the property that ranks higher in priority than the interest of the judgment debtor. In such a situation, it is necessary to resolve the relative interests of the third party and the judgment debtor before any execution proceedings are concluded on behalf of the judgment creditor.

For instance, a third party may be a bank or other holder of a chattel mortgage. A third party may also be a spouse or other person who claims that the property in question does not belong to the judgment debtor at all.

20.3.1 Procedure on third party claims against property

Whenever a third party claims entitlement to property that is subject to enforcement proceedings, s 178 of the *District Courts Act* provides that a Magistrate may direct a summons to each of the third party and judgment creditor. The purpose is to bring the issue before the court. Once the summonses are issued, the enforcement proceedings are stayed until the third party claim is resolved. Although the Act does not specify the issuance of a summons to the judgment debtor in relation to the resolution of third party claims, that party might be a useful witness in the resolution of third party claims.

The resolution of a third party claim takes place in accordance with the requirements of s 179. This section provides for service of the summons, the provision of particulars, the timing of the hearing and the awarding of costs in relation to the hearing.

20.4 ATTACHMENT OF DEBTS

A judgment creditor may utilise the provisions of Pt IX, Div 4 of the *District Courts Act* to, in effect, step into the shoes of a judgment debtor with respect to moneys owning to the judgment debtor. The process of discerning the details of any debt owing to a judgment debtor, and requiring payment of that debt to the judgment creditor, is referred to in the *District Courts Act* as the "attachment of debts". Section 180 defines a person from whom debts are owing or accruing to the debtor, and in respect of whom an order is made under s 182(1), as a garnishee. The same section defines a debtor as "the person liable under an order of the Court for recovery or payment of money or costs, or both". This chapter uses the expression "judgment debtor" to describe the same person.

Where a garnishee makes a payment to the clerk of the court, it operates as a valid discharge of any liability that the garnishee has to a judgment creditor, to the extent of the payment made.

The provisions relating to the imprisonment of judgment debtors do *not* apply to claims for the payment of money prior to judgment. No order for imprisonment may be made unless the person who is the subject of an application has already been ordered by a court to pay moneys or deliver goods to a judgment creditor.

20.4.1 Identification of moneys owing to judgment debtor

Proceedings in relation to the attachment of debts may be preceded by an examination of the debtor under s 181 of the *District Courts Act*, already described in 20.2.4. Such an examination may reveal the existence and details of moneys owing to a judgment debtor.

20.4.2 Order attaching moneys owed to judgment debtor

An application to attach moneys owing to a judgment debtor may be made to a Magistrate. An application for such an order may be made ex parte, pursuant to s 182 of the *District Courts Act*. The meaning of s 182 is unclear and does not appear to have been clarified by an available judgment of the National Court. However, it appears to indicate the following. An order attaching moneys owed may be made pursuant to s 182(2) where there is proof on affidavit, or otherwise, that:

an order for recovery of payment of money or costs is unsatisfied; and

another person who is in the country is indebted to the judgment debtor.

On an application for an attachment order, a Magistrate may order the garnishee to appear before the court to show cause why he or she should not pay moneys owed by him or her to the judgment debtor.

If a garnishee does not dispute a debt and does not pay the amount of the debt owing to the judgment debtor, an order may be made, pursuant to s 184, to order the payment of the debt, or that portion necessary to satisfy the judgment creditor, to the clerk of the court.

If a garnishee does dispute the debt, a hearing under ss 185, 186 and 187 takes place. The procedure for this hearing is that which would occur in a civil dispute between the judgment creditor and the garnishee in respect of entitlement to the moneys in question. Any third party with an alleged interest in the moneys may also be ordered to appear at the hearing.

A Magistrate, at the conclusion of a hearing, may make an order that determines the issue of liability of the garnishee to the judgment debtor and, in accordance with this finding, may order execution against the amount due from the garnishee. Section 188 also provides for a determination of related questions regarding a third party's claim to the moneys. Section 191 provides for the awarding of costs at the discretion of the Magistrate.

20.5 DELIBERATE NON-PAYMENT OF JUDGMENT DEBTS

The law does not normally permit the imprisonment of a judgment debtor as a means of enforcing an order for the payment of money. However, where a judgment debtor is clearly able to pay, but refuses to do so or takes steps to deliberately make payment of a judgment debt impossible, the law does provide for imprisonment in some circumstances. Division 5 of Pt IX of the *District Courts Act* contains provisions that govern the circumstances and procedures relating to the imprisonment of judgment debtors. The Act uses the word "fraudulent" in relation to judgment debtors. However, the range of circumstances that may give rise to an order for imprisonment goes beyond the strict meaning of the word "fraud".

20.5.1 Types of orders that may be enforced by imprisonment

Section 192 of the *District Courts Act* restricts the types of orders that may be enforced by an order for imprisonment.

They are orders for:

- payment of debts;
- payment of damages; and
- delivery of goods detained, or the value of goods detained.

20.5.2 Conditions for order for imprisonment

Sections 192 and 193 of the *District Courts Act* set out the grounds upon which an order for imprisonment of a judgment debtor may be made. These grounds are summarised as follows:

- A judgment debtor has, or did have, sufficient means to satisfy the order but has refused or neglected to do so.

- A judgment debtor is about to leave the country without satisfying the order for payment of money. (Exemptions apply in the case of persons about to leave for Australia.)
- A judgment debtor is about to depart for another part of Papua New Guinea with the intent of avoiding payment of the order for the payment of money.
- A person subject to an order for the delivery of goods has, after due notice and without reasonable cause, refused to comply with the order.
- A person subject to an order for the payment of money or delivery of goods incurred the liability that resulted in the order:
  - by means of fraud or breach of trust; or
  - wilfully, knowing that there was no reasonable expectation of being able to discharge the liability.
- A judgment debtor has deliberately transferred, disposed of or concealed property with the intent of defrauding creditors.

If a person has been declared insolvent (see *Insolvency Act*, Cap 253) since the order for payment of money or delivery of goods was made, that person is *not* subject to an order for imprisonment pursuant to the provisions of s 192 of the *District Courts Act*.

20.5.3 Procedure and proof

The onus of satisfying a court that conditions for the imprisonment of a judgment debtor are satisfied is on the party applying for an order for imprisonment. The judgment debtor may be summoned to court and examined in relation to the preconditions for imprisonment. The standard of proof required is not set out in the *District Courts Act*, other than requiring proof to be "to the satisfaction of the Court". Because the issue entails the possible deprivation of liberty of a person, a court will demand a high standard, beyond the normal civil standard of balance of probabilities. The evidence must be convincing and commensurate with the seriousness of the matter in question. The evidence must be real and substantial.

Because the result of an application under s 192 of the *District Courts Act* may be the deprivation of a person's liberty, it is also important that the judgment debtor is afforded all the benefits of natural justice. Section 192 provides that the judgment debtor (person making default) may be:

- personally served with a summons; and
- examined on oath.

It further provides for the summoning of witnesses, their attendance and examination under oath.

Proceedings in relation to an application for the imprisonment of a judgment debtor are judicial in nature. The examining Magistrate must record the evidence: s 197.

Section 195 provides that where *special circumstances* exist, an order may be made ex parte on the basis of affidavit or other evidence that may be permitted by a Magistrate. What constitutes special circumstances is not specified. Some guidance may be gained by reference to the occasions where an ex parte hearing might be held in other civil matters. For instance, where a judgment debtor wilfully fails to attend a hearing, despite being served, a Magistrate might consider proceeding ex parte. However, the requisite standard of proof also governs ex parte hearings: see 14.6.7 and 14.6.8.

20.5.4 Orders for imprisonment – term and effect

Where a Magistrate is satisfied on the evidence that an order for imprisonment should be made, the maximum term is two months. An order for imprisonment does not extinguish the liability of the judgment debtor pursuant to the original order for payment of money or the delivery of goods. However, a judgment debtor who has been imprisoned may pay the amount specified in the warrant of committal at any time, and when this is done must be discharged immediately from prison.

A Magistrate may also discharge a person imprisoned under Div 5 (even though payment has not been made) where he or she is satisfied that special circumstances exist.

20.6 ENFORCEMENT OF FINES

A fine imposed in a criminal matter against a natural person is always enforced by means of imprisonment. The term of imprisonment, often referred to as being "in default", is stated when the fine is imposed. Section 201 of the *District Courts Act* provides the scale of maximum terms of imprisonment that may be imposed in default of fines of various amounts.

Where a corporation is the legal entity that is convicted of a criminal offence, and a fine is imposed, the fine is not enforced by way of a default term of imprisonment. Rather, the fine is enforced in the same way that an order for the payment of a sum of money arising out of a civil judgment is enforced. Therefore, the provisions set out above apply to the enforcement of fines that are imposed on a corporation in a criminal matter.

20.7 CONTEMPT

District Court Magistrates do not have the inherent power to punish persons for contempt of court in the same manner as do National and Supreme Court Judges. Therefore, where an order is made directing a person to do or not do an act, and the person does not comply with the order, the consequences (either by way of punishment or enforcement) must derive from a specific statutory source: see 3.1.3 and 14.5.5. Section 277 of the *District Courts Act* provides measures that may be employed where a person behaves in an inappropriate manner in court. However, this section does not provide for a means by which orders to do or not do something *out of court* may be enforced.

The enforcement of orders to pay money has been covered above. However, in the case of an order directing a person to do an act, s 171 of the *District Courts Act* applies. This section can be applied to enforce such things as interim orders in the nature of injunctions, as well as final orders for the delivery of a thing or for some other act.

Section 171 provides that:

> "where …
>
> (b) a Court orders the doing of an act other than the payment of a fine or sum of money or costs and directs that, in case of the defendant's neglect or refusal to do the act, he shall be imprisoned and the defendant neglects or refuses to do the act,
>
> the Court or a Magistrate may issue a warrant of commitment for the imprisonment of the defendant for such time as the conviction directs."

Chapter 21 – Costs, Fees and Expenses

21.1 TYPES OF COSTS IN GENERAL

21.1.1 Actual expenses

In most cases, costs are the "out-of-pocket" expenses that a party has actually spent, or will have to spend in the very near future, in order to bring proceedings in court against someone, or to defend a prosecution or action that has been brought against the party. Costs may include such expenditure as filing and service fees and enforcement costs paid to the court, witness expenses, fees for medical reports, lawyer fees, and (in appropriate cases) the party's travelling expenses.

21.1.2 Costs and compensation

An order that one party should pay a sum towards the costs of the other party is a method of partially compensating the latter for having to fight the case. However, "compensation", as that term is usually used, can cover a range of different sorts of loss and damage, while costs are limited to the actual expenses referred to above. In all cases, Magistrates should be careful not to use a costs order as a means of adding to compensation otherwise ordered, or as a way of further penalising the party against whom the costs order is made.

21.1.3 The test

If a claim for costs is contested, the person claiming may have to produce receipts or support the claim with evidence on oath. In deciding what claims to allow, the Magistrate should consider whether each item of costs was reasonable necessary in order to properly conduct or defend the proceedings. The maximum may be fixed by fee schedules prescribed by law.

21.1.4 Lawyers' fees

Where a lawyer is acting for a party, the lawyer gives a bill or account to the party, and the lawyer's fees become part of the party's costs. In fact, the lawyer may also have paid the "out-of-pocket" expenses, so that the lawyer's bill will include both:

(a) the lawyer's fee or charge for the legal work and representation in court; and

(b) the expenses paid by the lawyer.

They are all costs of the party.

21.1.5 Party-to-party costs

A party in whose favour a costs order is made will not normally recover all of his or her own party costs, but only a contribution towards them, which is called "party-to-party" costs. The Magistrate usually fixes these, having regard to maximum fee schedules provided in court rules or regulations.

21.1.6 Costs in criminal cases

After a person has been found guilty and the sentence has been determined, the court may order the defendant to pay costs, but such costs are not intended to be paid to the state towards the salaries of police officers or for court services. These salaries and services are paid from the state treasury, into which fines are paid: see, for example, *District Courts Act*, s 177. Costs awarded against the defendant in criminal matters usually relate to items such as witness expenses and the out-of-pocket expenses of a private informant.

21.2 ORDERS FOR COSTS

21.2.1 General principle

The award of costs is the exercise of a judicial discretion, and any decision must always be made after taking each case on its merits, hearing each party and taking proper account of the law. There is no absolute rule that a party who loses a case must pay the costs of the successful party. Rather, it is a general principle in Papua New Guinea, as in the United Kingdom and Australia, that "costs should follow the verdict", thus penalising the unsuccessful party and reimbursing the successful one. However, this principle is always subject to the discretion of the court in the light of the circumstances of the particular case. For example, a party might win a claim for damages, but the delay and other tactics of that party might have caused such expense to the other party that the victor's costs should be reduced, or even denied. It is useful to regard the award of costs to the successful party as a strong presumption that can be rebutted in appropriate circumstances. In Papua New Guinea, a court's powers in relation to cost orders depend on the authority and discretions conferred by statute: see *PNG Pipes Pty Ltd v Mujo Sefa* (1997) SC524.

21.2.2 Awarding costs

As this is a judicial act, it is never automatic.

The Magistrate is required to consider the grounds on which a party should be ordered (if at all) to pay costs to the other party, such as:

- whether the party seeking the costs order was successful in the action; and
- whether the tactics or other conduct in the case on the part of the party seeking costs were such that the costs order should be reduced (perhaps to zero); or
- whether the conduct of the party liable for costs was such that he or she should pay the full amount permissible under the law.

In a criminal case, the court's duty is first to consider what is the appropriate sentence. If that is a fine, the offender's means to pay, so far as the court knows them, must be taken into account. The same applies to compensation orders: see 21.1.2. Costs should never be awarded as a disguised penalty. The costs awarded should bear some relationship to the level of any fine.

21.3 COSTS UNDER THE DISTRICT COURTS ACT

The District Court's power to award costs is implied and assumed in several sections, principally s 260 of Pt XII of the *District Courts Act*, but it should be noted that the costs power and the amount of any award are subject to that section. Other sections of the *District Courts Act* provide for costs in different circumstances. The *District Courts Regulations* (see regs 47-49) contain prescribed maximum fees in the following schedules:

- Schedule 3: Court Fees in the District Court;
- Schedule 4: Lawyers' and Agents' Costs;
- Schedule 5: Witnesses' Expenses;
- Schedule 6: Miscellaneous Fees (Court fees for providing copies of orders, etc).

21.4 COSTS IN CRIMINAL MATTERS

21.4.1 On conviction

Where the court enters a conviction, it may award such costs as it thinks just and reasonable to be paid by the defendant to the informant: *District Courts Act*, s 260(1)(a).

The principles governing the Magistrate's discretion, referred to in 21.1 and 21.2 above, apply. For example, natural justice requires that all parties present are entitled to be heard on the question of costs. Also, no order for costs can be made against a person unless there is proof of service of proceedings and the person has duly become a party to the dispute: *Leo Getsi v PNG Harbours Board* [1993] PNGLR 408.

The Magistrate must specify and fix the sums allowed for costs in the wording of the conviction: *District Courts Act*, s 260(1)(c) and (g). This is mandatory. The maximum amounts set in the schedules apply: see 21.3.

21.4.2 Time for payment or instalments

As in the case of a fine, the court may allow time for payment of costs. It may also direct payment by instalments, or direct that security may be given for the payment: *District Courts Act*, s 165.

21.4.3 Recovery of costs in criminal matters

When considering the recovery of payment of costs, it is necessary to read Pt XIII of the *District Courts Act* (on costs) together with Pt IX (on enforcement). Enforcement is by way of imprisonment, and the court must fix a term of imprisonment in default of payment, according to scale: ss 167, 168, 201 and 260(1)(h). Warrants of commitment (ss 170 and 171) and execution (s 173) may be issued. Moneys recovered and received by the court clerk are required to be paid by the clerk:

first, towards costs ordered in favour of a party (which may include the informant);

secondly, in accordance with any terms imposed on the conviction; and

thirdly, according to the law (if any) under which the information was laid; or

in default, to the Secretary for Finance: s 177.

21.4.4 Costs of successful defendant

Where the court dismisses an information, it may order the informant to pay the defendant such costs as it thinks just and reasonable, subject to the court's obligation to consider a list of **seven factors** relating to the prosecution's conduct of the investigation and prosecution of the alleged offence: *District Courts Act*, ss 260(1)(b) and 260A(1). These factors direct the Magistrate's attention to such matters as whether the prosecution acted in good faith in bringing and continuing the charge, and whether it conducted the investigation in a reasonable manner. The defendant's conduct may also be taken into account. Failure to consider the full list of factors may nullify any order as to costs.

The court must also take note of the fact that the withdrawal, dismissal or acquittal of a charge does not automatically entitle the defendant to costs, and there is no presumption either way: *District Courts Act*, s 260A(2) and (3). It seems clear that when a defendant seeks costs against the informant in reliance on s 260(1)(b), the Magistrate should first consider the wording of s 260A and apply that section to the facts. The court record of the decision should show that the Magistrate had turned his or her mind to the relevant parts of s 260A before making a costs order under s 260(1): *Leo Getsi v PNG Harbours Board* [1993] PNGLR 408.

The Act does not apply to a dismissal of a charge of an indictable offence: s 261. As far as court, witness and lawyer fees are concerned, the schedules apply.

21.4.5 Costs on sureties to keep the peace

Another example of statutory authority to award costs arises in relation to the Magistrate's jurisdiction to require a person to enter into recognisance and give surety to keep the peace. Section 218 of the *District Courts Act* provides that costs may be awarded in the same manner and to the same extent, and may be recoverable by the same process, as on a conviction.

21.5 COSTS IN CIVIL MATTERS

Where the court makes an order in favour of the civil complainant, it may award such costs as it thinks just and reasonable against the defendant in sums specified and fixed by the court, and the reverse applies where the order is in favour of the defendant: *District Courts Act*, s 260(1)(a), (b), (c) and (g). The schedules apply, and, in the case of the attendance at court of the complainant and defendant, a daily allowance to cover loss of wages and accommodation expenses, to a maximum of K85, is provided for in Sch 5.

Such costs and allowances are recoverable, without the direction of the court, by execution against goods and chattels under Pt IX, Div 2 of the Act.

21.6 ADJOURNMENTS

Where a case is adjourned, the court may order that the costs of and occasioned by the adjournment be paid by one party to another party: *District Courts Act*, s 260(1)(e). The schedules apply: see also the discussion of adjournments in Chapter 4. The power to order a party to pay costs that arise out of delay or other conduct interfering with the smooth running of the case is an important sanction. On the other hand, where adjournments and changes of venue are necessary in criminal matters, in circumstances for which an unrepresented defendant is not responsible, the Magistrate may need to take care that the defendant is aware of the right to claim reasonable costs.

In civil matters, the situation is sometimes different. By and large, it is up to the parties to protect their own interests by asking for, and objecting to, awards of costs. However, here again, the Magistrate may have to be vigilant to ensure that an unrepresented party knows the rules relating to costs, especially where the other party has a legal representative.

In the particular situation where proceedings have been brought in the wrong court, and the defendant satisfies the court that the matter could be more conveniently and properly heard in another court, the Act makes explicit provision. If it can be shown that the defendant has been brought to the wrong court vexatiously and oppressively, the court must immediately deal with the matter. Further, the court may order the person issuing the proceedings to pay the defendant, by way of compensation or amends, such reasonable sum as the court directs, together with the costs of the order: *District Courts Act*, ss 150 and 151.

21.7 WITNESSES

Witnesses who attend to give evidence or produce documents, whether they have been examined or not, shall, unless otherwise ordered by the court, be paid expenses covering travel and such matters as loss of wages and accommodation expenses to the maximum stated and in accordance with the details provided in Sch 5: *District Courts Act*, ss 260(1)(f) and 264.

21.8 LAWYERS' AND AGENTS' COSTS

The court may order a party to pay lawyer's costs to another party. This is within the discretion given by s 260 of the *District Courts Act*. However, the Act makes no distinction between the amounts of a party's own costs and party-to-party costs: see 21.1.4 and 21.1.5 above. No lawyer or agent is entitled to receive, in total, by way of fees for work done, any amount more than the fees prescribed in Sch 4: s 263. The schedule specifies the maximum costs and charges allowable in relation to items of work carried out by lawyers, according to a scale under which the fee increases in accordance with the amount recovered by the complainant and, in the case of the defendant, the amount claimed.

Schedule 4 also permits claims for such items as "money properly paid out of pocket", the "actual cost of conveyance", and a daily allowance when the lawyer attends court at a place other than that at which he or she carries on business. Where the lawyer attends court on more than one matter at the same sittings of the court, the schedule requires the costs and allowances to be rateably divided. This does not mean that a lawyer will recover all of his or her schedule costs from cases attended at the same sittings. In fixing costs to be paid for legal attendance in one case, the court is not obliged to take into account the possibility that the lawyer may not recover costs in the other cases heard at the same sitting: see, for example, *Leo Getsi v PNG Harbours Board* [1993] PNGLR 408. Clearly, claims for costs require careful scrutiny in light of the Magistrate's duties and discretions.

21.9 COSTS ON APPEAL

Appeal from the District Court to the National Court under s 219 of the *District Courts Act* requires both a notice of appeal and a recognisance or other security for costs: s 220. The Magistrate is called upon to determine judicially the amount that the prospective appellant must cover in order to ensure that the appellant will:

prosecute the appeal;

abide by such order as the National Court may make on the appeal; and

pay any costs awarded by that court: s 222.

The appellant has a choice – either to enter into a recognisance or to deposit the sum with the clerk of the District Court: see Chapter 26.

PART 6

Magistrates' Civil Liability and Case Management

Chapter 22 – Civil Liability and Protection of Magistrates

22.1 PRINCIPLE OF LIABILITY

A person who, by his or her physical acts, words or other actions, causes harm or loss to another person intentionally or in circumstances where a duty of care is owed, is liable to that person for damages in tort. Generally, officials are liable to persons affected by their decisions and, in the absence of any immunity or other protection at law, they may be sued for damages if they are negligent or cause harm by intentional acts.

22.2 PRINCIPLE OF IMMUNITY

In order to ensure the freedom of Judges, Magistrates, parties, lawyers and witnesses to act and speak in the interests of justice without fear of being sued for damages, the common law provides immunity for all those involved in the judicial process. This immunity protects them from being sued for anything said, written or done in the course of court proceedings or immediately preparatory to those proceedings.

As far as Judges are concerned, the common law immunity extends to:

acts beyond their jurisdiction, provided they act judicially; and

acts motivated by malice, provided the acts are within jurisdiction.

22.3 LIABILITY AND PROTECTION OF MAGISTRATES AND CLERKS

As judicial officers in the lower courts, Magistrates enjoy some of the immunity of Judges, but the Magistrates' common law immunity is limited in two important respects:

1. Magistrates are usually liable personally for acts done by them when those acts are outside their jurisdiction (**in excess of jurisdiction** – see, for example, the discussion of the criminal jurisdiction in 6.3 and civil jurisdiction in 14.2); and
2. Magistrates may also be sued for acts done **within jurisdiction**, where those acts are:
   (a) motivated by malice; and
   (b) done without reasonable and probable cause.

In Papua New Guinea, Pt XII of the *District Courts Act* gives general effect to the common law, but provides important procedural safeguards for Magistrates. It also extends the provisions of the Act to acts done by clerks of District Courts.

22.4 SCHEME OF PART XII OF THE DISTRICT COURTS ACT

22.4.1 Exceeding jurisdiction

Part XII of the *District Courts Act* deals with the two aspects of liability and protection referred to above, namely excess of jurisdiction and malice. As far as exceeding jurisdiction is concerned, the liability of Magistrates is emphasised by the language of s 247. This section declares that a person injured by an act done by a Magistrate "may maintain an action against the Magistrate" in circumstances where:

the Magistrate's act was done in a matter in which, by law, he or she had "no jurisdiction", or in which he or she had "exceeded his or her jurisdiction"; or

the act was done under a conviction or order made, or warrant issued, by a Magistrate in such a matter. (This seems to mean – an act done by another person in the course of carrying out such a conviction, order or warrant.)

In practice, the distinction between "acting with no jurisdiction" and "exceeding jurisdiction" is seldom important. For example, s 21(4) of the *District Courts Act* provides that a District Court "has no jurisdiction in the following cases ...", and the list includes such matters as the validity of a bequest under a will, and breach of promise to marry. A Magistrate who begins to hear such a case has no legal authority, and may be liable in damages for any harm caused. Other sections explicitly confer jurisdiction on the court, and, if the Magistrate goes outside the wording of the section, he or she is acting in excess of jurisdiction. An obvious example is where a Magistrate allows an amendment to increase a civil claim to a monetary figure above the statutory limit: s 21(1).

However, the consequences of a Magistrate acting contrary to sections like these are unlikely to be more serious than the consequences of mishandling a matter which lies within jurisdiction. Because the Magistrate's authority in any matter or process is dependant entirely on the wording of relevant statutes, any failure to observe the statute is an act in excess of jurisdiction. For example, failure to state "the offence" in a summons (s 44), failure to conduct matters in open court (s 57), or failure to explain the nature of the charge in ordinary language (s 96) will mean that all subsequent proceedings will be in excess of the Magistrate's jurisdiction.

In other words:

Once you step outside your jurisdiction, you can't just say "sorry" and carry on. You have to go back to the point where you stepped out, and start all over again.

22.4.2 Limitations on actions against Magistrates

One of the purposes of Pt XII of the *District Courts Act* is to place limitations on the circumstances in which actions can be brought against Magistrates.

No action can be maintained against a Magistrate for anything done under a conviction or order, or under a warrant leading to a conviction or order, until after the conviction or order has been quashed or set aside: s 247(2). If a warrant was issued to procure the attendance of a person who failed to appear on a summons, or if a warrant is not followed by a conviction or order, no action can be brought against a Magistrate for anything done under the warrant: s 247(3).

Where a warrant of execution or commitment is granted by a Magistrate bona fide (in good faith) and without collusion (secret agreement with one of the parties), in reliance on a conviction or order made by another court, it is that court alone which may be liable for any defects in the order or conviction: s 248.

Similarly, no action is maintainable against a Magistrate who acts in obedience to an order of the National Court or a Judge (s 249), nor is it maintainable in respect of a Magistrate's warrant of execution or commitment on a conviction or order that has been confirmed on appeal by that court (s 250).

A Magistrate, against whom an action, which the Act declares to be not maintainable, is brought, may apply to a Judge of the National Court to have the action stayed or set aside: s 251.

22.4.3 Actions against Magistrates in the execution of their office

A further purpose of the legislation is to set up strict procedural requirements in order to protect the Magistrate, as far as possible, from claims that are not based upon genuine grounds of complaint against him or her.

No action can be brought against a Magistrate who is acting in the execution of his or her duty as such, or in his or her capacity as a Magistrate as such, unless the provisions of ss 252-258 of the *District Courts Act* are complied with. The only grounds that can be successfully alleged under the Act are acts of a Magistrate that are "done maliciously and without reasonable and probable cause": s 256.

"Malice" requires an intention to cause harm – a spiteful or evil intention – and is difficult to prove against a Magistrate. Nevertheless, Magistrates should bear in mind that minor lapses of behaviour on their part may appear to be due to malice. They should remain aware of the very public nature of their daily contact with parties, both in court and on the court record. Magistrates are constantly interacting with people, and frequently making both minor and important decisions affecting parties, witnesses and the public. Everything Magistrates say and do (including on the occasions when they may be feeling ill, under pressure, angry or annoyed) will be watched and commented upon. People who do not understand the law and procedure may wrongly interpret the presiding Magistrate's comments or decisions. Disgruntled or unsuccessful parties may seek ways of hitting back at the Magistrate – and all of this can lead to reactions from the Magistrate which might be described as "malicious".

"Without reasonable and probable cause" means that a Magistrate has the opportunity to explain his or her actions. It is a reminder that Magistrates who conduct themselves with dignity and impartiality, and whose actions can always be shown to be based in law and common sense, have nothing to fear at the hands of those members of the public who pass through their courts: see also Chapter 1.

No action can succeed against a Magistrate for anything done in the execution of office unless:

- the special time limits, in s 252 of the *District Courts Act*, for bringing an action are observed;
- at least one month's notice of intended action is served on the Magistrate under s 253;
- the action is brought in the National Court (s 255);
- the grounds of malice and lack of reasonable cause are expressly pleaded (s 256); and
- compliance with the above requirements and the stated cause of action are proved (s 257).

Finally, if it is proved that the claimant was in fact guilty of the offence charged, liable at law to pay the sum which the Magistrate ordered, or has undergone no greater punishment than that assigned by law for the offence, the claimant is not entitled to recover any penalty or sum paid, and may not recover more than nominal damages of two toea for imprisonment or the cost of the action: *District Courts Act*, s 258.

22.5 OTHER JURISDICTIONS

While a Magistrate is acting as a Coroner (Chapter 19A) or sitting as the Court of Disputed Returns in local-level elections (Chapter 19B), he or she does so as a member of the District Court, and the above provisions as to liability and protection apply. While acting as an Assessment Officer under the *Motor Vehicle (Third Party Insurance) (Basic Protection Compensation) Act* (Chapter 19D), s 28 of that Act protects the officer in respect of any act done, which the officer believed in good faith to be within jurisdiction. It is interesting that this is the same "higher" protection that is afforded to Judges at common law: see 22.2 above.

Chapter 23 – Case Management

23.1 INTRODUCTION

Effective case management improves the quality of justice and enhances the public standing of the Magistrates' Courts.

This chapter will consider methods of case management in the District Courts, most of which could be adopted administratively within the existing framework of the *District Courts Act*. Experience elsewhere has shown that case management is implemented more effectively within a broad policy that all Magistrates feel they can support. It is also true that management methods are the responsibility of each Magistrate individually, who will apply the policy and methods in a manner that the Magistrate thinks is just in the light of the needs of each case.

"Case management" has a wide meaning, which may include such matters as registration procedures and record keeping. This chapter is mainly concerned with the flow of cases through the system, sometimes known as "delay reduction".

23.2 THE IMPORTANCE OF CASE-FLOW MANAGEMENT

Justice delayed is justice denied. It is recognised that delay in the court system can, and often does, have the following harmful effects:

- It prolongs and exacerbates disputes, anxieties and differences between people.
- It causes the memories of witnesses and parties to fade.
- It raises the expenses of litigation, thus excluding many people from pursuing their legal rights and remedies.
- It undermines genuine attempts to settle the cases.
- It devalues the effectiveness of judgements, decisions and orders.
- In criminal matters, it may breach the constitutional guarantee of a hearing "within reasonable time": *Constitution*, s 37(3) and see Chapter 3.
- In civil matters, it may cause parties to accept less than the full value for their claims.
- Accumulated delay produces backlogs of cases that waste court resources and create conflict in allocating Magistrates' time.

23.3 OBJECTIVES

The objectives of case-flow management are to:

- reduce delay and expense of the court system;
- dispose of each case in the most efficient manner;
- apply the same standards to all parties engaged in the court process; and
- increase public confidence in the court as an institution.

23.4 GENERAL PRINCIPLES

23.4.1 Ethical obligation

The magistracy has an ethical obligation to conclude all court proceedings promptly.

23.4.2 Unacceptable lapse of time

From the beginning of litigation[(1)] to the final disposition of the case[(2)], any time that elapses, other than time that is reasonably required[(3)] for the pleadings[(4)], evidentiary matters[(5)], mediation[(6)] and other court events[(7)], is unacceptable.

Notes on the above statement

1. *Litigation* includes criminal or civil litigation.
2. *Disposition* means disposition by settlement, guilty plea, dismissal, conviction, judgment or final order.
3. The Magistrate knows from experience what is *reasonably required.*
4. *Pleadings* include the laying of informations and the issuing of summons, complaints and statements of defence.
5. *Evidentiary matters* include the production of documents, preparation of depositions and pre-trial examination of witnesses.
6. *Mediation* and other forms of dispute resolution are often time-consuming, and a time-schedule should be fixed to bring unsuccessful attempts at mediation to a close.
7. *Court events* are any occasions when the parties attend before the court.

23.4.3 Control

In order to ensure the just and efficient resolution of cases, the court, rather than the parties or lawyers, must control the flow of cases. This is a fundamental proposition in any court, and, in the District Court, the ultimate responsibility lies with the Magistrates.

23.4.4 Determination

Reducing delay requires a strong commitment on the part of the Magistrates.

23.5 METHODS OF MANAGING CASE-FLOW

23.5.1 Supervision

Supervision by the court (the clerk of court) of all cases should begin from the time of filing of the first document. This might involve monitoring the steps taken in each case on a time-chart or calendar, perhaps with a line across the chart for each case, showing its progress.

23.5.2 Control of case-flow

Magistrates may control the progress of each case by techniques such as:

fixing short times between court events, such as:

- between the appearance of a defendant on a summons and the date of hearing; and
- when dealing with applications for further particulars of complaint or defence;
- never adjourning a case without fixing a further date (never indefinitely, or sine die, despite the wording of s 89(1) of the *District Courts Act*);
- when transferring a case to another court, arranging (wherever possible) a certain date for attendance at that court;
- fixing periods for adjournments which are as short as possible in the circumstances; and
    - after the close of evidence and argument at the end of a hearing, fixing as short a period as possible within which to consider and deliver the judgment, order or other decision.

23.5.3 Advice concerning adjournments

Magistrates should advise, and regularly remind, parties and lawyers that cases will be heard on the date fixed, and that, once hearings have begun, further adjournments will be firmly discouraged.

23.5.4 Early identification of problems

The Magistrate and clerk should review the list frequently to identify difficult cases, and cases which are likely to require more time (in preparation or in hearing), so that additional resources can be organised for them.

23.6 DEVELOPMENT OF A CASE-FLOW POLICY

This will usually involve:

- *preparing* data and/or examples which establish that delay is a problem;
- *analysing* causes of delay;
- *designing* a program to reduce delay, indicating the court's specific problems and how to deal with them;
- *planning* for implementation, including the administrative and training aspects, and the detailed methods to be put in place; and
- *putting* the plan into practice.

PART 7

Settlement, Decisions and Appeals

Chapter 24 – Out-of-Court Settlements and Alternative Dispute Resolution

24.1 INTRODUCTION

The primary focus of a Magistrate's attention concerns what takes place within the courtroom, particularly at a hearing or trial. However, it is important for a Magistrate to be mindful of the things that may go on between parties out of court, and what alternatives the parties have to a contested trial. In this chapter we look at the ways in which disputes that are commenced in a District Court can be finalised without a contested hearing and decision by a Magistrate. We will look at what a Magistrate should be aware of and what duties exist in relation to cases where there has been a successful or unsuccessful attempt to settle out of court. This chapter is primarily concerned with non-criminal cases. Criminal cases that are resolved without a trial usually involve a guilty plea. Guilty pleas are dealt with separately in Chapter 12.

24.2 ADVANTAGES OF OUT-OF-COURT SETTLEMENT

It is generally preferable for parties (other than those lacking legal capacity) to voluntarily enter into a settlement that they consider to be fair, rather than to bring their dispute to court for a Magistrate to decide.

Out-of-court settlements are not only in the interests of the parties, but are also in the interests of the justice system and society generally. As long as they do not conflict with other duties or with a sense of fairness in the particular circumstances, out-of-court settlements should be encouraged. However, out-of-court settlements should never be imposed against the will of any party.

24.2.1 Advantages to the parties

Consensus

Settlements are in the interests of the parties because they represent a consensus. A court judgment does not represent a consensus. In most cases, the decision goes against the wishes of at least one party. Sometimes all parties are unhappy with the result.

Greater range of possible outcomes

Out-of-court settlements are in the interests of parties to disputes because they are flexible. Whereas a court is limited in the sorts of judgments that can be made, an out-of-court settlement has the potential to be creative in addressing the needs and interests of the parties. For instance, if a person is suing another person for damages resulting from injuries suffered in a fall at a store, the owner may settle by giving the injured party a discount of 20 per cent on everything that the injured party buys at the store for a year. No court could order this. In a customary setting, an out-of-court settlement might take the form of a feast with an exchange of pigs, money or other types of wealth, real or symbolic. There many other ways that parties may decide to be flexible in how they settle disputes out of court.

Speed

A further advantage to parties in settling matters out of court is that a settlement can be made long before a scheduled court hearing. Parties can proceed with their normal activities and be saved months of uncertainty about the outcome of their dispute.

Cost

Out-of-court settlements also represent a financial saving to parties in most cases, especially where a lawyer is involved. In the District Court, legal fees can soon mount up to the point where taking the case to trial is uneconomical for both parties, regardless of the outcome.

Finally, there is an emotional saving in cases that are settled out of court. Parties have a better chance of reconciling, and even carrying on a productive relationship, where they have been able to work out a mutually agreeable solution to their dispute. The potential for this is often damaged where a case goes to trial and a judgment is imposed on the parties.

24.2.2 Advantages to the court

If all of the cases commenced in the District Courts proceeded to contested hearings before Magistrates, the backlog of cases would grow longer as the system struggled to keep pace. Each year there are more and more claims commenced in the District Courts. The cost of providing courtrooms and Judges to handle the increasing number of disputes is a major expense for the country.

The more cases that settle out of court, the less pressure there is on the court system to provide adjudication services for the public. The earlier that cases settle out of court, the sooner the justice system is relieved of the need to manage those files. The files that do have to be resolved by way of a contested court hearing can therefore receive greater attention and time. It is, therefore, in the interests of the justice system for cases to be settled out of court.

24.2.3 Advantages to society

The more cases that are settled by parties out of court, the greater the number of disputes that are settled by the parties in a consensual manner. A dispute that is settled in a consensual manner is less likely to give rise to complications in the future. Business and commerce is less likely to be disrupted, and individuals are less likely to carry grudges against each other. In this way the overall interests of society are served.

24.3 NEGOTIATION – THE MOST COMMON MEANS OF RESOLVING CASES OUT OF COURT

If a dispute is resolved out of court, it is most likely that a process of negotiation led to the settlement. Negotiation is a process that is part of every culture and is something that everyone does on a daily basis. We negotiate with friends, spouses, parents and children.

There have been a number of attempts to define negotiation. Two of these are:

- Negotiation is back-and-forth communication designed to reach an agreement when both sides have some interests that are shared and others that are opposed.
- Negotiation is a process of adjustment of existing differences, with a view to establishing a mutually more desirable legal relation, by means of barter and compromise of legal rights and duties, and of economic, psychological, social and other interests. It is accomplished consensually rather than with the force of law.

Negotiation requires the voluntary participation of all parties. Negotiation is not a process that always leads to a successful outcome. Even after protracted negotiations are conducted in good faith, a settlement may not be possible. The services of a Judge or Magistrate are required to impose a resolution in these types of disputes.

The evidential notion of privilege attaches to negotiations that are conducted between parties with a view to settling a court dispute. After a failed negotiation, the substance of any admissions, offers and counter-offers that have been made between parties or their lawyers in an effort to negotiate a settlement, if led by one party as evidence, may be properly objected to by the other party.

24.4 WHAT IS ALTERNATIVE DISPUTE RESOLUTION?

Alternative Dispute Resolution, or "ADR" as it has become popularly known, refers to the various ways that disputes are resolved without recourse to a Judge. Negotiation, as has been mentioned, is the most common means of settling disputes out of court, but is only one of several forms of ADR.

ADR is an area of growing interest on the part of lawyers, Judges and others involved in justice systems around the world. This is especially true in jurisdictions that have relied heavily on the adversarial system as a means of settling disputes.

The word "alternative" in "alternative dispute resolution" is appropriate in jurisdictions where the adversarial system of justice has a long history. In Papua New Guinea, where the formal justice system was introduced relatively recently, it might be argued that litigation is *itself* the alternative, that is, alternative to the customary means of resolving disputes that preceded it. Nevertheless, the expression "alternative dispute resolution", or "ADR", has become widespread and accepted.

24.4.1 Negotiation

Negotiation is the most flexible form of ADR. Only the parties (and their lawyers if they are represented) are required. Whether or not negotiation takes place is up to the parties. The pace, process and outcome of negotiation is completely in the hands of the parties to a dispute (and their lawyers). It does not require the involvement of any third parties.

24.4.2 Mediation

Mediation is a process of negotiation where the parties make use of a third party to assist them. The third party is neutral and has no authority to impose a solution on the parties, or even to advise them. The parties themselves retain ultimate control over the process. A mediator's job is to assist the parties to find their own solution. Like negotiation, mediation is a voluntary process that may or may not be successful in arriving at a settlement of the dispute. Mediators utilise specific skills to assist the parties in reaching a solution. We shall look more closely at mediation in 24.5.

24.4.3 Arbitration

Arbitration is an alternative method of dispute resolution that more closely resembles a contested hearing in court. Parties who agree to resolve their dispute by means of arbitration select a person or persons to hear both sides of the case. They agree in advance that they will be bound by the decision of the arbitrator and to the process that will govern the arbitration. The arbitrator or arbitrators manage the process in accordance with the rules that the parties agree to. The arbitration results in a finding by the arbitrator. An arbitrator performs an adjudicative role, much like that of a Judge.

The *Arbitration Act* provides some basic rules for the conduct of arbitration. Parties may agree to substitute some of their own rules, but they must do this by way of a written agreement. The *Arbitration Act* provides for the registration of arbitration decisions (sometimes called awards) as judgments of the National Court. Once registered, an arbitrator's decision may be enforced as a decision of the National Court. Arbitrators may be selected by the parties on the basis of their expertise in the subject matter of a dispute. In this respect, arbitrators are different from Judges, who are expected to be competent in all types of disputes that are within their jurisdiction. In some jurisdictions lawyers and retired Judges frequently act as arbitrators.

In many jurisdictions, arbitration is commonly resorted to in disputes that arise in construction cases. The arbitrator in this type of case is often a person who is experienced in the construction industry and able to understand the nature of construction disputes. This reduces the need for the parties to call experts to give evidence about the issues in dispute.

Similarly, in many jurisdictions, arbitration has long been a common method of resolving business and labour disputes. In Papua New Guinea, the Papua New Guinea Dispute Resolution Center (PNGDRC) provides mediation and arbitration services for business, commercial and international disputes.

24.4.4 Other forms of ADR

Sometimes ADR processes are based on combinations of mediation and arbitration. Parties can agree to attempt to reach a mediated settlement but, if this is not successful, to have the mediator or some other person take the role of an arbitrator and impose a decision on the parties. This is one way for parties to have some certainty that they will finalise their dispute without it dragging on and resulting in a contested court hearing. The PNGDRC is able to work with parties to arrive at an ADR procedure that suits the circumstances of the parties and their dispute.

24.5 MORE ABOUT MEDIATION

Of all the methods of alternative dispute resolution, mediation is the one that Magistrates are most likely to be involved with. The *Land Disputes Settlement Act* involves Magistrates in the mediation process. This statute does not define mediation or set out a procedure by which it is to be exercised, yet Magistrates may be called upon to act as mediators. It is therefore important that Magistrates understand the fundamental nature of mediation and the skills that are required to be a good mediator.

The easiest way to understand mediation is to think of it as assisted negotiation. A mediator, who remains neutral, provides the assistance. A mediator utilises some skills that are different from those of a Judge or Magistrate.

24.5.1 Mediation differs from adjudication in several fundamental ways

Mediators don't make judgments

One of the primary duties of a Magistrate is to make judgments, to communicate the judgments and to explain the reasons behind those judgments. A Magistrate who is acting as a mediator, on the other hand, is careful not to express judgment about the dispute in question. In some mediations, a mediator may make a suggestion about possible ways to resolve a dispute. However, care must be taken not to express suggestions in ways that reveal a judgment on the part of a mediator. A mediator remains neutral throughout the process of mediation.

Mediation is not a binding process unless the parties agree

Mediation is different from adjudication in that it is not binding on the parties. Parties who agree to mediation may or may not agree to a settlement of their dispute at the conclusion of the process. If the parties do reach an agreement, then they may proceed to express the agreement in the form of an oral or written contract or, in some cases, a consent order in court. Only then does the settlement become binding on the parties.

Mediation is less formal than adjudication

The process of mediation can be less formal than adjudication in court. Mediation, like negotiation, can take place at any location and at any time. Mediation is a means of dispute resolution that is frequently employed by Village Courts. These mediations often occur outdoors and sometimes involve groups of hundreds of people.

Mediation does not involve rigid rules of evidence or procedure. Even where lawyers represent parties, and the lawyers are present at a mediation, both the parties and the lawyers may speak informally and put forward evidence.

The role of a Judge is largely passive. It is up to the parties in court to define the issues, adduce evidence and make submissions. The parties, and lawyers for the parties, ask most of the questions in court. The rules of procedure and evidence govern when and how the questions are to be asked. Mediation is more flexible, and a mediator may enter into the process to a greater extent than a Magistrate normally does in court.

Mediators can meet with parties separately

In court, a Magistrate does not, except in exceptional circumstances, deal with the case in the absence of one of the parties. Ex parte applications are very much the exception. In mediation, on the other hand, a mediator routinely meets a party in the absence of the other party. This type of meeting is often referred to as a caucus. There are important guidelines that govern how a caucus is conducted.

24.5.2 What does mediation have in common with adjudication?

Rules of natural justice apply

The court process is based on the rules of natural justice, which in turn are based on a sense of fairness. A Judge or Magistrate must not have an interest in the matter in dispute. The same is true of a mediator. In both court hearings and mediation, it is important that both parties are treated equally, and that each party has an opportunity to give evidence and respond to the evidence and the arguments of the other party or parties. Mediation departs from the rules of natural justice in respect of separate meetings with a mediator. However, everything that a mediator does is done with the consent of the parties.

Parties may proceed with or without lawyers

In District Court hearings, the parties may or may not be represented by lawyers. Mediation can also be held whether or not the parties have a lawyer representing them. Even if the parties have had legal representation in the dispute in question, mediation may be held with or without the lawyer present, depending on the wishes of the parties.

The importance of listening skills

In order to impose a fair judgment in court, a Magistrate must be a careful listener. In addition to listening to the actual words that are spoken, a Magistrate must listen to how things are said, and sometimes must notice what is not said. This is important in order for a Magistrate to make findings of fact, especially where the credibility of a witness is an issue. Similarly, a mediator must also be a careful listener, although the reasons for this may vary from those that apply to Magistrates. A mediator must listen carefully to understand what interests underlie the position taken by a party, and what options might be acceptable to both parties. This type of listening is every bit as difficult as the listening that a Magistrate must engage in during a contested hearing. Both types of listening may be called "active listening", because they require the active attention and simultaneous thinking on the part of the listener.

24.6 WHEN IS MEDIATION APPROPRIATE (OR INAPPROPRIATE)?

Unless both parties agree to mediation, it is unlikely that it will be successful. It takes both parties to bargain in good faith to make mediation successful. It is, therefore, inappropriate to conduct mediation if one or more of the parties are not in favour of the process.

Where a mediator is not able to act in a neutral fashion, or where one or more of the parties have a perception that the mediator is not able to act impartially, then it is not appropriate for mediation to take place, at least until a more suitable mediator can be found. Section 22C of the *District Courts Act* provides that a Magistrate who has acted as a mediator in a failed mediation cannot later act as a Magistrate at a contested hearing, unless both parties agree.

Where one of the parties is a victim of an assault, harassment or some other form of intimidation at the hands of the other party, it is unlikely that the first party will be able to negotiate on an equal footing with the other party. In such circumstances, a serious power balance exists, and mediation is inappropriate. For instance, where a husband has physically abused a wife, there is a good chance that she will be unable to bargain on an equal footing in the mediation process.

Where there is a risk of violence or offensive behaviour during mediation, it is best not to proceed. The dispute is better handled in the more rigid and adversarial framework of adjudication.

Mediation is not appropriate for criminal matters. The main reason for this is that a criminal offence, even where there is an identifiable victim, is primarily an offence against society. In some jurisdictions there are alternative methods of dealing with offenders, mostly in the sphere of sentencing. However, these are beyond the scope of this chapter: see Chapter 13.

Mediation can take place at any stage of a proceeding. This means that a civil case that has commenced in the form of a contested hearing may be adjourned in order to allow mediation to take place.

24.6.1 The scope of mediation

Mediation may be successful in resolving some but not all of the issues in a dispute. For example, where a person is claiming damages as a result of the negligence of another party, there will be at least two issues. One is whether the defendant was negligent, and the other is that of whether the claimant has suffered damages and, if so, how much.

Mediation may tackle several issues but be successful in resolving only one. On the other hand, a mediation may only attempt to deal with some of the outstanding issues.

24.7 THE STAGES OF MEDIATION

Although mediation is a flexible process, mediators have come to recognise that a basic structure or model is helpful in conducting a successful mediation.

Thinking of mediation as a series of stages helps a mediator and the parties move through a process that is directed at the desired result of a negotiated resolution of the dispute in question. There are several *models* that involve a sequence of steps or stages. They are all similar in many respects. The differences are in the details.

Each stage of the process has a purpose and follows the preceding stage to achieve a specific objective. Used together, they enable a mediator to assist the parties to reach a principled settlement of their dispute.

No process should be adhered to rigidly in all circumstances. The circumstances of a particular mediation may require the mediator to move the parties back to an earlier stage in the process to readdress an issue or introduce a new one. For instance, while parties are brainstorming to search for a set of mutual goals (stage IV), it might become apparent that they have insufficiently canvassed some of their interests, and the mediator must move the parties back to stage III. Likewise, a new sub-issue might be revealed that requires the parties to move back to stage II. At times, it may be necessary for a mediator to move back to stage I to remind parties of the ground rules of the process.

The following are the stages of a mediation set out in point form. While it is hoped that it will be useful to Magistrates who are called upon to mediate, the skills of mediation are best acquired through face-to-face instruction with repeated practice and critique.

24.7.1 Preliminary steps

- The mediator should make sure that the parties know where and when to attend a mediation.
- Prepare an appropriate site with comfort, privacy and a place to hold a caucus.
- Ensure that parties are advised to bring all relevant documents.
- If a mediation is being attended by a representative of a party (for instance, if a party is a corporation), the representative should be advised that he or she must come to the mediation with authority to represent the party and authority to negotiate and settle on behalf of the party.

24.7.2 Stage I – Introducing the process

- Establish rapport and set a positive tone for the meeting.
- The mediator should display qualities that are desired of the parties (candour, fairness, patience).
- Describe the process, including the use of caucusing and the caucusing format.
- Clarify the roles (participant's and mediator's).
- Mediator's role:

• Not a judge
• Not an advocate or advisor
• Helps parties communicate and assists them to reach their own settlement
• Manages the process
• Disqualification from hearing case if mediation is unsuccessful

- Stress the need for movement and get express commitment from the parties.
- Verify time limits for the mediation (if any).
- Clarify that each party or representative has authority to settle.
- Address ground rules of the process:

- Only one party speaks at a time
- No insulting language or personal attacks
- Either party can ask for a time out or a caucus
- Need to listen carefully to the perspective of the other side
- Need for disclosure of information

24.7.3 Stage II – Identifying and framing the issues

- Allow each party an opportunity to tell their story in their own words.
- Summarise the issues and both sides' perspectives.
- Check out accuracy and seek clarification of facts and issues where needed.
- Identify the areas of agreement.
- Organise the information by separating issues and prioritising.
- Establish, and get an agreement on, the agenda by framing the issues.

At this stage the parties should have agreement on the issues (questions) that have to be dealt with.

24.7.4 Stage III – Exploring and resolving the issues

- Identify existing areas for potential movement by the parties.
- Clarify and ensure understanding of any new information shared.
- Identify assumptions and seek clarification.
- Invite the parties to make proposals based on objective criteria.
- Facilitate the exchange of information (using questions).
- Emphasise existing and emerging areas of agreement.
- Act as an agent of reality – help to dispel unrealistic expectations.
- Identify areas of progress and areas where movement is needed.
- Discourage parties from taking fixed positions, and encourage parties to discover common interests.
- Set and maintain an appropriate pace of negotiation.
- Break down larger issues into smaller ones.
- Utilise caucusing whenever appropriate.
- Stress the consequence of not reaching an agreement.
- Manage personalities to maintain a rational and positive momentum.
- Discourage "bottom lines" and ultimatums.
- Challenge the parties to continue negotiating.

24.7.5 Stage IV – Finalising the settlement

- Clarify each area of agreement and set it to one side.
- Summarise and ensure understanding of each agreement reached.

- Encourage the generation of additional options that will lead to agreement and closure.
- Test options by objective criteria already established.
- Provide a written memorandum of consensus to the extent needed.
- Discourage ambiguity by ensuring the parties clarify details.

If a comprehensive agreement is not possible, see if a partial agreement can be reached: see 24.9.

24.7.6 The use of caucusing in mediation

In many mediations, it can be productive for a mediator to interrupt the joint session and to meet with the parties separately. A meeting where a mediator meets separately with a party is called a caucus. Caucusing allows a greater amount of informality between the mediator and the parties compared to what goes on in joint session. Whereas caucusing would be highly improper where a Magistrate is acting as a judge, it is not improper where the Magistrate has no power to impose a settlement.

A caucus can be called at any stage of mediation by the mediator or by either of the parties to the mediation. When a caucus is called, the mediator provides separate space where each of the parties can talk privately with the mediator.

There are a number of reasons for holding a caucus during mediation.

1. **Reality testing:** The mediator may need an opportunity to discuss with a party how realistic or practical their expectations are. Doing this privately, instead of in front of the other party, allows the party to save face.
2. **Boundary testing:** The mediator may wish to discuss with a party the need to be flexible and open to alternatives. Doing this in caucus also allows the party to save face.
3. **Exploration:** Sometimes, a mediator is able to use caucusing to search for undisclosed facts or ideas. A mediator can also explore any personal issues between the parties that are withheld during joint session but sensed by the mediator.
4. **Dealing with emotions:** Parties in joint session can become overly emotional, withdrawn or simply exhausted. A caucus allows a mediator to meet with a party to re-orient them to the process, and allow them to rest, cool off and refocus.

There are several factors that a mediator must be aware of in order to make use of caucusing effectively.

The effect on the trust level of the parties

A mediator must always be seen by the parties to be neutral. A mediator must therefore be careful, when talking to a party during a caucus, not to give the impression that he or she is taking sides. If the mediator takes sides with one party during caucus, then that party is likely to wonder what is going on behind his or her back when the mediator meets with the other party. This can create a greater level of distrust between the parties.

The use of confidentiality

A mediator must reach an understanding about confidentiality during a caucus. This should be done at the outset of the mediation. The most common agreement is that what is disclosed to a mediator during caucus is confidential unless the party disclosing it agrees to allow the mediator to disclose it to the other side. Agreeing that what is disclosed during a caucus is confidential can encourage the sharing of more information during a caucus. On the other hand, it can create difficulties for a mediator in sorting confidential information from non-confidential information when back in joint session. A skilled mediator will encourage a party to authorise the disclosure of important information to the other side.

Managing the time spent with parties in caucus

The mediator should be aware that the party who he or she is *not* meeting with is waiting, and probably wondering "What are they talking about in there, it seems like hours." Therefore, a caucus should not last any longer than necessary.

Maintaining a balance in caucusing

A mediator should be careful to spend roughly equal amounts of time with each party in caucus. This balance helps maintain a feeling of impartiality and balance. Also, if there is more than one caucus in a mediation, it is a good idea to alternate the party who the mediator meets with first. This also helps to maintain a balance and a feeling of neutrality.

During a caucus, a mediator should try to generate an atmosphere of informality. It should feel like a "safer" environment for the parties to disclose information and concerns to the mediator. It is a good opportunity for a mediator to discuss with the party the best and worst alternatives to a negotiated agreement.

When going from a caucus back into a joint session, it is useful to positively reinforce the work done by the parties in caucus and to get any new (non-confidential) information "on the table" as soon as possible. Parties are usually anxious to know what was discussed in separate sessions.

24.7.7 Questioning in mediation

While a Magistrate acting as a judge must restrain himself or herself from becoming too involved in the process by asking questions, a mediator is free to ask questions of the parties. Questions should be non-confrontational. The skilful use of questioning is one of the most important tools that a mediator has. A mediator often uses "open questions". Open questions cannot be answered by a simple yes or no. They give the party being questioned the freedom to shape the answer and include information that a yes or no question does not allow. Open questions are useful for getting parties to disclose interests behind the positions they take, to detect clues as to hidden agendas behind bargaining positions and to get clarity.

There are several types of open questions:

Probing questions: These questions invite a party to go deeper into a matter that has been introduced.

- "I'd like to hear more about how you came to ask Peter to take an early retirement."
- "Can you tell me a bit more about how Mr Napa acted when you talked to him about the loss of the money?"
- "What was it like when the personnel manager called you back?"
- "What was important to you about getting the complaint dealt with before January?"

Clarification questions: These questions seek more information that allows a mediator to clarify an unclear meaning.

- "When you say 'the contract' what do you mean?"
- "When you said 'typical politician' what's that all about?"
- "I think you said a moment ago, 'Mr Manda is recovering.' I'm not sure I understand what you mean."
- "Can you tell me what you meant when you were talking about dealing with both estate agents at the same time?"

Justifying questions: These questions seek an explanation for an inconsistency that appears in what has been said by a party earlier.

- "Earlier you said that money was not the major issue in this dispute. Now you are saying that money is one of the keys to getting this resolved. Can you explain that to me?"
- "When we started this meeting, you said that the airline was putting unreasonable pressure on you to pay the money owed. Now you are saying that they asked you how much time you thought was reasonable. I'm a bit confused about that."

Consequential questions: These are used to ask about potential outcomes, that is, what might happen if a proposal that is "on the table" is incorporated into a settlement. These questions often use the word "if". They can be useful in assisting the parties to discover options of which they had not been previously aware.

- "You have said that you think the patient should hire a private doctor to deal with her complaint. If she did that, I wonder how you think that could affect the image of the health department in the community."
- "If the teacher accepted the proposal, when could you make the payments that he would be entitled to?"
- "What do you think would have happened if you had contacted Mr Johnny and made the suggestion directly to him?"
- "If the clan claiming the land where the garden is wanted to cross the land to get to the river, I wonder how that would affect your people."

24.7.8 Reframing

A mediator is often confronted by negative or unhelpful statements by a party during a mediation.

Examples of these may be:

- **Confrontational:** "I am entitled to two thousand kina and I am not going to take anything less."
- **Negative:** "There's no way that we will give an inch here."
- **Accusatory:** "Bertha will cheat anyone who is dumb enough to let her do it."

Sometimes, all three elements are combined in one statement: "There is no way that I am going to be so stupid and trust that lying cheating lawyer again."

When a mediator is confronted with these sorts of statements, the challenge is to recognise and state the underlying interest, and acknowledge that the party is seeking to have it met. Rewording the statement in a way that includes the underlying interest is known as *reframing*. It is most useful if, in reframing, a mediator can take some or all of the negativity out of the assertion.

Reframing is really a short process that invites the disputant to see, in a positive interest-based way, what will have to happen in order for them to contribute to agreement. To say reframing "names unmet needs" is to acknowledge the effect you can have in identifying building blocks of agreement.

Several steps can be required in reframing. This is an example:

Assertion: "I refuse to deal with Ronny. He is completely unreliable."

Step I - Listen, then restate or paraphrase: "You mean you don't want to deal with Ronny's non-dependability?"

Response: "That's right. I mean, he never does anything that he says he is going to do and he is never on time."

Step II - Listen for confirmation of the accuracy of your restatement, and then guess at the unmet need. In this sequence you might guess that the unmet need is the party's need to be able to rely on anything that Ronny agrees to.

So, to be able to deal with Ronny, you have to be able to count on his performing, particularly in the settlement of this dispute.

Here is another shorter example of reframing that leaves out the explanation of the process.

"I'm not increasing my offer until I see some movement from them."

"Well Jane, to increase your offer, you will need to be sure that this negotiation is a two-way deal."

"Yes, that's right."

24.8 THE DUTIES OF MAGISTRATES IN RELATION TO MEDIATION

24.8.1 Informing the parties about mediation

Many parties will not be aware of the Magistrate's potential role as a mediator, or even what mediation is about. Therefore, if a Magistrate waits for parties to request mediation, very few mediations will take place. It is appropriate for a Magistrate to advise parties that the services of a Magistrate as a mediator are available where this is the case. This could be done prior to the hearing by means of a notice posted in the courthouse, or by means of a pamphlet that is handed out to parties when a claim or a dispute is filed. Courthouse personnel should be aware that District Court Magistrates have this role, so that they too can advise parties that mediation services are available. Even if a formally trained mediator is not available, it may be appropriate to suggest that parties attempt to settle their dispute with the help of a pastor, an elder or some other person who has the respect of both parties.

24.8.2 Decision to act as a mediator

The following factors are relevant to a Magistrate's decision about whether or not to mediate in any given case.

Whether the parties wish to mediate

The parties can only make this decision once they are aware of what mediation is and that it is available. Unless the parties are willing to negotiate a settlement to their dispute in good faith, then it is probably a waste of time for a Magistrate to act as a mediator. On the other hand, where parties agree that mediation is a realistic means of settling their dispute, a Magistrate should make every effort to facilitate this.

Whether the resources of the court allow for mediation

It might be that there is only one Magistrate available. If that Magistrate acts as a mediator and the mediation is unsuccessful, then the Magistrate may be precluded from hearing the case as a contested hearing. It is only with the consent of the parties that a Magistrate can continue to act after an unsuccessful mediation. Parties who have already argued their case, and possibly disclosed their positions regarding settlement (evidence which is privileged in court), may be unwilling to allow the Magistrate to move from being a mediator to a judge.

Other factors are also relevant: see 24.6.

24.8.3 Changing roles

Whenever a Magistrate becomes a mediator, it must be made clear to the parties that the role of the Magistrate has changed. How the role has changed should be explained to the parties.

A Magistrate should also advise the parties that if the mediation is not successful, unless both parties consent, another Magistrate will have to preside at the hearing of the matter in court. Any delays that this is likely to cause to the parties should be explained.

Once these things have been explained, a Magistrate should re-confirm with the parties that they both wish to proceed with mediation.

The role of the Magistrate has changed, in that he or she will:

- not impose a settlement;
- not compel evidence;
- hear evidence that might be inadmissible in a contested hearing;
- not make a decision for the parties (It is up to the parties to reach their own decision); and
- probably ask more questions than if acting as a judge.

The role of a Magistrate has not changed, in that he or she will:

- listen carefully to the parties; and
- ensure that the process of mediation is fair and that both parties have an equal opportunity to have their say.

24.8.4 District Courts Act

District Court Magistrates are authorised by statute to mediate civil disputes that are commenced in the District Court. Section 2B of the *District Courts Act* provides that a District Court Magistrate, or some other person approved by the Judicial Services Commission, may act as a mediator of a civil dispute that is brought in the District Court.

The objective of such a step in the proceedings is to reach an amicable settlement of the matter.

24.8.5 When should a District Court Magistrate mediate?

The *District Courts Act* provides for a great deal of flexibility regarding the timing of mediation. Section 22B says that mediation can take place at any stage of a proceeding up to the conclusion of the hearing. We have seen that the advantages of a settlement are generally greater when they occur earlier in the proceedings. It is therefore preferable that mediation in the District Court takes place as early in the proceedings as practicable. However, in most District Court proceedings there are factors that often delay the prospects of mediation and settlement. One of these factors is that parties sometimes do not have very much contact with each other prior to the hearing. Unlike National Court proceedings, where there are a number of pre-trial steps that require the parties or their lawyers to communicate, the District Court procedure is straightforward. There is nothing that requires parties to communicate with each other prior to the hearing and, often, a formal hearing commences without the parties canvassing the prospect of a settlement with each other.

Another factor that inhibits any discussion of settlement in the District Court is that parties often do not realise that settlement is a realistic or honourable alternative to engaging in a contested court hearing. There is an attitude among many parties that once a court action is commenced, it is best to "let the Judge decide".

Further, many parties are not aware that mediation is a role that a District Court Magistrate is able to perform. It is up to the Magistrate to bring mediation to the attention of the parties as an alternative.

Even during a contested hearing, it may appear to the Magistrate that mediation could lead to a fair settlement. When this occurs, a Magistrate may interrupt the trial and discuss with the parties the prospect of mediation. If the parties agree to mediation, the Magistrate (provided that he or she is approved by the Judicial Services Commission to act) may change roles from that of a judge to a mediator.

24.8.6 Customary land proceedings

The *Land Dispute Settlement Act* deals with the resolution of disputes over customary land. There are three levels at which such disputes are resolved under the Act. They are by:

- Land Mediators;
- the Local Land Court; and
- the District Land Court.

Although Land Mediators involve themselves in mediation, Magistrates are unlikely to be required to act as Land Mediators. The District Land Court is not required or empowered to perform a mediation role. However, Magistrates who sit as Local Land Court Magistrates are likely to be involved in mediation either directly or indirectly. It is this level of dispute resolution with which we are concerned. The *Land Disputes Settlement Act* is examined in Chapter 17.

Where a Land Mediator resolves a dispute over customary land, any agreement reached may be referred to the Local Land Court for approval. A Local Land Court Magistrate, in fulfilling his or her duties under s 19 of the *Land Disputes Settlement Act*, may form the opinion that the agreement cannot be approved in its present form. In such a case, the Local Land Court Magistrate may mediate between the parties in order to reach a satisfactory agreement. If this is successful, then the agreement reached can be approved under s 19.

Where an agreement is not reached at the Land Mediator level, the dispute will proceed to the level of the Local Land Court. Although the court is given the power to make a decision where there is no agreement, the court is also empowered, by s 28 of the Act, to mediate between the parties at any stage of the proceedings. In making a decision about whether or not to mediate, a Local Land Court should have regard to the nature of the dispute, the wishes of the parties and any other factors that bear on the prospect of a successful outcome to a mediation.

If mediation is embarked upon by a Local Land Court under s 28, the mediation may or may not be successful in resolving the dispute. If the mediation is successful, then it will be approved as an order of the court. The approval of the settlement as an order of the court should only take place if the Local Land Court Magistrate who is presiding at the hearing is satisfied that all parties fully understand the terms of the agreement. The provisions of s 40 of the Act require a visit to the land in question by the Local Land Court upon making an order other than a temporary order. When approving an order that has been reached by mediation under s 28, the same procedure should be followed.

There is nothing to prevent a Local Land Court from continuing to preside and making an order, even after the members of the court have acted in an unsuccessful attempt at mediation.

Because a Local Land Court consists of a Land Court Magistrate and Land Mediators pursuant to s 23, mediation may involve several persons acting together as mediators.

As customary land disputes involve groups of people rather than individual parties, mediation over customary land may require the attendance of a number of people – sometimes in the hundreds.

24.8.7 Adultery and Enticement Act

District Court Magistrates often find themselves dealing with applications under the *Adultery and Enticement Act*. Section 10(1) of the Act says:

"(1) Before hearing an action under this Act, a Court shall endeavour to have the action settled by mediation".

At the least, this requires a Magistrate to inform the parties about mediation, how it might help them sort out their dispute without a court settlement, and the availability of the Magistrate to act as a mediator. Where the parties are willing to proceed with mediation, the Act says, at s 10(2), that the provisions of the *District Courts Act* dealing with mediation apply: see 16.5.4.

24.9 FORMALISING AN OUT-OF-COURT SETTLEMENT

Where parties are able to reach a settlement of their dispute prior to the hearing of a matter (by means of mediation or some other means), there are two separate methods for formalising the settlement. One method is to express their settlement in terms of a court order that is made by consent of all parties. The other method is to express their settlement in the form of a contract. One term of the contract is that the party who brought the proceeding will discontinue it or have it dismissed.

24.9.1 Consent orders

Although consent orders, by their nature, are sought by all parties to a dispute, Magistrates must remember that the approval of a consent order is a judicial act that requires careful scrutiny. In approving a consent order, a Magistrate must ensure that:

all parties have consented to the order being sought, and that their consent is expressed clearly, either in open court (in a manner that allows it to be reduced to writing in the form of a minute or memorandum by a Magistrate) or in writing;

the terms of the order being sought are within the jurisdiction of the court; and

none of the parties to the action are children or parties under some other legal disability: see 24.9.2.

24.9.2 Approval of settlements where a party is under a legal disability

Special considerations arise where one of the parties to a dispute where a consent order is being sought is an infant or a person with a legal disability.

A person who is under a legal disability does not have the authority to engage in binding agreements in the way that people who are not under a legal disability can. This prevents such people from entering into most types of contracts. A settlement of a court action by consent, either by means of a consent order or by means of a contract (and the withdrawal or dismissal of the action), is a type of contract and is, therefore, beyond the capacity of people under a legal disability. A Magistrate must be careful to ensure that sufficient evidence is heard to justify making the desired order on the merits of the case, rather than automatically endorsing the request of a party under a disability or their representative in court.

An agreement made out of court, which is not subsequently approved by the court, is not binding on the infant or person under a legal disability.

Chapter 25 – Decisions and Reasons

25.1 INTRODUCTION

Decision-making is an integral part of a Magistrate's job. In every matter that comes before a Magistrate, it is the Magistrate who must make decisions. Some decisions have the effect of imposing a final resolution of the matter. Other decisions do not resolve the matter, but merely allow it to proceed to the next step in the proceedings. In either case, a Magistrate cannot refuse to make a decision because it is difficult or unpopular.

This chapter is about making decisions and giving reasons for them. It deals with:

how Magistrates should make records of decisions;

the importance of giving reasons for decisions; and

how to communicate reasons for a decision as effectively as possible.

25.2 FORMALITIES OF RECORDING JUDGMENTS

25.2.1 Final orders

In the District Court, there is a statutory requirement that final decisions in any matter be recorded. Section 160 of the *District Courts Act* provides:

> "Where a Court convicts or makes an order against a defendant, a minute or memorandum of the conviction or order shall be made and signed by the Magistrate constituting the Court."

The words "memorandum" and "minute" are not defined in the Act. For our purposes, it is reasonable to think of a minute or memorandum as a carefully worded record of what is ordered by a Magistrate. The *District Courts Act* does not prescribe the use of a specific form for keeping minutes and memoranda. These should be kept as part of the overall notes that a Magistrate makes during a hearing. Alternatively, they may be drafted on a separate sheet of paper and retained in the court file.

The requirement that a minute or memorandum be made applies to decisions in both civil and criminal cases. There is good reason for this statutory requirement. A record of this sort of order is necessary in case a party requires confirmation of the terms of an order or that a formal order be drawn up. This might be needed where there is an appeal of a decision or where enforcement proceedings are undertaken.

In a District Court matter, where a decision takes the form of a dismissal of an information, complaint or set off, it is necessary to make a memorandum of the order with the same degree of care as where a conviction or other order against a defendant is made. A party may require a certificate under s 162 of the *District Courts Act* as proof that proceedings were dismissed. This requirement may arise some time after the hearing, when the Magistrate's memory of the exact terms of a decision has faded.

Regulation 10 of the *District Courts Act* requires that Magistrates keep a register of proceedings using a form that is prescribed and annexed to the Act. Form 1 specifies a number of details pertaining to a particular decision. There may be further particulars for which the form does not provide. In instances where this occurs, it is necessary for a Magistrate to make a separate memorandum of the additional information.

The minute or memorandum must be complete in every respect.

The following checklist may be a useful reference in ensuring that a record of a final decision is complete:

- The name of the party against whom the order of conviction is made. This is especially important where there is more than one defendant.
- The date that the order or conviction is made.
- The name of the Magistrate who convicts or makes the order in question.
- The specifics of the order made and the charge or allegation in respect of which it is made. This is important in cases where there is more than one charge or cause of action. For example, an information may include three counts of theft. A civil claim may be based on allegations of both negligence and breach of contract. In either case, a final order must specify which charge or allegation it relates to.

When a Magistrate makes an order that requires a defendant to do something, the Magistrate must be careful to ensure that all necessary terms of the order are included. For example, in making a final order in a family case where the defendant is ordered to pay maintenance, it is necessary to specify how, when, where and to whom the payment should be made. A defendant may try to frustrate the intention of the order. Any ambiguity in the order, or in the record that is made of the order, might enable him or her to do this.

If a decision involves an award of damages, matters that are ancillary to the main term of the order should be specified and noted in the memorandum. Ancillary terms could cover interest and costs and the details pertaining to each.

If an award of pre-judgment interest is to be included as part of a final order, the date from which it commences and the rate of interest should be specified. If costs are awarded, these too need to be specified, so that the party in whose favour the order is made can take steps to enforce it. The order and the memorandum of it should not be vague or omit anything that will allow the party against whom it is made to frustrate the court's intention.

If a sentence in a criminal matter involves a fine, the time to pay and any term of imprisonment in default of payment should be clearly specified and noted. If imprisonment is ordered in the first instance, and there is more than one information or more than one charge on an information, the record of the final order must specify whether the terms of imprisonment are to be served concurrently or cumulatively.

25.3 INTERIM DECISIONS AND ORDERS

The expression "interim order" refers to any order or decision in a matter that affects the parties' positions *prior* to a final order, or the procedure to be followed in arriving at a final order. It does not include the final decision. In a criminal matter, an example of an interim decision is the issuing of a summons or warrant. In a civil or criminal matter, it might be a decision about the admissibility of some evidence. It may also be a decision in relation to an adjournment application, even an uncontested one. There are a large number of possible interim decisions in both criminal and civil cases.

Some interim decisions create records automatically. An example is a decision to issue a warrant for the arrest of a person who has failed to obey a summons. The warrant itself provides a record of this decision.

Other decisions do not automatically create a record. It is these types of interim decisions that a Magistrate must take particular care to record. The record may simply be a memorandum in the bench book that is used to take other notes during the hearing or application. An example of a decision that does not create its own record is a decision relating to the admission or exclusion of evidence. For instance, a Magistrate might decide to allow a witness to give opinion evidence, even in the face of an objection by the opposing party. This decision occurs during a hearing and, unless a Magistrate makes a note of the decision, it may never be recorded. Of course, making notes of the evidence in a hearing is a routine part of a Magistrate's job. However, unless special care is taken, these notes might not reflect the fact that a decision was made during the course of evidence.

Examples of other interim decisions that do not automatically create a record are:

- a direction that a party provide particulars to another party (*District Courts Act*, s 31);
- a decision to close the court to the public in a particular matter or during part of a hearing (s 57);
- an order made where a witness refuses to be sworn or to answer questions (s 70); and
- a decision to proceed ex parte where a defendant in a civil proceeding does not show up and where there is proof of service.

25.4 REASONS FOR DECISIONS

25.4.1 The importance of reasons

It is important for a Magistrate to record each decision made in a case. However, it is not possible or desirable for a Magistrate to give detailed reasons for each decision that is made. An obvious example occurs at the end of a day of hearing when an incomplete matter has to be adjourned. It is not expected that a Magistrate will explain the reason for adjourning a case in such circumstances.

There are statutory provisions that require Magistrates to give reasons for some decisions. Section 16 of the *Bail Act* requires that a Magistrate who refuses bail to an applicant *must* give reasons for the refusal. Section 59 of the *District Courts Act* requires a Magistrate to give reasons where a law student from UPNG is refused leave to represent a person.

Apart from occasions where a Magistrate is required to give reasons for a decision, there are other occasions in court when it is desirable for a Magistrate to give reasons for a decision, even though there is no statutory requirement that the Magistrate do so.

Most interim decisions are of less consequence than final decisions in both criminal and civil cases. However, some interim decisions are more important than others, as they have a direct bearing on the outcome of a case. An example of such a decision is the admission of an out-of-court confession in a criminal hearing. The greater the effect that an interim decision has on the outcome of a case, the more desirable it is to explain reasons for making the decision.

It is always desirable for a Magistrate to explain reasons for a final decision in all types of matters. There are a number of reasons for this.

25.4.2 Reasons for a final decision

A party's right to know

The most important reason for giving reasons for a decision is that the parties who are directly affected are entitled to know that their case was carefully considered on its merits by the court. In some cases, the evidence and the manner in which the case proceeds gives some idea of why the final decision is the way it is. In other cases, this is not so. Even in cases where the Magistrate thinks that the parties follow the case in a way that makes the outcome self-explanatory, in fact, parties are not able to do this.

Shaping the law

Judges in the National Court routinely give reasons for the decisions they make, in particular, final decisions. These decisions are nearly all reduced to writing. Cumulatively, they help define the law in Papua New Guinea. They also allow law-makers and others to see into the workings of the justice system of the country. Problems or weaknesses in the law are more likely to become obvious when Judges give reasons for their decisions. When problems become obvious, solutions can be formulated. The more reasons for judgment that are recorded, the more quickly and completely the underlying law of the country can be defined. The District Court is an important institution in the process of development of the underlying law.

Guidance and predictability

The National and Supreme Courts are superior courts of inherent jurisdiction. The decisions of these courts have precedent value and, depending on the courts in which they are made and cited, they may have binding or persuasive authority in later cases that involve the same issues. Decisions of the District Court do not have this effect. They are not binding on any court. However, there are some areas of the law that only the Magistrates' Courts deal with on a routine basis. Although appeals of some of these cases go to the National Court, and possibly on to the Supreme Court, it takes a long time for a body of related decisions to build up. Written reasons of decisions made by Magistrates, even though not binding on other Magistrates, would be useful in creating non-binding precedents that could provide guidance.

25.5 COMMUNICATING REASONS FOR A DECISION

Reasons for a decision may be made either orally or in writing. Giving reasons orally is usually a quicker way to dispose of a case. Giving reasons in writing usually takes more time and effort. However, there are at least two reasons why giving reasons in writing is preferable to giving reasons orally:

1. The time and effort required to draft a written judgment can actually help a Magistrate to think about the decision. If there is vagueness or uncertainty in a Magistrate's mind, the act of writing out the reasons for a decision can help focus a Magistrate's mind and thereby clarify the reasoning behind the decision. The act of writing enables a Magistrate to look at what is written, evaluate it and consider improvements before the reasons are revealed to the world.
2. Providing written reasons reduces the chance of being misquoted. Oral reasons disappear as soon as they are given, and all that is left is the imperfect memory of the people who were present in the courtroom. In addition to having imperfect memories, parties may allow their vested interests to distort their understanding of the reasons. Even if notes are taken while the oral reasons are being delivered, they are seldom written word for word, and they too can be a source of distortion.

25.5.1 The audience

Whether giving reasons orally or in writing, it is useful for a Magistrate to first think about who the audience is. Depending on the particular case that is being decided, an audience will consist of one or more of the following groups of people:

- the parties;
- counsel for the parties;
- the legal profession generally;
- the media and the public;
- the makers of law and policy;
- other Magistrates;
- the appeal court.

The parties

The parties are the primary audience when a Magistrate gives any reasons. Reasons for a decision, whether oral or in writing, let parties know how and why the case has been decided as it has. In addition, conveying reasons will let both sides know that their case has been carefully considered before being decided. The parties are the most important audience in any case where reasons for a decision are given. Particular thought should be given to the party who is the "loser" in the matter before the court.

Counsel for the parties

This audience has the same interests as the parties themselves. In addition, the lawyer for the unsuccessful party will want to scrutinise the reasons for judgment to help explain the decision to that party, and, in the case of the losing party, with a view to possible appeal.

The legal profession generally

Even lawyers who have no involvement in a particular case may be interested in a decision and the reasons for it. They may have similar cases pending, or they may anticipate that they will have similar cases in the future. Knowing not only a decision, but also the reasons for it, may assist a lawyer to evaluate his or her own case. This understanding can help a lawyer to advise a client, and can significantly increase the chance of a case being settled.

The public and the media

Cases are often of great interest to the public and the media. The law can seem like a mysterious and complex matter for members of the public who have no legal background or training. In a participatory democracy, it is necessary for the public to know how public institutions operate, including the courts. Although few people may be interested in routine cases, it is appropriate that for those who are, reasons should be available and understandable. In significant cases that attract greater public attention, this is even more important.

The law-makers

Although members of parliament are unlikely to be sitting in a Magistrate's courtroom, the decisions that are made, and the reasons given for them (especially in significant cases), may circulate privately or be picked up by the press. It is unlikely that one case would lead to a change in the law. More likely, it will generate debate and discussion of policy matters. This is a healthy feature of any free society. If a pattern of cases demonstrates some weakness or deficiency in the law, it can lead to changes being made.

Other Magistrates

Magistrates have no time to sit in other Magistrates' courtrooms and observe proceedings. Even if they did, their presence in the courtroom might have a disturbing influence on the proceedings. If reasons for decisions are given in writing, other Magistrates will have access to those reasons. This will benefit Magistrates, as they will learn, by the example of others, how to communicate effectively. It could also help Magistrates to keep current on substantive law.

The appeal court

When a case is appealed, the appellate court will resort to the reasons given by the Magistrate who presided over the hearing of the case. If no reasons were given at the time of the decision that is being appealed, a Magistrate in the District Court is required, pursuant to s 224 of the *District Courts Act*, to provide reasons.

25.6 THE QUALITIES OF A GOOD JUDGMENT

The most important feature of any decision is the accuracy of the decision itself and the sense of justice and fairness that it conveys. This is so whether it is a final decision made after a lengthy hearing, or an interim decision made at some step of the process leading to a final decision. This accuracy and sense of justice can be characterised as the substance or the "what" of the judgment. In order to communicate the substance of a decision effectively, a Magistrate needs to pay attention to *how* it is communicated.

Experience and effort are important in developing effective communication skills in giving reasons for decisions. It also helps to keep in mind a number of key points when formulating reasons and in delivering them. The following text is designed to make Magistrates aware of these key points.

25.6.1 Language and grammar

Use short sentences

Long sentences, both written and oral, are more difficult to follow than several short ones. A reader or listener may become confused if he or she is forced to follow long sentences with interrelated ideas. Sometimes long sentences are difficult to avoid.

However, in writing or speaking, a Magistrate should try to avoid long sentences where possible.

Avoid legalese and archaic words

In every field of expertise, experts use jargon. Jargon can be useful in communications among people with the same expertise. When lawyers or Magistrates speak to other lawyers or Magistrates, legalese and jargon can be a way of achieving a concise and exact communication. It might actually enhance communication. However, when lawyers or Magistrates use this same jargon to communicate with those who have no legal background, it can have the opposite result. It can create confusion, a loss of interest and a loss of respect. The parties to most contested matters in the District Court have no legal background. When giving reasons, keep the audience in mind. Avoid the use of jargon that part of that audience cannot understand.

Use the active voice

Readers or listeners are usually better able to follow what is said or written if it is delivered in the active voice. The active voice places the subject in front of the verb in a sentence. Another way of saying this it that the doer of the action (subject) is mentioned ahead of the action (verb). The following examples demonstrate the difference between the active and passive voice.

Passive Voice	Active Voice
"The village elders were notified by the police superintendent about the search warrant."	"The police superintendent notified the village elders of the search warrant."
"The complainant was attacked by the defendant."	"The defendant attacked the complainant."
"Six bottles of beer were consumed by the accused."	"The accused consumed six bottles of beer."
"More money is needed by the applicant in order to send her daughter to school."	"The applicant needs more money to send her daughter to school."

25.6.2 Structure

The structure of a judgment, whether oral or written, makes an enormous difference to the ease of comprehension. A model structure can be applied to most instances, and may be adapted to suit other circumstances. The following model consists of parts arranged in sequence:

- Introduction and issues;
- The evidence;
- Findings of credibility;
- The facts;
- The law;
- The disposition.

The introduction and the issues

An introduction of a judgment is a short way of conveying to the reader or listener what the decision is about. It sets the stage for what is to follow. It will typically answer these questions:

- "What is the major issue or issues in this case?"
- "Who are the parties?"
- "How did this case get before the court?"

Where there is more than one question or issue, the introduction should set out clearly what they are. If there is an issue that has been conceded, this should also be set out in the introduction.

An example of an introduction that answers these questions is:

> "This is an application brought by Magi Jack, the applicant against Joe Hepi, the respondent. Ms Jack brought the claim against Mr Hepi, seeking a declaration of paternity and an order for support for their daughter, Juli Jack, born on 15 July 1992. The claim is made pursuant to the ... Act, Chap ... The application was filed on 30 October 1999 and was heard on 15 December 1999. Joe admits that he is the father of the child. He does not dispute Magi's right to claim maintenance. He says that he cannot afford to pay. The only issue is whether Joe can afford to pay maintenance, and if so, how much."

A judgment without an introduction can be confusing to an audience. In the case of an oral judgment, if there is no introduction, a listener may miss the significance of much of what follows. In the case of a written judgment, if there is no introduction, a reader might have to re-read part of the decision to understand the judgment.

The evidence

After the introduction, reasons should move on to deal with the evidence that has been adduced. Where the evidence is inconsistent, there should be an explanation of the inconsistencies. The reasons should go on to deal with issues of credibility, to indicate why some evidence is rejected and some is accepted.

The introduction in Magi Jack's case (above) might continue to deal with the evidence and the issues in the following manner:

> "During the hearing, the applicant gave evidence in support of her claim for maintenance. The respondent also gave evidence. No other witnesses were called.

Ms Jack gave evidence that she is a clerk, employed by Numbatu Trade Store in Boroko. Her evidence is that she works full time and earns K ... per month. Her job is secure and she will remain employed for the foreseeable future.

Ms Jack also gave evidence that her income is completely used up for the day-to-day expenses of life. The majority of her income is spent on rent, food and clothing. Her estimated expenses were itemised for the court, and the document setting them out was entered as exhibit 1. I have reviewed it carefully. The evidence indicates that she is spending more than she earns.

Ms Jack gave evidence that she has had to borrow money from her sister in order to meet the basic cost of living. Her evidence is that over the last three months, she has had to borrow a total of K240.

Mr Hepi, during his cross-examination of Ms Jack, challenged the applicant on this point, and suggested that she does not have to pay any money back to her sister. I accept Ms Jack's evidence that she is indebted to her sister in the amount alleged. In any event, whether or not Ms Jack has to repay the money to her sister does not alter the fact that she making less money than it takes to support herself and the child at a reasonable or even modest standard of living.

Ms Jack gave evidence that she hopes to enrol the child in school in the near future but has no money to meet the anticipated school fees. These fees will work out to K85 per month for 10 months of the year. This is a total of K850 for the year, or K71 per month if the school fees are spread out over the year.

Mr Hepi gave evidence that he works at ABC Motors in Port Moresby, where he is an assistant mechanic. He says he has been employed there for over five years. His evidence is that he is likely to be retrenched in the next month. He says there are rumours that some employees at ABC Motors will lose their jobs. When asked in cross-examination when he heard these rumours, he said is was six months ago. There is no evidence that anyone has been retrenched in the meantime. There is nothing but vague rumours to suggest that anybody might be retrenched. Even though this hearsay evidence was not objected to, I give no weight to these rumours. There is no evidence to suggest that Mr Hepi is specifically targeted for retrenchment."

This judgment would probably continue in this way to deal with evidence of Mr Hepi's income and expenses. It would be likely to conclude by making a finding of fact concerning whether or not Mr Hepi can afford to make a contribution to the support of his daughter.

Findings of credibility

As every experienced Magistrate knows, evidence often conflicts. It may be impossible to accept the evidence of everyone who gives evidence in a particular case. For instance, if the case concerns a car accident, and if four witnesses saw the accident, it is entirely possible to hear four inconsistent versions of what happened. However, this does not necessarily mean that somebody is lying. There are a number of factors that might account for the inconsistencies.

For example, in Magi Jack's case, the Magistrate did not accept the evidence of Joe Hepi relating to his alleged imminent retrenchment. This was clearly explained by the Magistrate when dealing with the evidence. It does not mean that Joe was lying. He might have had a genuine concern about being laid off.

A witness' memory of what he or she saw might be vague, and the evidence based on that memory might be inaccurate. A witness who was at the scene of a crime or some other relevant event might not have had an opportunity to get a good view of what was taking place. A witness might have bad vision. There are other reasons. Finally, a witness may be deliberately trying to deceive the court.

When giving reasons, it can be important to explain why a witness' testimony is not being accepted. This is especially so where the evidence of a witness is rejected despite his or her honest attempt to tell the truth. If a Magistrate does not explain why a witness's evidence is being rejected, that witness might go away thinking that the Magistrate thought he or she was deliberately lying. Here is an example of how a Magistrate might deal with this in his or her reasons:

> "Although the plaintiff says that the defendant's vehicle was travelling at 80 kilometres per hour, I find that the vehicle was travelling within the speed limit of 60 kilometres per hour. I do not think that the plaintiff deliberately lied to the court. However, he saw the vehicle for only a matter of one or two seconds before the accident. It is understandable that in the heat of the moment it would seem that the vehicle was travelling at a high rate of speed. An independent witness, Lola Mati, saw the vehicle from the time it turned the corner onto the street. She was not involved in the accident itself. She had a clear view. She says that the vehicle was travelling at a normal rate of speed. I accept this evidence."

At other times, it might be appropriate for a Magistrate to come out and say clearly that he or she rejects the evidence of a witness because that witness is lying. This might be done in words similar to the following:

> "The accused gave an explanation of his presence at the scene of the crime, which was incredible and which is fraught with inconsistencies that were brought out in cross-examination. (Here the Magistrate might itemise these inconsistencies). I find that the accused deliberately tried to mislead this court, and I do not accept his explanation."

If a case is very long and if there are various versions of what happened, it might take a long time to sort out each bit of evidence into what is accepted and what is rejected. To do this would make the reasons for the decision long and tedious. It is sometimes necessary for a Magistrate to strike a balance. In doing so, it should be at least acknowledged that there are conflicting accounts in relation to the issue in question. It may be appropriate to mention only some of these accounts.

The facts

After dealing with the conflicting evidence and credibility, a Magistrate should ensure that it is clear to a listener or a reader which evidence is being accepted and what findings of facts are being made. Some of the facts may already be apparent from what has been said by the Magistrate in dealing with credibility.

Sometimes the facts that are found by a Magistrate do not match any version given by the witnesses. The following is an example of an instance where a Magistrate does not fully accept the evidence of any witness:

> "I have listened carefully to the evidence of the complainant. She says that the defendant struck her repeatedly with a stick. Her evidence is that she was struck at least 20 times. The defendant, in his testimony, admitted that he had a stick and that he used it to strike the complainant. He says he hit the complainant only once. He says he did not use enough force to cause grievous bodily harm. I do not accept the evidence of the defendant. I find, after hearing all of the evidence, that he struck the complainant repeatedly with the stick, using a considerable amount of force. At the same time, I do not accept the evidence of the complainant that she was struck with the stick more than 20 times. It is understandable that she could easily think that she was struck that many times. However, after hearing all of the evidence, including that of the prosecution witness who heard the fight from the next room, I find as a fact that the defendant struck the complainant no more than10 times and that he used considerable force when doing so. The defendant did not tell the whole truth."

The law

After dealing with the evidence and the findings of fact that are made as a result of hearing the evidence, a Magistrate should consider the law. In many cases the law is quite simple and not in dispute. The entire case may turn on the facts. However, even in these cases, it is advisable to refer to the applicable law in giving reasons. In the instance of Magi Jack and Joe Hepi's case, the law is very straightforward. The Magistrate's reasons for judgment in that case might continue as follows:

> "The relevant statute sets out the law that applies in this case. [A citation of the relevant act and, if necessary, an explanation of what it means, should follow]. The law says that fathers of children are obliged to support their children where they are able to do so. The fact that Joe Hepi has admitted that he is the father eliminates the issue of paternity, and the case becomes a question of whether, in the circumstances of this case, the law requires Mr Hepi to pay, and if so, how much."

Although some cases, such as that of Magi Jack and Joe Hepi, turn on the facts, other cases may turn on the law. For example, in a contested case where the facts disclose that a child wandered near a car that a neighbour was backing out of the yard, and if the child was struck by the car and injured, a claim may be brought against the driver. The parties may be very much in agreement as to what happened. The main issue in this case would be whether what happened amounts to negligence on the part of the driver of the car. In giving reasons for judgment in such a case, most of the judgment will focus on the meaning of negligence (the law) and whether the facts, about which no one disagrees, fall within the definition. In this example, the issue of damages would also arise. It might turn more on the facts and less on the law than does the issue of negligence.

The disposition

The final step in most judgments is making the order that follows upon the reasons. As outlined above in the section of this chapter on recording decisions, it is important to include all the details that make the order complete and effective. In the case of Magi Jack and Joe Hepi, an order for payment of periodic maintenance might be made in the following words:

> "On the basis of the evidence before me, I find that Mr Hepi is liable to contribute to the support of the child. I order that Joe Hepi pay the sum of K50 every fortnight to Magi Jack for the support of Juli Jack born on 1 July 1992. Payment is to be made to the clerk of the District Court at Port Moresby. I order that the first payment be made on Friday 1 December 1999. Subsequent payments will be made on the first day of each month in subsequent months. If the first day of any month falls on a weekend or public holiday, payment will be made on the first weekday that is not a public holiday following the first day of the month."

The wording of this order may seem overly detailed, but it will have the effect of preventing Mr Hepi from trying to avoid making a payment due to a technical deficiency in the order.

The structure outlined above may not suit all cases. *It is not intended to be an inflexible formula for all reasons in all cases. It is a useful guide.* The structure makes formulating reasons easier. Many reasons are delivered orally from the bench without the luxury of time for quiet thought and reflection. It may be useful for a Magistrate to either memorise the headings, or have them available, so that even reasons that must be delivered immediately can be structured without difficulty.

25.6.3 What to leave in – what to leave out

Obiter dictum

Obiter dictum is a Latin expression (there does not seem to be a succinct English equivalent) that refers to an opinion contained in a judgment that is beyond what is necessary in order to reach a decision on the question before the court. Here is an example of obiter dictum that might have been included in the Magi Jack case:

> "I find that the defendant, Joe Hepi, has a secure job and that he is unlikely to be retrenched. However, if he was going to be retrenched, there would be some time before that happens and he would likely receive some severance pay. I would be inclined to make an order that he pay some maintenance in those circumstances."

It is easy to see how this obiter dictum could create confusion in the minds of the parties, and perhaps anger or resentment on the part of the defendant. There is no purpose for including it, as the decision is reached on other evidence. It should be left out.

As a general rule, all obiter dictum should be avoided. In giving reasons, Magistrates should confine themselves to the issues, and refrain from straying into areas where their opinions are not needed.

Self-reminders on evidentiary points

It is sometimes important for a Magistrate to include a specific reference to the rules of evidence. The rules relating to corroboration require that a jury be warned of the danger of convicting a defendant of a sexual offence without corroborative evidence. There is a similar need to warn about the danger of convicting solely on the basis of evidence of an accomplice. Where there is no jury (as is always the case in Papua New Guinea), the Judge or Magistrate is required to warn himself or herself of this danger: see Chapter 5. If a Magistrate fails to record this warning and if the defendant is convicted, the matter could be successfully appealed on the basis that the Magistrate failed to remind himself or herself. Magistrates should, therefore, be careful to include this warning to themselves in the memorandum or the decision and in the reasons for the decision.

It is also a good idea to include reference to the burden of proof and the standard of proof in the memorandum of a final decision and in the reasons that are given for it.

25.6.4 The Underlying Law Act

When writing a judgment or giving oral reasons for a decision, a Magistrate must apply relevant law to the facts of the particular case. In doing so, it is important for a Magistrate to be aware of the provisions of the *Underlying Law Act*. This Act took over the functions of Sch 2 of the *Constitution* in 2000.

If a decision requires only the application of a written law, a Magistrate will refer to the statute and the particular section or sections of the statute that are applicable in rendering a judgment. Section 23 of the *Underlying Law Act* provides that when interpreting a provision of any written law, a Magistrate *shall* give effect to any relevant customary practice, usage or perception recognised by the people to be affected as a result of the interpretation. In addition, a Magistrate *may* consider how courts in a foreign jurisdiction have interpreted identical provisions.

However, if either custom or the common law is relevant to the judgment in some way (either together with or separate from statutory provisions), a Magistrate must address these matters, even if they are not specifically applied in reaching the judgment. Section 4(4) of the *Underlying Law Act* states:

> "A Court which
>
> (a) refuses to apply a principle or rule of customary law, shall give reasons for its refusal in terms of subsection (2)(a), (b), or (c), or
>
> (b) applies a principle rule of common law (sic), shall give its reasons for the application in terms of subsection (3)(a), (b), (c), (d) or (e)."

In other words, if a Magistrate does not apply a rule of customary law, he or she must justify why this has not been done. There is a reverse onus with respect to the common law. Where a Magistrate *does* apply a rule of the common law, this must be justified.

The various grounds upon which the exclusion of a custom may take place, as set out in s 4(2), are:

- It is inconsistent with a written law.
- Its application and enforcement would be contrary to the National Goals and Directive Principles and the Basic Social Obligations established by the *Constitution.*
- Its application would be contrary to the basic rights guaranteed by the *Constitution.*

If the common law is applied in a judgment, this must be justified in accordance with s 4(3). The bases upon which common law may be applied are:

- It is consistent with a statute.
- It is applicable and appropriate to the circumstances of the country.
- It is consistent with the customary law as applied under s 4(2).
- Its application and enforcement would not be contrary to the National Goals and Directive Principles and basic rights guaranteed by the *Constitution.*

The *Underlying Law Act*, at s 16, also deals with the ascertainment of customary law, and, at s 17, the resolution of conflicts between different customary laws that apply to the parties or subject matter of a dispute.

A Magistrate should take care that a judgment explicitly covers the requirements of the *Underlying Law Act*: see also 2.3.8, 2.4 and 5.13.

Finally, where a court, other than the Supreme Court or National Court, has made a decision applying the underlying law, the customary law or the common law, in the manner set out in s 7 of the Act, it must forthwith send a copy of the decision to the

Chief Justice and the Chairman of the Law Reform Commission, to be dealt with by either of these under ss 12, 13 and 14: *Underlying Law Act*, s 8.

25.6.5 Dealing with submissions when giving reasons

In some cases, particularly where counsel represents one or more of the parties, submissions may be made to the Magistrate after the evidence has been called and before the Magistrate gives reasons. In giving reasons, a Magistrate should respond to the major points raised by counsel in argument. If counsel's submission relates to issues of evidence and credibility, the submissions should be dealt with in that part of the judgment. If part of the submission deals with the law, this should be dealt with in that part of the judgment.

25.6.6 Other factors relating to decisions and reasons

Delivery in open court

If a Magistrate decides to give oral reasons, those reasons are always given in open court, either at the conclusion of the hearing or after an adjournment.

If a Magistrate decides to write reasons for a decision, either interim or final, then, at the conclusion of the evidence and submissions, the matter will have to be adjourned in order for the Magistrate to write reasons. The case should be adjourned to a specific date. This exerts some discipline on the Magistrate to make sure reasons are available by that date. It also avoids the extra work that is required in having the registry contact the parties or their counsel to notify them of when the reasons will be handed down. When the court reconvenes, the Magistrate should read the written reasons from the bench. They should be read word for word in order to prevent the impression that there are two sets of reasons, one oral and one written.

It is bad practice to simply provide the written reasons to the registry and have the registry see that it gets into the hands of the parties. In addition, giving decisions and reasons in open court avoids confusion and the possibility that one or both parties will be unaware that a decision has been made.

Neutrality

It is of great importance that a Magistrate retains not only a real sense of neutrality, but also an outward appearance of neutrality. This is particularly important when making orders and giving reasons for them. Although there is no formula for neutrality, it is probably sufficient if a Magistrate simply reminds himself or herself of this requirement at the time of formulating reasons and when delivering them.

Emotions

In either a civil or a criminal hearing, emotions can run high. This is particularly so at the time that an order is made or reasons for an order are given. Some of the adverse emotion can be minimised if the reasons that accompany an order make it clear that the matter was considered fully and fairly.

A Magistrate should *never* allow himself or herself to display emotions in voice, gesture, or in the wording of the order or reasons that are given. It is helpful for a Magistrate to recognise that the office places the Magistrate in a position where he or she is, in a very real way, speaking for the community or the people of Papua New Guinea in making orders and giving reasons for them. A dispassionate measured tone of voice is essential, even if the Magistrate inwardly feels emotional about the matter at hand.

Security

Because some matters in Magistrates' Courts can be very contentious, there may be occasions when a Magistrate senses that communicating a decision or giving reasons will create emotions that could potentially erupt into violence. A Magistrate may feel vulnerable in this regard, or may recognise that one of the parties is vulnerable. In such circumstances, it is sensible for the Magistrate to adjourn the court and have the registry secure the attendance of one or more members of the police to be present in court when the order or decision is given. This is one occasion when it is best not to give reasons for the adjournment, as it could inflame an already volatile situation.

Timing

Some Judges and Magistrates who adjourn cases to formulate either written or oral reasons, allow other matters to take priority over this task. The result is that the matter is delayed. This only makes the task more difficult. Personal memory of the case fades, and a Magistrate is forced to rely more heavily on the notes taken during the hearing. Even if these notes are complete enough to piece together what the evidence was, it is difficult to regain impressions and findings of credibility without a clear memory of the proceedings. As time passes, the notes become less of a trigger to stimulate the memory and more of a substitute for memory. When this happens, a psychological block can develop which makes it even more difficult to arrive at a decision and formulate reasons. Not only does this make more work for a Magistrate, but the parties are left in suspense. The quality of justice suffers. The timely delivery of judgments is an ethical responsibility of a Magistrate: see 1.5.8.

It is very important, therefore, that Magistrates do not allow more time than is necessary to elapse between adjourning a case and giving the decision and reasons.

One way of preventing this from happening is to adjourn the case for only as long as is reasonably necessary to arrive at a decision and formulate reasons.

Chapter 26 – Appeals from the District Court

26.1 INTRODUCTION

Judges and Magistrates are human and, like all humans, sometimes make mistakes. It is therefore important that the justice system provides for appeals from decisions and orders that are made by Judges and Magistrates who preside at hearings and trials. Learning that a decision is being appealed should not trigger a negative response on the part of a Magistrate. It is simply part of the job. It is also a necessary safeguard that makes any justice system stronger and fairer. Appeals from the District Court also assist in clarifying the law, by producing binding precedents that interpret and apply statutes and cases.

Appeals sometimes require that *leave* first be obtained from the court to which the appeal is made. Appeals to the Supreme Court provide instances of this. However, an appeal from the District Court, subject to certain statutory limitations, may be made as a matter of *right*, that is, an appeal may be made without first obtaining leave of the court to which the appeal is being made. Appeals are made to the National Court. Most of the statutory provisions relating to appeals are found in Pt XI of the *District Courts Act*. It is important for Magistrates to be mindful of the possibility that any decision or order that is made may be appealed against. This assists Magistrates to perform their duties in a way that minimises the prospect of an appeal and, when one is made, to deal with it in a way that minimises stress and difficulty in responding in accordance with the procedural requirements.

This chapter is intended to assist District Court Magistrates in the way that they deal with appeals that are taken against decisions made by them. Appeals *to* the District Court are not considered in this chapter. They are dealt with in Chapters 17 and 18.

26.2 WHAT MAY BE APPEALED

Section 219 of the *District Courts Act* provides for appeals to be made by a person who is *aggrieved* by a decision of the court. A person aggrieved is almost invariably a party against whom an unfavourable decision has been made. The decision appealed against can take the form of a conviction in a criminal case, or the dismissal of an information or complaint. Other orders may also be appealed. For instance, a decision that awards damages to a party in a civil case, but which the party considers to be *inadequate*, may be appealed. Similarly, a custody or maintenance decision may not involve the dismissal of a complaint, yet a party may feel aggrieved and may appeal.

Section 219 provides that the Public Prosecutor may *not* appeal a dismissal of an information. This means that any error in the acquittal of an accused for a criminal offence is automatically resolved in favour of the accused. However, a *sentence* for an indictable offence triable summarily under s 420 of the *Criminal Code* may be appealed by the Public Prosecutor. A person who has been convicted in a criminal case may always appeal, regardless of the type of offence. Although the person *aggrieved* is normally one of the parties, the Secretary of Justice may, where he or she is of the opinion that a matter is of sufficient public importance, intervene in an appeal or pursue an appeal pursuant to s 219(3) without the party's permission.

An appeal must normally be commenced within a month of the date of the decision that is being appealed. However, the National Court may extend the time of appeal pursuant to s 231 of the *District Courts Act*. There is no limitation on the extension of time that may be granted. This means that it might be several months after a decision is made that a Magistrate first becomes aware that the decision is being appealed.

26.3 MINIMISING THE CHANCES OF AN APPEAL

Preparing for an appeal starts at the initial hearing or trial. Every decision, whether interlocutory or final, whether criminal or civil, is the basis of a possible appeal. Being conscious of this fact can assist a Magistrate in conducting a hearing in a way that is less likely to form the basis of a successful appeal.

Paying close attention to the evidence and the law, and carefully applying the facts to the applicable law, can minimise the chances of a successful appeal. An unsuccessful party who is satisfied that a Magistrate has considered the case carefully and has applied the law properly, is less likely to appeal that decision, even though the party may be unhappy with the outcome. Therefore, carefully explaining to the parties how and why a decision is made can minimise the chances of even an unsuccessful appeal.

When evidence is being given in court, it is important to make careful notes of the evidence and, where evidence is internally inconsistent or conflicts with that of other witnesses, to make findings of credibility and to make notes regarding these findings. This helps a Magistrate who later becomes aware of an appeal, but whose personal memory of the case has faded to some extent.

26.4 HOW AN APPEAL IS MADE

An appeal is commenced in accordance with s 220 of the *District Courts Act* by filing a notice of appeal in form 71. The notice of appeal must be filed with the clerk of the District Court that made the order appealed against. The notice must be served on the respondent and on the Registrar of the National Court. Section 238 sets forth requirements for service of the notice of appeal.

26.5 DUTIES OF MAGISTRATE WHEN APPEAL IS COMMENCED

26.5.1 Recognisance or deposit of money

One of the first duties of a Magistrate, after the filing of a notice of appeal, is to make a determination in respect of a recognisance and surety or deposit of money. Section 222 of the *District Courts Act* provides that a recognisance with a surety must be provided, or a sum of money deposited with the clerk of the court that made the decision being appealed against. This is to provide assurance that the appellant will:

- prosecute the appeal;
- abide by the order of the National Court; and
- pay costs that may be awarded against the appellant by the National Court.

The amount of money involved in this process should be determined in accordance with the circumstances of the appellant, and not in accordance with the Magistrate's opinion about the likelihood of success of appeal. In this respect, it is similar to the issue of bail in a criminal hearing, where the likelihood of conviction has little relevance.

26.5.2 Bail

If the decision being appealed against is a conviction or sentence that entails the incarceration of the appellant, the matter of the appellant's release from custody may arise. Section 223 of the *District Courts Act* provides discretion on the part of a Magistrate to grant bail. The onus of proof and other considerations relating to bail after conviction are covered in Chapter 10: see 10.3.3 and 10.5.2.

26.5.3 Documents and materials to be forwarded to National Court

In order for the National Court to consider an appeal, it is necessary that as many details as possible, about the decision being appealed, be forwarded to the National Court. Section 225 of the *District Courts Act* provides that the following be certified by the clerk of the District Court and forwarded immediately after the notice of appeal is lodged:

- Copy of conviction, order or adjudication;
- Copy of reasons for the conviction, order or adjudication if reasons were given at the time the decision was pronounced;
- Copy of the complaint (information);
- Copy of depositions;

- Copy of all other proceedings of the court that made the decision being appealed against;
- Exhibits, except in respect of those exhibits that are impractical to forward, in which case a list and description of the exhibits are required.

In cases where an appeal is against a decision for which reasons were not given at the time, a Magistrate has an obligation under s 225 to forward a report setting out the reasons for the making of the decision. In such cases, it might be a month (or even longer when an extension of time is granted) before a Magistrate is called upon to forward a report. With the passage of this amount of time, it is understandable that a Magistrate may have only faint personal recollection of the facts, the findings of credibility and other considerations that went into the making of the decision. For this reason, it is vitally important that a Magistrate has sufficiently detailed notes to be able to compose a complete report. Where notes are lacking in detail, there is a risk of a loss of completeness or accuracy in the report – either of which make it more difficult for the National Court to reach a proper decision on appeal. A lack of sufficient detail in the notes made by a Magistrate regarding the decision that is being appealed, inevitably creates stress for a Magistrate who is called upon to forward a report.

The obvious lesson from this is that Magistrates are best prepared for appeal when they have already given reasons for the decision being appealed against. Alternatively, it is imperative that detailed notes and records are kept that will allow a Magistrate to write a report with minimal recourse to his or her independent memory.

In cases where a person is brought before the National Court on habeas corpus, it is necessary, pursuant to s 239 of the *District Courts Act*, that a Magistrate, upon notice, provide to the National Court certified copies, or the original, of:

- the conviction on which the commitment was founded; and
- the depositions and information intended to be relied upon.

In cases where an application for judicial review is against a committal for trial or sentence, and, under s 118 of the *District Courts Act*, all relevant documents have been forwarded to the Public Prosecutor, the National Court may waive notice to the Magistrate to produce the documents.

26.6 AFTER THE APPEAL

Depending on the outcome of an appeal, there may be duties to be performed by the District Court Magistrate or clerk after the appeal. Sections 234 and 234 of the *District Courts Act* concern the payment of costs on an appeal. If the National Court makes an order for costs, it may or may not specify when the costs must be paid. Where no time is specified, the costs are payable within seven days of the making of the order for costs.

Costs are to be paid to the Registrar of the National Court. Where costs are not paid on time, the party entitled to costs may apply to the Registrar of the National Court for a certificate to that effect. The certificate, when produced to a Magistrate of the District Court, may be enforced as an order for the payment of money: see 20.2.

Index

[References are to page numbers]

LaVergne, TN USA
12 September 2010

196668LV00001B/8/P

9 789980 939524